MUSIC AND MUSKET

BANDS AND BANDSMEN OF THE AMERICAN CIVIL WAR

KENNETH E. OLSON

CONTRIBUTIONS TO THE STUDY OF MUSIC AND DANCE,
NUMBER 1

GREENWOOD PRESS
WESTPORT, CONNECTICUT • LONDON, ENGLAND

Library of Congress Cataloging in Publication Data

Olson, Kenneth E
    Music and musket.

    (Contributions to the study of music and dance; no. 1
ISSN 0193–9041)
    Bibliography: p.
    Includes index.
    1. Bands (Music)—United States.   2.   Military
music, American—History and criticism.   3.   United
States—History—Civil War, 1861–1865—Songs and music—
History and criticism.   I.   Title.   II.   Series.
ML1311.O47   785.06'71   79–6195
ISBN 0–313–22112–X lib. bdg.

Library of Congress Catalog Card Number: 79–6195
ISBN: 0–313–22112–X
ISSN: 0193–9041

First published in 1981

Greenwood Press
A division of Congressional Information Service, Inc.
88 Post Road West, Westport, Connecticut 06881

Printed in the United States of America

10 9 8 7 6 5 4 3 2 1

COPYRIGHT
ACKNOWLEDGMENTS

To Peg
who provides all of the music in my life

CONTENTS

ILLUSTRATIONS

FOREWORD

We stood in a ragged formation in front of the high school, just a block from my home, tootling our horns and poking at one another in the early morning sun, impatient for the parade to begin. It was Saturday 31 May 1939 and, for the first time, I was playing with the municipal band on Decoration Day. That's what we called it then—Decoration Day—not Memorial Day.

Before long Professor Knuppel arrived on the scene, wearing a white shirt, black pants, and sporting a natty bow tie. The visored cap of a German bandmaster crowned his gnarled features, an anachronism left over from his youthful service as conductor of the kaiser's orchestra in Berlin. Even though he had long ago replaced his own teeth with "store-bought choppers," he could still play all of the old double and triple-tongued cornet solos so popular when he was a young, barnstorming virtuoso. At age eighty the old man had lost most of his hearing, but to me he was the equal of a Toscanini on any podium. "Line oop!" he rasped, "Ve go!" Bill Garrett blew the whistle, swished his baton through the air, and "Ve vent!"

Directly ahead of the band was the American Legion Color Guard arrayed in an assortment of uniform parts. Simply to note the lack of precision in their execution of the manual of arms is a generous appraisal of their efforts. The most prominent features of the corps were their ample paunches and rather personal interpretations of Army Field Manual 10–40.

Directly behind the band was Jerry Halvorson's old black Packard with the yellow-spoked wheels. Jerry was an undertaker, and his pallbearers' car was often pressed into service as a limousine for distinguished persons at civic celebrations. On this day its lone occupant, except for the driver, was a gentleman even more ancient than Professor Knuppel. He sat slouched and shriveled in a dark blue uniform topped with a flat-brimmed hat. On the front of the hat was a golden wreath with GAR in the middle. The old gentleman was Elias Finster-maker, our last surviving Civil War veteran and proud member of the Grand Army of the Republic.

The open autos following the Packard displayed the few remaining members of the Women's Relief Corps all decked out in old-fashioned white dresses with colorful sashes slanted across their ample bosoms. They were followed by the high school band playing "Under the Double Eagle."

Behind them came still more open cars bearing the Gold Star Mothers of all of the past wars. The veterans of World War I, in uniforms that most had long since outgrown, shuffled along in company front, followed by the high school choir in their flapping robes. Bringing up the rear were the municipal digni-taries, the Boy and Girl Scouts in total disarray, various lodge groups, children on decorated bicycles and finally—the horses. Former parades placed the horses at the head of the column, but that didn't work out very well for the re-maining elements that were on foot.

The parade wound its way through town to the doleful strains of "The Van-quished Army." All drums were muffled as we entered the cemetery gates and silently filed between the stone markers to the speakers' platform. The bands and choir massed at the front of the rostrum.

The bands opened the ceremonies with the national anthem and the choir re-sponded with a hymn. They always managed to sing much better than they had marched. The valedictorian of the class of 1939, continuing a long tradition, delivered Lincoln's "Gettysburg Address," but he or she was always outdone by a leather-lunged professional orator hired for the occasion.

Finally, the veterans of past wars were called upon to hang the dedicatory wreaths upon the stark wooden crosses affixed to the end of the speakers' plat-form. Only a handful of veterans remained from the armies of the Blue and the Gray, but we were still privileged to have Mr. Finstermaker as a citizen of our town.

When it came time to dedicate the wreath to the dead of the Civil War Mr. Finstermaker, assisted by stronger hands, brought it shakily forward and hoisted it proudly up to the barren cross representing his long-departed com-rades. A World War I veteran paid similar homage to the dead of that conflict. A prayer brought a hush to the crowd. The silence was broken by the sharp report of the honor guards' rifles and by the equally sharp squall of several babies who forcefully voiced their disapproval of this unwarranted intrusion into their sleep. As the squalls diminished to whimpers, a trumpeter sounded an imperfect "Taps," echoed by another equally as shaky from somewhere over the hill.

I was always impressed by this homespun ceremony and particularly by Mr. Finstermaker, who seemed to me to be the world's oldest living human being. Occasionally, I had the pleasure of talking with him, and he took great delight in recounting some of his experiences during the War of the Rebellion.

As I grew older I realized that many of the cruelties he had witnessed had been dimmed by the memory of age, and perhaps his own contributions to the outcome of the war had been magnified through the perspective of too many wreaths laid on too many Decoration Day crosses. My fascination for this old soldier and his war stories continued long after he ceased to be a part of the solemn services and had become one of those veterans we memorialized.

Mr. Finstermaker had served as a drummer boy. It was he who piqued my interest in the role of the Civil War musicians. Were they, indeed, as important to the war effort as Mr. Finstermaker had indicated?

Hundreds of diaries, regimental histories, newspapers, and other sources attest to the truth that he spoke. Yes, Mr. Finstermaker, you and your fellow musicians were significant to the war effort, and, perhaps of greater importance, you were appreciated by your comrades-in-arms.

I hope this book will allow others to share in this bit of Americana and that this volume will do honor, not only to Mr. Finstermaker, but to all of the thousands of musicians who wore the Blue or the Gray.

KENNETH E. OLSON

PREFACE

Researchers into the growth and development of bands and band music in the United States have accepted willingly the statements of John C. Fitzpatrick and William C. White. Both claimed that civilian or military band music was virtually nonexistent prior to the end of the revolutionary period, and that army bands were not authorized in the regular service until 1834. This misconception has served as the basis for much contemporary research in the band field in spite of the conflicting evidence offered by O. G. Sonneck and S. V. Anderson.

This faulty hypothesis produced equally faulty conclusions, and prevented, or at least delayed, the development of an accurate account of the growth of band music in America. What is worse, it denied the band its rightful place at the center of the development of American music and relegated it to a peripheral position—if indeed historians mentioned the bands at all. One need only examine a popular music history text to determine how completely bands have been banished from all accounts of the growth of American culture. The few writers who mention them at all seem embarrassed by their presence and apologetically pass them off as of little consequence.

Fortunately, more recent scholars have successfully documented the enormous significance of band music to the development of American culture. Consequently, the band may yet achieve its rightful place in the history of American music.

Raoul F. Camus accurately and brilliantly traced the development of the military band in the United States Army prior to 1834. Clayton H. Tiede amply demonstrated the importance of the development of community bands during the nineteenth century. James W. Thompson provided further background through his studies of music in New England during the period 1800–1838. Kenneth Brungess currently is writing a history and repertoire of early

California brass bands, and Stewart Patrick has completed a study of military bands in Minnesota. Kenneth Carpenter wrote a history of the United States Marine Band and David C. McCormick a history of the United States Army Band from 1900 to the present.

David P. Swanzy explored analogous French developments in his work on the wind ensemble during the French Revolution. Older authors, such as James Farmer and Wilhelm Wieprecht, traced other European evolvements that were later transplanted to the New World. Richard F. Goldman wrote an early, but incomplete, history of the bands of America. William Bufkin completed a dissertation on the Union bands of the Civil War (including a valuable instrumentation and score analysis), while my own doctoral studies provided initial research for this volume.

Of all of these works, that by Camus comes closest to providing the yet to be written "History of Band Music in America." Since he proposed only to disprove the statements of Fitzpatrick and White, he terminated his study at the year 1834. He further limited his research to the development of military bands, ignoring the rather vigorous growth of civilian bands in America. By comparing his observations with those of Tiede, we can easily demonstrate the symbiotic relationship of early military and early civilian bands. When these two works are compared to Thompson's study, we can relate the development of bands to the growth of other musical activities in the United States. An understanding of these relationships is essential if we are to grasp fully the series of events that created the "Golden Age of the Brass Band" in America.

The year 1834 is significant to the study of American bands for two reasons. First, the army reduced the number and size of the bands then in service. Second, almost all American bands excluded woodwinds in favor of a totally brass instrumentation around 1834. The Civil War years represent the numerical peak of this Golden Age of the Brass Band.

After the war, gradual changes in instrumentation transformed these groups into units of mixed instrumental families. This was due to many factors, but a list of the most important causes would include a greater demand for indoor performance, and the efforts of bandmasters to enlarge the musical potential of the wind ensemble.

The brass band marched proudly through the war, but it could only limp into the early decades of this century. Appomattox signaled the end of its years of robust exuberance. By 1900 the old soldier's health was clearly failing.

Although this volume records the history of the military music of the Civil War, it can also be regarded as a history of the brass band in America. In this way, it continues the story so eloquently told by Camus. I leave it to others to complete the history of America's bands from 1865 to the present.

ACKNOWLEDGMENTS

A very special thanks is due Fred Benkovic of the Heritage Musical Foundation for his gracious hospitality and generous assistance in the early research for this book. His broad knowledge of Civil War music is spread throughout its pages. The materials, information, and photographs he so kindly shared were the basis for all subsequent research.

I also wish to give a very special thanks to William Bufkin who so kindly shared the products of his extensive research. I am particularly in his debt for the materials dealing with the history of the Fort Sumter band. It was his sleuthing, not mine, that provided the details of the band's history after it left Fort Sumter. He managed to uncover the muster rolls in the National Archives that had somehow eluded my most diligent efforts. Other references to his excellent dissertation will be found throughout this book.

All research would have come to a standstill were it not for Jack Robson, librarian at Southwest Minnesota State University, and Art Goldsmith and Robert Ragin of the library staff at Austin Peay State University. Their untiring cooperation in searching out sources and negotiating the waters of interlibrary loan has been greatly appreciated. The anonymous librarians all over the nation who responded to requests for materials deserve special thanks. The staff members of a number of other libraries and historical societies aided greatly in my search for materials. Their responses to written inquiries were always warm and generous. Their names are too numerous to list here, but that does not diminish my appreciation.

To my lovely wife Peg goes a special thanks for the meticulous task of proofreading this manuscript throughout all its drafts. Even after a hard day's teaching, she always read with great care and polished up my wayward prose. My friend and distinguished colleague Willis Hackman deserves a medal "for services above and beyond the bounds of friendship." He has read this work so many times he knows the material at least as well as I do. His own impeccable scholarship, respect for detail and the well-turned phrase, wit, and general excellence have served as benchmarks for many of these pages. His untiring cooperation has been one of the joys of writing. I would also like to thank Janet Brown for her excellent editorial work.

A final thank-you is due to Lavern Wagner of Quincy College who recently discovered the W. H. Shipman Collection of music in the Iowa Historical Library and persuaded that institution to microfilm this valuable collection so that it will be easily available to other Civil War buffs. I appreciate his sharing the fruits of his research and look forward to a detailed examination of this fine collection.

AUTHOR'S NOTE

In the mid-nineteenth century, authors, newspaper reporters, and other professional writers were rather casual about spelling, punctuation, and grammar. Inconsistencies, errors, and variations were common even in the most literate works.

If professional writers were vague about the rules, semi-literate soldiers weren't even aware of their existence but that did not prevent them from writing to their friends and loved ones. The trooper who wrote an entire paragraph extolling the virtues of his "scolin" without spelling a single word correctly merely represents an extreme case.

Rather than make corrections and add brackets that impede the flavor of the language, I have quoted all sources exactly as they were written. The result reflects the language and educational level of the period, and I hope, offers the reader an opportunity to participate in the social milieu of the war years.

MUSIC AND MUSKET

THE MUSICAL LEGACY
OF EARLIER WARS

In 1856 John Sullivan Dwight—who in a period of only four years had established himself as the "Boston Oracle" on all matters musical—felt compelled to write:

> Brass! Brass!
>
> In these dog-days the only music is of one sort, and that not the most refreshing. "The heavens are as brass above us," and the *airs* are all as brass about our ears.[1]

He continued this biased harangue against brass bands in the next issue of his journal, firing a terse, verbal salvo against "the hoarse, martial sound of brass, smothered by drums and cymbals."[2] To reinforce his position, he enlists the author of a letter to the *Musical World* "whose style sounds wondrously familiar."

> Last week we had commencement—commencement at old Harvard—and as usual, a Boston band assisted at the exercises. But—Ichabod!—the glory has departed. Brass, brass, brass,—nothing but brass. Brass led the procession from the library to the church—brass stood in the entry, and blew and blew—as we advanced to our pews. Brass clashed, and drums cracked the drums of our ears as we entered the doors. Brass led us to the dinner in Harvard Hall—brass gave us sentimental melodies in the President's yard in the evening—all is brass now-a-days—nothing but brass.
>
> Brass plays upon the Common in Boston, evenings.—Brass leads off our military and civic and political processions—brass is everywhere, and nothing but brass. God grant, that the disease among the bands do not become chronic. . . . In the history of Tom Thumb, we read that he was the son of a tumpeter, in Queen Anne's service, who might have lived to this day had he not blown his breath away! When I hear the continual braying of brass, I silently pray that the fate of the elder Thumb soon overtake these followers of Sax.[3]

Dwight continued to wage a losing battle against the proliferation of brass bands until the final issue of his journal in 1881, when his equally unpopular opposition to the music of Wagner contributed to the demise of the publication. He was obviously out of step with the public taste of both continents.

Dwight made two observations pertinent to the study of Civil War bands. First, by 1856 the band was the most-often-heard medium of musical performance in Boston. Second, these groups employed a totally brass instrumentation.

Other literature from this period confirms the fact that brigades of bandsmen were blowing, blaring, and blasting all across the land in complete disregard of Dwight and his oft-expressed bias against them. With the surrender of Fort Sumter, both the Rebel and Yankee armies found that they could readily accommodate most of these musicians on active duty.

Indeed, the sheer numbers of musicians enlisted by the Union and Confederate forces is astounding. Most were organized into brass bands, while the military instrumentalists of previous wars had been primarily woodwind players.

These observations posit three questions. First, where, in a country that was supposedly unmusical at best, did the two armies find enough musicians for hundreds of bands? Second, what events occurred that caused both military and civilian bands to change their instrumentations from woodwind to brass? Third, did Civil War musicians inherit an earlier musical tradition that governed both their numbers and their employment? The remainder of this chapter answers these three important questions and provides other background material pertinent to the study of Civil War bands.

AMERICAN BANDS AND THEIR EUROPEAN INHERITANCE

Music has long been associated with European military traditions. By the seventeenth century, drums, fifes, bugle horns, and trumpets were the common property of all European military musicians, and their rank and social position had been clearly defined by the musicians' guilds. The military musician's calling was an honorable one, and he was an esteemed member of all royal households.

Today we would classify these guildsmen as "field musicians." They sounded the calls and alarms essential to the day-to-day operation of the army. The musicians' functions continued unabated until 1918 when their role was reduced from one of necessity to one of tradition and ceremony.

These European musical traditions were transferred to the New World and to the revolutionary armies of George Washington. Indeed, they were reinforced by the musical requirements of a military structure unique to our democratic form of government and were expanded during the decades immediately preceding the Civil War.

In addition to the field musicians, several European armies had "Bands of Musick." Most bandsmen were enlisted as "privates of the line," and not as field musicians.[4] The term "musician" was reserved as an exclusive designation for a field musician.

American citizens of the Revolutionary period had ample opportunity to hear British bands of music. Most of the ninety-five "regiments of foot" serving in the colonies from 1755 to 1783 had bands of music attached, as did the elite colonial militia units.[5]

While field musicians were paid according to the rights and privileges of their military assignments, members of early bands were not provided for in the tables of organization. Support of these bands was accomplished by the methods previously utilized in the British armies.

Either of two methods was acceptable. In rare instances, the total expense of a band was borne by the regimental officers, or by the commanding officer personally. In effect, the officers simply hired a band. More often, bandsmen were carried as privates in the line units. Thus, their basic pay and allowances were provided by the government. However, the cost of their musical services was borne by the commanding officer personally, or by an assessment against all regimental officers. These expenses included the purchase of instruments and music and the hiring of an instructor, if the fife major (from the field music) was unable to accomplish this task.

It was possible to muster bandsmen as privates of the line because of the rather widespread practice of carrying phantom enlistees on all military rolls to provide extra emoluments for a regimental fund. Salaries accruing to these nonexistent soldiers were used for other purposes. This had been a long-accepted practice in European armies. Washington's Continental Army simply followed the tradition.[6] This is indicated in a letter dated 20 December 1778 from George Washington to General Sullivan.

It is not however my desire to remove the band in case it has been procured at the cost of the officers, and is kept up at their private expense. This is a prerogative I could not think of assuming. But on the other hand, if it belongs to, and is supported by the public, I shall adhere to my former order. . . .A Band is no part of our establishment, to indulge one Regiment therefore and refuse another (equal in pretensions) is setting up invidious distinctions which cannot be productive of any good but may [be] of much evil and ought to be avoided.[7]

The band in question was attached to Jackson's Continental Infantry. The fife major served as bandmaster. "Sullivan as commander could order the bandsmen to serve as soldiers, since they received soldier's pay, but to function as a band was the prerogative of the Regimental Officers at whose expense the musical skills were maintained."[8]

Since bandsmen performed no line duties, the system guaranteed that someone else would do the work of two men, his own, plus that of the nonexistent private who had been replaced by a bandsman. Washington questioned the propriety of this in a letter to Brigadier General John Stark: "How happens it that there are musicians returned as rank and file in Col. Webb's Regiment who do no duty in the line? This seems to be an abuse and requires a remedy."[9] When the abuse was remedied and the musicians forced to serve in the line, Camus notes that five chose to take a discharge.

This seemingly felonious arrangement was not unusual in the Continental Army. For example, Fobiger's Second Virginia Continental Infantry Band was under the musical direction of Thomas Sheldon who served as "Fife Major, with additional duties of teaching a Band of Musick."[10] This band was supported by the regimental officers.

Washington's questioning whether "[the band] belongs to and is supported by the public," implies that some revolutionary army bands were totally supported by government funds. If such is the case, it has not been documented.

The instrumentation of the field music and the bands of music was standardized during the eighteenth century, when certain instruments became associated with specific types of regiments. The trumpet, which could be heard over great distances, was assigned to mounted units, while the drum and fife became the property of troops of foot. The elite dragoons were allowed a degree of latitude in these matters. They used the fife and drum or the oboe and drum when serving primarily as troops of foot. The trumpet (or the bugle horn) was used when the unit was mounted. "In addition, the combined trumpeters [of the British Dragoons] were expected to form a 'band of music' consisting of 2 oboes, 2 horns, and a bassoon, when serving a fort."[11] Band performances, in this instance, were an added duty assigned to selected field musicians who had to double on the instruments of the band.

The instrumentation of eighteenth-century bands of music had roots in the double reed traditions of the Renaissance. The most common eighteenth-century instrumentation employed two oboes, two horns, and two bassoons. With the advent of the clarinet, two clarinets were added. These eight instruments, termed "harmoniemusik," were quickly adopted by eighteenth-century British and French army bands.

Since the army of colonial America was patterned on European models, and since the Continental field musicians used British manuals (later standardized by Stuben's Regulations), it seems safe to assume that early American bands employed an instrumentation similar to that found in Europe.

Near the end of the eighteenth century, western Europe hosted a number of janizary bands (Turkish military bands) which used bells, triangles, drums and cymbals as a part of their instrumentation. These percussion instruments were quickly adopted by the western musical establishment, appearing first in the harmoniemusik and later in the symphony orchestra. The added volume of sound provided by the percussion in the harmoniemusik necessitated an increase in the number of winds. By 1800 groups numbering from twenty to twenty-five musicians were not uncommon.

Other instruments were added during the final decades of the eighteenth century. The piccolo replaced the fife, and the serpent and trumpet were used by some bands. "The effect of the [four keyed] serpent in militia marches of the 18th century is excellent. The usual English Band combination was 2 B^b Clarinets, 2 Horns, 2 Bassoons (mainly in unison), one Trumpet with an exhilarating, epiphenomenal fanfare-like part, and Serpent *ad libitum* written rather low, an octave below the Bassoons where possible."[12]

As an instrument used on the march, the serpent was cumbersome at best. Around 1800 it was straightened to form a bass horn, which then continued in use with the original form, until both were replaced by the ophicleide, and still later by valve instruments.[13] The widespread acceptance of the augmented harmoniemusik attracted the efforts of Europe's finest composers, including Haydn, Mozart, and Handel.

Although colonial militia bands were patterned on British models, the models themselves had been altered by other Continental traditions. There is a long history of foreign musicians associated with British military bands. "Bands of Negro musicians were brought back from the crusades, and...[by] the beginning of the eighteenth century, black trumpeters and drummers were a feature of the British Army."[14] Janizary instruments were frequently played by corps of Black musicians in British bands.

Although these Black musicians were an important part of the history of early British military music, the German musicians playing in British bands were more significant to the development of military music in America.

In 1749, the band of the 1st Regiment of Foot Guards, commanded by HRH, the Duke of Cumberland, was dismissed and replaced by a band of Germans. They were the first musicians to be enlisted as soldiers, and for the next hundred years the bands of the British Army consisted almost entirely of Germans.[15]

It is obvious that many of the musicians of the ninety-five British regiments of foot in America during the eighteenth century were of German origin, and that a number of these remained to find their fortunes in the New World. "By the mid [18]50's more than half of the foreign-born musicians in New York had come from Germany."[16]

Although it would be difficult to overstate the importance of British army bands in the development of American military music, the vast number of Civil War bands would never have existed had they not inherited an equally lively civilian instrumental tradition. Both civilian and military music grew slowly in seventeenth-century America, but it is unlikely that the religious outcasts who settled in New England were completely unmusical. It has been widely held that instrumental music was ecclesiastically banned to the Puritans.

When reading the histories of music in America we almost gain the impression that the emigrants of the seventeenth century detested not so much the religious, political or economic atmosphere of Europe as the musical and we feel overawed by the constellation of mysterious motives prompting Providence to send to our shores out of all the millions who inhabited Europe just those few thousand beings who had no music in their souls.[17]

This was not the case for, although banished from the divine service itself, instruments were at least tolerated in private worship. In 1647 the Reverend John Cotton published a defense of singing in churches and in private devotions. In this he wrote: "Nore doe we forbid the private use of an instrument of Musick therewithall; so that attention to the instrument, doe not divert the heart from the attention to the matter of song."[18] Such a comment would have been unnecessary had society as a whole agreed upon the prohibition of instruments.

Indeed drums, trumpets, and horns were used in seventeenth-century New England to summon worshipers, to give an alarm in case of attack, and probably to augment the rather rudimentary military training common to these early settlements. Although references to instruments in early America are rare, those available include the notation of a virginal belonging to the wife of Judge Samuel Sewell of Boston, that was repaired on 1 December 1699;[19] and the disposition of bass viols in the will of the Reverend Edmund Browne of Sudbury, Massachusetts, who died in 1678.[20]

If the majority of instrumental activities of seventeenth-century America was left unrecorded, eighteenth-century writers provided rather comprehensive accounts of the music of their day.

In the midst of Spotswood's term the colony was called upon to mourn the passing of Queen Anne and the accession to the British throne of George I, November, 1714. Public mourning in the Dominion rivaled that of the mother country. Previously, the death of William III had furnished the occasion for an elaborate ceremonial. On May 18, 1702, Governor Nicholson had called to Williamsburg not only the colonial militia, but a number of Indian chiefs. Reviewing stands and batteries were placed in front of the college. In the upper balcony were buglers from warships; in the second balcony were placed oboeists, and below those were violinists, who separately and together played "very movingly." Men in somber black bore flags covered with crepe, followed by the Governor seated upon a white horse caparisoned in black.

After the funeral sermon by Dr. James Blair, the Governor withdrew, to return in blue uniform and gold braid, whereupon the bugles, violins and oboes struck up lively airs, and Queen Anne was proclaimed with artillery salutes, and the rattle of musquetry.[21]

Other references to instrumental music before 1750 give little evidence of more than an avocational interest in music. Although music as a hobby was the norm, a study of the art was still considered essential to a gentleman's education. After 1750 gentlemen amateurs frequently joined with semiprofessional and professional musicians to present public concerts.

A musical avocation was not the exclusive domain of the gentleman. Slaves and indentured servants participated on an equal footing with persons of greater means, and when slaves escaped from their masters the fact that they were musicians was an important part of their identification.

Charles Love, a runaway Virginia slave, was a "singer, violinist, and hautboisist," who was wanted by that state in 1757, "for running away from . . . Phillip Ludwell Lee with . . . a very good bassoon."[22] Vincent Hudson, a lad who "sounds the fife well, for which he was enlisted,"[23] was wanted as a deserter by the authorities of the 7th Virginia Regiment of the Continental Army.

One of the most interesting assessments of eighteenth-century American instrumental music is contained in a letter from Thomas Jefferson to Alberti. Writing from Williamsburg in 1778 Jefferson berated all music in his own country. "If there is a gratification, which I envy any people in this world, it is to your country its music. This is a favorite passion of my soul, and fortune has cast my lot in a country where it is in a state of deplorable barbarism."[24] Jefferson's purpose in writing was to inquire about hiring a group of servant musicians from Italy.

The bounds of an American fortune will not admit the indulgence of a domestic band of musicians, yet I have thought that a passion for music might be reconciled with that economy which we are obliged to observe. I retain among my domestic servants a gardener, a weaver, a cabinet maker, and a stone cutter, to which I would add a vigneron. In a country where, like yours, music is cultivated and practiced by every class of men, I suppose there might be found persons of these trades who could perform on the French horn, clarinet, or hautboy, and bassoon, so that one might have a band of two French horns, two clarinets, two hautboys and a bassoon, without enlarging their domestic expenses. A certainty of employment for a half dozen years, and at the end of that time, to find them, if they chose, a conveyance to their own country, might induce them to come here on reasonable wages.[25]

No evidence exists to confirm the success of this venture, but the idea was rather rare for both its time and place.

Eighteenth-century American amateurs did not limit their music to purely secular pursuits. Many eighteenth-century churches employed instrumentalists in their divine services. In one New England church an instrumental band (usually composed of clarinet, flute, and violoncello) was used to accompany choral singing.[26] The trombone choirs, and other instrumental groups, at the Moravian settlements of Bethlehem, Wachau, Lititz, Nazareth, and Salem are well-known. The Moravians cultivated instrumental music from the very inception of their settlements.

A reasonably active civilian and military instrumental milieu existed by 1789. In that year the newly-elected president, George Washington, traveled throughout the northeastern states where he was greeted by bands of music in nearly every village and city.[27] The limited number of revolutionary army bands could not possibly have been the source of all of the bands of music that greeted the new chief executive. Civilian bands must have been part of eighteenth-century American culture.

The American theater provided an important source of support for the eighteenth-century instrumentalist. Plays were introduced to American audiences in 1703 at Charleston, South Carolina. The first opera was advertised for performance in 1735 in the same city.[28] *Flora* or *Hob in the Well* and *The Devil to Pay* were both premiered in 1736. Except for a brief episode in Charleston the following year, "no further references to theatrical affairs appear in the old sources until 1749."[29] There were plays in Philadelphia in 1749, and the actors moved to New York in 1750.[30]

Thespian interests attempted to establish a theater in Boston in 1750, but laws were immediately passed by the most conservative elements prohibiting such exhibitions. The theater was equated to the antechambers of hell. In March of that year the General Court in Boston passed an act "for preventing and avoiding the many and great mischiefs which arise from public stage-plays, interludes, and other theatrical entertainments."[31] These laws were re-enacted as late as 1792 in spite of efforts by the less conservative elements to repeal them. To skirt this problem, theater productions were frequently advertised as moral lectures or tableaux. Theaters were built while the laws prohibiting their erection and use were still on the books.

Originally music was sandwiched between other dramatic presentations, but it soon achieved billing in its own right. Secular concerts were performed in Boston theaters as early as 1720.[32] Musicians soon found theatrical billing easy even if they did create "great mischiefs."

Civilian instrumentalists continued to find ready employment in the expanding musical markets of the 1780s, but army musicians were not as fortunate. The Continental Army disbanded immediately after the Revolution, and the bands that had been a part of it ceased to exist. The threat of Indian wars forced Congress to reconsider this hasty action, and in 1789 it established a small regular force to confront this unexpected menace. The revival of the military encouraged the organization of civilian as well as regular army bands, and the newly formed militia became one of the most demanding consumers of civilian band music.

Evolution of the Military Organization.

If we are to understand why a revival of the American military stimulated the growth of bands, we must first understand how the army evolved. The Yankee and Confederate forces were not legatees of a single military organization. It was, in fact, a tripartite structure. One of these components, the Unorganized Militia, had nearly expired by 1860. Another, the Organized Militia, a citizen-soldier organization, was philosophically more social than military in purpose. The third component was the smallest of the three, the Regular Army.

It was the development and organization of the citizen-soldier units that promoted the expansion of band music in America. Their gradual growth and evolution guaranteed that the Civil War would be musical as well as bloody. Since the very structure and purpose of these military organizations are so closely entwined with the development of American band music, it would be well to trace briefly the most salient features of their history.

A military officer, Captain John Smith, disembarked in 1607 to help establish the colony of Virginia. Smith's commission as a captain was not obtained from the Crown. It was granted by a corporation chartered for merchant ventures. In short, Smith was a soldier of fortune plying his trade. With the exception of these few chartered mercenaries, America looked to England for guidance in military matters. Britain's military institutions, and the legal concepts that supported them, were quickly adopted by the colonists.

Captain Miles Standish and a small group of armed volunteers who landed in Massachusetts in 1620 were members of the civil body created by the Mayflower Compact. They functioned in a role similar to that of the trainbands (companies of trained citizen-soldiers) of England, defending their counties, towns, and cities.

As the colonies prospered, three types of military organizations developed. These were: the Organized (or Volunteer) Militia of the various colonies; the units of the Unorganized Militia; and the Regulars of the British Army.

The troops of the King's First Guards (called Grenadier Guards since 1815) were the first British Regulars in the colonies. They arrived, under the command of Colonel Herbert Jeffreys, to quell Nathaniel Bacon's abortive revolution.

Some regiments of the King's Regulars were partially raised in the colonies. George Washington's older brother, Lawrence, was commissioned as a captain in the King's Regulars in 1740. On the other hand, George's commission was in the Organized Militia of the colony of Virginia. When he found that a Regular first lieutenant always outranked a provincial major, he vigorously sought a Crown commission. By the age of twenty-seven, he was commanding a brigade as a full colonel of militia, and consequently lost interest in obtaining a commission from the Crown.

When the revolutionary government was seeking troops in 1775 it turned to the Organized Militia of the various colonies. These regiments were recruited by officers named by their colonial governments. The regiments carried their colonial designations to the end of the war. The Organized Militia was the prototype of our National Guard. The bands of music of the revolutionary army were attached to these militia regiments.

In addition to the Organized Militia, other units of only local significance (the Unorganized Militia) served a home-guard function. Although they were not called for service in the Continental Army, they did participate in the war. When a given locale was threatened, they rose up beside the Organized Militia regiments of the Continental Army. When the threat was routed, the personnel demobilized themselves and returned to the towns and farms from whence they had come. Hence, these were limited-duty units that did not pursue the enemy. Generals Stark at Bennington and Herkimer at Oriskaney were part of the Unorganized Militia. Without these units we would probably still be British subjects.

After independence was won the Continental Army was disbanded, with the exception of one artillery battery assigned the detail of caring for government property at West Point. This battery, originally organized by Alexander Hamilton in 1776, became the first unit of America's present-day Regular Army.

Except for this single unit, a standing army of any kind found little support for at least the next decade. Indeed, Jefferson thought it would be impossible to support one since there were not enough paupers to fill the ranks. Other minds prevailed, and the First Congress on 29 September 1789 passed an act for the establishment of troops in the service of the United States. The officers, then as now, swore allegiance only to the United States.

In addition, a Federal Militia Act was passed in 1792. This was really nothing more than a system for counting the able-bodied men in America. All males between the ages of eighteen and forty-four were enrolled. From this census each state was to organize company, regimental, and division-sized districts and to form Enrolled Militia units appropriate to each district. The Enrolled Militia was similar in function and organization to the Unorganized Militia of colonial days with one significant exception. Unlike the Unorganized Militia, the Enrolled Militia was to be available to the federal government during wartime. Until federalized, the individual states were responsible for supplying and equipping these units. By 1811 the Enrolled Militia showed a strength of over 1,000 regiments under some 300 generals. These units met once each year for an annual encampment.

What is more important than the actual formation of the Enrolled Militia is the stimulus that it provided for the organization of purely voluntary companies and regiments that formed *active* military units. Some states encouraged these active bodies and tried to organize at least one within each regimental district of the Enrolled Militia.

The flank companies of the Enrolled Militia regiments of that day were comprised of specially selected men. One flank was held by the Grenade Company or Grenadiers. They led the charge against fixed positions. The other flank was held by a Light Infantry Company that performed local security duties and provided skirmishers for the regiment when in marching order. These elite units were organized within the Enrolled Militia as active militia. With statehouse encouragement, a plethora of "Sea Fencibles," "Pioneer Rangers," "Rough and Ready Grays," and "Invincible Tigers" continued to grow in number until the Civil War. These active units became known as the Organized Militia.

It is important to note that two distinct types of useful, active, military organizations developed prior to the War of 1812: the Regular Army, which was a
small core of professionals, and the Organized Militia, comprised of uniformed
units within the various states. The remainder of the Enrolled Militia gradually
decayed into a state of alcoholic and forensic uselessness. A member of the
14th Regiment of New Hampshire Volunteers, when discussing the raising of
the army by the Union, observed that the Enrolled Militia had long since
ceased to be a source of manpower in case of an emergency. "The traditions of
war had faded from the American mind. The militia was an ancient joke, and
'trainins' were obsolete; the only reminiscences of them cherished by the fighting generation of 1861 being those of bear-skin caps, burlesque soldiering,
pandemonium of drums, gingerbread, and beer."[33]

The Military and the Bands

Although the Enrolled Militia had disintegrated into a pandemonium of
drums and gingerbread, the Organized Militia grew and prospered. By 1800 it
had become common practice for regiments of Organized Militia to associate
themselves with civilian bands of music. In addition, the federal government
provided bands for all Regular Army regiments.

Militia bands received legislative stimulus near the end of the eighteenth
century. Prior to this, bands had been funded by the unit officers since none of
the federal or state militia acts made financial provisions for militia bands.

The instructions of General John Wilkinson, Jr., demonstrate the tendency
around 1800 for a single brigade or regiment to become associated with a band:

The Gentlemen of the 2nd Regiment Inf. having proposed to purchase the instruments
of the Band, which are the General's property, the performers are henceforward to be
considered an appendage of the 2nd Regiment, and are not to be detached from it, but by
the consent of the Commanding Officer of the said Corps present.

John Rogers, having enlisted for the band, is transferred to the 2nd Regiment from the
Artillery, and will be assigned and mustered accordingly from the first instant.[34]

From this we can see that the band was attached, in quasi-official manner, to
the 2nd Infantry Regiment. Musicians were still enrolled as privates, but it is
obvious that John Rogers was to function as a bandsman and not as a soldier of
the line.

A Massachusetts enactment of 1800 provided further official impetus for
the formation of bands: "Each Brigadier General or Command Officer of
Brigades of the Militia of the Commonwealth is authorized, by volunteer enlistment, to raise and organize a band of music in each Brigade, and when so
raised, to issue warrants to them accordingly."[35]

In 1808 New York provided regimental militia bands through the passage of
a similar act. It was amended in 1810 to relieve the regimental officers of the

financial burdens of purchasing the instruments from their private funds. The amendment authorized the purchase of band instruments from the fines collected in the regiments.[36] Similar laws had been enacted in most states by 1810 and bands became an integral part of the Organized Militia.

The United States Congress did not overlook the Regular Army in these matters. General Wilkinson organized a band for his regiment in 1797, and other Regular Army units had similar quasi-official bands from 1800 onwards. The War of 1812 spurred the increase in their number. The regulars were impressed by the bands of the federalized volunteer regiments. When the Regular Army was reorganized in 1821 legislative action insured that bands would be a part of the regular forces as well. The legislation allowed bandsmen (attached to regiments) to draw the pay and allowances of privates officially. The officers of the Regular Army were still required to provide the necessary instruments, but this financial burden was eliminated by regulations issued in 1825. These allowed the surtax on sutlers' receipts to be used to support bands.[37] Bandsmen were still line troops, but could now be formed in a separate squad, at the discretion of the commanding officer. By 1832 all but two regular regiments of infantry, and two of artillery, had bands numbering from fifteen to twenty-four musicians each.[38]

In 1832 the number of musicians allowed each band was reduced to "10 Privates in addition to the Chief Musician allowed by law." An artillery regiment was allowed "one Sergeant to act as Master of the Band, and one Corporal, in addition to the 10 men."

The number here specified and allowed to act as musicians, is not to be exceeded under any circumstance, excuse, or arrangement whatsoever. The men who may compose the Band are to be mustered in their respective companies and will be perfectly drilled and liable to serve in the ranks, and on any occasion of emergency are always to be effective to the service as soldiers.[39]

This regulation is significant, for it is the first to provide for a "Master of the Band" separate from the junior principal musician of the field music. Thus, through legislative action, bands were established for the Regular Army as well as for the Organized Militia.

Still other federal bands existed that were not associated with the infantry regiments of the Regular Army. An artillery school was established at Fortress Monroe in 1824. The 4th Artillery Band arrived at the fortress in 1825 when the parent regiment was assigned to the school. In 1828 the 1st Artillery Regiment assumed responsibility for the school, and the band was detached from the 4th Regiment and assigned to the "School of Practice" as it was called.[40] The group, twenty-four in number, continued service as a post band to the end of the Civil War, through the simple expedient of attaching it, for administration and logistics, to the various artillery units assigned to the school for training. Two bands were present if the unit in training had one of its own.

Other permanent posts had similar musical organizations. The Charles Town Navy Yard at Boston had a band prior to 1853. In that year John Phillip Pfeiffer was transferred from the Navy Yard Band to Annapolis to organize a band for the Navy Academy.[41]

Another important wartime band was that of the United States Marine Corps, stationed in Washington. The group performed a concert on 21 August 1800 when it had an instrumentation of two oboes, two clarinets, two horns, two bassoons, and a drum (the harmoniemusik with one added janizary instrument). It had previously performed on 10 July 1800 in Philadelphia.[42] Its first director was Drum Major William Farr.

In 1840 General Requirement 2-154 was published as a part of the *Marine Corps Manual*. It states that "no person shall be enlisted or reenlisted in the Marine Corps except as a Private or Field Music. All enlistments or reenlistments, other than those for the Marine Band, will be informed that they must enlist or reenlist for general service." Although this general requirement clearly implies that one could enlist in the Marine Corps as a bandsman, such was not the case in actual practice. Congress did not provide funding for the band until 1861, so the Corps revived an old tradition to provide the necessary pay and allowances for the bandsmen. The enlistment of one of its most famous members demonstrates how well the system worked.

Francis Scala, director of the Marine Band during the Civil War, joined the U.S. Navy at Naples, Italy, in 1841, playing clarinet in the band of the *Brandywine* as it sailed to the United States. On 11 August 1842, two years after the publication of Requirement 2–154, he enlisted in the Marine Corps as a field musician. Although he was "officially" a field musician, his letters make it clear that he was to serve as a bandsman. He wrote: "Soon I secured a place in the Marine Band. It wasn't much of an organization then. Congress had made no provision for the Band, so that the ten or twelve members were enlisted as fifers or drummers, there being no leader, a Fife Major and a Drum Major served as leader."[43] Congress unwittingly paid the bandsmen as field musicians, while the corps itself excused them from any requirements for general service.

Scala was appointed bandmaster around 1850, and nine years later Lieutenant C. A. Henderson recorded the effects of his leadership.

Francis Scala, the bearer of this, was appointed leader of the Marine Band about eight years ago. During most of this time, the band was immediately under my charge. The band was not in good condition. Under his direction it at once began to improve and has continued to improve....He was first placed in this position on trial and succeeded so well that he has kept the place without much difficulty.[44]

Although the band gained much from his leadership, it must have performed with some proficiency prior to his appointment, since President Tyler instituted a series of Saturday night concerts on the White House lawn, beginning on 7 January 1845. The concerts continued to the end of the Civil War.[45]

The history of the West Point band is yet to be written. We have already noted that Alexander Hamilton's artillery battery was assigned to West Point immediately after the Revolution. In a few years, attrition and official neglect reduced the unit to an ineffective handful of men. In 1784 Congress assigned fifty-five men to this housekeeping detail and took steps to insure its permanence and well-being. Although music was associated with the unit early in its history, the date when musicians were assigned cannot be established with certainty. Probability suggests that the earliest musical unit was the massed field music rather than a band. In White's account of the West Point band field, musicians are confused with bandsmen. The possibility exists that these men did double duty, since the precedent had already been established. This account notes that martial music was played for George Washington on 31 May 1872 and that the congressional acts of 1792 and 1812 provided "musicians" for the cadet corps, but it is obvious, from both their designation and number, that they were field musicians and not bandsmen.

The first authentic reference to the West Point band is contained in an old book that is a part of the records of the academy. It notes the appointment of Second Lieutenant George W. Gardiner, Artillery, as commanding officer of the band, from 12 October 1816 to 15 September 1817.[46] Since Lieutenant Gardiner was an artillerist it is possible that he was assigned as the commander of an artillery band stationed at the Point, rather than as commander of the West Point band. It cannot be ascertained that "leader" and "commander" are synonymous. In any event, a band was present at the Point early in the nineteenth century, and was still there during the Civil War.

The Naval Academy Band is another pre-Civil War unit. The academy was founded in 1845, but a band was not authorized until 22 November 1852. In spite of its authorization by the Bureau of Ordnance and Hydrography, the band was not actually established until the following year. In 1853 the acting secretary of the navy transferred John Phillip Pfeiffer from the Charles Town Navy Yard band to Annapolis, where he was charged with the organization and direction of a band at the academy. When the band became operative the field musicians were relieved of their duties. Early in the Civil War, the band and the academy were transferred to Newport, Rhode Island. While there, five brass players were added to the instrumentation, bringing the total to eighteen. In 1866 the band was changed from an enlisted status to civil service, but it remained under the baton of Mr. Pfeiffer. It continued as a civilian unit until 1910 when Congress again established it as an enlisted organization of forty-eight performers.[47]

Although the naval academy band was established rather late, the navy had assigned bands aboard its vessels long before the Civil War. Scala's musical career began with the band aboard the *Brandywine*. This ship had musicians on board as early as 26 July 1825. On that date, James F. Drapers's name appears as a musician on the frigate payroll. Taking a cue from the army, the navy had bandsmen mustered as seamen. This practice makes it impossible to determine the size of shipboard bands.

George Jones, a schoolmaster who sailed on both the *Brandywine* and the *Constitution*, described receptions, balls, and funerals at which a band was present during voyages. In 1826 he wrote, "We have a fine band on board containing about twenty excellent musicians." The ship's log of the frigate *Constellation* indicates that John H. Page was promoted to master of the band on 31 August 1826.

On 5 April 1820 William Raymond enlisted at Norfolk, Virginia, as a musician for the United States Navy. On the thirtieth of January of the same year, Julian Gonzales was promoted to first class musician. Whether these men performed as a band, or were part of the field music, cannot be ascertained. The first official recognition of the navy band is recorded in the pay table of the Navy Register for the year 1838, where one bandmaster and several musicians were listed as having received pay.[48]

Eighteenth-century naval records are mute on the matter of bands, but they do indicate that field musicians were assigned aboard United States ships of the line as early as 1775. The muster rolls of military musicians from Pennsylvania[49] include forty-seven "drummers of the navy" and seven "musicians of the navy." The musicians of the navy were probably fifers. Several of these musicians were assigned to the USS *Thunder* and others to the USS *Ranger*. Musicians John Edwards and Stephen Hayny were escaped slaves. The muster indicates that they were "taken away by their masters" in October 1777 and October 1766 respectively. James Webb was "discharged by the Muster Master" on 1 March 1777 because he was too small. John Geyer was only eleven years old when listed as missing on 27 August 1776 after being wounded in the heel. If Geyer was accepted for combat at age eleven, Peter Puttan must have been a mere babe-in-arms when he was discharged in 1777 for being under age.

All of the army, militia, navy, post, academy, and civilian bands had been patterned upon British models; but Napoleon's brilliant successes changed the focus of American military thinking, and French tactics and military traditions became important in United States military circles. While the Regular Army slowly and thoughtfully assimilated those French tactical elements that seemed useful and appropriate, the Organized Militia impetuously and precipitously adopted the most flamboyant aspects of the French military. Since these elements were mostly ceremonial, their adoption transformed the Organized Militia into a gaudily uniformed group of public entertainers. From the point of view of the bandsman, this turn of events presented an unparalleled opportunity. Ceremony, pomp, circumstance, and display required more military music than ever before. Musicians and militiamen soon developed a mutually profitable relationship that lasted to the end of the Civil War.

In 1815 a board of officers encouraged the adoption of French regulations and tactics for the United States Army.[50] What began as a slow and orderly process turned into a tidal wave of change as American military men became acquainted with events associated with the Crimean War of 1854–56. Colorful gallantries, such as the charge of the Light Brigade, in combination with the variegated, gaudy uniforms and fancy precision drills (originated by the Chasseurs de Vincennes in Algiers in 1830), captured the imagination of America's organized militiamen.

Elmer Ephraim Ellsworth of Chicago was an exceptionally avid fan of these Crimean Zouave units. Ellsworth assumed command of a Chicago infantry company known as the National Guard Cadets (renamed the United States Zouave Cadets) on 29 April 1859. Due to the general apathy of its membership, the unit had reached an all-time low prior to his assumption of command. He soon worked out an American adaption of the Algerian-French uniform, and instructed his men in the complicated and precise formations, drills, and manuals of the French models. In a matter of months, the unit reached full wartime strength with additional recruits assigned to a waiting list. Because of his success he was able to enforce a Spartan discipline that banned alcohol, tobacco, profanity, consorting with lewd women, billiards, masked balls, and other dissipations.

Volunteer militia companies like Ellsworth's bound up in themselves much of the social and recreational interest of the day and attracted the youth of the best families. Their armories were the clubrooms of the period, and membership signified social position. Public interest in and adulation for an excellent unit were akin to those granted athletic teams of today, and drill contests attracted huge crowds.

Zouave drills were based upon the maneuvering of four-man squads, and their evolutions included circles, triangles, crosses, double crosses, bayonet drills, and loading and firing exercises; all executed with inconceivable rapidity on the march, on the run, lying or kneeling down, and even lying on the back. The drills were a splendid gymnastic exercise, and when executed in unison formed a continuous and beautiful design. The drill presented by Ellsworth's company required four and one-half hours to complete. Performed without audible cadence, it required both concentration and physical stamina.

In an untitled article in *The Chicago Sunday Mercury* Doestick summed up his observations of the Zouave on 15 July 1859:

A fellow with a red bag having sleeves to it, for a coat; with two red bags without sleeves to them for trousers; with an embroidered and braided bag for a vest; with a cap like a red woolen saucepan; with yellow boots like the fourth robber in a stageplay; with a moustache like 2 half-pound paint brushes, and with a sort of sword-gun, or gun-sword for a weapon, that looks like a cross between a broadsword and a musket—that is a Zouave. A fellow who can "put-up" a 110 pound dumbbell; who can climb an 80-foot rope, hand over hand, with a barrel hanging to his heels; who can do the "giant swings" on a horizontal bar with a 56 pound weight tied to each ankle; who can walk up four flights of stairs holding a heavy man in each hand at arm's length, and who can climb a greased pole feet first, carrying a barrel of pork in his teeth—that is a Zouave. A fellow who can jump 17 feet, 4 inches, high without a springboard; who can tie his legs in a double bowknot around his neck without previously softening his shin-bones in a steam bath; who can set a 40-foot ladder on end, balance himself on top of it, shoot wild pigeons on the wing, one at a time, just behind the eye, with a single-barreled Minie rifle, 300 yards distance and never miss a shot; who can take a five-shooting revolver in each hand and knock the spots out of the ten of diamonds at 80 paces, turning somersaults all the time and firing every shot in the air—that is a Zouave.

Ellsworth's shows attracted the attention of other military units and soon his unique and dazzling company of athletes was in demand throughout Illinois. On 15 September 1859 he entered his unit in an "international" competition sponsored by the United States Agricultural Society at their seventh annual fair held in Chicago. Only one other unit appeared in competition, but when the cadets won the championship flag Ellsworth claimed the title of national champions for his unit. Not a little adverse criticism was evoked by this action. Units from other sections of the country objected that the National Agricultural Society was hardly representative of the entire nation, and that, after all, only one other company had competed.

In reply, Ellsworth issued a challenge to any military company in the United States or Canada, and in the summer of 1860 he toured twenty eastern cities to take on all comers. None could match the speed and precision of the cadets, and the eastern tour was a triumph.

Ellsworth relinquished command of the unit when he returned and moved to Springfield to read law in the office of Abraham Lincoln. He was active in the presidential campaign of 1860 and in 1861 accompanied the president-elect to Washington, where he was charged with the organization of a proposed federal militia bureau.

With the outbreak of hostilities he was given command of a regiment from his native state of New York, which promptly adopted the name "Ellsworth's Zouaves" (officially the 11th New York Infantry). The unit was recruited from the ranks of New York City's firemen.

On 24 May 1861 Ellsworth became the first federal officer killed by gunfire. He had boldly led his unit to the Marshall House, in Alexandria, Virginia, where he raced up the stairs to the third floor and thence by ladder to the roof. There he cut down a Rebel flag said to be visible to Lincoln from his office in the White House. Ellsworth followed Corporal Brownell back down the stairs, but when they reached the first landing J. T. Jackson, the proprietor of the inn, sprang out of the darkness and discharged one barrel of a double-barreled shotgun squarely into Ellsworth's chest, killing him instantly. Brownell returned the fire. Jackson was blown back with a wound in the head, but before he could hit the floor the corporal ran him through several times with his bayonet. Needless to say, he too was dead. Ellsworth had pitched forward down the stairs where they found him lying face down on the now blood-stained Rebel flag.

Ellsworth's exhibitions and tours between 1857 and 1860 created a near-hysteria for Zouave units and served to revitalize the Organized Militia. Wherever his regiment appeared, public-spirited citizens organized similar groups. Existing units quickly adopted his methods, and the nation was soon alive with these flamboyantly named and costumed groups. A band was considered essential to their programs, and a brisk business soon developed between the Ellsworth-type units and civilian bands.

Some observations by John S. Dwight in 1860 can tell us much about this relationship.

In view of the rapid advances in the art of *militaire* made by our citizen soldiery throughout the United States, during the past few years, and the spirit in which they emulate the imposing appearance, pomp of parade, and brilliant martial attractions of the regular army, it strikes us that the subject of military band music merits the attention of the critic. In the military countries of Europe, the martial orchestras include many of the finest solo performers of the continent. . . . As ours is not a military country, our government brass bands do not amount to much, and it is left to our citizen soldiery to possess martial musicians equal to those of the old world.[51]

To provide the requisite "brilliant martial attractions," the militia regiments contracted for the services of the best civilian bands available. Bands were in such demand that most accepted contracts from several different units. Regiments, unsuccessful in hiring well-known civilian bands, quickly organized their own from the available pool of unemployed civilian musicians. The band business suddenly became profitable. Musicians rushed new groups into being, and bands proliferated at a dizzying pace. The revitalization of the militia movement was accompanied by a revitalization of the musical marketplace. Soon "martial music resounded from everywhere."[52]

Fortunately, there were enough musicians available to meet these increased demands. They had been trained by musician-teachers from several different sources. The British and Continental army bands were early wellsprings of musical instruction. These army musicians frequently turned to teaching after being discharged from their military obligations.

John Hiwell, who was continental inspector and superintendent of music under George Washington, moved to Providence after the war. There he established a school of instrumental music and gave concerts. Later, he moved to Savannah where he offered to teach "the clarinet, German flute, hautboy, French horn, concert fife, bassoon, teneroon, guitar etc." He brought with him "a sufficient number of instruments to form a complete band, also a choice collection of musick in the newest taste."[53] Early military bands provided one source of musical instruction. Their numbers were augmented by immigrant European musician-teachers.

The Influx of European Musicians

By 1810 the revolutions of the Old World had driven a large number of

European artists and musicians to the United States. Conditions in America were more stable, giving rise to an active cultural life. A letter from an unidentified German musician, dated 27 July 1828, helps to explain why these artists came in such numbers. When he arrived in New York, he found four theaters, "the Park, Bowry [sic], the Lafayette and the Schottam [Chatham]." He found instant employment at the Lafayette and attended productions in the other theaters as well, all of which he described in a letter to a friend in Germany.

A complete and fully appointed opera is not to be thought of; they have no orchestras for that, for the orchestras here are in the highest degree bad, as bad as it is possible to imagine, and not then complete; oft-times they have two clarinets—but that is a great deal—generally but one. One sees nothing of bassoons, oboes, trumpets or drums [?]; perhaps, now and then, one of the former. Oboes are entirely unknown in this country; there exists but one oboist in North America, and he is said to live in Baltimore.

But in spite of all their incompleteness they play the symphonies of Haydn and grand overtures; and when there comes a gap, they think to themselves—only a passing matter—all right as soon as all cracks again.

In every one of the orchestras you are sure to find a trombone; this instrument serves only to strengthen, and therefore never plays its own proper part, but that of the violoncello; and if the subject is suitable, it plays now and then a passage with the violin. This instrument and the double bass are also the best paid; sixteen or seventeen dollars a week is not uncommon; the others have ten; some of the better twelve, and the very highest for a first clarinet is fifteen, because the usefulness of this instrument comes next to that of a contrebass and the trumpet; but the player must be able to *blow strong*.

It is a matter of course that the director of the orchestra accompanies every solo with the violin; therefore one never hears a solo performed alone; one reason of this is probably to strengthen the voice.

In all of these theatres they perform six times a week; Sunday is a day of rest. The performances begin at 7 1/2 and last till 12, often till one in the morning. If a rope dancer comes, or one who can play the clown well, or jump about a little something like dancing, and in addition can make up all sorts of faces, and farther, one who can grind a hand-organ, blow the panpipes, beat a pair of cymbals and a big drum, and jingle a string of bells upon his hat, and all this at once,—these are the men that are good for the treasury of the theatrical lessees, and who make enormous sums.

Such is the condition of music here, so far as I have been able to learn it during my short stay in New York. I am now going to see if it is better in Boston; I have my doubts of it.

In a pecuniary point of view, music is a lucrative business for men who in addition to their regular engagements can give lessons on the piano or guitar. Such persons can save up a small fortune in a short time;—but only on these two instruments; nobody finds time for any other. Good teachers get one thaler (75 cents) a lesson; others get eighteen thalers ($13,50) for twenty-four lessons.

Living is not very dear here; young musicians from Germany, even those with only moderate talents, who could scarcely keep soul and body together at home by their music, find good incomes here, and if economical, make their fortunes; and moreover, they find themselves placed in the first rank of artists. However, for lesson giving, the English tongue is an indispensable necessity.[54]

European musicians arrived on our shores singly and in groups. The success of two of these groups, during the decade of the fifties, encouraged still others to make it big in the New World.

The first of these was the Germania Society. It was organized in Berlin in January 1848. The members "determined. . .as soon as possible, to undertake a journey to the United States of America; with a view of arousing in the hearts of this (politically) free people, by successive performances of the master-pieces . . . a love for the beautiful Art of music."[55] After a few concerts in Berlin and a three-week stay in London, they arrived in New York in September 1848. They presented their first concert on 5 October in the Astor Place Opera House. They had performed over 900 concerts by 1854, including perfor-mances with local choral societies in the production of numerous oratorios.

The group partially disbanded in 1854. "Mr. Bergmann, the conductor, re-sisted all offers from Boston and moved to Chicago, a city full of music-loving Germans...where he is engaged as conductor of the Philharmonic Society, as organist in one of the principal churches, and as a teacher."[56]

Carl Zerrahn, the principal flutist, became the conductor of the Boston Handel and Haydn Society, and later of the Boston Philharmonic Society. He took about a dozen of his old associates with him, including Schultze, Meixel, Hehl, and Buchheister, all violinists, and Balke, the contrabassist.

Schulz, the principal clarinetist, Zoehler, the second flutist, and Thiede and Hunstock, two bassoonists, joined the orchestra at the Boston Theater. Sentz, the principal trumpet, joined the faculty of the Young Ladies' Academy in Worcester. The third trumpet, Ahner, took a similar position in Providence.

Rudolph, a vocalist and superior hornist, remained in Boston. The other hornist, Kuestenmacher, and Moritz, the second trumpet, joined the Boston Philharmonic under their old leader Bergmann.

The manager of the orchestra, Brandt, went into business in Chicago as an impresario of sorts, while New York received the services of Meyer, an oboist, Luhide, a violoncellist, and Thomas, a trombonist.

Philadelphia enlarged its musical resources with Plagemann, second hornist, and Koppitz, a flutist. Mr. Albrecht, second clarinetist, who pos-sessed, according to *Dwight's Journal of Music* in 1854, an "ideal, artistic and social, and fraternal, self-sacrificing sentiment," moved to Nauvoo, Illinois, to join Mr. Cabet's Icarian Community. This was one of the many social/reli-gious experiments popular during the nineteenth century, and one especially interested in music. The Icarians had an orchestra of forty instruments, two singing societies (one male and one female), and a mixed chorale. They performed an extensive annual concert series. Albrecht also donated his 665-volume library to that community.

The second significant group to arrive on our shores was under the baton of Monsieur Jullien. Jullien (pronounced Julee) was always respectfully addressed as Monsieur Jullien in France, and this title was frequently abbreviated as Mons. Jullien on his printed programs. The Americans anglisized the abbreviation and simply referred to him as "The Mons." The "T" was always capitalized. This was also a mark of esteem from his adoring public since in France, the eldest brother of a reigning monarch had been routinely called Le Monsieur (*The* Monsieur) since the sixteenth century. This set him apart from all of the other Monsieurs at court. He was then referred to as Le Mons (The Mons) when discussed by the courtiers.

After a successful sojourn in Paris as director of the concerts at the Champs-Elysées and the balls of the Academie Royale, he moved to London, where he met with equal success as director of the promenade concerts at Drury-Lane Theater. Jullien, in 1847, organized a "*troupe* of *artistes* of celebrity," and attempted, according to the December 1852 *Dwight's Journal of Music*, to establish in London an English opera "in a style of splendor unprecedented in the annals of the English lyric stage." By the end of the season The Mons (as he was adoringly known to his disciples) was broke, having lost the fortune he had accumulated during the previous fifteen years. It was then that he met P. T. Barnum, who suggested that he bring his not inconsiderable talent and his monster concerts to the United States.

He arrived in the fall of 1853 and by the end of the year had accrued considerable wealth. He then returned to England where his fortune, library, and health were consumed in the flames of the Drury-Lane Theater fire. Returning to his native Paris, he died in an asylum, broke in fact and in spirit.

When Jullien returned to the continent, many of his musicians remained to secure their futures in the United States. It is difficult to estimate the far-reaching effects of these artist-musicians upon the cultural life of America.

Frank Danz, for example, had played violin with Jullien. He became professor of violin at the College of the Brothers at Manhattanville (later Manhattan College), along with a former orchestral comrade, Professor Armand. In 1866 Danz left New York. He traveled to St. Paul, Minnesota, where he replaced Munger as director of the Great Western Brass and String Band and as director of the St. Paul Music Society. A short time later he married the daughter of George Seibert, a prominent figure in band activities in St. Paul. Seibert had organized bands in several Minnesota communities. In response to an ever-growing demand, he organized a Great Western Band for Minneapolis to complement the Great Western Band of St. Paul, which had enjoyed much success under the leadership of Munger and Danz. Danz had just completed a short term of service with the 20th Infantry Band at Fort Snelling when Seibert was seeking a conductor for this new endeavor. Who better to fill the bill than his son-in-law Frank Danz? Danz continued as an active Minnesota bandmaster well into the 1890s.[57]

Bufkin noted that several musicians from the Germania Society joined with the 33rd Massachusetts Band in Savannah after the capitulation of that city on 18 December 1864. These men had been playing and teaching in Savannah since the demise of the society.[58] Musicians from these and other noted European organizations remained in the New World and continued to influence American music as performers and teachers.

Germany was the source of a large number of musical organizations whose members later scattered throughout the United States. All of the inhabitants of a German community, Salzgitter, seem to have made their living during the nineteenth century as wandering musicians who functioned in an incredibly well-organized manner.

The probable origin of these wandering ensembles was the gradual impoverishment of the Salzgitter population by wars that destroyed the town and robbed the men of their customary employment in the salt mines. By the end of the Napoleonic wars the community was at the end of its rope. Total ruin seemed imminent. It was then that the men decided to become musicians.

In 1780 the Salzgitter church register did not list a single individual as a practicing musician. By 1800 sixteen were listed, and in 1812 forty-one were recorded. By 1845 there were seventy-four Kapellen, of four to eight players each, working out of Salzgitter.[59] The Kapellen were quick to adopt the all-brass instrumentation of Wieprecht, and many musicians who had played under him in the German Guards Corps Band joined the Salzgitters.

Those who emigrated wrote home of their experiences. Soon a well-organized system was developed that eased the travel of the less-experienced musicians. Neophytes were provided with traveling companions who, among other things, helped them learn the language of their new country en route.

Homebound families of deceased musicians also received help, and old musicians could return to Salzgitter and find employment at the headquarters of the organization, helping other emigrants, teaching languages or music, or repairing defective instruments. They developed their own "Klesmer" language which they used for recording secret information between Salzgitter groups.

By 1830 most of the traveling Kapellen numbered from twelve to fourteen musicians. Larger groups were found only under contract to British and United States military forces. The United States was a favorite country of the Salzgittern. Their letters indicate that they traveled quite far west. (Several Kapellen were attacked by Indians, one of the Kappellen girls married an Indian chieftain, and another married the chieftain's grandson.)

Several Kapellen were made up of women. "Among the other novelties now in St. Paul is a band composed of women, who perform on brass instruments—the only one of its kind in the country. The ladies have a reputation for 'blowing up' delinquent husbands sometimes, but this is the first instance we have known them to supply surplus wind to metal mouthpieces. . . . They are said to be accomplished performers."[60]

Yet another German organization influenced music in America.

The "little German band" was once an institution of the United States. Composed usually of a half dozen or more tolerable musicians, of whom one was always a seasoned immigrant who knew his way about, while the rest were "green horns", the little German bands, dressed in blue German cap, came into many American cities as regularly as the flowers of spring. These musical immigrants came in droves via steerage, of course.[61]

Prior to 1860 the number and influence of civilian bands were far greater than historians have been wont to admit.

The whole social atmosphere of the midwest...was one that was very receptive to the band, mentally, socially and economically. Furthermore, with the paucity of military bands, so abundant on the east coast, the Minnesota civilian community band was able to evolve and develop without having its growth stunted by the overshadowing military units....The band was a constant ingredient of civil celebrations and as a socializing element, the band drew the masses together for moments of diversion and social intercourse.[62]

There were more than fifty civilian bands in Minnesota prior to 1860. The northern half of that commonwealth was hardly a cultured civilization. It was Indian country, defended by a row of forts running diagonally across the state. Fort Abercrombie, near Moorhead, Minnesota, anchored the left flank. Fort Ripley, just south of Brainerd, held the middle of the line, and Fort Snelling, located in Minneapolis, held the eastern flank.

By 1852 the number of immigrant and home-grown musicians in the United States was staggering. Dwight notes that in New York,

It is said that there are two thousand and eighty-five persons, male and female, . . that live by their musical labors. Some teach vocal music; some teach instrumental music; some sing; some play the piano; some fiddle; some give concerts; some sing in church; some sing in opera; some sing in both church and opera; some play the bugle, flute, haughtboy, French horn, cornet á piston, opheiclide, banjo, brass drum, kettle drum, tenor drum, triangle, cymbals, fife, violoncello, clarionet, flageolet, guitar, melodeon, organ, tamborine, trombone, or other noisy instrument; and all of them blow their own trumpets.[63]

Most of these musicians were available to the regiments of the Civil War.

THE BRASS BAND REVOLUTION

The St. Paul female band, like almost all of its contemporaries, performed on brass instruments. So did the little German bands. Early military bands were comprised of woodwinds. What developments occurred in the nineteenth century to alter so radically the eighteenth-century harmoniemusik?

The first development occurred in 1810 when an Irish bandmaster, Joseph Halliday, applied five keys to a bugle constructed in the usual trumpet shape. By opening the key holes, a full chromatic scale of over two octaves could be achieved. This instrument was named the Kent (for the Duke of Kent) or keyed bugle.[64]

William R. Bayley, who played with the band of the Pennsylvania State Fencibles during the war years, was an amateur musician whose career began in the early 1830s, with the band of Bailey's Circus and Menagerie. During the early 1840s he learned to play the bugle and trumpet while operating a music store in Cincinnati. In 1893, in a brief history of music in Pennsylvania, written for the *Philadelphia Evening Star*, he spoke very highly of the bugle.

I played in one [band] which was attached to Bailey's Circus and Menagerie in 1833, and the following year in another which my father organized and taught in Chillicothe, Ohio.

Brass instruments had in the meantime been generally introduced, and it was here that I met the superb E-flat bugle soloist, Edward Kendall,...This man was indeed a wonderful performer and was justly noted as the prince of buglers. For quality of tone, power, and execution he has never been surpassed. Among the first bugle players in this country were Willis and my father, William Wood Bayley, over seventy years ago. Willis was at West Point and my father at Norwich, Vermont, afterwards Middletown, Connecticut, at Capt. A. Patridge's Military College.

Professor Willis had three sons, James, Richard, and John. The first two named were bugle players, the latter a flute player; all well known leaders in New York City.[65]

Kendall, who served as director of the Boston Brigade Band, was unquestionably the most famous Kent bugle player in the nation. His performances established the standard for interpretation and execution for all of the bandsmen of America. Aspiring bandmasters and performers alike sought instant public approval by advertising themselves as students of the noted Ned Kendall. Mr. Gayety, for example, described himself as a pupil of the noted Kendall when he sought to organize Gayety's Brass Band in St. Paul, Minnesota, in 1849.[66]

The Kent bugle, popular in American bands from 1820 to 1855, was at best an awkward instrument. By 1860 it had been virtually replaced by valved brass, although a few Civil War bandmasters continued to use it. It was a rather delicate instrument, not given to the rigors of field duty, and was not commonly found in regimental bands.

Frank Jackson was bandmaster of the regular army's 6th Regimental band, stationed at Fort Snelling. His bugle was said to be "well known throughout the length of the Mississippi."[66] The director of the band of the 2nd Minnesota Regiment of Volunteers, Robert Rhodes, was first known as a celebrated bugler, but adopted the cornet for wartime service, and continued to use it with the minstrel troop he organized after his return to civilian life.

Since valved instruments were demonstrably less cumbersome and more durable for field service, they quickly replaced all of the keyed group that had preceded them. The serpent, for example, and its replacement, the bass horn, as well as its successor, the ophicleide, were quickly relegated to oblivion by the valve tuba.

Piston virtuosi soon appeared to challenge the Ned Kendalls of the keyed brass world. Harvey Dodworth was accepted as a master of the instrument by 1840, and the celebrated Arban was world-renowned as a master of the cornet á pistons by 1850.

Other authors have provided detailed histories of the valved brass instruments. Large numbers of manufacturers experimented with this promising development during the first decades of the nineteenth century. The musical world was soon confronted and confounded by "clavicors, althorns, bombardons, tenorhorns, basstubas, burdons, saxotrombas, saxtubas, neo altos, bombardons contrebasse, cornophones, sudrephones, ebocornos and cornotinos," to mention but a few. Adam Carse had the final word on this subject when he wrote that:

Most of these [instruments] would probably fail to establish a claim to any individual existence, for the field is limited, and there is not room for any great variety between the tone-quality of the cornet and that of the bugle, whether large or small; nor does the admixture of trumpet-, horn- or trombone bore, and their characteristic mouthpieces, supply sufficient variety to provide very many new and clearly different tone-qualities. Many claimants . . . within this restricted field have had to give up their pretended individuality and throw in their lot with the common types which are in use to-day. . . . [The instruments may] be differently named . . . but their nomenclature is always more varied than their tone-qualities.[68]

One type of valve was patented by Stoelzel and Bluemhel in 1818,[69] but this was not the first valve added to an instrument. The Prussian Rifle Regiment already had a complete valve-brass band in 1814 for which Cherubini had written parade marches, quicksteps, and other music of a similar type. Around 1830 Wilhelm Wieprecht, then director of the bands of the German Guards Corps, revolutionized Prussia military music by converting all the bands to valve brass. He standardized the instrumentation so that any number of corps bands could be combined. It was then practical to print music for these groups, and the hand-copying of parts was no longer necessary.

It is difficult to document the first all-brass band in America. The Boston Brigade Band was founded in 1783 as the Massachusetts Band. In 1810 it was reorganized as the Green Dragon Band, and in 1821, under the auspices of Major Daniel Simpson, proprietor of the Green Dragon Tavern, it was again reorganized under the baton of Asa Fillebrown as the Boston Brigade Band. It made its first public appearance, at a brigade muster on the Boston Common, on 23 September 1821. In 1824 its instrumentation included six clarinets, a flute, a bassoon, a keyed bugle, two trumpets, two horns, a serpent, a bass horn, a brass drum, and cymbals. In 1830 E. H. Weston of Belmont became the bandmaster. In 1835 the band under its new leader, Ned Kendall, adopted an all-brass instrumentation consisting of one Kent bugle (Kendall's), four cornets, two trumpets, two altos, three trombones, an ophicleide, and a bass. Although all are brass instruments, they represent a mixture of valved and keyed types.[70]

It would seem that Dodworth's group could perform as a brass band as early as 1837.

In the course of their long and brilliant career, Dodworth's Band has made great improvements in the plans and machinery of brass instruments generally. The Nova Ebor Corno (New York Horn) was invented and used by them twenty-three years ago, to supply the important desideratum of a medium harmony in brass band music. They also invented those curious instruments composed of bells turned backward, and first used them in 1841.[71]

DOUBLING ON BRASS: CIVILIAN AND MILITARY MUSICIANS

A professional musical organization was expected to perform as a brass band for parades and excursions, as a mixed wind band for outdoor concerts, and as a string unit for the dances that followed these entertainments. Riverboat bands frequently paraded as brass bands, played as theater orchestras during the show, and then played as string bands for the dances that followed. Indeed, a three-faceted program was the norm for all professional bands. Hall's Brass Band appeared in concert on Wednesday 13 June 1858 "after the Protean fashion set by other bands, in the three forms of Brass Band, Reed Band, and Orchestra...."[72] The Boston Brigade Band performed a concert in the Boston Music Hall on 15 May 1858

in which they appear[ed] both as a Reed Band of twenty-five instruments and [as] a Brass Band of eighteen....We rejoice to see other Bands following the example of the Germania in this good direction of a return to clarinets and oboes, and bassoons and French-horns: but pray take care to have enough of them, for this noisy, bullying and unregenerate Sax family requires a deal of softening and subduing, if not snubbing into utter silence sometimes.[73]

Dwight could not overcome his prejudice against brass bands. "We did not stay to hear the all-brass portion of the programme, the waltzes, Galopades, &c., nor the Potpourri descriptive of a battle. Such claptrap is indeed childish, and a degradation of the art of music."[74]

Whether Dodworth's Band or the Boston Brigade Band was the first to convert to brass instruments, they were two of the best-known and most highly respected groups in the east. Both were associated with crack militia units.

When they adopted brass instruments for their military duties other groups quickly emulated them.

Civilian instrumentalists generally performed with several different militia units to increase their earnings. He who could double on several instruments was the epitome of commercialism. In addition, many performers advertised themselves as teachers or professors of music, stating that they were competent to teach almost anything that was blown, struck, plucked or strummed. One went even further, claiming that "forming bands [was] a specialty."[75]

The brass revolution that began in Prussia was transplanted to this country, where it flourished and prospered. By 1850 nearly every hamlet in the nation could claim its own brass band, and any modestly-competent brass player could find employment. Indeed, bandsmen were in short supply.

The shortage of field musicians was, if anything, even greater. The modest success of the Organized Militia during the late eighteenth century had already absorbed the available supply of field musicians. During the first half of the nineteenth century more field musicians were trained, and an adequate musical competence prevailed. The success of Ellsworth's tours, begun in 1857, produced an explosion of new units, and a rejuvenation of those already in existence. By 1860 there weren't enough field musicians to go around, and many regiments, entering service, actively recruited young boys as field musicians in spite of their musical illiteracy.

A 1789 exchange of letters between Lieutenant Robert Rankin and Colonel Barrows, the commandant of the Marine Corps, paints a vivid picture of the difficulties facing recruiters in search of competent field musicians. Lieutenant Rankin, recruiting in Baltimore on behalf of the corps, reported his lack of success in these matters. "I am sorry to inform you that I can neither enlist a drummer or fifer in this place, as they are engaged at the different Regts of Militia of Baltimore and are generally paid by the individual complements here from 2 to 3 dollars for attending on them for one evening only."[76]

Since Baltimore proved to be a barren recruiting ground, the commandant turned to Lieutenant James Weaver as a more promising source of musicians. He instructed him to go to New York where "you are to procure as many drummers and fifers as you can. If they are really capital and can not be had without a bounty, you must give it. The Officers here have agreed to advance Ten Dollars each to enable the Regiment to procure music."[77]

The desire for music was truly compelling, for a lieutenant's pay was only eighteen dollars monthly. Lieutenant Weaver experienced the same lack of success in New York that Lieutenant Rankin had experienced in Baltimore. Colonel Burrows now sought the help of higher office and placed his problem before the secretary of the navy. "It appears impossible to procure music without a bounty. I wish you would give me liberty to extend such sums as I shall think fit for the Corps. We at present, have agreed to raise three hundred dollars amongst ourselves, until your pleasure is known. Other troops give a bounty and volunteer Corps expend large sums in this way, which makes it difficult to procure musick of any kind. I enlisted a fifer out of my own pocket and the villain went off in a few hours afterwards."[78]

The commandant betrayed feelings of hopelessness and even frustration as he continued his efforts to recruit musicians. He sought a fresh source of inspiration and turned the entire problem over to his newly appointed executive officer, Lieutenant Jonathan Church. "I wish you success in musick," he wrote. "I should suppose you might get some lads enlisted and have them taught, but they must pay for their being taught out of their own money. . . . I shall leave these matters to your own judgement, observing that it will not be worth while to enlist boys unless you can procure men of musical talents to instruct them. I should prefer them being taught by note than by ear."[79]

Lieutenant Church was partially successful, and really deserved an award for the ingenuity he displayed in attacking this seemingly hopeless problem. He replied to the commandant's letter. "Music I am not so successful in, have three fifers, one of whom plays the violin, and one drummer. Except my little son who is imperfect yet . . . the whole number [of Marines] recruited is one hundred and eighteen, but three has since been discharged and some dessertions. It will impede recruiting to be without musick very much."[80]

By now nearly seven months had elapsed, and only three fifers had been enlisted in addition to the lieutenant's son, who did not seem to count for much. Two months later the search continued. The commandant, now driven by total desperation, was even willing to bend the regulations a little in order to accomplish his musical purposes. He instructed Lieutenant Keen that, to be marines, "all men must be sound, above 18 and not exceeding 40 when enlisted. They may be enlisted from 5 feet 4 to any height above. No foreigners or vagrants are to be enlisted. Drummers and Fifers may be enlisted of any country but they must be white men. . . . The first necessary thing to be done is to get a good sergeant and good musick."[81]

The yearlong search for field musicians eventually paid dividends. On 10 July 1800 under the direction of Drum Major William Farr, "the fife and drum corps . . . played 'Yankee Doodle,' 'Rural Felicity,' and 'Washington's March' with as much noise and vigor as any other military band of the Revolution."[82]

The opening of hostilities at Fort Sumter turned an acute shortage of musical talent into a veritable famine. Since most bands and field musicians served several different regiments of militia, there was not enough talent to go around when all of these units rushed into active service. For this reason, a regiment securing the enlistment of a fine band was the envy of the entire army, and the musicians were the pride and joy of every soldier, from the commanding officer to the lowest private.

In spite of the mutually profitable prewar alliance between militiamen and musicians, professional civilian bands could not have existed had their fiscal well-being been solely dependent upon their military commitments. It was the success of, and demand for, their civilian performances that made these organizations profitable.

Although eastern bands received a great deal of publicity when they appeared with the gaudily uniformed militia units, many bands existed without noticeable support from the military. If most western hamlets were too small to support an active regiment, they could still boast about their brass band. In all probability bands were introduced into frontier areas by the army, but they were quickly outnumbered by professional and amateur civilian groups. In 1852 Minnesota "which, four years ago heard no music but the hi-i-e-hi-i-e of the Indians, accompanied by the instrumental thump upon the parchment head of a hard keg, and the stirring airs of the Fort Snelling Band—now has a variety of professional talent."[83] Lavish editorial praise had been heaped upon the band of the 6th Regiment stationed at the fort; their performances transcended the simple ends one might expect from an art form. "Unquestionably there is much music in the 6th Regimental Band. What triumph of Art seems more wonderful than this? . . . It is the most powerful element of influence amongst us for good, next to the pulpit and the press."[84]

It was not long after the arrival of the band of the 6th Regiment that a cacophony of civilian brass bands swarmed through the territory. Tiede documents the formation of Mr. Gayety's Band in St. Paul in 1849. It was followed by J. C. Lawrence's Brass Band, organized in Saint Anthony in 1852. N. P. Ingalls organized a band (attached to the Minnesota Pioneer Guard) in February of 1855 and still others made their appearance in other parts of the state. The Red Wing Brass Band and Taylor's Brass Band were organized in 1854, the professional "Old Gents" Band in 1856, and in 1858 Russell Munger (a St. Paul music store owner) organized the famous Great Western Band of St. Paul. Others of pre-Civil War origin included Wagner's Band, the Concordia and Germania Bands of Mankato, Butt's Band, Sidwell's Union Quadrill Band, the Saint Peter Amateur Band, the Young Gent's Band (also in Saint Peter, Minnesota, in 1858), the Owatonna Brass Band, the New Ulm Band, Hazen's Cotillion Band, the Mankato Tin Horn and Tin Pan Band, the Red Wing Brass and Cotillion Band, and the German String Band of Dubuque, Iowa; not to mention several nomadic "German Bands" that periodically passed through the territory. Other bands were organized during and after the war. Most of these bands operated in communities no larger than villages. With the exception of St. Paul and St. Anthony, Mankato was the largest town in Minnesota. By 1875 it had a population of only 5,402.[85]

This vast array of community bands could not have been supported solely by the militia units on this far-flung frontier. Their civilian pursuits paid their way. Many were sponsored by societies such as the Turners, or by fire departments. A few were organized by churches. A number of others were established on a professional or semi-professional basis by individual bandmasters.

They performed for vaudevilles, minstrel troops, circuses, excursions, dime concerts, and at political rallies. They blew civic celebrations in, and national holidays out. They played for wedding dances, cotillions and balls, open-air promenade concerts, steamboat excursions, and dances in the public "Lust Gardens," as one moralizing editor labeled these German pleasure spas. They played in theaters, and to a lesser extent, in concert halls. They serenaded citizens, regardless of rank, and played benefits for all sorts of worthy causes.

Even the more noted eastern bands, attached to volunteer militia regiments, were not restricted to performing solely for these military units. They were free to accept as many civilian engagements as their leaders could contract. A band that caught the fancy of the fickle public could earn a bundle.

By 1837 Lothian's New York Brass Band had become a favorite of society, commanding sixty to eighty dollars for each performance. In 1845 Dodworth's Cornet Band replaced Lothian's as the musical representative of the famed 7th Regiment of New York Volunteers. Success followed success until Dodworth held a near monopoly in both the civilian and military markets, contracting for all sorts of musical endeavors in New York, Boston, Philadelphia, and other eastern cities. His success encouraged active competition from other groups.

Clean execution, nifty uniforms, versatility of style, and a substantial library of music in the public taste were essential elements of success. Engagements, such as dances and cotillions, defined the type of music required. Parades and civic celebrations called for rousing renditions of the national airs, marches, and other stirring music. "Negro songs" were the stock in trade of the vaudeville minstrel bands, while other popular songs of the day provided concert fare for open-air performances.

Concert bills show that performances were mixtures of vocal and instrumental pieces, frequently interspersed between moral lectures or tableaux. They invariably included arrangements of popular operatic airs. Although these arrangements did not please the sophisticated Mr. Dwight in Boston, they were the only culture available in the outer regions of the growing republic, and the public regarded them highly.

We hope that Mr. Jackson, the leader of the 6th Regt's Band, will not discard those admirable compositions of Rossini which the band performs so well, when we inform him that Rossini, that sweet gentlemanly composer, has stripped all the romance from his character, by putting up pork for the Balogna market, being extensively engaged in that trade. He should visit our great market in Cincinnati and take lessons in killing and packing the grunters.[86]

The long-accepted practice, especially among German musicians, of doubling on several different instruments, made this wide variety of musical styles possible.[87] Professional groups could provide indoor music, as well as the more blaring brass variety better suited to the out-of-doors.

Civilian bands performed for the military whenever they could. Bands were significant and essential ingredients in any successful regimental display. Unit officers would not have expended the necessary sums to hire brass bands had they been regarded as merely decorative. This alliance of bands and the military was not simply a manifestation of patriotism. Commercially-minded musicians capitalized upon the faulty military concept that substituted pomp and circumstance for sound military training.

A band's Civil War service, however, was not the result of financial need coupled with opportunity. The compelling expectations of their fellow soldiers prompted musicians to enlist. The tradition of associating band music with all civil, social, and community celebrations was established long before the war. When the regiments entered upon active service, the enlistment of a band of music allowed the men to take a little of the comfort of home into the field. It was the performance of these civilian musical traditions by the military bands that most inspired the authors of regimental histories and the diarists from the ranks.

The music aroused a pleasant recall of home, of wife and family, of childhood sweethearts and beloved companions, of incidents of the past, and of pleasant civilian pursuits. Music could inspire a fever of patriotism and simultaneously anesthetize the mind from thoughts of the bloody tomorrows that came in endless succession.

The enlistment of hundreds of bands seemed sensible to the citizen-soldiers of 1860. When they entered active service officers and enlisted men burdened themselves with tons of civilian impedimenta, from sleeping caps to personal servants. Amongst all this bric-a-brac from home, a small band of music to lighten lonely hours paled to a logistical insignificance. The soldiers wanted—even needed—the bands. Multitudes of musicians responded to their urgent pleas and marched off to war.

Once in the field the musicians quickly realized that their civilian musical pursuits were not adequate preparation for the rigorous demands of field service. Military incompetence was not limited to the newly commissioned officers or neophyte enlisted men. Rampant musical nincompoopery was the natural concomitant of the acute shortage of trained field musicians and bandsmen. Indeed, the musicians were often the first members of a unit to attract the personal attention of a commander. Faultering fifes, bleeting brass, and ragged drum rolls were difficult shortcomings to keep secret from even the most tone-deaf officer. Drum majors and bandmasters were called to task, and they quickly organized crash programs to improve the performance of their charges.

Musicians of the Volunteer Militia regiments had to master a substantial body of music and military ritual that had become established tradition in the Regular Army during the revolutionary war. The field musicians were particularly important in these matters. Some calls served to regulate daily army routine. Others, more ceremonial in nature, were meant to insure that war would be both ritualized and civilized. Rendering an opponent hors de combat is less like killing if it can be accomplished in a ritualistic frame. Military musicians were a part of this ritualization.

Many internal military functions had been codified, sanitized, and civilized through the addition of ceremony. Funerals and executions had long employed appropriate music. The "Dead March" from *Saul* was already traditional in the British Army by 1775 and was routinely used in the colonies as well.

Other ceremonies were calculated to instill the troops with the proper fear and respect. The "Rogues March" was traditionally used for "drumming out" incorrigibles. During the siege of Boston, Daniel McCurtain chronicled the treatment given a thief. First the scoundrel endured thirty-nine lashes with a cat-o-nine-tails. Then, "after having his number, he was drummed out of camp by fifty and two drums and as many wifers. This was the first time that ever I heard such a number of drums beat all together, they made such a report in my ears, when accompanied by such screaking of whifes that I could not hear the next man to me, or however, could not hear what he said."[88]

The surrender of a besieged garrison or post was another occasion for ceremony. Defenders were to hold out until the wall was breached and until the commander had made an honorable defense. When it became evident that he would lose the battle, he was to surrender his command in a manner commensurate with the determination of his resistence. After the flag had been respectfully lowered and saluted by cannon fire, the "Garrison [was to] march out through the breach, with their arms, baggage, spare carriages, horses; drums beating, fifes playing, matches lighted on both ends, flying colours."[89] The vanquished, as a demonstration of respect for his conqueror, performed a march common to the victor. If the defense had been brilliantly executed, the victor permitted the performance of patriotic airs common to the defenders. All of this sounds terribly familiar to anyone knowledgeable of the events accompanying the surrender of Fort Sumter.

European traditions governing the employment of military bands had also been firmly established long before 1776, and these traditions were honed and refined during the French Revolution.

The wind band in France. . .had always been associated with military music. . . .Its major activities were on the battle field or parade ground, but the Band of the Francaises also gave occasional serenades on the boulevards of Paris. . . .With the revolution, the situation changed dramatically. Both the size. . .and the concept of its use expanded considerably to accomodate new political purposes. Thus in the early 1790's wind bands not only fulfilled their former responsibilities, but they performed serious music. . .written expressly for them. . .and accompanied the gigantic choruses of the patriotic festivals as well.[90]

French armies used two types of bands. The first, called "Une Fanfare," consisted only of brass instruments without valves. Since these were limited to

the overtone series, their stock in trade was battle music and ceremonial flourishes. The French employed a second type called variously "Une Orchestre
de Fanfare," "Une Harmonie," "Une Musique d'Harmonie," or "Un
Orchestre d'Harmonie." These groups covered the gamut of woodwind and
brass instruments and were thus not confined to a limited repertoire. An additional term "Une Musique Militarie," was used in a generic manner to include
all types of military music. Gradually this last term acquired greater spe-
cificity until it was generally accepted as referring only to a band of mixed
instrumentation. Following the French Revolution, the valveless brass
groups were abandoned in favor of the more flexible "Un Orchestre d'Harmonie." The French had added janizary instruments late in the eighteenth
century. Other winds were added early in the nineteenth century, and their
parts were provided into the traditional designations of first, second, and third.

Governing powers of the French Revolution encouraged concerts of gigantic proportion to help inflame the impassioned bourgeois heart. The finest
French composers wrote for these wind groups. *Musique d'Harmonie*, published during the revolution, includes works by Francois Joseph Gossec,
Charles-Simon Catel, Estienne-Nicholas Mehul, Louis Emmanuel Jadin,
Franchois Devienne, Estienne Solere, Rudolph Kreutzer and other notables
who wished to display their patriotism. Patrick Gilmore's monster concert (including 1,000 school children, 2 batteries of field artillery, a 300-piece band, 2
fire companies with anvils, all the regimental bands and church bells in the city,
and several soloists) in New Orleans during the Civil War and the Peace
Jubilees that he staged in later years amply demonstrate the durability of traditional French military music.

Traditions of the French revolutionary period were adopted by American
bands during the first two decades of the nineteenth century. The Salem Light
Infantry Band, organized in 1806, adopted this early nineteenth-century
French instrumentation. The Boston Brigade Band, when it first appeared in
1821, employed six clarinets, one flute, one bassoon, one keyed bugle, two
trumpets, two French horns, a serpent, a bass horn, and the janizary bass drum
and cymbals.

French influences were never totally abandoned by American military
musicians. Even during the Golden Age of the Brass Band, some military
bands clung to the older French traditions. Professional civilian bands had
always had the capability of performing as a mixed ensemble or as a brass
band. The United States Marine Band and the bands of Grafulla and Dodworth are cases in point.

The Scala collection of music (from his tenure as conductor of the Marine
Band) demonstrates his affinity for the mixed wind ensemble. From the surviving scores it is obvious that this was his favorite instrumentation. It was this
mixed ensemble that played the popular concerts on the White House lawn
during the Civil War. A few post bands took their cue from Scala and used a

similar instrumentation. All Civil War regimental bands performed the same musical functions as the bands attached to the French armies of the revolution.

Three facets of the development of American military music have been established. First, America was filled with instrumentalists long before the Civil War required their services in large numbers. Second, the increasing use of brass instruments by German military bands and a parallel French movement led to the establishment of mixed brass and woodwind ensembles in America. Although both instrumentations were used during the Civil War, it was the German tradition that prevailed in most regimental bands of the Civil War period. Third, the military musical traditions of Europe moved to our shores. These traditions were adapted to the peculiar needs of our militia system that, in turn, stimulated the development of civilian bands. When these militia musicians donned the Blue or the Gray, they were not only representative of their age, but were also part of a line of military musicians extending back to the Roman Legions. Both civilian and military bands became cultural and social touchstones for the vast majority of the noneastern population of the United States.

Bandsmen established themselves in both the civilian and military communities. The public came to expect—indeed to demand—the presence of a band at all social, civic, or ceremonial functions. An army of citizen-soldiers expected a band to be present for similar occasions during their active military service. Band traditions, established long before the Civil War, were simply transferred to the two armies.

Even older traditions governed the employment of field musicians in all branches of the service. These men were not mere entertainers. They were essential to the regulation of daily routine. Their roles had been clearly defined prior to the holocaust, and their music had become part of America nearly a century before the Civil War.

The number of Civil War musicians is astounding. It was impossible for the Union or Confederate soldier to escape the sound of music. A band of music accompanied the drama as it unfolded at Fort Sumter. Bands were present, or near at hand, during every major engagement of the war. Bands played incessantly in "The Old Camp Grounds." They eased the suffering of the wounded in the hospitals and accompanied the unfortunate to their final rest. They celebrated victories and mourned defeats. They provided dignity for ceremonial occasions but were sometimes a cause of levity when dignity would have been more appropriate. Bands fanned the flames of burning cities and paced the withdrawal of the troops from the ashes. Bands accompanied combatants as they exchanged tobacco for coffee and sometimes brought the Blue and Gray together, if only briefly, in a common religious or human experience. Brass bands accompanied the miscreants and recalcitrants, the goldbricks and thieves, to their places of punishment. They drummed in the recruits and drummed out the misfits. They mourned the dead and cheered the living. They accompanied awards and executions with equal solemnity. They measured the tread of an army through a vanquished land and paced the last Grand Review. Some played from horseback. Others sloughed through the dust and the mud on foot. They serenaded the mighty and the lowly without distinction. Some were first-rate musical organizations. Others were truly horrible. But good or bad, large or small, they were loved by the common soldiers.

NOTES

1. John Sullivan Dwight, ed., *Dwight's Journal of Music*, 41 vols. (1881; reprint ed., New York: Johnson Reprint Corp., 1968), 9, no. 16 (19 July 1856): 126 (hereafter cited as *DJM*).

2. *DJM* 9, no. 18 (2 August 1856): 141.

3. Ibid.

4. There is at least one period in the history of American military music when this may well have been the norm.

5. Raoul F. Camus, "The Military Band in the United States Army Prior to 1834" (Ph.D. diss., New York University, 1969), Appendix A.

6. Camus quotes from a number of letters between Washington and his field commanders that question the propriety of certain expenses from these regimental sources.

7. Washington to Sullivan 20 Dec. 1778 in John C. Fitzpatrick, ed., *The Writings of George Washington from Manuscript Sources, 1745–1797* George Washington Bicentennial Commission (Washington, D.C.: Government Printing Office, 1931–1944), 13:440.

8. Camus, "Military Band," p. 311.

9. Washington to Stark, February 1780 as cited in John C. Fitzpatrick, *Writings of Washington*, 13: 63–64.

10. Camus, "Military Band," p. 314.

11. Robert Hind, *Discipline of the Light Horse* (London: W. Owen, 1778), p. 206.

12. Anthoney Baines, *Woodwind Instruments and Their History* (New York: W. W. Norton, 1957), p. 308.

13. Camus, "Military Band," p. 379.

14. David McBain, "The Royal Military School of Music," *Musical Times* 98, no. 1372 (June 1957): 311–12.

15. Ibid., p. 311.

16. Robert Ernst, *Immigrant Life in New York City, 1825–1863* (New York: Columbia University, King's Crown Press, 1949), p. 97.

17. Oscar George Theodore Sonneck, *Early Concert-Life in America, 1731–1800* (Leipzig: Breitkopf and Haertel, 1907), p. 7.

18. John Cotton, *Singing of Psalmes...A Treatise....*(London: printed by M. S...., 1647), p. 15.

19. James W. Thompson, "Music and Musical Activities in New England, 1800–1838" (Ph.D. diss., George Peabody College for Teachers, 1962), reprinted from *Proceedings of the American Antiquarian Society* (October 1939): 24.

20. Henry Wilder Foote, "Musical Life in Boston in the Eighteenth Century," re-

printed from *Proceedings of the American Antiquarian Society* (October 1939): 5.

21. Matthew Page Andrews, *Virginia, The Old Dominion* (Garden City, N.Y.: Doubleday Doran & Co., 1937), p. 191.

22. Oscar George Theodore Sonneck, *Early Opera in America* (Boston: G. Shirmer, 1915), p. 26.

23. *Virginia Gazette*, 13 June 1777.

24. Adrienne Koch, *The Life and Selected Writings of Thomas Jefferson*, ed. A. Koch and Willien Piden (New York: Modern Library, 1944), pp. 262–64.

25. Ibid., p. 263.

26. Samuel Gilman, *Memoirs of a New England Village Choir, With Occasional Reflections By a Member* (Boston: S. G. Goodrich and Co., 1829), p. 38.

27. *Pennsylvania Gazette*, 22 April 1789. *Boston Independent Chronicle*, 5, 12 November 1789. Camus makes a similar observation in "The Military Band," p. 404.

28. Sonneck, *Early Opera*, pp. 5–12.

29. Ibid., p. 14.

30. Ibid., p. 13.

31. Thompson, "Music and Musical Activities," p. 533.

32. Lloyd F. Sunderman, "Sign Posts in the History of American Music Education," *Education* 62 (May 1942): 519.

33. Francis H. Buffum, *A Memorial of the Great Rebellion...the Fourteenth Regiment New Hampshire Volunteers* (Boston: Franklin Press, Rand, Avery & Co., 1882), p. 141.

34. "General Order No. 12," July 1803 from *General Wilkinson's Order Book*, p. 404, microfilm M–645, roll E, Record Group 94, National Archives, Washington, D.C. as cited by Camus, "The Military Band," p. 429.

35. State of Massachusetts, *Laws for Regulating and Governing the Militia of the Commonwealth of Massachusetts* (Boston: Young and Mimms, 1800), Section 14.

36. The State of New York, "An act to organize the militia of the state of New-York." *Laws of the State of New York* (New York: Southwick and Pelsue, 1809), 334, n.p.n. With this is "An act to ammend the act entitled: 'An act to organize the militia of this state.' " [n.p., 1810?] Both of these are reprinted in The State of New York, "An act to organize the militia of the State of New-York....with the acts ammending the same." *Laws of the State of New York* (Albany: Websters & Skinners, 1821), 356, n.p.n.

37. U.S. Department of War, *General Regulations of the Army* (Washington, D.C.: Davis and Force, 1825), p. 351.

38. Camus, "Military Band," p. 485 and passim.

39. U.S. Department of War, "General Order No. 31," 5 April 1832, *General Orders and Records of the Adjutant General* Record Group 94 (Washington, D.C.: National Archives). This order was incorporated into the General Orders of 1834. Camus points out that this regulation served to reduce the size of the Regular Army bands and that White had misunderstood the intent of the order of 1834 which was to add emphasis to that published in 1832. White saw the order of 1834 as the beginning of bands in the United States Army. *See* Camus, "The Military Band," p. 480 and William C. White, *A History of Military Music in America* (New York: Exposition Press, 1944), p. 37.

40. U.S. Department of War, "General Order No. 58," 29 October 1828. *General*

Orders and Records of the Adjutant General, Record Group 94, National Archives, Washington, D.C.

41. White, *History of Military Music*, p. 211.
position Press, 1944), p. 211.

42. *Philadelphia Universal Gazette*, 10 July 1800. *See also* Kenneth W. Carpenter, "A History of the United States Marine Band" (Ph.D. diss., University of Iowa, 1970). Carpenter traces the complete history of the band, but finds it difficult to define precisely its origins or date of organization. Musicians for the band were enlisted as field musicians who then did double duty as bandsmen. The early Marine Band was under the direction of the principal musician, i.e., the drum major. It is difficult to establish at what time the duties of field musician and bandmaster were separated from each other. The Marine Band did not receive official sanction until Lincoln provided for it in 1861.

43. Commandant of the Marine Corps to Representative Frothingham 27 July 1927, "Letters from the Commandant of the Marine Corps," Music Division, Francis Scala Collection, Library of Congress, Washington, D.C.

44. C. A. Henderson, First Lieutenant of Marines, 19 November 1859, Music Division, Francis Scala Collection, Library of Congress, Washington, D.C.

45. The concerts were suspended for a brief period of mourning following the death of Lincoln's youngest son Tad.

46. White, *History of Military Music*, pp. 203–04. A copy of the original manuscript source cited by White was kindly furnished to me by an old classmate, the Reverend James Ford, Chaplain to the Cadets at West Point and more recently Chaplain to the Congress of the United States.

47. Ibid., pp. 211–19.

48. Ibid., pp. 83–108. White discusses shipboard bands rather thoroughly.

49. "Soldiers of the American Revolutionary War from the State of Pennsylvania," *Pennsylvania Archives*, ser. 1 (1884), vol. 10; ser. 2 (1887), vols. 1, 12–14; ser. 5 (1906), vol. 1.

50. "Report of a Board of Officers" 25 February 1815 as cited in Charles K. Gardner, *Compend of the United States System of Infantry Exercise and Manoeuvers*, (New York: William W. Merclin, 1819), Preface. *See also* Camus, "The Military Band," p. 397.

51. *DJM* 16, no. 26 (24 March 1860): 412–13.

52. *New York Times*, 14 June 1861, p. 2.

53. *Gazette of the State of Georgia*, 20 February 1785, as quoted in a letter of Lilla M. Hawes, Director, Georgia Historical Society to Raoul Camus, as cited in Camus, "The Military Band," p. 402.

54. *DJM* 3, no. 5 (7 May 1853): 38. The original source of this letter is Gottfried Weber's musical periodical, *The Caecilia*: 9 (1824). It had been translated from the original German for Dwight's reprint.

55. *DJM* 5, no. 24 (16 September 1854): 187–88.

56. Ibid., p. 189.

57. For a complete account of the growth of civilian bands in Minnesota *see* Clayton Tiede, "The Development of Minnesota Community Bands During the Nineteenth Century" (Ph.D. diss., University of Minnesota, 1970).

58. William F. Bufkin, "Union Bands cf the Civil War (1862–1865)," (Ph.D. diss.,

Louisiana State University, 1973), p. 130.

59. *See* Alfred Dieck, *Die Wandermusikanten von Salzgitter* (Gottingen, BRD: Heinz Reise Verlag, 1962). A brief summary of Dieck's work is contained in Jean-Pierre Matheg, "The 19th Century Wandering Musicians from Salzgitter," *Brass Bulletin* no. 13 (1976): 106–115.

60. *St. Paul* (Minn.) *Pioneer and Democrat*, 10 June 1858, p. 2.

61. Louis C. Elson, *The History of American Music* (New York: MacMillan Co., 1915), pp. 374–75.

62. Tiede, "Minnesota Bands," p. 6.

63. *DJM* 1, no. 7 (22 May 1852): 52. This is a reprint taken from *Music World*.

64. Adam Carse, *Musical Wind Instruments* (reprint ed., New York: Da Capo Press, 1965), p. 285.

65. Article written by William R. Baley for the *Philadelphia Evening Star* in 1893, as cited by White, *A History of Military Music*, p. 59. The *Philadelphia Evening Star* ceased publication in 1900 according to The Philadelphia Public Library check list of Philadelphia newspapers. The article was never published by the newspaper.

66. White, *A History of Military Music*, p. 203–04, and Tiede, "Minnesota Bands," p. 90.

67. *St. Paul* (Minn.) *Chronical and Register*, 13 October 1849, p. 12.

68. Carse, *Musical Wind Instruments*, p. 315.

69. Adam Carse, *Musical Wind Instruments*, reprint Introduction by Himie Voxman (New York: Da Capo Press, 1965), pp. 64–65.

70. David Hamblen, "Early Boston Bands," *Journal of Music*, 24 (December 1966): 32–33.

71. *DJM* 16, no. 26 (24 March 1860): 412–13. It should also be noted that the over-the-shoulder instruments, that Dodworth claimed to have invented, were not a totally new idea. The earliest bands held the valveless French horns in hunting fashion, which put their bells nearly directly to the rear. It is interesting to note that, Dodworth's claim notwithstanding, the United States Patent Office has no record of ever issuing him a patent for the invention of the over-the-shoulder horns.

72. *DJM* 13, no. 10 (15 June 1858): 78.

73. *DJM* 13, no. 7 (15 May 1858): 55.

74. *DJM* 13, no. 8 (22 May 1858): 63.

75. *Minneapolis Pioneer Press*, 22 June 1879, p. 7.

76. Rankin to Burrows, 1 September 1789, in an anonymous "Chronology," an unpublished typewritten manuscript in the Marine Band Office, pp. 1–9.

77. Ibid., Commandant to Weaver, 19 September 1789.

78. Ibid., Burrows to Secretary of the Navy, 10 October 1789.

79. Ibid., Burrows to Church.

80. Ibid., Church to Burrows, 27 March 1799.

81. Ibid., Burrows to Keen, 21 May 1799.

82. Charles V. Forman, "A Thumbnail History of the Marine Band," *Jacob's Orchestra Monthly* 23, no. 2:89. Forman indicates that he in turn quoted from the *Philadelphia Universal Gazette*, 10 July 1800.

83. *St. Paul* (Minn.) *Pioneer and Democrat*, 9 December 1852, p. 2. The Fort Snelling band was that of the Sixth Regiment of the Regular Army Infantry Band.

84. *St. Paul* (Minn.) *Minnesota Pioneer*, 30 January 1850, p. 2.

85. Tiede, "Minnesota Bands," p. 2 and *Mankato Weekly Review*, 13 April 1875.

86. *St. Paul* (Minn.) *Minnesota Pioneer*, 27 February 1850, p. 1.

87. Johann Ernest Altenburg, *Essay on...Heroic and Musical Trumpeters*, trans. Edward H. Tarr (Nashville, Tenn.: Brass Press, 1974), p. 114. In discussing the requirements and duties of the teacher, Altenburg states that he should "be a good trumpeter, and play the violin as well because in most cases it is indispensable. [The teacher] should instruct his pupil to a certain extent on the latter instrument also." He later notes that ". . . some instruction in singing would also be very beneficial to the trumpeter."

88. Daniel McCurten, "Journal of the Times at the Siege of Boston Since our Arrival at Cambridge Near Boston," in Thomas Balch, *Papers Relating to the Maryland Line During the Revolution* (Philadelphia: Seventy-six Society, 1857), pp. 20–21 as cited by Camus, "The Military Band," p. 324.

89. Thomas Simes, *Military Guide For the Young Officer* 1 (1772; reprint ed., Philadelphia: J. Humphries, R. Bell & R. Aitken, 1776), pp. 158–59.

90. Walter S. Dudley, Jr., "Orchestration in the *Musique D'Harmonie* of the French Revolution," (Ph.D. diss., University of California at Berkley, 1968), p. 2. The discussion that follows represents a brief summary of the extensive and detailed study of French military music presented by Dudley.

THE BAND AT
FORT SUMTER

As the night of 26 December 1860 turned to inky blackness, several small boats with muffled oars set out to navigate the murky waters of Charleston harbor. The lack of channel markers and the presence of secessionist patrol boats made this a hazardous expedition, and the need for secrecy was urgent. This clandestine voyage effected the transfer of Companies E and H (both understrength) and the band of the 1st Regiment of Artillery from Fort Moultrie to Fort Sumter.

Major Robert Anderson had assumed command of the unit on 21 November, arriving at Fort Moultrie with little information and even fewer instructions from Washington. He was to hold all federal property in the harbor. Beyond this, he had been offered only a vague hope for reinforcement of his meager command. It did not take him long to assess accurately his military position.

In spite of their rather long history, both forts had suffered from neglect and only periodic maintenance. Fort Moultrie was a land-based fortification. The *New York Times* reported that sand had drifted up against the south wall so as to render the parapets easily accessible. Only recently some of the sand had been removed from the sea wall to keep out stray cows, but this did not prevent hostile Charleston civilians from strolling in and out through the gaps in the landward wall. Major Anderson succinctly stated his position in a letter dated 26 December 1861.

When I inform you that my garrison consists of only 60 effective men, that we are in very indifferent works, the walls of which are only about 14 feet high, and that we have, within 100 yards of our walls, sand hills which command our works, and which afford admirable sites against our batteries, and the finest covers for sharp shooters, and that besides this, there are numerous houses, some of them within pistol shot, you will at once see that if attacked in force, headed by anyone but a simpleton, there is scarce a possibility of our being able to hold out long enough to enable our friends to come to our surrender.[1]

Fort Sumter, only partially completed, offered only modest strategic improvement. The fortress had long been unoccupied with the exception of workmen recently assigned to make repairs. The barracks had no roof and none of the artillery pieces had been mounted. As political conditions worsened, Anderson ordered the construction crews in Sumter to expedite their work.

When the legislature of South Carolina passed an ordinance of secession Anderson felt compelled to assume a more defensible stance. Not quite one week later, he transferred his tiny command to the island fortress. Sumter was obviously a more defensible position, and it did offer the remote possibility of reinforcement by sea.

Anderson did not realize that this simple transfer of troops between two federal forts violated a tacit agreement between the federal government and that of the Palmetto State. On 20 December 1860 President Buchanan had courteously received a group of commissioners from South Carolina. Their polite conversation centered upon the possible transfer of all federal property within the state to Governor Pickens' administration. Although little of substance resulted, both parties did sense a tacit understanding that no changes would be made in the strength or disposition of federal troops in the Charleston harbor. Thus, when Major Anderson moved his command Governor Pickens and all South Carolinians regarded his action a clear violation of their gentlemen's agreement.

Conditions disintegrated almost daily during the next three and one-half months. By 4 February the Southern Confederacy had become a reality. Federal forts in other parts of the South quickly surrendered to their respective states until by 1 April only Forts Jefferson and Pickens in Pensacola Bay, Fort Taylor at Key West, and Fort Sumter still flew the federal colors. With each passing day the demands for Anderson's surrender grew more pressing and urgent. Most wondered why he did not follow a course similar to that taken by the commanders of other federal forts, but to a large degree Major Anderson was both governed by and a victim of military tradition.

Anderson was a Kentuckian and a Regular Army officer. Secretary of War Floyd thought that he could be relied upon to carry out the "Southern Program," but Anderson would not have worked for its success even had he been aware of it. He was perfectly willing to chastise South Carolina for any revolutionary measures, but his outlook was less violent when all of the southern states joined the Confederacy. He regarded the conquest of the South as a hopeless undertaking. In spite of this belief, he felt obliged to defend Sumter. Politics aside, this action can be explained by two military concepts: duty and tradition. Anderson's employment of the military band was also governed by tradition.

Norman Dixon, in an excellent study of "military incompetence" describes the role of tradition.

The academies which produced the men whose incompetence has sometimes cost society dear cannot be entirely held to blame for the ethos and values which they maintain. Equally culpable are those who encouraged them. Even as recently as 1949, after a war which was nearly lost through the effect of the cerebral millstone of archaic tradition, Admiral of the Fleet the Earl of Cork and Orrery, having taken the salute at Dartmouth, urged the cadets to "absorb tradition"—rather as one might adjure a sufferer from rheumatism to absorb some ancient well-tried liniment.[2]

The military traditions that were to be upheld at Sumter had been clearly described by Thomas Simes in 1776.[3] The traditional elements governing the surrender of a beleaguered fortress required that: 1) the defenders hold out until the wall was breached and until the commander had made an honorable defense; 2) the commander, when it became evident that he would lose the battle, surrender his command in a manner commensurate with the intensity of his defense; 3) the flag of the besieged garrison be respectfully lowered and saluted by cannon fire; 4) the garrison be allowed to march out through the breach with their arms, baggage, spare carriages, horses, drums beating, fifes playing, matches lighted on both ends, and colors flying; 5) the vanquished, to demonstrate the proper respect, perform a march common to the enemy army; 6) the victor, in turn, honor the brilliance of the defense by allowing the band of musicians to perform one of the patriotic airs of its own army. All of these traditions were observed in the Charleston harbor. Lamentably, the observance of these very traditions reinforced the "picture book" concept of the war and indeed served as a cerebral millstone to further preparations by both the North and the South.

The participation of the 1st Regiment of Artillery in these events is important to this study only because of the small and unique group attached to the regiment—the band. These instrumentalists were part of a long military tradition, but they simultaneously established precedent that would remain constant to the end of the war. A brass band was present at nearly every battle. Although its presence seldom affected the outcome, it was usually considered of sufficient significance to have the band's actions recorded by someone present at the time. The band of the 1st Regiment of Artillery received its share of coverage as the drama unfolded at Sumter.

The regiment and the band had occupied Fort Moultrie since 1857, and the soldiers were well acquainted with the citizens. Life was reasonably comfortable, and the officers were frequent guests in the summer homes of the best families of Charleston. The band reciprocated with concerts, and Fort Moultrie itself was frequently open to visitors.[4]

As tensions in the harbor increased, the Charlestonians had gone out of their way to avoid any incidents with the military that would upset the delicate political balance. Although officers had always been Southern favorites, enlisted men had long been regarded as social outcasts—the dregs of the earth. But now almost any action on the part of a soldier was excused or tolerated by the citizens of Charleston no matter how gross.

In November of 1860 South Carolina held elections to fill the state's offices. Each candidate generally gave a barbecue or feast of some kind, at which stump speeches were delivered in a florid style. The whole body of voters attended these entertainments and, it is feared, decided rather upon the merits of the feast than the fitness of the candidates. At one of these entertainments on Sullivan's Island, the regimental band was hired as an attraction, and soldiers holding passes gathered around the fringes of the crowd which surrounded an open-air table.

The supper was over, and the speaking had begun. Everything eatable had been devoured except a remnant of ham which rested on a platter in front of the chairman....The chairman was speaking and the audience was enthusiastic. A storm of applause had just broken out...when a soldier, who had his eyes on the fragment of ham for sometime,...mounted the table at the lower end, and carefully picking his steps among the dishes, walked to the chairman's end, picked up the coveted fragment and started on the return trip. The audacity of the man stunned the audience, but indignation soon got the better of astonishment and the soldier was in some danger of rough treatment. But the chairman had his revolver out in a second, and holding it aloft proclaimed: "I'll shoot the first man who interferes with that soldier." And the soldier carried off the fragment. Of course he was drunk, but he could not have done the same thing without a drubbing in 1859.[5]

This kind of tolerance came to a sudden halt when Major Anderson transferred his command to Fort Sumter.

The move to Sumter had been accomplished in haste. Even so, "the band instruments had not been forgotten but other important items had."[6] If all instruments were accounted for, other impedimenta got lost in the shuffle. The Thirty-seventh Congress, in September of 1861, appropriated $1150.00

... to remunerate soldiers and members of the band stationed at Fort Sumter, in South Carolina, for the losses of private property incurred in the removal from Fort Moultrie to Fort Sumter on the evening of December twenty-six, eighteen-hundred and sixty, namely:

To the band $400.00
To Co. E, 1st Arty $500.00
To Co. H, 1st Arty . . . . . $250.00[7]

The morning of arrival in Fort Sumter was spent bringing order out of chaos. By noon of 27 December 1860, Major Anderson was ready to raise his flag.

It is known that the American Flag brought away from Fort Moultrie, was raised at Sumter precisely at noon on the 27th ultimo....It was a scene that will be memorable reminiscence in the lives of those who witnessed it. A short time before noon, Maj. Anderson assembled the whole of his little force, with the workmen employed on the fort, around the foot of the flag staff. The National Ensign was attached to the chord, and Major Anderson, holding the end of the lines in his hands, knelt reverently down, the Officers, soldiers and men clustered around, many of them on their knees, all deeply impressed with the solemnity of the scene. The Chaplain made an earnest prayer—such an appeal for support, encouragement, and mercy as one would make who felt that man's extremity is God's opportunity. As the earnest, solemn words of the speaker ceased, the men responded Amen with fervency that perhaps they had never before experienced. Major Anderson drew the Star Spangled Banner up to the top of the staff, the band broke out with the national air of "Hail Columbia," loud and exultant cheers, repeated again and again, were given by the Officers, soldiers and workmen.[8]

Two other performances by the band, prior to hostilities, are recorded. On 22 February a salute of thirty-four guns was fired in honor of the birthday of George Washington, and on 4 March a thirty-four gun salute marked the inauguration of Lincoln. The band performed national airs for both occasions.[9]

The band gained one additional musician during those tedious weeks, but it is not known if this man performed with the group. Davin was a Frenchman who had been practicing his musical profession in Charleston for some time prior to the war. It took very little for a foreigner to become suspect as tempers grew white-hot in the crucible of events. Davin was labeled a spy for an inconsequential act. A Charleston resident, Mary Chesnut, recorded the events.

In Camden I found myself in a flurry of women, all excited over Davin. "Traitors" they cried. "He'll be hung; never you mind." "For What?" "They caught him walking on the trestle work in the swamp, after no good, you may be sure." "They won't hang him for that." "Hanging is too good for him!" "You wait till Colonel Chesnut comes! He is a lawyer," I said gravely. "Ladies, he will disappoint you. There will be no lynching if he goes to that meeting today. He will not move a step, except by 'Habeas Corpus,' and trial by jury, and a quantity of bench and bar to speak long speeches."

Mr. Chesnut did come, and gave a more definite account of poor Davin's precarious situation. They had intercepted a treasonable letter of his at the Post Office. I believe it was not a very black treason after all. At any rate, Colonel Chesnut spoke for him with might and main at the meeting. It was composed (the meeting) of intelligent men with cool heads; and they banished Davin to Fort Sumter. The poor Music Master can't do much harm in the casements there! He may thank his stars that Mr. Chesnut gave him a helping hand. In the red-hot state our public mind now is in, short shrift for spies!

Judge Withers said that Mr. Chesnut never made a more telling speech in his life than he did to save this poor Frenchman for whom Judge Lynch was ready. As for me, I had never heard of Davin in my life until I heard he was to be hung.[10]

Conditions continued to worsen after the arrival of Davin in the fort, until on

6 April Lincoln brought matters to a head. He informed Governor Pickens that an attempt would be made to reinforce Fort Sumter. Pickens responded on 10 April ordering General Beauregard to "at once demand its evacuation, and if this is refused, [to] proceed in such manner as you may determine to reduce it."[11] Beauregard's demand for surrender was communicated to Major Anderson on 11 April to which he replied:

I have the honor to acknowledge the receipt of your communication demanding the evacuation of this Fort, and to say in reply thereto that it is a demand with which I regret that my sense of honor and my obligations to my government prevent my compliance. . . . I will await the first shot and, if you do not batter us to pieces,[we] will be starved out in a few days.[12]

It is evident that Anderson realized his position was indefensible. Indeed, the steamship *Star of the West* had entered the harbor on 9 January with provisions and additional troops, and was turned back after being struck twice by cannon fire. Major Anderson displayed an unusual lack of imagination by not returning fire in support of the ship. He idly watched his only chance for reinforcements sail out of the harbor.

Following this abortive reinforcement mission, General Beauregard scuttled two hulks in the harbor entrance and removed the remaining navigational aids from the harbor making it difficult for vessels to enter or leave without the greatest circumspection. The best pilots were barely able to pick their way by daylight. Navigation at night was impossible. To make matters worse, ships entering the harbor had to pass within three-quarters of a mile of the guns of Fort Moultrie, as well as those on Cummings Point at the northern extreme of Morris Island. Knowing this, Major Anderson still clung desperately to his post and to the obscure hope that yet other ships might come to his aid.

Since Anderson had already admitted to the futility of his efforts, LeRoy P. Walker, the Confederate secretary of war, offered him an out, in a telegram to Beauregard.

[I] do not desire needlessly to bombard Fort Sumter. If Major Anderson will state the time at which, as indicated by himself, he will evacuate and agree that in the meantime, he will not use his guns against us unless ours should be employed against Fort Sumter, you are authorized thus to avoid the effusion of blood. If this or its equivalent be refused, reduce the Fort, as your judgment decides to be the most practicable.[13]

Anderson was to be allowed to carry all arms, personal baggage, and company property of every description with him, and the flag which he had maintained with "so much fortitude" could be saluted when hauled down.

The major consulted with his medical officer as to the probable time the men would be able to make effective resistance after their bread had given out.

Being told that "owing to the enthusiasm of the men, they could probably hold out for five days,"[14] he made written reply that he would evacuate the fort at noon on the fifteenth, provided that he did not receive supplies or controlling instructions from his government to the contrary. He agreed that he would not open his batteries unless "the flag of his country was fired upon," or unless some hostile intention on the part of the Confederate forces should be manifested. It was on this point that negotiations broke down.

Anderson realized that he had blundered earlier in not supporting the arrival of the *Star of the West*. To agree not to fire, unless fired upon, would tie his hands should another ship attempt his relief. General Beauregard wanted to resolve the question of Sumter before further efforts towards reinforcement could be accomplished. When he received Anderson's reply, he determined to reduce the fort. At 4:30 A.M. a shell arched across the sky from Fort Johnson and exploded directly over the flag pole in Sumter. The war had begun!

The bombardment continued for the next thirty-four hours, and was conducted "according to all of the rules of civilized warfare."[15] Beauregard noted in his informal report that "our brave troops, carried away by their naturally generous impulses, mounted the different batteries, and at every discharge from the Fort, cheered the garrison for its pluck and gallantry, and hooted the fleet laying inactive just outside the bar."[16]

On 16 April The *New York Times* noted that "during the fire, when Major Anderson's flag staff was shot away, a boat put off from Morris Island, carrying another American flag for him to fight under—a noteworthy instance of the honor and chivalry of South Carolina Seceders, and their admiration for a brave man."[17] The indomitable observer, Mary Chesnut, gleefully recorded this incident. "Willie Preston fired the shot which broke Anderson's flagstaff. Mrs. Hampton from Columbia telegraphed him: 'Well done, Willie'."[18]

Another newspaper stated that "one of the aides [to General Beauregard] carried brandy to Major Anderson in a boat after the fires, and the latter said it was very acceptable as the men were completely exhausted by their labors. I mention this to show the kind and chivalrous relations between the Officers."[19]

During the bombardment, the members of the band spent most of their time filling cartridge bags with powder and carrying ammunition.[20] Since bags were in short supply, several dozen pairs of Major Anderson's wool socks were filled as substitutes. As the shelling increased in intensity a Confederate round set fire to a powder magazine, and "the musicians streamed out of the casemates and onto the shot-torn parade ground to see what could be done."[21]

When it became obvious that the entire interior of Sumter was in flames, Beauregard dispatched a boat to talk of surrender. Anderson graciously received the delegation and reluctantly accepted the same terms offered him before the bombardment, presenting his sword as a token of his capitulation. General Beauregard declined the gesture as inappropriate to the surrender of such "a brave gentleman."[22]

Anderson communicated his defeat to Washington. "Sir—having defended Fort Sumter for thirty-four hours, until the quarters were entirely burned, the main gates destroyed by fire, the gorge wall seriously injured, the magazine surrounded by flames, and its door closed from the effects of the heat, . . . I accepted the terms of evacuation offered by General Beauregard. . .prior to the commencement of hostilities, and marched out. . .with colors flying and drums beating, bringing away company and private property and saluting my flag with fifty guns."[23]

In spite of the intensity of the thirty-four hour bombardment, a horse tethered behind a sand dune on Morris Island was the only casualty. Sergeant Thomas Kernan and Privates James Hays and Edward Galloway (also spelled Gallway and Galway in the sources), were slightly wounded by flying masonry on 12 April, as was John Swearer, a laborer who had remained with the garrison. None were injured seriously enough to exempt them from duty.

Two days later, events took a more unfortunate turn. When the garrison's baggage was on board the transport (the soldiers remaining inside the fort under arms), a portion of the command "told off" as gunners to fire a one-hundred gun salute during which time the flag was to be slowly lowered from its place of honor on the parade. The bore of the piece was not sufficiently swabbed following the forty-ninth discharge. When the powder bag for the fiftieth was rammed home, it exploded prematurely, igniting the remaining powder bags that had been piled in front of the gun. Private Daniel Hough fell dead in his tracks. Private Edward Galloway, who had been wounded by flying masonry two days earlier, had his right arm jaggedly torn from his shoulder. He died in Gibbes Hospital in Charleston on 19 April. Privates James Fielding, John Irwin and John Pritchard (George Pinchard, according to Doubleday) were all burned rather severely, and Private James Harp (James Hayes, according to Doubleday) was slightly wounded. Fielding was admitted to Chisholm hospital and was later sent north without exchange. The other wounded men were evacuated with the rest of the command.

The projected one-hundred gun salute was cut short at the fiftieth round and several hours later, Private Hough was buried in the parade with full military honors. The band performed a "moving hymn" as a part of the interment services. This done, the command marched out, the band playing "Yankee Doodle" and "Hail to the Chief," to board the *Baltic*.

To Major Anderson, the fifty-gun salute was a moving experience that satisfied a point of honor, but to Colonel Wigfall, who had appointed himself as Beauregard's aide and general "go-fer," it was nothing but an empty and meaningless gesture. Newspaper accounts of the surrender, released by Anderson after his return to New York, depicted Wigfall's role as bumbling at best, and Wigfall responded acidly to this black mark against his family escutcheon. "Catch me risking my life to save him again. . . .He might have been man enough to tell the truth to those New Yorkers, however unpalatable to them a good word for us might have been. We did behave well to him. The only men of his killed, he killed himself, or they killed themselves, firing a salute to their old striped rag."[24]

The trip north was uneventful, but their arrival in New York harbor was accompanied by every possible demonstration of enthusiasm. Harbor shipping dipped their flags as the *Baltic* passed and New York's citizens cheered themselves into a patriotic frenzy.

The *New York Times*, commenting upon the battle, noted that "a fortress may become untenable, even though every man in it may remain untouched. The world has outlived that vulgar taste for slaughter which measures the importance of the battle by the number of corpses left upon the field. . . .The only defense required was such a one as should vindicate the honor of the garrison. . .and this has been accomplished."[25]

The Sumter Band was transferred to the *Isabel* and followed the regiment to a heroes' welcome in New York. They were assigned to Fort Hamilton (in the New York harbor) where the tri-monthly report indicates that their military appearance was "pretty good," their discipline "good," and their clothing "lost." Under *Instructions*, the report indicated "none—want instruments."[26]

The band was a group of regulars, most of whom enlisted for a five-year term at Moultersville, South Carolina.[27] The actual size of the band is difficult to determine since different sources provide different information. Major General Abner Doubleday (who was at Sumter as a captain during the bombardment) wrote of a group "of thirteen musicians of the regimental band," but he only lists the names of eight of them in the appendix of his book.[28]

The monuments in Fort Sumter compound the confusion. The small one on the parade lists eight men under the heading of "Band." A second monument by the flagpole lists thirteen men. The muster roll of the 1st Regiment (for January, 1861) lists nine men as bandsmen, one of whom is the quartermaster sergeant, William H. Hamner.

The newspapers give varying accounts of the size of the band as well as of Anderson's command. *The New York Times* of 4 January 1861 states that fifteen musicians were present. The *Baltimore Sun* indicates the same number. Captain James Chester, in *Battles and Leaders of the Civil War*, lists only the NCO's of the Band, Sergeant James E. Galway and Corporal Andrew Smith.[29]

These differences could have several explanations. Charles Hall and Robert Foster were assigned as Field Musicians to Companies E and H respectively. In addition to these two men, quartermaster sergeant William Hamner could well have performed with the band, not to mention the deported music master, Mr. Davin. Perhaps other men with musical backgrounds were assigned to the band for extra duty.

The tri-monthly reports list the following eight men as permanently assigned to the band, and their names are on the monuments in the park and are included in Doubleday's accounting.

NAME	DATE MUSTERED
Sgt. James E. Galway (Leader)	24 Nov., 1858
Cpl. Andrew Smith	17 Nov., 1858
Pvt. Patrick Murphy	2 Sep., 1859
Pvt. Fedochi Onovatto	1 Oct., 1856
(Fedeschi Onoratti according to Doubleday)	
Pvt. Henry Schmidt	9 Nov., 1859
Pvt. Peter Rice	24 Nov., 1859
Pvt. John Urquhart	9 Jul., 1858
Pvt. Andrew Wickstrom	10 March, 1860

The lost instruments must have been replaced. On 4 June 1861, six regular army bandsmen from Fort Collis were added to the roster of the 1st Regiment Band. Now numbering fourteen, the band was transferred to Fort Columbus.[30] Finally, in October of 1861, it was transferred to Fort Warren (in the Boston harbor) where the men served out the remaining time of their enlistments.[31]

On 22 July 1864 the band was still at its post. The 13th Regiment of Massachusetts Volunteer Infantry was reassigned and was "escorted by the Band of the First United States Artillery. . .from Fort Warren."[32]

No pictures of the 1st Artillery Regimental Band seem to exist, and the instrumentation cannot be determined from available records. Pension records for two of the original bandsmen, Peter Rice and John Urquhart, show that the band remained at Fort Warren as a permanent post band to the end of the war.

Rice initially enlisted in Battery D, 1st Artillery Regiment on 8 November 1854 and was transferred to the band on 1 March 1858. His final enlistment, at Fort Adams, Rhode Island, was on 11 March 1877. On 12 January 1879 he attended the regular Sunday morning inspection of the band and then left the garrison for his home. At 9:30 A.M. on the fourteenth his body was found "floating three feet from the steam launch landing pier." It was believed "from the appearance of his dress that Rice had gone there to obey a call of nature, and owing to the ice on the ground at the time, had slipped, fallen forward, and being stunned, was unable to recover himself."[33]

His wife Margarette Rice (nee Farley) was fourteen years old when they were married on 29 January 1859 at Fort Moultrie, South Carolina. Following his death, Margarette and their four children moved to San Francisco where she applied for his pension on 22 August 1888. Her application was denied when the adjutant general determined that Rice was not in a duty status while traveling from the garrison to his home since he lived off-post by choice and not necessity. The pension commission ruled in favor of Margarette's claim on 11 February 1889, and the matter was then submitted to a review board for resolution. The board supported the adjutant general, but Margarette's death rendered the ruling moot. Her eldest son, Peter Rice Jr., then filed for the pension on 14 December 1892 in behalf of the youngest minor son,

Stephen. His application was also denied. Rice's twenty-five years of faithful service did not provide a single benefit for his survivors.

John Urquhart originally enlisted with the 1st Artillery Regimental Band at Fort Columbus, New York, on 9 July 1858. Except for a two-year period between 17 July 1871 and 18 November 1873 he served continuously until his discharge on 8 April 1881. From 1876 to 1878 he was at Camp Douglas, Utah Territory (Wisconsin), where he suffered debilitating hard-ships and exposure during the Ute Indian expedition. Discharged for disability, he was assigned to the Soldiers' Home in Washington, D. C., and awarded a pension of five dollars monthly. As his condition worsened, his pension was increased by two-dollar increments until he received twenty dollars monthly. Suffering from partial blindness, partial deafness, loss of teeth, and varicose veins in both legs and his left foot, he died on 2 April 1896. He never rose above the rank of private during his twenty-one years of active service.[34]

Norman Dixon observed that "being a gentleman" was one of the most prized traits of a nineteenth-century military officer. He discusses the creation, maintenance and importance of military ceremony in a chapter rather irreverently entitled "Bullshit." He notes that "bull" is not a total loss in the structure of the military since it ensures a level of orderliness, cleanliness, discipline, personal pride, obedience, and morale which could not be met by reasoned, as opposed to compulsive, behavior. He postulates that all of this would be good but for one thing—the addition of ritualization that tends to transform means into ends. Once ritualized, "bull" becomes addictive. It then becomes a substitute for doing something different, and resists totally the adoption of new battle drill.[35]

The events at Sumter had precisely this effect upon further preparations for the war. The scenario had already been standardized in Simes' day. The "vulgar taste for slaughter" was not yet obvious, and the concept of a "gentleman's war" was reinforced. Bands were important elements in the ritualized ceremonies that created two armies modeled after those of the Crimean War. Bands were principal ingredients in the recipes for successful recruiting, for war meetings, for flag raisings, for sword presentations, for parades on the barracks square, and for many other institutionalized and ritualized military ceremonies.

Along with the promotion of the officers at Sumter (Anderson became Brigadier General) came the necessity for bringing an entire army into existence. With Washington, D.C. threatened, the basically ritualistic militia units were rushed into federal service. As each was accepted by its government, the Union or Confederate Armies gained another brass band. Completely new regiments were organized on the familiar model, and young men, reflecting upon the glorious defense of Sumter, rushed forward to become a part of this patriotic and chivalric undertaking. Regiments and bands multiplied in dizzy profusion until it could be said that martial music resounded everywhere.

NOTES

1. *Boston Journal*, 26 December 1860, p. 6.

2. Norman F. Dixon, *On the Psychology of Military Imcompetence* (New York: Basic Books, 1976) p. 160.

3. Thomas Simes, *Military Guide For the Young Officer*, vol. 1 (1772; reprint ed., Philadelphia: J. Humphries, R. Bell & R. Aitken, 1776), p. 158.

4. Roy Meredith, *Storm Over Sumter: The Opening Engagement of the Civil War* (New York: Simon and Schuster, 1957), p. 27.

5. James Chester, "Inside Sumter in '61," *Battles and Leaders of the Civil War*, ed. Robert Johnson and Clarence Buell, 4 vols. (1887; reprint ed., New York: Thomas Yoseloff, 1956), 1:51.

6. W. A. Swanberg, *First Blood, The Story of Fort Sumter* (New York: Charles Scribner's Sons, 1951), p. 172.

7. *National Intelligencer*, 19 September 1861, p. 4.

8. *New York Times*, 10 January 1861, p. 8. Doubleday claims the band played "The Star Spangled Banner" for the ceremony. *See* Doubleday, *Reminiscences of Fort Sumter and Fort Moultrie 1860–61* (New York: Harper and Brothers, 1867), p. 71.

9. *National Intelligencer*, 23 February 1861; 4 March 1861.

10. Mary Boykin Chesnut, *A Diary from Dixie*, 2d ed., ed. Ben Ames Williams (Boston: Houghton Mifflin Co., Riverside Press, Cambridge, 1949) pp. 55–56.

11. U.S. Department of War, *Official Records of the War of the Rebellion* (Washington, D.C.: Government Printing Office, 1898), ser. 1 vol. 1 p. 297 (hereafter cited *OR*). *See also New York Times*, 11 April 1861, p. 1.

12. *OR*, ser. 1 vol. 1, pp. 13, 14, 59, 301. *See also New York Times*, 12 April 1861, p. 1. The newspaper account includes verbal statements made by Major Anderson to Colonel Chesnut.

13. Stephen D. Lee, "The First Step in the War," *Battles and Leaders* 1:75. *See also OR*, ser. 1 vol. 1, p. 301.

14. *New York Times*, 13-14 April 1861, p. 1.

15. Ibid., 14 April 1861, p. 2.

16. Ibid., 16 April 1861, p. 1.

17. Ibid., 16 April 1861, p. 4.

18. Chesnut, *Diary*, p. 41.

19. *Baltimore Sun*, 16 April 1861, p. 2.

20. Swanberg, *First Blood*, p. 308.

21. Ibid., p. 329. Spaulding claims that Major Anderson lost all his socks in this manner. See Oliver Lyman Spaulding, "The Bombardment of Fort Sumter 1861," *Annual Report of the American Historical Association for 1913* (Washington, D.C., 1913), 1:192. Chester claims several pairs. *See Battles and Leaders*, 1:54.

22. *New York Times*, 16 April 1861, p. 8.

23. Ibid., 19 April 1861, p. 1. *See also OR*, ser. 1, vol. 1, p. 12.

24. Chesnut, *Diary*, p. 46.

25. *New York Times*, 16 April 1861, p. 2.

26. "Tri-monthly return from 28th day of February to 30th day of April 1861," from Fort Hamilton, New York, National Archives, Washington, D.C. I am indebted to William Bufkin for the military records regarding the assignment of the band fol-

lowing their duty at Fort Sumter.

27. "Muster Roll of the Field, Staff and Band," First Regiment of Artillery, January 1860, National Archives, Washington, D.C.

28. Abner Doubleday, *Reminiscences of Fort Sumter and Fort Moultrie, 1860–61*, p. 15 and Appendix.

29. Chester, "Inside Sumter," *Battles and Leaders*, 1, p. 67.

30. "Monthly Return, Muster Roll of the Field, Staff, and Band," First Regiment of Artillery, 4 June 1861 from Fort Collis.

31. "Tri-monthly Return, Muster Roll of the Field, Staff and Band," First Regiment of Artillery, from 31st day of October 1861 to 31st day of December 1861, from Fort Warren, Mass.

32. Charles E. Davis, Jr., *Three Years in the Army: The Story of the Thirteenth Massachusetts Volunteers* (Boston: Estes and Lauriat, 1894) p. 384.

33. General Index to the Pension Files 1861–1924. Peter Rice, no. WO379987, National Archives, Washington, D.C. I am indebted to William Bufkin for this source and the one that follows.

34. John Urquhart, no. SC200773. General Index to the Pension Files 1861–1934, National Archives, Washington, D.C.

35. Dixon, *Psychology of Incompetence*, p. 178.

BANDS AND THE RECRUITING EFFORT

The initial reaction to the bombardment of Fort Sumter was one of great excitement—even exhilaration. In Washington the *National Intelligencer* trumpeted "The Civil War has at last begun!"[1] as if it were a long-anticipated garden party that had finally arrived. The *Baltimore Sun* observed that "even in our little villages, the war spirit is fully aroused."[2] The historian of the 75th Illinois Infantry Regiment, intoxicated with the exuberance of his own verbosity, pompously observed that it was time to "gird on the armor, march forth to battle and, breasting the leaden and iron hail of the enemy, stand the avowed champion of the national honor and safety."[3] Mary Chesnut was certain that God's grace was bestowed only south of the Mason-Dixon line and asserted: "Of course, He hates the Yankees."[4] She summed up the southern feeling nicely when she wrote: "I felt a nervous dread and horror of this break with so great a power as the United States, but I was ready and willing. South Carolina had been rampant for years. She was the torment of herself and everybody else. Nobody could live in this State unless he were a fire-eater. Come what would, I wanted them to fight and stop talking. South Carolinians had exasperated and heated themselves into a fever that only blood-letting could ever cure."[5] Mary coquettishly observed that men whom she had previously found dull and uninteresting were transformed into witty, brilliant conversationalists, grown handsome in their army gray.

Although both sides seemed to have understood that war was imminent, neither had done much in the way of preparation. The South had been purchasing military supplies from abroad since January 1861, and individual states had confiscated the arms at the federal installations within their borders. The newly formed Army of the Confederacy slowly expanded its commissioned ranks as federal officers resigned from the Union to accept commands from their home states. This number included Lieutenant R. K. Meade who had been a Union officer at Fort Sumter.

The North was but slightly better prepared. A long period of relative contentment and peace had made tactically-sound military organizations seem unessential. Although the Regular Army appeared formidable on paper, it consisted of but nineteen regiments with a total enlistment of around eighteen thousand men. Of the nearly two hundred companies, one hundred sixty were performing duty in the territories of Nebraska, Texas, Utah, and Kansas with some in areas still farther west.

The security of Washington had been left to the three to four hundred marines stationed at the Washington arsenal. The commanding general was the "Hero of Lundy's Lane," General Winfield Scott, whose most conspicuous features were his age and his weight. It was evident to President Lincoln and President Davis that other immediate sources of manpower were required. They turned to the organized militia of the individual states.

We have already noted Ellsworth's contributions to the expansion, if not the effectiveness, of the Organized Militia. Other events had encouraged the formation of these uniformed, armed, regularly drilled (if not tactically sound) voluntary military associations.

Their formation was encouraged by Southern governors who feared the tensions created by slavery. In the north, the bigoted Know-Nothings had rioted and destroyed property even in the smaller towns. The Astor Palace Riot of 10 May 1849 had been suppressed by New York's famous 7th Infantry Regiment. The high-brow devotees (exemplified by the Astor Opera House), and the low-brows of the Bowery Theater (supported by Irish immigrants with a natural animosity toward England and English actors), were easily fanned into ethnic revolts. These and other refugees of the barricades of Europe instinctively associated street riots with freedom. As a consequence, New York City was in a constant turmoil between 1848 and 1860. In California civil authority collapsed when lawless elements were opposed by secret vigilante committees. William Tecumseh Sherman was appointed adjutant general of California and charged with the creation of sufficient Organized Militia units to restore order. It was these various state militias that responded to President Lincoln's urgent call for seventy-five thousand men to serve for a period of three months.

The president's call was allocated among the northern states according to the census of 1860. New York and Pennsylvania were to furnish seventeen and sixteen regiments respectively. Arkansas, North Carolina, Tennessee, and Virginia (all of whom joined the Confederacy) were asked to supply eight regiments among them. The border states were to furnish twelve more. Massachusetts, whose governor, John A. Andrew, had worked to upgrade the militia, had thirteen thousand troops immediately available.

The flamboyant designations of these units were exceeded only by their gaudy uniforms and complex parade-ground drills. All were colorful, but surely one of the most bizarre was the mounted Rush's Lancers, named after their commander, Colonel John Rush. Armed with seven-foot pikes topped by foot-high steel blades, they were startlingly effective on parade. These were quickly replaced by the standard cavalry sword after a charge through heavy underbrush proved the impracticability of the lance as a contemporary weapon.But the war had not yet begun in earnest, and on 1 January 1862 the Lancers created a tremendous stir as they paraded through Washington one thousand strong, headed by their "fine mounted band."[6]

Brass bands were indispensible to the parade performances of these crack drill units. Each drill unit presumed a band to be equally essential to service in the field. The army was soon awash in a sea of brass bands.

One of the first units to respond to the call of arms was the 6th Massachusetts Militia Infantry Regiment. It raced toward Washington to prevent seizure of the capital by secession forces. These troops had paraded through Philadelphia and Boston to the cheers of a wildly enthusiastic public, and in New York their drum major attracted considerable attention:

The Drum Major of the Regiment is Henry J. White, who belongs to the Eighth Regiment, but who requested to be allowed to accompany the Sixth, for fear that his own Regiment would not be called into service. He is 89 years old, and has served 40 years in the United States Marines and in the Massachusetts Militia. Not withstanding his extreme age, he has all the martial spirit and not a little of the youthful appearance of a soldier of 20. As might be expected, he is the pet of the Regiment, and the echoes of the Revolutionary Era resounded from the tap of his drum.[7]

The regiment, band, and drum corps were accompanied through New York by the Lowell Brigade Band, with George Brooks as leader. The brigade, stationed in New York, always formed at the railhead to greet newly arriving regiments. The 55th Regiment (Lafayette Guard) together with detachments of the New York 7th Regiment joined to escort the 6th Regiment to their quarters. Civilians cheered themselves hoarse as the troops passed through the city. Two full regiments with parts of a third, a full drum corps, and two brass bands made quite a parade.

The ceremonies were repeated when the 6th Regiment left for Philadelphia the following day. They were again escorted to the "new ferry boat John P. Jackson." At the dock they were met by Mayor Van Vorst of Jersey City, Chief of Police Martinus, Sheriff Francis, and by an immense crowd of Jersey men and women who provided a welcome as tumultuous as that in New York. "A hardier looking or better trained Regiment of Militia has never visited this city, and should it be their fortune to encounter the rebels and conspirators of the CSA, they will, doubtless, prove themselves abundantly able to withstand the 'smell of southern powder and the touch of southern steel'."[8]

The regiment's first encounter with "rebels and conspirators" occurred sooner than anticipated. Although cheered in New York and feted in Philadelphia, the tumult created by their passage through Baltimore was of a different sort. As the regiment neared that city, it received word that its passage would be contested by individuals loyal to the Southern cause. Ammunition was issued and strict orders given to the band to confine its music to a bipartisan program. It was specifically told not to play "Dixie."[9]

Passage of trains through Baltimore required that the engines be detached at one depot, and that the cars be pulled by horses to another. This was accomplished in piecemeal fashion since horses could not pull a full-length train. The operation went smoothly until only about one hundred fifty of the troops, and the band, remained at the initial location.

With the majority of the regiment across town, Southern sympathizers barricaded the tracks. The mob immediately set upon the remaining cars. The band, being unarmed, at first refused to leave the train. Against their better judgment, they finally left the cars and the mob was on them instantly. They fought back as best they could but were compelled to retreat to safer positions under the rail cars. Their attackers forced them out. The police, who seemed to regard the entire incident as a big joke, told them to "run like the devil." They ran— unceremoniously dumping their instruments and other impedimenta enroute.

About a half-mile from the encounter the band met a group of German and Irish civilians who took them into their homes. Once safely inside, they removed all insignia from their uniforms and finally left the city under the protection of four hundred policemen via the crosstown railroad as was originally planned.[10] Most of their instruments were eventually located around the Philadelphia station, but the band returned home while the remainder of the regiment went on to Washington.[11] One frightened drummer stowed his instrument under a nearby haystack and never was able to recover it. Some weeks later, the 20th New York Volunteer Infantry was camped near the site of the disturbance and the wayward drum caused some difficulty for one of its men. "One night my company. . . .found a quantity of arms concealed under a haystack, and a drum belonging to the Sixth Massachusetts Regiment. The man in whose posession the drum was found was arrested, taken to headquarters, and asked to explain how he came by the drum. It was found that the Sixth Massachusetts had been fired upon by a disloyal mob while marching through the streets of Baltimore on their way to Washington."[12]

The entire incident was hardly a joke. When stones were followed by pistol shots, the regiment responded in kind. Several of the mob fell. Four soldiers died and thirty-six were wounded before order was restored.

The 6th Regiment finally arrived in Washington to a thunderous ovation. "The Regiment has paraded two or three times in Washington, attracting marked attention. They are much mortified at the loss of their band, and tried hard to get their commanding officer to let them form in Baltimore, after they reached the Washington Depot, and countermarch through the city, despite the mob, but the colonel replied that his orders were to bring them to Washington, and they could go nowhere else."[13]

Subsequent groups parading through Baltimore learned much from the experience of the 6th Massachusetts. When the famed 7th New York Regiment left for their training camp, the bandsmen carried revolvers as protection against the Baltimore mobs. On 27 May when the 1st New Hampshire marched through that city, Fife Major F. H. Pike, "knowing that he was supported by a thousand loaded muskets, beat right and left with his baton, clearing the way before him, while Baldwin's Cornet Band played 'Yankee Doodle,' the first National Air that had greeted the ears of the people since the passage of the Massachusetts Sixth."[14]

Though the president's initial call for men was quickly oversubscribed, it became evident that existing militia units would be unable to supply sufficient troops to prosecute the war. By 1864 Lincoln had issued eleven more calls. The first was in April 1861, the last in December 1864. In the period between, 2,573,748 Union soldiers were called to their country's service.[15]

Since existing militia regiments were unable to meet the demands for manpower, new regiments were organized in response to these calls from the federal government. The federal troop levy on the states established the size and type of each regiment and provided its table of organization. The quota for each state was transmitted to its governor. The governor, in turn, announced the acceptance of a specific number of volunteer regiments. Prominent individuals responded by raising a company or a larger-sized unit. Successful citizens were rewarded with an officer's commission.

Units were often raised from a single segment of the population, Ellsworth's "Fire Zouaves" having previously set the example for this practice. Others were composed of men of a single ethnic origin. Prior military experience was not a prerequisite for participation in any of these matters. One writer noted that "in the early days little regard was paid to military training. Almost anyone who could persuade eighty, or sometimes fewer men to enlist could secure a Captain's commission; almost anyone [who] could raise a regiment could attach the title of colonel to his name."[16]

Although the initial call was oversubscribed, it was evident that still more men were needed, and that time was a critical factor. On 28 July 1862 Lincoln appealed to the governors, asking what progress had been made and how soon new regiments would be available. Then, on 4 August, he issued his second call for troops—this time for three hundred thousand men to serve for a period of nine months. Every city and hamlet responded. Committees were organized. Bounties were offered. Great war meetings were held to stimulate enlistments. Much of this stimulation was provided by the music of the bands.

On 6 August the bells rang all over Washington and a thirty-four gun salute was fired. Businesses closed early. By 5:00 P.M. a crowd of nearly ten thousand had gathered before the steps of the capitol building to hear the serenade played by the Marine Band. Leather-lunged orators and bands discoursing national airs encouraged potential recruits to determine their duties. The slaughter on the field at Bull Run had already tarnished the picture book concept of war, and potential recruits were less eager, having discovered that soldiers bleed and die. The orators and bands sought to overcome the understandable reluctance of these young patriots and to encourage them to fall in behind their flag.

The Washington war meeting of 6 August was typical of those held throughout the nation. The assembly was addressed by a formidable array of speakers including George S. Boutwell, Leonard Swett, and L. E. Chittenden. The first two were well-known in Washington for their professional rhetoric, while Chittenden was the father of the persuasive member of Congress who had tried to avoid the war with the Chittenden compromise.

The program was interrupted by the late arrival of President Lincoln who was greeted by the band playing "Hail to the Chief." He spoke a few words without a prepared text. Other men with proven propensities for verbosity prolonged the program well into the night. The meeting finally concluded in a blaze of fireworks and patriotic songs. The songs were led by first one and then another of the several brass bands present, in addition to the United States Marine Band. The cumulative effect whipped the crowd into a patriotic frenzy.[17]

Band music contributed greatly to the success of these appeals to patriotism. U. H. Farr recorded their effect when he recounted the events leading to his own enlistment. "The fife was playing, the drums were beating, and the new soldiers fell into line. When I saw among them boys no larger than myself, I suddenly resolved to see if they would take me, and stepped into the ranks with the others. I kept the step till the war was over."[18]

John Casler responded to the same emotional appeals when he enlisted in the Confederate service. He was absolutely elated as he marched off to his training camp. "As we marched out of town the brass bands were playing, the drums beating, colors flying and the fair ladies waving their handkerchiefs and cheering us on to 'victory of death.' Oh! How nice to be a soldier."[19]

Not all recruiting was as magnificently staged as that in Washington. Captain Wright of the 8th Kentucky Volunteer Infantry recalled that on "the 26th of September, Capt. R. Winbourn and myself left Estill Springs on a recruiting tour...to the farm of Mr. Willis, where our first appointment to beat up for volunteers had been previously announced. The surrounding hills reechoed the sound of our martial music, the music of which was not of the best, but the patriotic ardor being augmented by the rumored invasion of the State, caused men, women and children to collect from all directions....The poor music was followed by an equally poor speech...and this was followed by loud and boisterous cheering. We hoisted our flag, headed by our three amateur musicians, playing their one and only tune, 'Sally is the gal for me.' As each recruit fell into the moving line, loud cheers rent the air. In a short time we had about eighteen recruits."[20]

The enlistment of a son was a crushing separation to fathers and mothers, while a man leaving his wife and children experienced inexpressible anguish. But the only distress felt by boys in the flush of youth was the fear that they could not meet the requirements for muster. Amidst the bombast, rhetoric and blaring bands, young sons cajoled and begged—and parents relented. One mother smothered her misgivings with bravado when she told a reporter, "I could not have felt he was my son had he hesitated."[21] A recruiting officer reported that a boy—an only child—wished to enlist and asked his mother to gain her consent. She "displayed an indescribable radiance on her beautiful face as she replied, 'yes, he may go. How can I refuse to give my son to the country when I remember that my Heavenly Father gave his only son to save the world?' "[22]

In rare instances the emotion of the moment turned to acid as long-smoldering differences rose to the surface. Mary Chesnut operated an early car pool on her way to a recruiting meeting. "I drove Jesse James and we picked up a Mrs. Willie Knox whose husband beats her. She was wishing he would go to Pensacola and be shot!"[23]

The general feeling of the public toward the young soldiers, no matter what their circumstance, was perhaps better stated in a later entry in her diary. She wrote that "a Negro girl who brought a note from Madame Togno was in a great state of excitement."

She had witnessed a frightful outrage on the street. She was so graphic, she had to be silenced. She said a drunken soldier assulted "a lady, a real lady dressed fine. She fought like a tigress, and two Negroes ran to help her, but the soldier drew his pistol and held the lady by one leg and his pistol in the other hand, and such a crowd was tearing up, and she was yelling like a stuck pig, and dancing and prancing!" The ladies in the drawing room made allowance for the luxuriant black imagination. The soldier was carried off to the guard house. The unknown lady in fine cloths went her way at double-quick speed. It is hard to be forced to think ill of a soldier, drunk or sober.[24]

A good band was a great help in promoting enlistments. A new regiment that could announce the enlistment of an already well-known civilian band had a noteworthy edge in recruiting. Units that could not secure a professional band quickly set out to organize one from whatever musicians were available.

When the 20th Regiment, Massachusetts Volunteers, arrived in New York the commander, Colonel William R. Lee, felt compelled to explain that "a band is now recruiting in Boston which will follow the Regiment in a few days."[25]

By 12 June 1861 Colonel Baker's California Regiment had met the requirements for federal recognition and was at Fort Schuyler to begin training. "The men are in uniform now," he wrote, "and present an extremely fine appearance, being stalwart, tough-looking customers, who can give quite as much as they are ever likely to take, and perhaps a little more. A grand parade will take place at Fort Schuyler on Saturday next, when the Regiment expects to 'see company.' A Regimental Band is now in the course of formation and will make its debut on that occasion."[26]

Advertisements for field musicians appeared in most newspapers as the competition for their services grew more intense.

The National Zouaves are well organized, but a Drum Major and Buglers are wanted for this Regiment.[27]

ADVANCED GUARD ZOUAVES, Col. Duryea Commanding, six drummer-boys wanted. Apply at No. 564 Broadway Avenue.[28]

Most established militia units held contracts with local professional bands. In some instances these musicians performed exclusively for a single unit, but most often they hired their services to several different regiments. Bands that played for several military organizations obviously could enter service with only one of them. The lucky regiment invariably publicized its good fortune.

The City Cornet Band beg to have us announce to their friends and public generally that they have joined the Maryland Guard Battalion and hence-forth will assume the name of the Maryland Guard Band. They solicit a continuance of the patronage heretofore so liberally bestowed upon them.

Signed, D. Feldman, Captain.[29]

The advertisement indicates first, that the band had built a substantial reputation and second, it intended to continue limited civilian appearances even though it was now a part of the regiment. If the musicians counted upon very much "continued patronage," they were soon to be disappointed. The regiment and band were quickly sent to the field, but not before additional performances established their latest composition, *The Maryland Guard Quickstep*, as a successful publication for the house of Metter and Beechains.

New regiments quickly discovered that not all musicians responding to their advertisements were equally talented. Mr. James A. Emmerton, who wrote the record of the 23rd Regiment of Massachusetts Volunteer Infantry noted that "certain men, such as could afford to leave their civilian occupations for the enlisted man's pay and were, in their own estimation capable of earning that pay as musicians, had collected at [the camp]. When. . .[some of these men were] put to the trial. . .they were [found to be] utterly incapable. They were summarily sent to their homes. A successful search was made for qualified musicians; the Regimental Officers agreed to contribute to extra pay for the Band members, and a good band was organized which performed with credit."[30]

In this instance the officers did not object to the extra assessment, but this was not always true. The 44th Massachusetts Infantry Regiment had no band of its own. The officers hired the Boston Brass Band with Patrick Gilmore as leader for one occasion, and passed the assessment on to the enlisted men without prior consultation. The enlisted men complained that perhaps "some of our rich friends from Boston should get together to help defray the cost."[31]

The Lincoln Cavalry could not secure a band prior to its departure for camp, so it hired the famous Dodworth Band to accompany its march to the point of embarkation. "As the Regiment marched on to the pier, Dodworth's Band, which had escorted them, played 'Dixie Land,' while some of the more jolly in the ranks struck out into kind of a shuffle, and went forward in the liveliest manner. The Band then changed to 'Old Lang Syne' when the scene became really affectionate. Wives and husbands, brothers and sisters, were for a time locked in each others arms, and the last good-by and parting kiss was given. . . . The Unit will receive its horses and equipment in Washington."[32]

The 44th Massachusetts Infantry Regiment paid $3,000 to Flagg's Band for its services—a sizeable fee even by today's standards.[33]

In other instances musicians were perfectly willing to enlist but once in service found that there was no money for instruments. The regiment then appealed to the public for support. The 1st Regiment of New York Volunteers was in this predicament. A letter appeared in the *New York Times* entitled "A Patriotic Appeal" describing the plight of the band.

Ladies and Gentlemen of New York, I appeal to you on behalf of the Band belonging to the First Regiment, New York Volunteers. They have been for several weeks now in the field without their instruments. On the day of the Battle at Great Bethel, these noble spirits shouldered the musket and stood in the thickest of the fight, and there, on the altar of their country, offered up the first blood of the First Regiment.

You know too well the elevating, enervating and cheering effects of good band music to need any comment upon that subject from me or anyone else.

Our soldiers feel the need of those elevating and inspiriting strains which give life and fervor to the soul. Will you aid in giving this great blessing to the weary and dispirited soldiers? They are willing to suffer and die, if need be, for your country and your homes.

I saw them stand, like men of iron nerves, before the cannon's fire for one hour and forty minutes on that day without broken ranks or confusion. They will not fail you— they will not disappoint you.

Any person willing to aid in this cause may leave the amount they propose to give with Mr. Stetson, at the Astor House, where every farthing will be accounted for.

As I am under orders to return to Fortress Monroe within ten days, what is done, must be done quickly. $1200.00 will be needed.

Respectfully, etc.

P. Franklin Jones

Chaplain, First Regiment, NYV[34]

Chaplain Jones, like most men of the cloth, was adept at fund raising. Eastern newspapers were soon heaping accolades upon the band of the 1st Regiment of New York Volunteers.

So many regiments sought musicians that demand quickly exceeded supply. The historian of the 104th Pennsylvania Infantry wrote in September 1861 that "the demand was so great that it was somewhat difficult to obtain a good band; but I engaged one at Emaus, Lehigh County, composed of young Germans, which soon became quite skilled in playing."[35]

When a new regiment reached full strength, the neophyte colonel notified his governor. The governor then ordered the unit to assemble at the nearest training camp where it was armed and equipped at state expense. The regiment was then mustered into federal service.

War meetings were replete with pompous rhetoric and bravado, and the resulting enlistments produced the painful partings of loved ones. But these emotions were quickly replaced by others once the troops left the railhead or pier. Cyrus Stone, a New York farm boy, wrote to his mother on 22 October 1861 from the deck of a ship as he sailed down the Mississippi to his first encampment. "After we got out of their hearing the boys acted as if they had forgoten their mothers and. . .wives, that they had just. . .left. . .with tears in their eyes Not but a few minutes before the band boys handed wround the whiskey bottle among themselves. . .one of the members of the band got drunk."[36]

A Wisconsin farm boy, who had never been far from home, wrote to his parents after completing the first leg of his journey by rail:

We came in the cars to Madison from LaCrosse. It was a new experience for me, I was wide awake the whole day. I was afraid we were off the track every time we crossed a switch or came to a river. At the towns the girls swarmed on the platforms to ask the boys for their pictures and to kiss the best looking ones. One young Frenchman, we called him the pony of the regiment because he was so small and quick, got the most kisses. He was so short the boys held him by the legs to he could reach down out the windows to kiss the girls. Many times some old fellows held the girls up so she could be reached. It was fun anyway.[37]

Generally, new regiments were presented with a stand of colors when they were accepted into federal service. Groups of locally prominent ladies sewed the ensigns or raised the necessary funds for their purchase. When completed, they were bestowed upon the regiment at solemn ceremonies consisting of patriotic speeches, music, and the actual presentations.

On 8 October 1861 Mrs. Maria Lydig Daly, a New York social gadfly, a judge's wife, and a personal friend of Colonel Corcoran (who had recently been given command of the 69th New York Regiment of the Irish Brigade), was wrestling with the financial burdens of this patriotic purpose. "I have been busy today in assisting to raise money for standards for the Irish Brigade. Three US standards and three green flags with Irish emblems and mottos and the guide colors. They will cost about $600.00."[38]

Six hundred dollars was no mean sum, being roughly equivalent to the annual income of a law clerk or minor government bureaucrat of 1861. Funding problems were compounded by the pressures of time. The brigade had only recently reported to New York but was to be moved to another location within a few days. On 14 October Maria Daly summed up the results of her earnest efforts. "I have been engaged in raising some money to aid in presenting the Irish Brigade with stands of colors. I have altogether sixty-five dollars, and as that is one-eighth part of the whole, I shall make no further effort."[39] Someone else must have taken up the burden she so quickly relinquished, since the brigade did eventually receive a beautiful stand of colors.

Flag raisings and ceremonial presentations were accepted with mixed emotions by the soldiers. Some felt these ceremonies were primarily to gratify the home folks. Others greeted them with genuine enthusiasm. Many felt, especially in 1861, that their unit did not really exist until it marched behind wind-whipped colors that each man had sworn to defend to the death. This romantic attitude gave way to sterner reality by 1864. On 16 February of that year Major James Connolly wrote to his wife. "I am at Chattanooga and happened to be present at a flag presentation today in the camp of the 11th Ohio. The flag was an elegant silk one, presented by the ladies of Troy, Ohio, and purchased with funds from a Ladies Aid Society. The citizen, delegated by the ladies to present it made a spread eagle speech. I would rather listen to Bragg's cannonade than to a citizen urging soldiers to stand by their flag."[40]

Not all presentation ceremonies were marked by eloquence and beauty. One of the less-pretentious affairs was described by a Massachusetts lieutenant who was a participant. "This eve we were presented with a flag by the ladies of this town. A very homely young lady (though she was the best looking one in town) made a speech which she learned (at least she thought so, but I did not for she went through with [it] about as smooth as one might come down a rocky hill in the dark). Col. Gordon then answered it. Three cheers were then proposed for him which sounded a good deal as old bad Fali [the Lieutenant's cat] did when her tail was stepped on. The officers of the regiment then gave the ladies three cheers which made them turn pale. The band play[ed], we took the [flag]. . .and went home."[41]

Flag presentations grew less frequent as the war dragged on, but they continued as long as new regiments were mustered into service. Recruiting activities, on the other hand, intensified as the two bloody war machines efficiently dispatched thousands of earlier enlistees to hospitals—or to their Maker.

Neither government established a regular system for the replacement of battle casualties. Although the draft did provide some replacements of questionable quality, the recruitment of sufficient men to return depleted units to full strength was left pretty much to the ingenuity of regimental commanders. Their most vigorous efforts could not stem the reduction of many regiments to company or even platoon-sized units by the end of the war. Commanders at all levels dispatched their adjutants, and attendant musicians, to nearby communities where every effort was expended to encourage the available men to enlist in the battle-hardened regiments. A band was a valuable asset in these proceedings, and a regiment with a superior ensemble always fared better in the competition for the incessantly dwindling supply of available recruits.

From our point in time, several wars removed from 1861, it is difficult to understand how a brass band could be so important to the war effort. Indeed, it is well-nigh impossible for us to project a band into the mainstream of military thought—not to mention a social milieu—when present-day bands have so long been abandoned to the world of sports and academia. But in 1860 society clutched the wind band to its bosom. T. H. Rollison in 1886 could still write that "the Military Band . . . belong[ed] to the public in general. A merry-making, no matter of what description, held out of doors, appears incomplete without a Military Band."[42] The brass band had long been a part of our national culture. Civilian soldiers naturally associated band music with any sort of civic or patriotic demonstration. The close relationship between militia units and bands was one of long standing. The tables of organization for the expanding armies were simply extensions of the models at hand, and the militia organizations provided these models.

In addition to this practical explanation for the proliferation of bands, a more philosophical reason could be offered. The nation had experienced a long period of prosperity prior to 1860, and citizens tended to hold a rather romantic view of life. Most felt that they truly lived in the best of all possible worlds, and as Mary Chesnut so aptly observed, their concept of war came from reading *Ivanhoe*. Young men rushing to join the volunteer regiments, believing that the war might end if they did not hurry, represented the view of a majority of citizens. Bruce Catton accurately described the resulting conflict as a "picture-book war" fought by two amateur armies in his book, *The Army of the Potomac: Mr. Lincoln's Army*.

The Organized Militia reinforced this romantic concept. The colorful and picturesque unit names, the Arabian Nights uniforms, the variegated silken flags, the bombastic rhetoric and oratory, the "gentleman's-club-like" atmosphere of the units (Ellsworth's unit did not allow drinking, cussing, or chewing), the posturing chivalry at Sumter, the appearance of town folk (with picnic baskets) to watch parades and even battles, the newspaper articles stressing that "battles in civilized war could avoid the sabbath," the paroled POWs with gentlemen-officers keeping their side arms, the ceremonial surrender of the sword upon defeat, and the twelve and thirteen-year-old drummer boys were all part of a make-believe world that could only be described as romantic.

The Civil War, more than any other in history, was begun with the vain hope that it could and would be fought according to the rules—rules taken from the days of King Arthur—rules that would keep war civilized and ritualistic. Although other wars had similar aspirations, the Civil War distilled this yearning into a concentrated palliative. This universal desire of mankind persisted until World War I. Even when that global conflict reduced itself to a bloody contest of attrition in the trenches, the fledgling air force remained a final bastion of Civil War romanticism. The leather helmets, long silk scarfs, goggles, and jennies were as colorful as anything that the Civil War could offer. The posturing "Red Baron" air aces, saluting their downed opponents, or breaking off the dogfight when one had exhausted his ammunition, were anachronisms belonging more properly to the year 1860. This naivete produced the atmosphere that allowed the bands to flourish during the Civil War. Indeed, the picture-book concept was essential to their well-being.

By 1863 the last vestige of idealism had been eradicated in a diluvium of blood. Bands continued to perform, but in greatly reduced numbers. By government edict regimental bands were replaced by brigade bands, producing at least a modest reduction in number.

As the war grew in ferocity and devastation, romanticism offered a means of escape. In modern warfare killing is accomplished at an impersonal distance, but in 1861 the individual soldier observed his fallen foe at close proximity. Perhaps a romantic view was an essential ingredient of conscience for the young recruit who snuffed out the life of his fellow man in spite of the Ten Commandments. The task was accomplished with efficiency and dispatch— but seldom with hatred. Exigencies of service compelled it, but Billy Yank or Johnny Reb could not easily forget the exhilaration of battle nor the torment, pain, fear, anguish, and death of his fallen foe. Dolor could not subsist if framed in a picture book of ritualized heroics. Ritualization and romanticism furnished the essential, but distorted, perspectives that allowed the average soldier to separate his battlefield actions from the conscience of his childhood education. Unfortunately, the war outlasted his ability to fantasize. As the glory and whitewash were stripped away, it was revealed in all its ugliness. The romanticism of the bands became less and less important.

But in 1861 none of this had come to pass. Bands fanned the flames of patriotism and followed the recruit into service. Music resounded from everywhere and all were anxious to go.

NOTES

1. *National Intelligencer*, 16 April 1861, p. 1.

2. *Baltimore Sun*, 21 April 1861, p. 2.

3. William Sumner Dodge, *A Waif of the War, The History of the Seventy-fifth Illinois infantry, embracing the entire campaigns of the Army of the Cumberland* (Chicago: Church and Goodman, 1866), p. 28.

4. Mary Boykin Chesnut, *A Diary from Dixie*, 2nd ed., ed. Ben Ames Williams (Boston: Houghton Mifflin Co., The Riverside Press, Cambridge, 1949), p. 22.

5. Ibid., p. 38.

6. *National Intelligencer*, 2 January 1861, p. 2.

7. *New York Times*, 19 April 1861, p. 1.

8. *New York Times*, 20 April 1861, p. 1.

9. George W. Mason, *Minute Men of '61* (Boston: Smith and McCance, 1910), p. 188.

10. Ibid., p. 210. Additional accounts of the Baltimore incident were carried in the *New York Times*, *Baltimore Sun*, *National Intelligencer*, and several other newspapers around 19 April 1861.

11. Mason, *Minute Men*, p. 201. *See also* Frank Moore, *The Civil War in Song and Story*, 2d ed. (New York: O. F. Collier, 1889), p. 36 and William A. Bufkin, "Union Bands of the Civil War (1862–1865)" (Ph.D. diss., Louisiana State University, 1973), p. 24.

12. Enos B. Vail, *Reminiscences of a Boy in the Civil War* (Brooklyn, N.Y., privately printed, 1915), p. 25.

13. The *New York Times*, 25 April 1861, p. 1.

14. The *New York Times*, 27 May 1861, p. 2; *National Intelligencer*, 27 May 1861, p. 1.

15. Mason, *Minute Men*, p. 28.

16. Ella Lonn, *Foreigners in the Union Army and Navy* (Binghamington: Vail-Ballou Press, 1951), p. 72.

17. *National Intelligencer*, *Washington Star*, and the *New York Times* all carried accounts of the great war meeting.

18. Samuel Merrill, *The Seventeenth Indiana Volunteer Infantry in the War of the Rebellion* (Indianapolis: Bobbs-Merrill Co., 1900), p. 4.

19. John O. Casler, *Four Years in the Stonewall Brigade* (2d ed. 1906; reprint ed., Marietta, Ga.: Continental Book Co., 1951), p. 19.

20. Capt. T. J. Wright, *History of the Eighth Kentucky Regiment Volunteer Infantry* (St. Joseph, Mo.: St. Joseph Steam Printing Co., 1880), p. 19.

21. *National Intelligencer*, 7 December 1861, p. 3.

22. Ibid., p. 2.

23. Chesnut, *Diary*, p. 9.

24. Ibid., p. 189.

25. *New York Times*, 6 September 1861, p. 2.

26. *New York Times*, 12 June 1861, p. 2.

27. *New York Times*, 5 May 1861, p. 3.

28. *New York Times*, 8 May 1861, p. 8.

29. *New York Times*, 1 September 1861, p. 2.

30. James A. Emmerton, *A Record of the Twenty-third Regiment Massachusetts Volunteer Infantry in the War of the Rebellion, 1861–1865* (Boston: W. Ware & Co., 1866), p. 48.

31. Francis A. Lord and Arthur Wise, *Bands and Drummer Boys of the Civil War* (New York: Thomas Yoseloff, 1966), p. 35.

32. *New York Times*, 27 August 1861, p. 1.

33. Account book of the unit fund of the 44th Massachusetts Infantry, National Archives, Washington, D.C., n. p. n.

34. The *New York Times*, 20 June 1861, p. 3.

35. W. W. H. Davis, *History of the 104th Pennsylvania Regiment (Ringgold Regiment) August 22, 1861 to September 30, 1864* (Philadelphia: James B. Rodgers, 1866), p. 113.

36. Bell Irvin Wiley, *The Life of Billy Yank* (Indianapolis: Bobbs-Merrill, 1952), p. 31.

37. "Letters of a Badger Boy in Blue," *Wisconsin Magazine of History*, 4 (1920–1921): 209.

38. Harold E. Hammond, ed., *Diary of a Union Lady 1861–65* (New York: Funk and Wagnalls, 1962), p. 60.

39. Ibid., p. 63.

40. James A Connolly, *Three Years in the Army of the Cumberland*, ed. Paul M. Angle (Bloomington, Ind.: Civil War Centennial Series, Indiana University Press, 1959), p. 169.

41. F. M. Abbott to his brother 22 July 1861 as cited by Bell Irvin Wiley, *The Life of Billy Yank*, p. 30.

42. T. H. Rollinson, *Treatise on Harmony, Counterpoint, Instrumentation and Orchestration with Appendix Treating Upon the Instrumentation of Military Bands* (Philadelphia: J. W. Pepper Co., 1886), p. 257.

THE ORGANIZATION
OF THE BANDS

As early as 7 December 1862 Secretary of War Stanton recommended that "the employment of Regimental Bands should be limited; the proportion of musicians now allowed by law being too great, and their usefulness not at all commensurate with their heavy expense."[1] Since raising an army did not proceed in earnest until after Lincoln's call for seventy-five thousand volunteers on 5 April 1861 we can conclude that the musicians, who were the object of Stanton's complaint, had accumulated during a period of only twenty months.

The bands of the regular regiments were not the source of the secretary's grief. It was the bands of the volunteer regiments that had gotten totally out-of-hand.

Recruiting for the Regular Army has not been attended with the success which was anticipated.... While it is admitted that soldiers in the Regular Army, under control of officers of military education and experience, are generally better cared for than those in the volunteer services, it is certain that the popular preference is largely given to the latter. Young men evidently prefer to enter a Corps officered by their friends and acquaintances, and, besides the bounty granted to volunteers in most of the states, inducements are often directly offered to them by those whose commissions depend upon their success in obtaining recruits. In addition, the volunteer is allowed to draw his full pay of $13.00 per month, while by law $2.00 per month are deducted from the pay of the regular to be returned to him at the end of his term of service.[2]

Newly raised volunteer regiments followed the precedents established by the older units of the Ellsworth type. Each brought a full brass band into service if possible. The federal government itself created this flood of bands when it formulated the tables of organization for the combat arms.

General Order Number 15, issued 4 May 1861, was the first to affect the volunteer regiments.[3] It called for thirty-nine regiments of volunteer infantry and one of cavalry. Companies were to number from eighty-three to one hundred one officers and men, with ranks distributed according to the following tables:

Minimum		Maximum	
1	Captain	1	Captain
1	First Lieutenant	1	First Lieutenant
1	Second Lieutenant	1	Second Lieutenant
1	First Sergeant	1	First Sergeant
4	Sergeants	4	Sergeants
8	Corporals	8	Corporals
2	Musicians	2	Musicians
1	Wagoner	1	Wagoner
64	Privates	82	Privates
83	Aggregate	101	Aggregate

Regiments were to include ten companies, a regimental staff of twelve officers and men, and a band of twenty-four musicians. Ranks were distributed according to the following tables:

Minimum		Maximum	
1	Colonel	1	Colonel
1	Lieutenant Colonel	1	Lieutenant Colonel
1	Major	1	Major
1	Adjutant	1	Adjutant
1	Regimental Quarter-master	1	Regimental Quarter-master
1	Sergeant Major	1	Sergeant Major
1	Regimental Quarter-master Sergeant	1	Regimental Quarter-master Sergeant
1	Regimental Commissary Sergeant	1	Regimental Commissary Sergeant
1	Hospital Steward	1	Hospital Steward
2	Principal Musicians	2	Principal Musicians
24	Musicians for a band	24	Musicians for a band
830	Company Officers and enlisted men	1010	Company Officers and enlisted men
865	Aggregate	1045	Aggregate

Calvalry regiments substituted buglers for the drummers and fifers of the infantry at both company and regimental levels. For some unexplained reason cavalry bands were limited to sixteen musicians.

If all musical vacancies were filled the 40 regiments would include 80 principal musicians, 780 company musicians (infantry), 20 company buglers (cavalry), 39 brass bands of 24 bandsmen each, and one cavalry band of 16 members. These 1,832 musicians represent 2.5 percent of the total troop levy.

Support troops, such as sappers and miners, were generally assigned piecemeal to combat units, and no bands were assigned to them. Bands were the exclusive property of the combat arms.

It is interesting to postulate the total number of musicians who served in the Union army. In December 1861 the United States Sanitary Commission conducted an inspection of the Army of the Potomac. The Commission was concerned with living conditions in camp, including comfort, sanitation, and morale. Its report notes that "of 200 Regiments inspected in the Army of the Potomac, 143 had bands, 43 had no band and nothing is available on the other Regiments."[4] The total musical vacancies in the inspected regiments would include 400 principal musicians, 4,000 musicians, and 3,436 (143 x 24) bandsmen. If all vacancies had been filled, 7,836 musicians would have serenaded the Army of the Potomac.

It is difficult to establish an average size for one of these 143 bands. Some were as small as 8 musicians, while the Maryland Guard Band far exceeded the regulations with its 30 bandsmen. If we arbitrarily select 18 musicians as an average figure, the Sanitary Commission *Report* accounted for 2,574 bandsmen in the Army of the Potomac alone.

Dyer's Compendium can provide an estimate of the musical vacancies existing in the entire Union army. Dyer indicates that 272 cavalry regiments, 61 artillery regiments, 13 engineer regiments, 4 sharpshooter regiments, and 2,144 infantry regiments saw service with the Union army during the four years of the war. In addition, he lists 1,066 units of less than regimental size. Some of these served independently, while others were grouped into regimental-sized commands. Even some of these provisional regiments had bands.

By multiplying the number of musicians allowed each type of regiment by the number of regiments of that type, we can conclude that vacancies existed for a total of 104,234 musicians during the course of the war.[5]

The total number of musicians who actually served with either army is a moot issue since many bandsmen served with several different units, and a number of bands entered and left the service several times. The Repaz Band of Williamsport, Pennsylvania, served three enlistments, each time with a different regiment. Bufkin mentions more than two-hundred rosters of bandsmen, mustered out between April and September 1862, and more than two-hundred additional bands have been identified in other Civil War sources as having served in the Army of the Potomac during this same period.[6]

One thing is certain, the cost of the regimental bands was staggering. As early as 1855 Augustus Meyers was already concerned about the cost of his regimental band on Governor's Island. Under the leadership of Bandmaster

Bloomfield, they performed at guard mount, and for dress parades, musters, and general inspections. On warm summer evenings, they played in front of the commanding officer's quarters or hired out to play in New York City, a lucrative opportunity for the musicians. Meyers wrote that "one of the largest expenses was the band whose members were paid extra (according to their ability) over and above their grade of soldiers's pay. Their instruments, which the Government did not furnish, had to be purchased, as well as music and a showy uniform. . . .Indeed [the bandsmen] were much petted and pampered and enjoyed many privileges. . . .all of which had to be paid for out of the post fund. . . .From all this the officers received the greater benefit and yet they were not required by army regulations to contribute to the fund."[7]

By 5 December 1861 the paymaster general of the Union army felt compelled to observe that the bands were "far more ornamental than useful," and he recommended that they be abolished. He estimated that this would provide an annual saving of five million dollars.[8] The paymaster's estimates are not unreasonable.

The first session of the thirty-seventh Congress established the pay scale for bandsmen. It stipulated that "one fourth of each [band] shall receive the pay and allowances of Sergeants of Engineers; one fourth those of Corporals of Engineer Soldiers; and the remaining half those of Privates of Engineer Soldiers of the First Class. The Leader of the Bands shall receive each the pay and emoluments of a Second Lieutenant of Infantry."[9]

A lieutenant of infantry received fifty dollars per month, four rations per day, and one servant. Officer's subsistance was computed at thirty cents per ration and forage at eight dollars per month per horse actually owned and kept in service. A bandmaster of infantry or cavalry received eighty-six dollars per month plus one servant. An engineer sergeant drew thirty-four dollars per month, an engineer corporal twenty dollars per month, and a first class private eighteen dollars per month. Bandsmen were payed similar amounts. While drum majors of infantry received twenty-one dollars per month, principal musicians of cavalry were paid sums equal to those received by sergeants of cavalry. This provided an added benefit since cavalry sergeants received an additional seventeen dollars monthly as a type of hazardous-duty pay in addition to their basic pay of thirty-four dollars per month. A drum major of infantry received thirty dollars less per month for performing the same duties as the principal musician of cavalry. This gross inequity cannot be explained in terms of cavalry forage payments since these were established at eight dollars per month per horse throughout the army. Company musicians were paid as privates of the first class in all branches of the service.[10]

Using these figures, the monthly cost for the musical establishment of a single corps, had all vacancies been filled, totaled $33,217. Multiplying this by the twenty-four corps of the Union army, and extending that figure on an annual basis, gives a total annual expenditure of $6,643,400. This does not include the additional costs of outfitting these organizations with instruments, music, and special uniforms. The paymaster's estimates were conservative. Morale building was indeed expensive.

In an effort to reduce expenses the adjutant general's office on 2 October 1861 banned the further enlistment of bands of volunteer regiments. Additionally, it ordered the mustering out of all bandsmen who were not musicians. (One can only speculate why these incompetents were enlisted in the first place.) Finally, it froze all existing vacancies for bandsmen in the volunteer regiments already in federal service.[11]

Less than two weeks later, Benjamin F. Larned, Paymaster General, answered a query from Henry Wilson, of the United States Senate, who, like all politicians, was seeking areas of the military budget that might lend themselves to a prudent paring. Larned suggested that the abolishment of the regimental bands would save about $5,000,000 annually.[12] The paymaster suggested that still further reductions could be achieved by exploring other areas of the military as well. He felt that cavalry regiments might be replaced with infantry, thus eliminating the forage costs for all those "hay burners." Further, he suggested weeding out incompetent chaplains, tightening accounting procedures to reduce excessive forage, increasing the tax on the sutlers, revoking a recent pay increase, and reducing the number of horses permitted each officer.[13] Eventually, some degree of economy was achieved in all of these areas, but the regimental brass bands stood the brunt of the retrenchment.

In January 1862 the inspector general of the army was authorized to discharge all bandsmen who were not competent musicians.[14] Finally, in July 1862, the adjutant general ordered that all bands of the volunteer regiments be mustered from the service, stipulating that "so much of the aforesaid act. . .as authorizes each regiment of volunteers in the United States service to have twenty-four musicians for a band. . .is hereby repealed; and the men composing such bands shall be mustered out of the service within thirty days after the passage of this act."[15]

Those seeking economic relief were clearly justified. Edwin O. Kimberley, bandmaster of the 3rd Wisconsin Volunteer Infantry Regiment, estimated that the upkeep of their band "including pay, rations, and clothes, is over $50.00 per day, $1400.00 per month,"[16] and this figure did not include the costs of the field musicians assigned to his unit. If we use Kimberley's figures the costs of the bands, army-wide, would exceed $15,000,000 annually.

Bandsmen soon became aware of considerations relating to their discharge. In early December 1861 Kimberley wrote to his parents. "We expect to hear something this week in regard to bands, don't know how it will come out yet."[17] In spite of these early rumors nearly eight months passed before the discharge of bands was an accomplished fact.

Most writers accept July 1862 as the date ending the regimental band period and beginning the brigade band period. In fact, however, the situation is much more confused than the general orders indicate. On 15 April 1862 General Buell ordered that all bands in his command be mustered from the service.[18] The historian of the 48th Ohio Infantry recorded the effect of General Buell's order upon the band of his regiment. "On the 15th of April, a general order was issued to discharge all regimental bands. . . .When the battle of Shiloh commenced, our band discarded their fine instruments, armed themselves, and went into the fight with the regiment. The result was, they lost their instruments. . . .They were one of the first bands discharged."[19]

Buell continued to muster out bands as his command moved south in pursuit of the Confederates. The band of the 2nd Regiment of Iowa Volunteer Infantry was discharged at Pittsburgh Landing. The historian of the 2nd Minnesota Volunteer Infantry's recorded that his "band was mustered out on the 24th of April, by order of General Buell. . . .They were good musicians but did not take kindly to actual soldiering, and were quite willing to quit there."[20]

One authority, commenting that "whatever authorization was assigned to General Buell at Shiloh must have also been extended to other commands of the Union Army," lists a large number of bands, under Buell's command, that were mustered out over a period of only a few weeks.[21]

The mustering out of regimental bands did not enjoy support from all bureaucratic levels. Although the secretary of war had said the bands' "usefulness was not at all commensurate with their heavy expense" the secretary of the sanitary commission did not agree. He concluded that although "these bands are not generally of the first order . . . they are sufficiently good to please and interest the great majority of the soldiers. The men are almost universally proud of their band, particularly so if it be of more than average respectability."[22]

Although many soldiers could intellectually understand the requirements for economy, most felt that the bands were the wrong place to achieve it. The historian of the 13th Maine spoke for many of his comrades when he wrote, "There is room for a reasonable doubt as to whether that measure of cheeseparing economy accomplished any real savings."[23] Another historian questioned the conflicting efforts to achieve economic relief: "All of the regimental bands have been mustered out. . . .Ours left the first of this month. . . .I understand that this is in the interest of economy. . . .I also learn that the officers' pay has been raised, so just where the savings comes in does not appear."[24]

A band's quality strongly affected the opinions of the troops. The 24th Massachusetts Infantry enjoyed the services of Patrick Gilmore's band, one of the best in the army. The regimental commander thought the mustering out to be "a great mistake."[25] On the other hand, the band of the 2nd Michigan Volunteer Infantry was not so good. Charles B. Hayden recorded their departure with a great sense of relief. "The band has been discharged, right glad we were to be rid of the lazy grumbling loafers."[26]

The Ohio regiments did not receive the order to muster out their bands. As a

result, some of the Ohio bands served in the battles of Turner's Gap and
Antietam while officially mustered out from the service. When the orders
finally caught up with them, they were outraged to find that they were to
receive no pay for the elapsed time, combat notwithstanding.[27]

The general order under which substantial numbers of bands were mustered
out also provided for the formation of bands at the brigade level. Paragraph six
states that "each brigade in the volunteer service may have sixteen musicians
as a band, who shall receive the pay and allowances now provided by law for
regimental bands except the leader of the band who shall receive forty-five
dollars per month with the emoluments and allowances of quarter-master sergeant."[28] Bandmasters must have been less than elated to receive simulta-
neous reductions in status, pay, and rank, not to mention the loss of the servant
(by the infantry bandmaster) that went with his commission as a second lieutenant. Bands were to exist at brigade level only—but this is not what occurred. Not only did regimental bands continue to exist, but the order had no
effect at all on post bands, bands in prisons and hospitals, bands of the unorganized militia, and of the regular army. Nor did the order prevent a regiment
in a cantonment area from hiring a nearby civilian band for the duration of its
encampment.

Brigade bands were envisioned as furnishing music for all the regiments of a
single brigade. In practice, some furnished music for an entire division, while
other brigades had the services of regimental bands in addition to their own.

Information on brigade bands is scanty at best. Most regiments published
postwar histories, but only a couple dozen brigades saw fit to do so. Nevertheless, there is evidence that "at least a hundred or more brigade bands existed at
one time or another."[29]

Regimental bands serving during the brigade band period were no different
from those that had served earlier except, of course, that they were no longer
authorized. To circumvent this rather minor inconvenience, some older military traditions were revived in order to maintain them.

The band of the 2nd Minnesota Volunteer Infantry got around the order
quite handily. Although Private Hayden questioned their worth, the remainder
of the regiment must have missed the band. Shortly after their discharge, the
regiment formed a bugle band. The field musicians served as the nucleus for
this group, and other musicians were added from the ranks of the companies.
This new organization enjoyed modest success. Bishop noted that the "Bugle
Band had, as opportunity was afforded for practice, so improved in time that
we became quite proud of them."[30] Efforts toward improving their musical
competence grew quite naturally from this general feeling of esprit de corps.
"Having some money in the regimental fund, a complete set of brass instruments was ordered [for them] from Cincinnati. Principal Musician R. G. G.
Rhodes was announced as bandmaster, and for the next few weeks the woods
about the camp were full of practicing musicians."[31] Although the regiment as

a whole appeared pleased by these developments, Private Timothy H. Pendergast could see little good in the return of the band. He wrote: "Misfortunes never come singly and on the next day a wagon load. . .of brass instruments, varying in size from a dinner horn to a cart wheel arrived for our band and peace fled, for the next two weeks the braying of the horns from one side. . . would be answered by the braying of the mules from the other. . . .The poor mules no doubt thought another wagon train was parked over there. Whether the mules ever learned their mistake or the band boys. . .that it was not a portion of their crowd answering. . .I cannot say."[32] Mules and bandsmen were eventually sorted out, and the regimental historian proudly recorded that "three out of four of the regiments in our brigade now have bands, ours [is] the best of the three."[33]

After two years of service, this unauthorized band was discovered by a corps inspector. When it was demonstrated that the band was not supported by federal funds, and that the bandsmen also served in other military capacities, the inspector ruled that all was according to regulations and the band was allowed to continue.[34]

The 2nd Minnesota was not the only regiment that evaded the intent of the adjutant general's order. In 1862 Smith's Brigade contained two regimental bands. In compliance with orders, the band of the 73rd Ohio Regiment was designated as the official band for the brigade and the second one was sent home. The 33rd Massachusetts and 55th Ohio Infantry Regiments, with their bands, were added to Smith's Brigade when it was assigned to Hooker's XI Corps in the fall of 1864. Instead of losing bands, Smith's Brigade actually gained one.[35] This was probably atypical. The overall number of regimental bands was reduced, but not all of them were eliminated.

The band of the 14th Regiment of New Hampshire Volunteers had never been officially mustered into federal service. It was organized on 16 October 1862 three months after the issuance of General Order No. 91, and just ten days before the regiment left for the "seat of the war."

The largest number which the band ever mustered was twenty-one, seven of them coming from one company, G. Some of the members enlisted with the express understanding that they were to be detailed as band-musicians; but there was no band enlisted as such. George A. Day of Company F was engaged to organize the band, remuneration to be guaranteed him out of the regimental funds. George W. Hodgdon of Company D was the first leader, and held that position until his discharge in June, 1863; when Mr. Day was appointed to succeed him, but did not assume direction because of absence on account of sickness. Mr. W. H. Bolster, a non-enlisted man from Keene, was hired to conduct the band; and he remained its leader until July, 1864, when he left the regiment on its arrival at Fortress Monroe from Louisiana. While in New Orleans, a French-citizen musician, James Maurepas, was hired by the regiment; and he served faithfully during the remainder of the war, coming home to Concord with the band, and then returning to Louisiana. The band of the Fourteenth was highly prized,

and its members faithfully performed their every duty. In battle they did brave and
efficient work in succoring the wounded. Five of the original members, who attended
the first rehearsal in the woods at Concord, served at their posts throughout the war, and
played in the State-House yard the night after the regiment's final discharge.[36]

The circumvention of the mustering-out order even extended to the Veteran
Reserve Corps, an organization formed for duty on the home front. Veterans of
the line regiments whose wounds or illness rendered them unfit for further duty
in the field were assigned to this organization. They wore distinctive uniforms
and were organized into military units paralleling the structure of the army in
the field. Bands were assigned at Brigade level, but it wasn't long before most of
the regiments of the VRC could also boast of a brass band.

Alfred Bellard, assigned to the 1st Regiment of the VRC, wrote that on "the
5th [of June 1864] our new band played for us on dress parade for the first time
and did very well."[37] Bellard's regiment was not the only one in the VRC with a
band, and the cost of supporting them at regimental level remained as a burden
for the officers and the regimental funds. "Our band were [sic] getting along
nicely and were handsomely uniformed. . . .but the company funds had to
sweat in rigging them out. The officers paid an assesment for that purpose and
the funds did the rest."[38]

Another interesting circumvention of the regulations was accomplished by
the 24th Regiment of Michigan Infantry, a part of the Iron Brigade. Shortly
before the battle of Fredericksburg the regimental officers decided that the cost
of supporting both the field music and the band was too great. As a result, "the
fife and drum majors were. . . .sent home as excess baggage which the regiment
could no longer afford. The band, however, was retained."[39] This was an
atypical situation. The unit historian does not specify who sounded the necessary calls, but it seems obvious that the bandsmen must have served as field
musicians. Thus they functioned in an opposite capacity to the field musicians
of the 2nd Minnesota, who were used to reorganize a brass band. An adequate
accommodation must have evolved, since the band was still with the regiment
in March 1863.

Although the bandsmen had been retained in preference to the field musicians, this hearty group of instrumentalists may well have regretted the signal
honor bestowed upon them. The 24th Regiment of Michigan Infantry entered
service 1000 strong in 1862, but after Spotsylvania they could muster fewer
than 150 men. The band was then disbanded, and its members "distributed
among woefully thin companies. . . .A band was a luxury the unit could no
longer afford."[40]

Assigning musicians to line units for combat duty became more commonplace as the war took its toll of men. Had they sought them out, the bandsmen
of the 24th Michigan could have easily found their counterparts in several
other regiments that had seen heavy duty.

Another band, interesting for both its quality and lack of conformity, was that of the 7th New York State Militia. Unquestionably, it was one of the finest ensembles in the service, having established a substantial reputation long before the war. Its prewar service was unusual in that, unlike most professional civilian bands, it was contracted exclusively to the 7th Regiment. Its wartime service was equally irregular. It enlisted initially in June 1861 for a period of three months and was mustered from the service with the regiment in September of that year. In May 1862 it was again mustered into service for a period of one hundred days, to combat Stonewall Jackson's threat to Washington. Finally, in June 1863 it was again mustered for a thirty-day period when Robert E. Lee invaded Pennsylvania. This famous band exceeded regulation size during all three periods of federal service. In 1861 it numbered thirty-five members. During its second and third periods of service it numbered twenty-nine musicians.[41] The 7th Regiment was always treated as a state militia unit. Since its service was so limited no effort was ever made to insure that it conformed to federal regulations, even when it was on active duty. It had been a white glove outfit prior to the war, and the regiment continued to be treated as if it were more decorative than useful. The band of the 7th Regiment was the pride of the Army of the Potomac during the periods of its active duty.

There were other post bands, such as that at Fortress Monroe, that exceeded sixteen members, but these existed without regimental associations. Orders governing regimental and brigade bands did not apply to them.

The band of the Maryland Guard numbered thirty members, but such large groups were rare. The majority of bands failed to muster the total membership allowed by law. Large bands were most common during the early months of the war. Willing musicians became less available as the pages of the picture-book were blurred by blood and gore.

Bandsmen were never impressed into service, even though the governments of both the North and the South resorted to drafting enlisted men for all other types of military assignment. Bandsmen enlisted because they wished to do so. Although a bandsman held a less hazardous assignment than an infantryman, bandsmen were frequently under fire, and served on every battlefield of the war. Some led cavalry charges. Others played concerts on the front line while the battle raged around them. Nearly every regimental bandsman saw service as a stretcher bearer, both during and after the bloodiest of battles. The average trooper was rightfully proud of his band, and whether it was large or small, good or bad, the soldiers wrote of this pride.

The 5th Regiment of New Jersey Volunteers was in winter quarters on Christmas of 1862. In order to make the day as festive as possible, some tentmates put up a small tree in front of their quarters and "decked [it] off with hard tack and pork. . . .Our band of 15 pieces arrived. . .and the boys were highly elated at the prospect of plenty of music. And it was noticed that when the Regt. marched out. . .with our band at the head of the line, the boys had more rubber in their heels than formerly."[42]

F. H. Buffum of the 14th New Hampshire spoke for all of his comrades, both

North and South, when he wrote: "We were fond of the burly whole-souled leader; and we became attached to the physiognomy of every member. Yes, the High Private who tailed the bass drum, and boasted (when away) that he played in the band; his ramrod erectness and solemn tread, became a cherished feature of the programme."[43]

NOTES

1. *National Intelligencer*, 7 December 1862, p. 2.

2. Ibid., p. 21.

3. U.S. Department of War. Adjutant General's Office, "General Order No. 15," *General Orders Affecting the Volunteer Force, 1861* (Washington, D. C.: Government Printing Office, 1862), p. 1.

4. U.S. Sanitary Commission, *Report to Secretary of War: Operation of the Sanitary Commission in the Volunteer Army—Month of September and October* (New York: U.S. Sanitary Commission, 1866), doc. 11, nos. 1–40, p. 37.

5. Frederick Dyer, *A Compendium of the War of the Rebellion*, 3d ed. (New York: Thomas Yoseloff, 1959), 1:37.

6. Bufkin, "Union Bands of the Civil War (1862–1865): Instrumentation and Score Analysis," (Ph.D. diss., Louisiana State University, 1973), pp. 28–29.

7. Augustus Meyers, *Ten Years in the Ranks, U.S. Army* (New York: Stirling Press, 1914), pp. 17, 20–21.

8. U.S. Department of War, *Report of the Paymaster General* (Washington, D.C.: Government Printing Office, 1861), p. 3.

9. *National Intelligencer*, 19 September 1861, p. 8.

10. The figures given for the pay of the musicians and soldiers are drawn from various newspapers which reprinted general orders issued by the Department of War. No single order governed the pay for all members of the military.

11. U.S. Department of War. Adjutant General's Office, "General Order No. 91," *General Orders and Records of the Adjutant General, 1861* (Washington, D.C.: Government Printing Office, 1861), par. 3, p. 43.

12. U.S., Department of War, *Official Records of the War of the Rebellion* (Washington, D. C.: Government Printing Office, 1898), ser. 3, vol. 1, p. 728.

13. Ibid.

14. Ibid., p. 803.

15. U.S., Department of War. Adjutant General's Office, "General Order No. 91, Section 5," *General Orders Affecting the Volunteer Forces, 1862*, (Washington, D. C.: Government Printing Office, 1862), p. 63.

16. Letters of E. O. Kimberly, n.d. (front page missing), 1861–62 series, State Historical Society of Wisconsin, Archive Division, Madison, Wisconsin, p. 2. I am indebted to Bufkin for drawing my attention to this series of letters. *See* Bufkin, "Union Bands," p. 65, for his discussion of this same group of letters.

17. Kimberly, letter, 6 December 1861.

18. Bufkin was the first to mention General Buell's order discharging the bands of his command. He notes that "by what authority he was allowed to do so remains a mystery." *See* Bufkin, "Union Bands," p. 65.

19. John A. Bering and Thomas Montgomery, *History of the Forty-eighth Ohio Veteran Volunteer Infantry* (Hillsboro, Ohio: Highland News Office, 1880), p. 39.

20. Judson W. Bishop, *The Story of a Regiment . . . Second Minnesota* (St. Paul, Minn.: N.P., 1890), p. 55.

21. Bufkin, "Union Bands," p. 66.

22. U.S. Sanitary Commission, *Report to the Secretary of War*, p. 41.

23. Edward B. Lufkin, *The Story of the Maine Thirteenth* (Bridgeton, Me.: H. S. Shoney and Son, 1898), p. 4.

24. David L. Day, *My Diary and Rambles with the Twenty-fifth Massachusetts Volunteer Infantry* (Milford, Mass.: King and Billings, 1884), p. 66.

25. Alfred S. Roe, *The Twenty-Fourth Regiment Massachusetts Volunteers* (Worchester, Mass.: Twenty-fourth Veteran's Association, 1907), p. 146.

26. Diary of Charles B. Haydon, 1861–1862, Michigan Historical Collections, Bentley Historical Library, University of Michigan, Ann Arbor, Michigan. I am again indebted to Bufkin for this source.

27. Bufkin, "Union Bands," p. 68.

28. U.S. Department of War, "General Order No. 91," p. 63.

29. Bufkin, "Union Bands," p. 74.

31. Ibid.

32. Ibid., p. 41.

33. Ibid.

34. Ibid., p. 178.

35. *New Bedford Evening Standard*, 8 July 1912, pp. 1, 10, as cited by Bufkin, "Union Bands," p. 79.

36. Francis H. Buffum et al., *A Memorial of the Great Rebellion. . .the Fourteenth Regiment New Hampshire Volunteers* (Boston: Franklin Press; Rand, Avery & Co., 1882), p. 304.

37. Alfred Bellard, *Gone For a Soldier. . . Civil War Memoirs*, ed. David Herbert Donald (Boston: Little, Brown & Co., 1975), p. 264.

38. Ibid., p. 266.

39. Donald L. Smith, *The Twenty-fourth Michigan of the Iron Brigade* (Harrisburg, Pa.: Stackpole Co., 1962), p. 48.

40. Ibid., p. 200.

41. Emmons Clark, *History of the Seventh Regiment of New York* 2 (New York: Seventh Regiment, 1890): 245 fol.

42. Bellard, *Gone For a Soldier*, p. 37.

43. Buffum, *Fourteenth New Hampshire*, p. 134.

THE FIELD MUSICIANS

Similar scenes were enacted on both sides of the Mason-Dixon line in the spring of 1861. While trains stood at the ready village bands played martial music, and small knots of relatiyes gathered about the male members of their families. These men had already completed the first step of the process that would transform them into soldiers. They had affixed their names or marks to the rolls of one of the many companies that filled up so rapidly following the opening of hostilities. The young recruits were then granted a few days of freedom until further enlistments would bring the units to full strength—a time spent in arranging personal affairs and in bidding farewell to kith and kin.

But now it was time to take their leave. The rosters were full, and the units were ordered to training camps where the men would be sworn into federal service. Then, after a woefully short training period, they would move to the "seat of the war," a euphemism for the field of battle.

Mothers, daughters, wives, and sweethearts bade tearful farewells to sons, fathers, husbands, and fiances, while younger brothers skulked about the peripheries, downcast faces reflecting their desires to join up with their fathers or older brothers.

A surprising number of these lads, mere boys, did succeed in going, if not during the first year of the war, then in 1862 after the appalling casualties of early battles had depleted the ranks of both armies. Most, but not all, enlisted as field musicians. Many other youngsters carried a rifle and some assumed command responsibilities. Galusha Pennypacker was breveted a major general in the Regular Army at age seventeen. He was too young to vote until the war ended.

The Marion Rifles of the Stonewall Brigade was composed entirely of Americanized Germans, generally referred to as "old Germans." They were labeled "The Boy Company," since only five of the original eighty-seven members were over twenty-one years of age. "When Louis J. Fletcher, aged eighteen, became its Captain in late 1861, he was nicknamed 'Jackson's Pet' and the 'Boy Captain of the Stonewall Brigade'."[1]

George Ives, father of the famous composer Charles Ives, is another case in point.

George Ives . . . in 1861, although he was barely seventeen years old . . . undertook to recruit and organize a volunteer band, drawing especially upon German-American musicians of his acquaintance. The youthful leader then led his band through the remainder of the war. It was attached to the First Connecticut Artillery . . . and it served as a siege artillery brigade band during the Union siege of Richmond. It was during this siege that General Grant is supposed to have remarked to President Lincoln that Ives's band was the best in the Union Army. The war must have been a hard, as well as a maturing experience for the young man, for he later recorded in a notebook: "A space of three years servitude as leader . . . and one year sick, from Sept/62 to Sept/63."[2]

On the Confederate side, John Cheeves Haskell received his initial commission as a lieutenant at the age of nineteen, and by the age of twenty-one was a full colonel. He was ordered to the north side of the James River when Fort Harrison was taken by the Union. There he lost his right arm leading his troops. Haskell, in spite of his youth, was a superior officer, but commissioning youth did not always work out that well. Austin C. Stearns, a sergeant with Company K of the Thirteenth Massachusetts Infantry, appraised his superiors forthrightly:

William B. Bacon was the name of the boyish looking fellow; he was mustered in as our 1st Lt. . . . He was a young man, just from school, without any knowledge or experience of the great principles one should have who is called upon to command. In fact he was a boy; boyish principles and boyish impulses governed all his acts. To put such a boy in command . . . was one of the fatal mistakes of the Executives of Mass. . . . Of Capt. Blackmer, I have but a word to say. He entered at the big end of the horn, with a loud flourish, declaring he would "wade in blood to his ears," and then in three months came out at the little end, from a hole too small to be seen with the naked eye.[3]

Age differentials of the soldiers in both armies were very much alike. In every regiment, young boys marched and fought beside men old enough to be their grandfathers. An analysis of the age patterns of 11,000 Confederate and 14,330 Union soldiers concluded that eighteen-year-olds comprised the largest group in both armies, with about four-fifths of the total sample falling between the ages of eighteen and twenty-nine. One Confederate soldier was only thirteen, three were fourteen, and thirty-one were fifteen when they entered service. The Union roster revealed three who enlisted at the tender age of twelve. At the other end of the age spectrum the oldest Confederate in the sample was seventy-three, while his Union counterpart was a spry sixty-five.[4] Twenty-five boys enlisted in the Union army at age ten or under.[5] We have already noted Drum Major Henry White, who at the age of eighty-nine headed the 6th Massachusetts Regiment as it paraded through New York.

Federal regulations required that a boy be eighteen before he enlisted to shoulder a rifle, but a parent's permission easily nullified that requirement. Several young men resorted to the simple expedient of lying about their age. Even younger boys were allowed to enlist as musicians. Army regulations of 1863 allowed the superintendent of recruiting depots to cause "such of the recruits as are found to possess a natural talent for music, to be instructed on the fife, bugle, and drum, and other military instruments; the boys of twelve years of age and upward, may under his direction, be enlisted for this purpose. But as recruits under eighteen years of age and under size must be discharged, if they are not capable of learning music, care should be taken to enlist those only who have a natural talent for music."[6]

It may seem unreasonable that children were allowed to enlist, but recruits of one hundred years ago came chiefly from farms where even the youngest members of the family were routinely put to work at an early age. Early employment, and the consequent lack of schooling, contributed to the illiteracy so common in both armies. It was unusual to find a regiment that did not contain from one to a score of men who could not sign their names.

Adults regarded children with both an extravagant sentimentality and a hard-eyed realism. Their helping hands were essential in making a living. Parents manifesting this realism actually encouraged younger sons to enlist, and boys sixteen and under were accepted almost without question as field musicians.

Field musicians were well represented among the last few survivors of the war although the last surviving veteran had been an infantryman. Albert Wolson of Duluth, Minnesota, a federal drummer, was the last Union veteran. John B. Salling, his Confederate counterpart, was the last musician and penultimate survivor when he died on 16 March 1959 in Kingsport, Tennessee at age 113. Confederate "General" Walter W. Williams (14 Nov. 1842–17 Dec. 1959) of Franklin, Texas was the last surviving veteran of the war.

The army had maintained a training school, the School of Practice, for young field musicians for some years prior to 1860. A touching reminiscence was written by Augustus Meyers, who at the age of twelve, joined the United States Army, on 31 March 1854, as a drummer boy in the general service.[7] His first military assignment was at this training school.

After his enlistment he was rowed over to Governor's Island from the Battery in New York City in an eight-oared barge manned by soldiers from the island. Upon debarking he was thrown into the company of fifty or more boy-musicians, ranging in age from twelve to sixteen. All were quartered at the Old South Battery on the east side of the island opposite Brooklyn. They were crowded into double-deck bunks with insufficient space for comfort or convenience. They slept on large sacks stuffed with straw where, on cold nights, they shivered under two blankets in an unheated building. No one but the corporal-in-charge had a pillow. These had to be purchased by the boys, and Meyers looked forward to the day when he could afford this modest item of comfort.

Knapsacks and other military impedimenta were in confused disarray on shelves above each bunk. The outer hall contained a row of tin basins hung on hooks, one for each boy. Each morning the basins were filled with pump water cold enough to make the performance of personal ablutions both expeditious and invigorating.

When dressed the boys gathered outside the sally port to sound *reveille* in unison. They then marched to the mess hall for a breakfast of cold salt pork and four ounces of bread, washed down with a cup of black coffee. A foul-smelling dish of grease was available as a butter substitute for those who could stomach it.

Returning to the parade outside the sally port, they beat *Three Camps*, followed by *Guard Mount* at eight. A general police of the grounds and quarters followed this performance. School began promptly at nine, continuing until eleven. A free hour before lunch was consumed by individual practice.

The noon meal, showing little improvement over breakfast, consisted of a bowl of rice or bean soup mixed with assorted desiccated vegetables, accompanied by the ever-present ration of bread.

After a second hour of practice, from 1:00 to 2:00 P.M. the boys gathered for two additional hours of class. At 4:00 P.M. they received instruction in the "School of the Soldier" (saluting, facings, etc.) followed by squad and company drill. At 5:00 P.M. they returned to the mess hall for a supper of stewed dried apples, another slice of bread, and the evening bowl of black coffee. *Retreat*, the final call of the day, was sounded en masse.

Weekdays followed the same schedule, while most of Saturday was absorbed by an inspection of person, quarters, and gear. Sunday afternoon was reserved for divine service.

Ashworth's *Fife Instructor* was used in the early days of the school. This text was superseded by Scott's *Instructor for Drum and Fife*. Both texts seem to have fallen into disuse around 1860 and had "long been out of print."[8] In 1862 Bruce and Emmett's *The Drummers and Fifers Guide* was adopted as the official text for the school. Its selection was guided by a rather distinguished board of bandmasters and composers.

In addition, Emmett had written a *Fife Instructor* which was advertised as a "thorough and progressive method, embracing the rudiments of music, and a complete collection of all the calls and tunes as used in the Regular Army of the United States, to which is added several of the most popular marches, quicksteps, waltzes, side-beats etc., the whole forming the most perfect and best selection of fife music ever offered to the public." Privately published, it was probably used by the author for his own instructional purposes.

Both men were well qualified to write such a work. George Bruce had served as drum major for the band of the 7th New York Militia Regiment under the baton of C. H. Grafulla. Bruce was a first-rate drummer having studied with Ashworth, and was drum instructor at the School of Practice when Meyers was in attendance. Daniel Emmett had served for many years as principal fifer of the 6th Infantry Regiment of the Regular Army, and was regarded as somewhat of a virtuoso on the instrument. (He achieved greater fame as a minstrel show impressario and as the composer of "Dixie.")

Earlier texts contained instruction for either the drum or the fife. None dealt with both instruments and all lacked information on the camp duty. Consequently, musicians could learn to play their instruments and still be ignorant of the duties required of them in actual service. Bruce and Emmett, through their collaboration, sought to fill this void.

Both men were genuinely concerned about the quality of training received by the field musicians. Meyers noted that most instruction, given by the older fifers, consisted solely of rote learning. Bruce, a trained musician, noted with regret that "the old system of thorough Rudimental teaching is apparently becoming obsolete; and the standard of Drum and Fife playing is therefore rapidly deteriorating. Without this rudimental instruction, we can only have indifferent players, comparatively ignorant of the nature of the very instrument they play upon. . . . The present war has revealed the fact that our militia drummers and fifers are but very imperfectly acquainted with camp and garrison duties."[9]

Their book is well organized. Beginning with rudimental music reading, it continues with progressive studies for each instrument. It contains all of the regular and irregular calls and beats of the camp duty, ending with a set of fancy quicksteps, side-beats, and troops that could be inserted into the duty for special occasions. The total comprises one hundred forty-eight compositions exclusive of instructional materials. The young boys had their work cut out for them since all music was performed from memory.

Many soldier-diarists decried the quality of the field music, but memorizing this many scores would tax even a professional musician. For a musically illiterate recruit of twelve it must have been nearly impossible. During the war these quantitative demands were compounded by the element of time. Volunteer regiments in particular were provided with little training, and field musicians were expected to be perfected in their art at the time of their enlistment. There was precious little practice time for the development of polished individual technique.

The School of Practice continued to train field musicians to the end of the war. As late as 17 February 1869 a board of officers was convened at Fort Columbus (now Fort Jay on Governor's Island in the harbor of New York

City) to investigate the system of training employed at the school. This board approved Strube's *Drum and Fife Instructor* as the sanctioned text.[10] (After the Civil War no school was organized on this site until October 1911 when, through the efforts of Frank Damrosch and Arthur A. Cleppe, ten scholarships for study at the Institute of Musical Arts of New York City were placed at the disposal of the secretary of war for the training of officers to serve as army bandmasters.[11]) Although the school trained regular army musicians, musicians of the volunteer regiments were expected to learn their duties and art through what would now be called on-the-job training.

Certain members of the field music had individual responsibilities in the performance of the camp duty. At guard mount, one drummer and one fifer were designated as orderlies by the drum major. They accompanied the guard to the guard tent. The drummer remained there, giving signals to alert the remaining regimental musicians for the performance of certain calls. He was admonished not to leave his post under any circumstance since his duty was very important.[12] The smooth performance of the entire corps was dependent upon his cues.

The orderly fifer was to "attend to the marque" (the quarters of the regimental adjutant or the officer of the day) after he had escorted the guard to the guard house. He served as a runner for the adjutant and, when dismissed by him, returned to the guard tent to wait until relieved.

The leading drummer and fifer were important to ensemble performances. Stationed on the right of the massed field music, they gave the necessary signals for the commencement of the music, and established new tempi. The leading drummer set the tempo for the entire corps. He was also the disciplinarian for the day, reporting all misdemeanors of individual members to the drum major. This duty alone must have kept him fairly busy in some regiments.

The leading drummer was further designated "the leader," and was to be recognized as such by the other members. His role was akin to that of first sergeant, while the drum major held duties similar to a commissioned platoon leader. The leader was also responsible for instrumental repair, and he inspected individual musicians to insure compliance with uniform regulations.

The drum major's duties were extensive. His was a position of overall authority. He was directly responsible for the musical and military training of all of the field musicians in his regiment. He wrote necessary requisitions, and organized and assigned the calls for each day, after consulting with the regimental adjutant. He saw to the training of new recruits, and submitted requests to the adjutant for replacement personnel. He established times for practice and supervised its execution. He was the first man of the regiment up in the morning and the last one to bed at night. The first and last calls of the day were performed by the massed musicians under his direction. The time between these two performances was filled with music.

The number of beats (compositions) for the normal duty day was fixed at eighteen. These were frequently augmented by others pertaining to special events, such as funerals or drumming-out ceremonies, and were further extended by a large amount of parade music.

The drum major, in addition to mastering the music, had to master the baton. Baton movements were divided into three basic categories. A fourth group pertained to special ceremonies. There were seven movements requiring musical responses from the corps, seven that required physical movements of the field music and band, four that pertained to the drums alone, and three which were used only for parades and battles.

One of the parade movements resulted in the only left-handed salute prescribed for use in the United States Army.

When within ten paces of the reviewing Officer, make numerous revolutions with the staff until arriving directly in front of said Officer, when, with a quick motion, the staff will be brought under the right arm, pommel and right arm extended upward and obliquely to the front; at the same time the back of the left hand will be carried to the front of the cap, head and eyes turned towards the Officer until the salute has been acknowledged by him; after which, make a few revolutions with the staff, and return it to its former position before giving up the salute.[13]

Most drum majors did not use a whistle. They depended upon the attention of the musicians for snappy execution and prompt response. Since regimental muster rolls frequently note that "John Doe, musician, was drunk on duty and incapable of performing his music," it is not difficult to understand why parades did not always achieve states of perfection.

All of these activities came together to form the camp duty that regulated the soldier's workday. The day began at 5:45 A.M. for the orderly drummer at the guard tent. The hour was often earlier during the summer. He opened the day with a solo performance of the *drummers' call*, signaling the other musicians to assemble. When all were gathered at the foot of the flag pole, the call was performed a second time en masse. The orderly drummer's performance was referred to as *first call* and when played in unison it was called *second call*. The fifers were tacit during both performances.

Second call was the signal for the troops to fall out and form by units in the company streets. Roll was called and announcements made. When all reports had been properly rendered the massed field music played *reveille*. This was not a single call, but a series of six compositions that were frequently augmented by one or more appropriate pieces. They were strung together by the long roll which commenced at the end of one call and lasted until the drum major signaled the beginning of the next. *Reveille* began with *Three Camps*. The leading drummer established the tempo by tapping a stick on the edge of his drum. The *Slow Scotch*, the *Austrian*, the *Hessian*, the *Prussian*, and the *Quick Scotch* followed in rapid succession. The *Dutch* was sometimes inserted between the *Prussian* and the *Quick Scotch*. The performance of *reveille* marked the beginning of the soldier's duty day. The disgruntled and worn-out soldier questioned the beauty of the calls at the time of his service, but when old age left him little but his memories he wrote of the rapturous melody and the tantalizing drum, as he ruminated upon the excitement of his youth.

There are no more exhilarating bounds from the rest of night into the duties of day, no finer inspiration thrilling the entire nervous system of a vigorous man, than the first burst, crash, and roll of reveille when a crack drum-corps with melodious shrill fife rallies upon the color line, and rouses an entire regiment as by an electrical shock. On a bright morning, or in the midst of storm and bluster, nothing so fittingly ushers in the day and stirs to activity as the reveille in a military camp. It is incomparably better than five glasses at Congress Spa before breakfast. The effect is intensified when, in a great army stretching out for miles, a single bugle-note gives the signal, and then, as by magic, from every direction break out and roll on in one mass of accelerating sound the roll of drums, the screech of fifes, and the blare of artillery and cavalry bugles. Where is the human being who can compete with an accomplished trumpeter in waking the music out of a crisp morning atmosphere?[14]

At 6:15 A.M. *pioneer's call or fatigue call* turned out work parties to police the area and to complete other housekeeping duties. The call was also used to drum "scarlet women" from the camps. Perhaps a philosophy is revealed in the application of *fatigue call* to their removal. When used as a duty call it was performed by drums alone. Fifes were added when it accompanied the departure of the women.

When the *assembly* was beat at 6:30 A.M. the troops formed by companies to receive instructions. A few minutes later, the entire corps sounded *surgeon's call*. This announced to the sick, the lame, and the lazy that they were to march to the hospital under the command of a noncommissioned officer. One veteran regarded *surgeon's call* with semi-contempt, since those genuinely in need of medical aid always seemed outnumbered by the camp goldbricks.

Then came . . . the mournful, ludicrous procession gathered from each company. . . . There was seen the faithful soldier who had fought off disease, and stood at his post until nature, in a good physique, had quite succumbed. . . . Beside him fell in the man who was not sick but discouraged. Next to him was the tricky fellow who simply wanted a furlough, and intended to "play off" just enough to secure it.

But in that procession were always to be found the cronic "dead-beats,"—the most contemptible vermin that ever infested our grand army; the worst rubbish that could encumber ambulance, hospital, or barracks. They deliberately cheated the government, the cause, and everybody concerned. They were selfish animals, lazy scamps, and errant cowards. They shifted every burden of duty on to their overworked comrades, and day after day limped to the tune of the surgeon's call. . . . There was a great deal of peculiar music in the surgeon's call.[15]

In his weekly report, Captain W. H. Waldron (Commanding Officer, Company I, 16th Maine Infantry) minced few words in defining the source of these "ludicrous processions."

I have the distinguished honor to submit for your consideration and approval, the following statement respecting the departure from Co. I . . . of sick men and *bummers*, since my last weekly report. I very much regret the necessity I am under of stating that the bummers far exceed the numbers of genuine sick. I will add in this connection that the bummers, in my opinion, have been very materially aided and abetted in their nefarious practices through the overflowing (but mistaken) kindness of heart which our two amiable and esteemed surgeons exhibited toward this rascally set of men who are drawing sustenance from Uncle Sam's plethoric purse, but who persistently refuse to render any aid in crushing the infamous and cussed rebellion.
Sent to General Hospital sick, 4.
Sent to General Hospital bumming, 6.[16]

At 6:45 A.M. the orderly drummer repeated *drummers' call*, the signal for the musicians to form at the guard tent. *Breakfast call* was beat en masse at 7:00 A.M. This was fondly referred to as "peas on a trencher" by the always-hungry troops. One soldier wrote, "The breakfast call. . . . was more suggestive of slab bacon than of aestheticism; but the accompaniment of tin plates, quart cups, and iron spoons was perfectly attuned to the stomach's sentiment."[17]

After gulping breakfast the orderly drummer again beat *drummers' call*. All repeated the performance at 7:45 A.M. as *second call* followed immediately by *adjutants' call*. This summoned the adjutant to the parade as well as those troopers detailed as a part of the guard. After the guard was formed, inspected, and instructed, the adjutant commanded, "Troop—beat off!" The musicians moved to the right of the line, playing "Three Cheers." They returned to the left, passing between the adjutant and the guard, while playing *the troop*. Here, they countermarched and returned to their original positions. "Three Cheers" was repeated while the old and new officers of the day saluted the adjutant. The drum major signaled a quickstep, and the corps continued to play until the guard had passed to its front, on the way to the guard tent. The field music wheeled to the right and marched to their quarters, the orderly drummer and fifer excepted. Many troopers looked forward to guard mount (providing they were not assigned as one of the guards), for it was suggestive of a pleasant parade. "A good drummer had the fullest opportunity for displaying his skill while playing the detail to the guard-house, when the band had ceased its escort, the review before the officer of the day being passed, and the parade dismissed. There, too, the dummy musician—who enlisted for a drummer, but who never would know a roll from a drag if he rattled the sticks to all eternity— on those occasions passed a good examination for promotion to the ranks."[18]

The *assembly* was beat once more, following guard mount. This dispatched the remaining troops to their duty stations. The musicians spent the remainder of the morning in rehearsal.

At 11:45 A.M. all musicians responded to *drummers' call*, followed by *dinner call*, wishfully entitled "roast beef" by the troops. This ended morning duty, and the musicians hurried to their respective messes to gulp a quick meal. *Assembly* sent the regiment to the parade for noon drill. *Pioneers' call* sounded at 12:45 P.M. It was followed by another quickstep while the troops completed afternoon housekeeping.

Musicians were now free to practice or were called to assist the surgeon. Formal dress parade was accompanied by the same series of calls used at guard mount and took place about an hour and one-half before sundown. Additional quicksteps were added as the entire regiment passed in review. Dress parade was the high point of cantonment area service. It was meant to be a culminating military spectacle, a poetry of tactics—indeed, a show-stopper that was to ring down the curtain at the end of a busy day. A unit commander, on dress parade, found his entire career was justified by the few minutes that elapsed between the *adjutants' call* and the call to form on the colors.

The drummers beat first the musician's call, then the assembly on the color-line; and the stereotyped warning of the orderly-sergeant follows, "Company A fall in for dress-parade!" Then there are brought forth the white gloves and the brightened brasses of accoutrements; boots are polished; and the daughty warrior issues from his stockade or tent, cleaned up, and respectable in attire for half an hour in the day, if no more. . . . There is nothing of the imposing grandeur of an army-corps review: the sublime inspiration of the battlefield with its crushing tumults and heroic struggles, is not even hinted at, save as the portentous steadiness and terrible reserve power, masked in the quietness of a battalion at parade-rest, may suggest the lion crouching for a spring,—a prophecy of invincible energy yet under the potent check of discipline. But there is a rounded completeness in the spectacle as a whole, a charm and beauty in every tributary movement and motion, which is surpassingly attractive. . . . It was never determined whether a crack drum-corps or a fine band appeared to best advantage on those occasions. For martial music, purely, a drum-corps stands "par excellence," unrivalled; while a band possesses obvious advantages, and constantly tends to promote morale, strengthening the discipline and elevating the sentiment of the organization. One thing was observed: no regiment with a band maintained a first rate drum-corps.[19]

Following dress parade, the troops formed in the company streets for *retreat*, sometimes called *at sundown*. This included, in quick succession, "The Lamplighter," "Pretty Girl Milking the Cow," and "Erin's Green Shore," all linked together by the long roll. It terminated with the "Three Cheers."

The supper hour followed. Musicians were free to clean equipment until 9:00 P.M. when they returned to the parade, and the troops fell out in the company streets for a final roll call. At 9:15 P.M. the orderly drummer sounded three distinct taps from the parade to signal lights out. Then began the evening *tattoo*.

This erupted with the "Three Cheers" followed by "The Doublings," "The New Tater Jack Quickstep," "The Doublings," "The Slow March, "The Doublings," "The Downfall of Paris," "The Doublings," "My Lodging's on the Cold Ground," "The Doublings," "The Trust to Luck Troop," "The Three Cheers" and finally, "The Doublings." *Tattoo* was sometimes short-ened in winter but in summer other works were added according to the drum major's bent for embellishment. Then the entire enterprise took on the propor-tions of a small concert. Finally the exhausted musicians could turn in for a well-earned rest.

All of the calls, marches, and airs of the bands and drum corps entered into the very life of a regiment, but the evening calls were particularly appreciated by the men.

The evening calls of supper, tattoo, and taps, were full of music and meaning, and each breathed forth its own suggestions. A military camp at the hour of tattoo was a study; games, letter-writing, reading, mending, lounging on bunks, story-telling, pondering on objects far away but near to a soldier's heart—these were intruded upon by the ra-a-at-tat-tat-tat of the drum-major, in his preliminary flourish, as he initiated the stereotyped measures of the bed-time concert. A little imagination reproduces the circumstances, the familiar faces, all the accessories and incidents, even to the oddities, hilarity, and banter which relieved the sober tedium of camp monotony, and the painful strain of exposure and danger. The tattoo-calls seemed to wake a thousand memories, only to soothe and lull to rest. It was a master-spirit that invented tattoo.[20]

In addition to the duty calls, there were a number of irregular calls used in battle. The most often heard was the *general*, a signal for a movement of the entire command. This was repeated any number of times at the option of the drum major. It began with the drum corps attached to a major command head-quarters, and quickly spread through the huge camps, as first one and then another of the regimental corps took it up. It always created a great deal of excitement, due to the anticipation of new events and to the stereophonic effect that it generated as it welled up from positions all over the camp.

There were other special calls such as *church call* (which was also used to signal the *parley* during battle), *to the colors* (which signaled formations by battalions instead of by companies and was used to advance the colors), and at least a dozen others.

In camp many calls were coordinated between units of an entire army corps. The music, beginning on the extreme right, was taken up in turn by each musi-cian, until the air was filled with shrieking fifes, all slightly out of tune, and splattering drums—few of which were in ensemble. The effect was at once magnificent and horrifying.

Delavan Miller, a drummer boy with the 2nd New York Heavy Artillery Regiment, performed the calls as one of the massed musicians of his division.

The massed drum corps were followed by the massed brass bands. Miller described the concert as follows:

This afternoon all the bands and drum corps of the division were ordered to report to division headquarters. . . . Numbering in all about one hundred and seventy-five, and under the leadership of Mr. Higgins, of the division band, played "Hail to the Chief," and "Hail Columbia," after which the brass bands played the "Grand March from Belsaria," "Garry Owen," "Larry O'Gaff" and "Yankee Doodle," and if there was any lack of harmony there certainly was not of noise.[21]

A number of calls were employed to control the movements of lines of combatants: one list cites sixty-seven bugle calls.[22] Several hundred other bugle calls existed because of the lack of standardization throughout the army. The camp duty varied in all services, according to the wishes of individual commanders; cavalry and artillery regiments used calls inappropriate to infantry.

Of the hundreds of calls, *taps*—the final call sounded over the mortal remains of every soldier since July 1862—is the best known. A now-unfamiliar version had been borrowed from the French armies of the War of 1812. By 1862 there was a tendency towards confusion when regiments or brigades were drilled and maneuvered in close proximity. A call for one unit was likely to be heard and responded to by another.

To forestall this in his own brigade, General Butterfield composed a brigade call. This was a brief series of notes which was sounded twice before the call for any operation or movement to be executed by the 3rd Brigade. The men put words to it: Dan, Dan, Dan, Butterfield, Butterfield; or sometimes, if the going promised to be rough, Damn, Damn, Damn, Butterfield, Butterfield.[23]

Butterfield instructed the bugler at his headquarters to substitute the entire call for the French version of *taps*. Musicians from other units quickly picked it up, and it soon came into general use throughout the Union armies.

Although we think of *taps* as the restful and melodic close to a busy day, the soldiers found the call hopelessly incongruous to the events that it accompanied. The call was always either too late or too early.

If the sergeant of the guard, who perambulated every company street immediately after taps, commanding "Lights Out!" would but gather the comments which were occasionally hurled after him, he could present the public with a most remarkable and startling collection of ejaculatory literature. It often occurred that said executor of taps-law was not more than three tents away before candles were lighted again, and penny-ante progressed, necessitating another tour of the camp by the irate sergeant. And something else sometimes happened, for the audacious gamester exchanged his fun for a night in the guard-house.[24]

Several volumes could easily be filled with the drum-and-fife music of the

Civil War. It is small wonder that, long after the war, many veterans were awakened in the middle of the night by the memory of one of their favorites. A quarter-century after the war, the veterans of the 20th Maine attended a reunion at Gettysburg.

A bugler went up on Little Round Top and sounded the old Dan Butterfield call. Veterans who had been scattered all over, examining half-remembered positions, came hurrying to the hill in answer to the call, many with tears in their eyes. Echoing sharp and clear among the rocks and trees where they had fought, it had awakened the memories they were seeking with a sudden and breath-taking sense of reality.[25]

If the memories of the calls gave the veterans fitful sleep, the final sounding of *taps* over their graves brought eternal rest to each member of the Blue and the Gray.

Diarists and regimental historians assessed the music as ranging from excellent to pitiful. The music was incidental to other military functions, and the average soldier laid no claim to the title of music critic. Most came from rural areas where an amateur brass band represented the musical epitome. One drummer boy, Delevan Miller, was sure that only his comrades-in-arms could really share in the excitement.

War has its fascinations as well as its horrors, and there is an enchantment that thrills in the movements of large bodies of soldiery with their bayonets glistening in the sun, the flags and guidons flying, the trumpets of the cavalry ringing piercingly and thrillingly, the field batteries rattling and rumbling along the road, with a score or more bands playing. Nothing can make so striking or enchanting a picture. Artists can portray such a scene on canvas, but they cannot make you feel the thrill you experience when you are an active participant, touching elbows and keeping step with a thousand comrades whose hearts are young and gay.[26]

Martial music had encouraged his enlistment, it sustained his years of heroic service, and it placed a final lump in his throat when Gracey, his favorite bugler, intoned the final call for his regiment:

There never was such another bugler in the whole army of the Potomac as our little Gracey. Small of stature, gentle by nature, but a marvel with his trumpet. . . . Gracey was at our last dress parade. . . . After the parade the guns were stacked for the last time, and then Gracey sounded "taps" . . . and on this occasion our old bugler seemed to breathe his very soul into his trumpet, for the tears were trickling down his cheeks while strong, bronzed men who had walked up to the cannon's mouth . . . were not without emotion as they broke ranks for the last time.[27]

Nor did the passing of forty years dampen his enthusiasm. Bands were all right for city slickers, but it was the field music that stirred the heart.

For a marching column there is nothing like martial music of the good old-fashioned kind. . . . such as rallied the boys of '61, and later led them in all the marches through the South.

Martial music seems to have gone out of fashion in these up-to-date days, and what little there is, is but a poor apology with. . . . drummers who hardly know their a b c's about snare drumming.

I have heard but one good drum corps since the war, and that was at the G. A. R. gathering at Buffalo a few years ago. . . . Many of the crack brass bands of the country were there, but they were not in it with the old martial band. Their music. . . . caught on with all the swell people of the city. . . . [but] the veterans went wild as they heard again the reveille and tattoo and the old familiar strains of "Yankee Doodle," "The Girl I Left Behind Me," "Rory O'More," "The Campbells Are Coming," "Hail to the Chief," and many other reminders of the old days.[28]

Enos B. Vail, another veteran, felt that field musicians had been an important part of the army. He lamented the little notice they received in regimental histories: "I have never read any work on the Civil War which mentioned anything about the fife and drum corps. The fife and drum corps constituted an important part of the army."[29]

Edwin B. Houghton, of the 17th Maine Infantry, thought that the stereophonic performance of *reveille* was a splendid way to introduce a new day.

As the first beams of the rising sun began to tinge the eastern skies, the clear notes of the bugle, sounding reveille from headquarters are heard—repeated in turn by the regimental buglers. The drums of one regiment commence their noisy rataplan, which is taken up by the ear piercing fife and spirit stirring drum of another, til every drum corps of the brigade, with the accompanying bugles and fifes, join in the din, and the morning air is resonant with the rattle of drums, the shrill notes of the fife, or the clarion tones of the bugle, sounding reveille.[30]

A cavalry private named Pete Malloy offered his own prelude. "He was noted for amiability and for his singing. Possessing a deep bass voice, he was wont to arouse the Fourth Kentucky boys by singing, 'Awake, awake, ye drowsy sleeper,' in the early morn before Tom Hayden sounded reveille with his bugle."[31] Described as "a splendid soldier, and athlete,"[32] Malloy's resonant bass voice was stilled when his "head [was] torn off by a cannon ball."[33]

Not all performances were accomplished with polish and perfection. The field music of the 148th Pennsylvania Volunteers was under the command of Drum Major R. A. Cassidy. The corps included ten fifers, ten tenor drummers, and a bass drum played by Billy Ishler of Company G.

No opportunity was offered for the regular organization of the drum corps, and concerted drill and discipline therein, until after the arrival of the Regiment at Cockeysville, Maryland. . . . Our indescribable lack of knowledge of military tactics at that time

can hardly be better depicted than by . . . the first guard mount [held] at Camp Beaver....
After going into camp, Sergeant Major Muffly passed up and down the company streets
proclaiming "guard mount". . . . We don't recall who it was that summoned the drum
corps, but it was done and the scene disclosed to Colonel Beaver, when he came on the
ground to witness the first formal evolution of his Regiment, in the language of the
Apostle, literally "beggars description." There was an entire absence of uniformity in
the attire and equipment of the men detailed for duty. Several of the fellows who "knew
something about war" exercised the precaution to bring their arms with them. Others,
not apprehending any danger from resident "secesh" or prowling "rebels," did not.
Some were in their shirt sleeves; others, as happened to be easiest, were attired in
blouses, dress coats or overcoats, etc. We remember Colonel Beaver administered his
first rebuke to the Drum Major for appearing on that "auspicious occasion" in his shirt
sleeves, without equipment of any kind, and topped out with a brilliantly variegated
sleeping cap for a headgear. He was in such a state of exasperated military disgust that
his early piety and soldierly restraint, . . . alone, prevented a sulphurous explosion. . . . It
is scarcely necessary to remark that "guard mount" the following morning was "turned
off" with an exactness of attire and equipment and precision of ceremony that would
have challenged. . . . much older commands.[34]

The field music continued to benefit from the assiduous attention of the
colonel. Some weeks after the ill-fated guard mount, the colonel determined
that the corps should acquire a better quality of instrument, and ordered a
special set from a company in Baltimore. Gradually the varied musical dia-
lects of the individual members were integrated into a unified corps. Indeed,
improvement was so great and so rapid that on 7 January 1863 the brigade
commander ordered that the miscreant drum major assume responsibility for
all brigade musicians and tutor them in both music and military drill. General
Hancock later advanced him still further, placing him in charge of the consolidated field music for the entire division when they performed en masse.

There is little wonder that some of the field music got off to a faltering start,
considering the background and training common to most of the musicians.
Dan Owen Mason had been a bugler with Company D, 6th Vermont Infantry,
during a brief period in 1862. He was at Camp Griffin, Virginia, on 5 February
of that year and had already been promoted to the rank of corporal. The regiment was in need of a bugler. Mason seemed a little hazy about the details of
the job when he wrote to his "Darling Harriet" of his assignment to that post.

I like camp life very well and why shouldnt I it is so muddy that I dont have to drill but
very little I have not been on guard duty for a number of weeks. a great many days we
have nothing to do but eat read write play chequers practice on my Bugle & have a good
time generally. . . . A little more than 2 weeks since our Col sent to Washington for a
new Bugle. the next question was who should play it. one of our tent boys from Brown-
ington happened to be Cols orderly (as he is called) & heard the conversation he told the
Col that he knew a fellow in Co D that had played on the Alt Horn considerable in a
Band. the Col siad he thought the one mentioned was the one he wanted. I happened to
be the chap. I got Lieut Dwinell to intercede for me & I got the Bugle with orders to go to

my tent and practice the calls for skirmishing. I practice on it every day. it has been so muddy for several weeks that we have had no drill to amount to much . . . I expect to be Regimental Bugler. I dont know how much pay I shall get. some say i shall get more than I now do & some say i get the same. Lieut Dwinell thinks I shall get $27.00 per month if so well and good. if I get no more I shall get clear of all guard duty both Picket and Home which is the most tedious duty that we have to perform. I shall also be exempt from all drill. When the mud drys up . . . we shall drill in skirmishing & then I shall find out how much pay a Bugler gets. at all events it is considered quite an honor to be Bugler for a Regt. When an army is advancing through the enemies country it is frequently necessary to send out a portion or a whole Reg to search the woods a little in advance of the main army so as not to meet with a sudden surprise from the enemy. in skirmishing the Capts and Lieut stand several paces behind their Cos the Col stands or rather sits on his horse on an eminence where he has a fair view of the men perhaps 50 or 100 rods behind them. the Bugler sounds the call used to represent the command. the Capts have to be familiar enough with the calls so they can tell one from an other. they give the command to their Cos. some of the calls are short & some are quite tunes I have learned to play nearly all of them.[35]

Mason had enlisted in October 1861 and was promoted to sergeant on 1 May 1862. On 30 March 1864 he was commissioned a captain in the Regular Army, and assigned to Company H, 19th Regiment, U.S. Colored Troops. On 20 March 1865 he was furloughed to Glover in Orleans County, Vermont, where he married Harriet B. Clark, his childhood sweetheart. On 20 November 1865 while waiting to be mustered out of the service, he died of yellow fever in a camp near Brownsville, Texas.

Although Mason was an excellent soldier and did learn to play nearly all of the calls, this was not always the case. William Anderson was appointed first bugler in Captain Eli Lilly's 18th Indiana Light Artillery Battery in July 1862. "Anderson practiced regularly on his calls but admitted that he had trouble remembering them."[36] He was frail in both physique and spirit and was a regular on the sick list at Camp Morton. He should have been discharged as physically unfit, for any kind of physical exertion was beyond him. His diminishing health deteriorated with alarming rapidity under the stress of training. He had only been at Camp Morton for a few weeks when he wrote to his mother. "We had to walk downtown and back which is two miles & a half; and the boys walked tolarbly fast which maid the walk more laborious, and caused me to sweat heartly which I was afraid would impare my health more than ever."[37] He died of erysipelas on 28 December 1862 at Gallatin, Tennessee.[38]

Another bugler who had trouble learning the calls was Tom Hayden of the 4th Kentucky. One afternoon the regiment had halted after crossing a mountain, waiting for the rest of the brigade to close up. General Marshall, riding up from the rear, stopped at the head of the regiment, where for the first time he saw Tom Hayden. Tom had belonged to a brass band before the war, and when he went into the army he took his cornet along to keep in practice. He was an accomplished musician and could play on almost any instrument. But Tom neglected to learn the various regulation cavalry calls, and usually, when sounding *reveille*, *boots and saddles*, etc., he would simply play some popular air, a favorite being "Sweet Ellen Bayne." The cornet's valves were frequently out-of-order, and often it was difficult to blow the instrument at all. General Marshall examined Tom's horn and then pleasantly commanded him to sound the calls. Tom, afraid to confess that he did not know them, said the old horn was out-of-order and could not be blown. The general then told him to whistle the calls. Tom said he could not whistle. The General then laughingly said that "a bird that could sing and wouldn't sing should be made to sing," and then he rode away, much to Tom's relief.[39]

Tom didn't always play, even when the horn was in working order. On 1 January 1864 the regimental historian wrote, "there was no sounding of Tom Hayden's bugle. The old horn had a bad cold, likewise Tom. However, if there was no blow in the horn, old Boreas was giving us a blast, the very memory of which makes us shiver on a midsummer day."[40]

Tom Hayden was a generous person when it came to the posessions of others and had a mildly larcenous bent. Hayden and Musgrove, the regimental historian, were close friends. Musgrove wrote that on a particularly cold night when "my teeth were chattering and my frail frame was shaking like an aspen leaf, Tom Hayden, the bugler, cautiously approached me, placed his arms affectionately around my neck and—blew his breath in my face."

Do you think I was insulted? Not much. That breath was laden with the fragrant fumes of "moonshine brandy," and wonderingly, but unquestioningly, I heeded his mute signal, "dropped to all fours," and following his lead crept through the grass to a pack-mule, which I recognized as one belonging to Dr. Scott, the surgeon. . . . I knew, instinctively, that I was in the presence of the "elixir of life". . . . I kept my eyes on Hayden, and saw him crawl to the gentle and generous mule. I did likewise. Two canteens, dangling from the pommel of the saddle, glistened in the pale moon-light. Hayden. . .inverted one of the canteens, and let the contents thereof flow in an uninterrupted stream down his throat. No words were spoken. None were necessary. All I had to do was to imitate my comrade and I imitated him until those canteens were sucked dry. Is there a Good Templar living who would have acted differently under similar circumstances? I think not. The fire-water had a wonderfully exhilarating effect upon us. That was a really generous act in Hayden. He might have appropriated to himself the two canteens, but he preferred to divide "the find" with a comrade. Good old Tom![41]

The 20th Maine Infantry was another regiment with a musical problem. Colonel Ames, its commander, was as ill-tempered as a goat and very short on patience. At the first formation of his command he barked: "This is a hell of a regiment!" and then set to work to straighten it out. After some preliminary training, he decided to brave a dress parade.

This was interrupted, noisily. In their martial ardor the men had organized a fife and drum corps in which the fifers and drummers all seemed to fife and drum independently but with great power. Just as the Colonel took his place in front of the drawn-up troops, the fife and drum corps suddenly and prematurely moved from its position and came tweetling and thundering down the line, making an appalling racket. To the company commander nearest him Colonel Ames shouted, "Captain Bangs, stop that damned drumming!" Captain Isaac S. Bangs couldn't hear him for the noise, nor could anyone else. In a rage, Colonel Ames charged the drum corps with his sword, and scattered it sufficiently to make himself audible.[42]

Of course not all field musicians were bunglers. Many mastered their art and performed to perfection. The historian of the 1st Rhode Island Light Artillery Battalion wrote enviously of the infantry, as his unit marched to the first battle of Bull Run in July 1861. He found it to be "an inspiring scene to see the different Infantry Regiments filing into camp, and to hear the different Drum Corps beating tattoo, the Artillery and Cavalry Buglers sounding the same calls."[43]

Lack of instrumental technique was not the sole cause of failure. Professional pride sometimes got in the way of efficiency, producing friction that prevented perfection. This was the problem in the 7th Pennsylvania Cavalry which had two first buglers." One of the two first buglers was subsequently carried as a deserter on the muster roll of the regimental history.

Professional pride was a source of conflict between the Regular Army and volunteer militia units. For example, George Townsend, a British reporter, found a general of volunteers wounded, following the battle of Cedar Mountain.

I found General John White Geary, a Pennsylvania brigade commander, in the dwelling of a lady near the end of the town. . . . He had received a bullet in the arm. . . . He was lying on his back, with his shattered arm bandaged, and resting on his breast. Twitches of keen pain shot across his face now and then. . . . He did not speak of himself or his services. . . but [that] McDowell had insulted him, as he rode from the field, and Geary felt the sting of the word more than the bullet. He had ventured to say to McDowell that the Reserves were badly needed in front, and the proud "regular" had answered the officious "volunteer" to the effect that he knew his own business. Not the least among the causes of the North's inefficiency will be found this ill feeling between the professional and civilian soldiery. A regular condemns a volunteer; a volunteer hates a regular.[44]

This intraservice rivalry often involved the essentials of life. Henry Campbell was bugler with Captain Lilly's 18th Indiana Light Artillery Battery. He was sixteen when he enlisted at Crawfordville, Indiana on 12 July 1862. His naivete was showing when he welcomed the arrival of an "old regiment" to his brigade of volunteers on 24 December of that year. "The 17th Ind., Col. Wilder's com'd joined our Brigade today. The 17th is an old, well-tried regiment and we gladly welcome them to our brigade."[45] The next day, Christmas, he noted: "Today is a delightful one, warm as a May day. . . . Some of the boys had about half their things stolen last night, the consequence of camping near the 'old' regiment. They swear they will get even before long."[46] When this midnight "requisitioning" finally touched him personally on 10 February 1863 Henry wrote: "Some cuss stole my brand new horse blanket off my horse last night. Somebody has to lose one tonight."[47]

Similar rivalries affected the efficiency of the field music of the 17th Pennsylvania Cavalry. The chief bugler was "Regular Army" to the core. He was well-qualified in every respect, but personal ambition produced a harsh discipline, and his disciples resisted his efforts to improve them. The problem was temporarily resolved in favor of the Regular Army when the chief and one of his subordinates resorted to the manly arts. The solution was ephemeral, for a second round favored the volunteer forces. Before another round could be fought, the regimental commander solved the entire problem by threatening to reduce both buglers to the ranks.[48]

Not all such differences resulted in violence. Sometimes a solution was achieved through the application of more democratic principles. Daniel Harris, a member of the band of the 12th New Jersey Volunteer Infantry, described a conflict that had arisen between the band and the drum major.

30 Jan 1863. Pleasant day. There is a mess brewing between the Band and the Drum Major who is trying to show off his authority over us. He has today issued an order requiring us to attend roll-call at reveille in the centre of the camp. This had created quite a breeze among us, and the strength of his authority.

31 January 1863. The plot deepens. We attended roll this morning and afterward drew up a petition and presented it to Col. Johnson, setting forth the fact that we were decidedly averse to being ruled by a man of his principles and that we would prefer returning to the ranks. Col. J. has promised to settle it. At guard mounting this morning the Adjutant informed us that we were under the Drum Major, and that he wished to hear no more from us on the subject. We said nothing but we are of a *different opinion*, and think the matter remains to be tested. The [Drum] Major, taking courage from this, has issued another mandate with all the dignity of a despot requiring us to play every night at 8 1/2 o'clock in the centre of the camp.

1 February 1863. A memorable day for the band. Victory has perched upon our banners and the would-be tyrant, like Icarus in soaring too near the sun, melted his wings and has suffered a most ignominious fall. Col. Johnson decided that we are to be under the control of the Drum Maj. when on duty or under orders, but at all other times we are to be ruled by one of our own number who is to call the roll and report all absence or sickness. The [Drum] Maj. was brought before the Col. with us and his misdeeds were shown up and proved in his teeth. He is considerably crest-fallen and in all probability will trouble us no more.[49]

Musicians did not always win out in disciplinary matters. A Massachusetts fifer, "for some petty offence, was sentenced. . .to play upon his instrument for two hours in front of headquarters. The sentence failed to prescribe the program, it having been supposed that it would be varied, as the performer was skilled in his profession. He. . .saw his opportunity, and selected a doleful air entitled, 'On the Road to Boston,' and inflicted it upon his hearers until his time had expired. . . . The Field and Staff endeavored to conceal their discomfiture, but did not succeed."[50]

Bugler Buck Cole of the 7th Kansas Cavalry was even more impudent. He was a man of infinite jest and complemented his unchangingly sober commander, Colonel Herrick, who nevertheless, did appreciate a good joke. He enjoyed Buck's sense of humor so much that he had him assigned as his bugler, an appointment that would keep him near at hand.

Buck took advantage of the situation and played the court fool to his heart's content. He was notoriously sloven in his dress, but used to say "that he was bound to dress well if he didn't lay up a cent." He was not always amenable to discipline, and once, while he was carrying a log . . . as a punishment, [he] was accosted by the chaplain, who had come for a book he had loaned Buck. . . . The chaplain was a recent appointment, and as yet guileless, and when Buck suggested that he hold the log while he went after the book, the Chaplain absent mindedly took it, and, ten minutes later, when the captain appeared on the scene, was pacing up and down, thinking over his next Sunday's sermon, with the stick still on his shoulder. Buck was found peacefully sleeping in his tent; he stated that. . .he supposed the idea was to have the log carried, and as the chaplain was doing it he thought it would be all right.[51]

While bugler Buck Cole was merely impudent, the field musicians of the 148th Pennsylvania Volunteers were out-and-out insubordinate. Encamped near Falmouth in the early spring of 1863, the musicians were called out on a particularly dark and disagreeable night. A muddy wagon road ran directly through the center of the camp. Drum Major Bob Cassidy wanted *tattoo* beaten on the north side of the road, but the leading fifer decided it should be performed on the south side. The fifer, claiming two colleagues (one being the leading drummer), maintained that because of their rank they represented a majority of the twenty members of the corps.

The result was what might be expected of two divisions of a band of music thirty feet apart trying to play so complicated a production as tattoo at one and the same time. Before we were half through, the stentorian voice of the Colonel was heard, "If you don't stop that infernal racket I'll put you all in the guard house." We slunk away in the dark, but not far enough to prevent our hearing the Drum Major's report to the Colonel, nor the sending by the Adjutant for the corporal of the guard, nor the orders to the corporal to take a file of men and arrest Harpster and Otto of Company C, and Mattern of Company D, and put them in the guard house. It is needless to say, Harpster and Otto could not be found, but Mattern, not being so well posted, languished in the guard house until the next day.[52]

Drummer boys were rarely involved in serious breaches of military law, but a few did desert. Two, who took French leave from the School of Practice on Governor's Island, were caught after a time. They were tried by courts martial and sentenced to receive "twenty-five strokes with a rattan well applied to their 'bare buttocks'," and to be confined in the guard house at hard labor for two months. They forfeited their pay for the same period.

We were turned out and formed in ranks. . .to witness the punishment. . . . They were marched to the place under guard. The adjutant read the sentence. . . . Then one of the boys was laid face down on a long bench and held by a member of the guard at his head and another at his feet. His clothes were removed sufficiently to expose his buttocks, and. . .a corporal commenced to apply the rattan, which. . .made the boy squirm and groan and finally cry out with pain before the Adjutant cried "Halt" at the twenty-fifth blow. While the blows were not inflicted with anything like full force, yet they were cruel enough if only by their number.

The unfortunate second victim was obliged to witness his comrade's punishment and then endure the same himself. . . . The trembling and sobbing boys were reconducted to the guard house, and we marched back to quarters after this distressing scene.[53]

Another case of rank insubordination occurred in the 148th Pennsylvania Infantry Regiment. Major General Barlow set out to reorganize the field music of his division in order to better utilize "the wasted energy of the sheep-skin batteries" as he so often called them. He consolidated all of the musicians into a single unit and placed a mounted lieutenant in overall command. This large group was subdivided into four platoons, each containing the musicians from one of the four brigades of the division. A sergeant was detailed to supervise each platoon. The combined unit numbered one hundred sixty men. Musicians who had lost or thrown away their instruments, as some frequently did during a summer's campaign, were sent to their companies and placed in the ranks as privates. The remainder were marched in a body at the rear of the division. When the command entered combat, the musicians were put to work erecting hospital tents under the direction of the surgeon.

Friction developed from two sources. First, the principal musicians, who outranked the sergeants, were stripped of their command authority. The musicians, in turn, resented the sergeants who were somewhat imperious in their manner. Soon, several of the boys, contrary to orders, went on a foraging expedition.

They had captured a Confederate calf and appropriated it to their own use, being short of rations. Taken to division headquarters they were "bucked and gagged" and all the musicians of the division assembled to witness the penalty imposed by General Barlow. Six strokes on the shoulder with an ox gad as they sat in their cramped and helpless position, were given each, and as the last stroke fell the tall form of the General crowded through the outer circle and inquired:

"Who administered those blows?"

The executioner saluted and replied, "I did General."

"Well, Sergeant," retorted the General, "you may report to your company; I will not have a Sergeant in my provost guard who does not obey orders. Those blows were not nearly so heavy, nor the stick so large as I ordered."[54]

A roster of rascals would have to include Joe Boner of the 1st Minnesota Volunteer Infantry who, along with a comrade, died in a jail they had set afire with a view to effecting their escape. Boner was a bugler but was so frequently in confinement that his associates called him "Guardhouse Joe." After his Gotterdammerung a comrade wrote, "Boner was a fidler. He was about 30 years of age, a very small man he was always drunk when he could get a chance."[55]

Not all field musicians displayed the vicious bent of Guardhouse Joe. Some of the younger boys were merely mischievous. Susie King Taylor served with the 33rd United States Colored Troops and recorded the antics of the young regimental musicians.

I must mention a pet pig we had on Cole Island. Colonel Trowbridge brought it into camp one day, a poor thin little pig. . . . The pig grew to be the pet of the camp and was the special care of the drummer boys, who taught him many tricks; and so well did they train him that every day at practice and dress parade, his pigship would march out with them, keeping perfect time with their music. The drummers would often disturb the devotions by riding this pig into the midst of evening praise meeting, and many were the complaints made to the Colonel, but he was always very lenient towards the boys, for he knew they only did this for mischief.[56]

Augustus Meyers, a fifer himself, wrote of the impish nature of the young boys in his corps.

Tricks were played upon us boys once in a while. We played our calls at the flag staff in front of the commanding officer's house, where, when commencing to play, some fifer would nearly burst himself trying to blow his instrument. Upon investigation he would find it stuffed with paper or rags. Sometimes a drummer would find the drumhead greased or the snares loosened. The bandsmen also had their troubles. Their brass instruments were filled with water or stuffed with rags; these experiences soon taught us to examine our instruments before going to the parade ground.[57]

This "boys will be boys" attitude on the part of many commanders would seem to imply that these young men retained the innocence of youth during their terms of service, but this was generally not the case. More than one fell victim to his surroundings. In a letter dated 9 March 1863 Private Davenport assessed the effects of the army upon the boy musicians of his regiment.

The more vulgar a man is, the better he is appreciated and as for morals. . .[the army] is a graveyard for them. . . .If you think soldiering cures anyone of wild habits it is a great mistake, it is like Sending a Boy in the Navy to learn him good manners. We have Drummer Boys with us that when they came at first could hardly look you in the face for diffidence but now could stare the Devil out of contenance and can't be beat at cursing, swaring and gambling.[58]

George Ulmer, a young field musician, was left in camp during one of the battles. Finding a green spot, he stretched himself out and listened to the awful din of musketry from the front. The debris of a deserted camp surrounded him on all sides—empty cans, broken bayonets, parts of weapons, fragments of bursted shells, and occasionally a whole shell that had failed to explode. As he sat observing events, he was joined by another drummer boy from a Pennsylvania regiment.

I thought he was the most profane lad I had ever met. Most every other word he uttered was an oath. I asked him if he wasn't afraid to talk so.

"What the h____l should I be afraid of?" he asked, at the same time picking up an old tent stake and sticking it into the ground, trying to drive it in with the heel of his boot. Failing in this he reached over and got hold of an unexploded shell and used this on the stake. . . .

"I wonder if this was fired by those d_____d rebs," he asked.

"I guess it was," I replied, "and you better look out, or it might go off."

"Off be d_____d, their shells were never worth the powder to blow 'em to h____l, see the hole in the butt of it, it would make a G____d_____d good mawl, wouldn't it?" and looking around at the same time he found an old broom. . . . "I'll make a mawl of it and drive that d_____d rebel stake into the ground with one of their own d_____d shells be d_____d if I don't." Inserting the broom handle into the end of the shell he walked over to a stump, and taking the shell in both hands commenced pounding the stick against the stump; "d_____d tight fit," he hollored to me, and the next instant I was knocked down by a terrific explosion. I came to my senses in a minute and hastened to where he had been standing. There the poor fellow lay unconscious and completely covered with blood, there was hardly a shred of clothes on him his hair was all burned, and both hands taken completely off, as if done by a surgeon's saw. . . .

The sight was horrible, but I quickly regained my composure, knowing that something must be done and done quickly. So taking the snares from my drum I wound them tightly around his wrists to stop the flow of blood, then I hailed an ambulance, and we took him to the field hospital about a mile to the rear.

On the way the poor fellow regained consciousness and looking at his mutilated wrists, and then with a quick and bewildered glance at me, said "G____d_____d tough, ain't it?" Then the tears started in his eyes, and he broke down and sobbed the rest of the way, "Oh my God! What will my poor mother say? Oh what will she do!"[59]

Some weeks later Ulmer visited his young comrade in the hospital and offered whatever help he could.

He had changed wonderfully, his little white pinched face told too plainly the suffering he had endured. I asked him how he was getting along.

"Oh I'm getting along pretty d_____d fast. I guess I'll croak in a few days. . . .I'm a goner; I know it. I don't want to live, anyhow. What in h____l is the good of a man without hands?. . .Say Cully, reach under my pillow and find a little book there; it's a little Testament that my dear old mother gave me; read a little for me, will you please? You'll find a place mother marked for me, read that please."

I turned the leaves over till I found a little white ribbon pinned to a leaf, marking the verse beginning. "Suffer little children to come unto me." I started to read for him, but the tears filled my eyes. I had to stop. . . .I glanced at him and the open, staring eyes and the rigid drawn features told me too plainly that the little fellow was out of his sufferings:—he was dead![60]

If some of the boys grew profane, others remained uncontaminated by their surroundings. Ransom Powell was confined to Libby Prison when but thirteen years of age. Captain Wirz, the infamous prison commandant, felt sorry for the boy and took him into his office as his orderly. The boy's bright face and winning manners fascinated the women visitors at the prison headquarters, and numbers of them tried to adopt him, but with poor success. He claimed that he could see few charms in an existence under the Rebel flag, and turned a deaf ear to all of their blandishments. He was allowed to move freely between the headquarters and the camp and acted as a purveyor of information for the soldiers imprisoned there. He was "a bright, blue-eyed, fair-haired little drummer boy, as handsome as a girl, well bred as a lady, and evidently the darling of some refined living mother. . . . We called him 'Red Cap,' from his wearing a jaunty gold-laced crimson cap. Ordinarily, the smaller a drummer boy is the harder he is, but no amount of attrition with rough men could coarsen the ingrained refinement of Red Cap's manners."[61]

Young drummer boys were not the only ones caught in the struggle between the contaminating influences of army life and the upbringing of their youth. Older men, especially those with strong religious convictions, wrestled mightily with their consciences while they participated in the seamier side of army life. Many found their surroundings so evil that they refused to allow their wives and sweethearts to visit them in camp.

Joseph Whitney wrote of the struggle occurring in his regiment, but reassured his wife of his own salvation.

You ask is the doctor a professor of religion. I think not, but he is a very good man, a moral man. I mean, he uses good language, always. There are a good many in the regiment that are still trying to serve God and with them I have good sessions. We have no Chaplain, each one has to be his own preacher. Some get worse or more wicked and others get better or have a greater desire to love and serve God. As for myself, I am still striving to serve God and making my calling and election safe. I never forget to give my fellow soldiers good advice. I feel thankful to God that in the person of my beloved wife, I have a praying friend....Kiss Clara for Papa.[62]

An army Sabbath fell short of his expectations. In an earlier letter he wrote, "Today is Sunday. You would not think so if you were here. Every day is alike.

The longer men are in the service the weaker Sunday seems to get. There is not one minute a day you do not hear cursing and swearing. No one in our tent swears. I thank God for it. We are in the midst of wickedness. We do not have prayer meetings, because it would be like casting pearls to the swine. Thank God, we can still pray in secret."[63]

Whitney's appraisal of his colleagues changed when he fell in with more compatible companions, all of whom regularly attended prayer meetings conducted by the newly appointed chaplain. "We have five regiments here now," Whitney wrote, and ". . . . we have first rate prayer meetings twice a week in our barracks. Preaching three times on Sunday and twice during the week. So you can see the time is well filled up. There are all kinds of folks here, just the same as at home. . . . If a man wants good company, he can have it."[64]

Older married men, like Whitney, had established their life styles prior to their induction, and were more likely to shun the temptations of military life. On the other hand, young drummer boys, recently loosed from paternal restraint, seem to have abandoned all of the principles of life that they had learned at their mother's knee.

A famous photo in Miller's *Photographic History of the Civil War* shows a young drummer boy playing bluff with a mustachioed sergeant, while a still younger lad observed the result of the betting.[65] "An Ohio Cavalryman reported seeing a fifteen-year-old win $120.00 in one gambling session."[66]

A great religious revival swept through both armies during the winter of 1863–1864, and more than one young soldier repented the evil of his ways.[67] Henry Campbell attended a prayer meeting but shunned the call to repentance.

Lt. Rippetoe and some of the men built a "church" last week out of hemlock poles, covering it with a wagon sheet and stuffing hemlock branches in the cracks between the logs. It was dedicated today, most all the boys attending.

In the evening we had prayer meeting and "Old Uncle Jo" (our black Hd. Qr. teamster) "lead" in the prayer and a right good effort the old man made. He is the only man in the Department that can drive a mule team *without swearing*. Uncle Jo will plant himself by the side of his camp fire at the end of his wagon, all by himself. He dont "sociate" with the other "common niggers." Here of evenings you will hear him "line out" a line of some old darky hymn, in a monotonous tone, as if he had a large congregation before him. Then he will sing over the line with all the pomp and flourishes of the country singing teacher.[68]

Some men were sincerely moved by this religious renewal. Alburtus Dunham wrote to his mother that Marietta, Georgia, in June 1864. "Never did I know what it was to be away from home until I came into the armey. Oh, I hope Eugene or Hiram wont come in to the army. Thare was too of our come and that is enough out of one family. Dear mother you said you would be so happy to heare that I was one of the ones that was converted in our Regt. Ma I feal as iff God was on my side. It useless for me to try to express my fealeings. I have resolved to be a christon the rest of my life. Doo pray for me. I know you do P and Hercey too."[69]

If Dunham was moved to immediate repentance, William Bardeen was much slower in responding to the call. Bardeen was a field musician with Company D of the 1st Massachusetts Infantry. He was only fourteen when the war broke out, but the firing on Sumter really excited him:

I remember walking up and down the sitting room, puffing out my breast as though the responsibility rested on my poor little shoulders, shaking my fist at the south and threatening her with dire calamities which I thought some of inflicting on her myself. I joined the military company of Orange country [sic] grammer school and took fencing lessons. As men began to enlist I wished I were older. I don't know why I did not happen to think of getting in as a drummer boy; perhaps because I didn't know how to drum or have any means of learning, though as I afterward discovered, that was no obstacle.[70]

On 3 December 1861 Bardeen tried to enlist through the aid of Captain John F. Appleton of the 12th Maine, a part of General Benjamin Butler's brigade. Appleton, a cousin of Bardeen's mother, took the boy to see the general. He introduced him to Butler and said: "This boy is rather young, but he is healthy and strong and intelligent, and I should like to have him in my company."[71] Butler's response was short and to the point. "Take the damned little snipe away, we've got babies enough in this brigade already."[72]

Bardeen had better luck six months later when his second cousin returned home from the front as a recruiting sergeant. He arranged to enlist him as a drummer. He passed the physical and on 21 July 1862 at the age of fourteen was assigned as a musician in Company D.

Bardeen's father had died in 1859, and his mother had remarried. The boy was a "disturbing" element to this new union. He readily admitted that he was "conceited, boastful, self-willed, disobedient, saucy, and always wanting to do something else than the duty of the moment, a liar and generally wholly disagreeable."[73] He had been expelled from Orange County Grammar School, and his last recollection of Fitchburg High School was of Miss Anna Haskell rather maliciously telling him that he had not passed geometry. He had run away from home, gone to Boston, bought some portraits of war generals on credit, and worked his way to Randolph selling the pictures. His mother had even threatened to put him in reform school, but she relented at the last moment. He was more appreciative of his mother's attitude in later years. "I can see how it was a relief to her to have me really in the army, under authority that could control me, with the responsibility off her mind."[74]

Once enlisted, Bardeen eagerly set out to learn the tools of his trade. He borrowed a drum from the quartermaster, and went over to a hill, between his camp and Tufts College, to practice. He had no one to teach him. "I think that I have never succeeded in anything less than in learning to drum. My sense of rhythm was keen and I could keep time, but I could never get an even roll. That double stroke I never mastered. It was partly because a drum was so awkward to carry on the march that I soon sent for a fife and learned to play that, and in December got transferred from Drummer to Fifer, but I was glad enough to turn in an instrument that I played so poorly."[75]

Bardeen easily adapted to army life in spite of his youth. A vagabond childhood made him self-reliant, and once in service, he became an entrepreneur of sorts. He bought postage stamps wholesale and retailed them to his comrades. He stenciled knapsacks at a quarter apiece, and when business grew brisk he sent for his eleven-year-old brother to help him keep up with the demand. He pilfered candles from the commissary and stole pies and cakes. Untouched by the religious revival, he wrote on 27 January 1863 "I got a fine Bible and Diary from home. I have the Diary still: the Bible with hundreds of others, fell by the way on my first long march."[76]

Bardeen learned all of the games of chance and became so expert that only the professionals would play with him. He meticulously kept books on his winnings and frequently sent home amounts of up to $200.

On 2 October 1863 he got a pass to go fishing "within sight of the guards," but quickly went over-the-hill to Harlem. He did catch three fish before he took leave. He bought additional fish in Port Morris to round out his stringer so that he could fool the guards into thinking he had been fishing all day. While in Harlem he "played billiards and drank rum. . .and had a good dinner. . . .Spent a 3 dollar counterfeit bill. . .and had a pretty good time altogether."[77] Passing a three-dollar bill speaks highly of his abilities as a con man.

By 1863 he was such an accomplished gambler that he expanded his sphere of operations to include his entire division. On 25 November he "set up a sweat board among the Excelsiors, and after getting about $50.00 ahead was cleaned out, having vest torn and losing all [his] money. Big thing!"[78]

The accumulation of years did not dim his youthful exuberance.

My greeness could not have been better illustrated than by my venturing off alone into another brigade, of New York toughs at that, and expecting to get away with any winnings I might make. I grabbed my money tight between my fingers, and after I was knocked down I was kicked and beaten considerably before I let go my clutch. They got the money in my waistcoat, but did not happen to think of an inside shirt pocket in which I had a hundred dollars or so stowed away. As it was I did not lose much more than my winnings and was not seriously bruised, so I learned a good lesson more cheaply than I deserved to.[79]

Perhaps he would have exercised greater caution with a clear head, but he had been robbed of a good night's sleep before his "lesson." Indeed, his card playing had been none too sharp the previous evening. He summed up the problem in his diary. "Lost my night's rest by eating beans before I went to supper last night. Orders to move and after we had got on line and were wet through, they were countermanded. Lost $20 at Bluff."[80]

Bardeen was a compulsive gambler who would go to any length to win a buck. He won eleven dollars at bluff and used his winnings to buy a raffle ticket from a comrade. He tied for the raffle and successfully shook dice to break the tie and win the watch. He raffled off the watch the following day, clearing twenty-five dollars on the series of transactions.[81]

His gambling finally came to an end when he "signed the temperance pledge" on 17 March 1864.[82] He had considered the errors of his ways and had already recorded his pangs of conscience on the previous New Year's Eve. The thirty-first of December 1863 was a rainy, drizzly day. Bardeen mustered into camp at 3 P.M. and stayed up to ring in the New Year. "Slow pass the hours, 7, 8, 9, 10, 11, 11 1/4, 11 3/4, and down to seconds. 1863 is a thing of the past. A happy new year to all. The year that has passed was passed by me in the Army. I bear witness to its contaminating effects. Many an evil habit has sprung up in me since Jan 1st, 1863. God grant that the year on which we have now entered be not so."[83]

His new life style confirmed his seriousness. He continued to attend temperance meetings, and on 21 February attended "the best meeting I ever attended in the Army, at Holy Jo's tent."[84] He regarded Miss Gilson, who spoke at this meeting as "an angel on earth." The meeting ended with a serenade by the band of the 120th Regiment.

His renewal of the spirit was accompanied by a renewed interest in education. He attended spelling school at night where he got spelled down on "reception." He played checkers and chess to stimulate his mind and enrolled in boxing class and a physical fitness program to stimulate his body. His nights were given to culture. He participated in singing class. He bought a flute for eighteen dollars and tried to teach himself to play the "Lancer's Quadrille."[85]

He held to his new way of life until the very end of his term of service, when the temptation for a bit of bravado was more than he could suppress. A fall against a hot stove, when a child, had left a scar on the top of his head. When discharged, he sought the services of a purveyor of tonsorial arts to prepare him for his return home. The barber, noting the scar, asked, "Get this in the army?" He returned to his early dreams of valor and answered, "Yes, at Chancellorsville. Our color-bearer fell, and just as I seized the flag a rebel cavalry officer cut my head open with his sword. Fortunately one of our boys shot him and we got away with our colors."[86] The barber was interested and wanted to hear all of the particulars. Bardeen had been at Chancellorsville, but not in the fighting and had the necessary facts at his disposal. He met the expectations of his credulous and sympathetic audience. But alas "as I got down from my chair and glanced into the long mirror I caught sight of Holy Jo, who had been sitting in the chair next but one. There must have been appeal in my look, for he gave no sign of recognition and I hurried away. But I fancied he looked discouraged, and I have no doubt so far as he ever thought of me afterward it was as the boy who told those whoppers in French's Hotel barber-shop."[87]

Joe Phillips played the drum that accompanied Bardeen's fife in Company D. Bardeen regarded himself as an accomplished instrumentalist but had little good to say about the other members of his corps. He thought highly enough of Hull, the regimental drum major, and Drum Major Hart, the regimental principal musician, but found John C. Prest of Company I to be a "born blunderer."[88] On 28 August 1863 he blamed Prest for his own errors. "Sixteen years old today," he wrote. "Made a bad mistake at Guard Mounting occasioned by Prest who is too big a fool to do as he ought."[89] Age did not improve his generosity towards Prest, and he later wrote, "I don't know why mistakes of the drummers annoyed me so much. I had no responsibility beyond my own fife. But guard mounting and dress parade seemed to me about the only places we earned our pay and I did like to get through them decently and in order."[90]

Two weeks after Bardeen's sixteenth birthday, Mayor Lincoln and Generals Canby, Cowdin, and others came out to present the regiment with a city flag. Bardeen thought the flag was a "very handsome one, [but] our drum corps done nothing right as usual."[91] The other members of the corps were Joe Welch (Company C), Sawyer (Company H), Charles C. Perkins (Company K), George Allen (Company A), Dearing (Company G), and his two good friends, the Mingle brothers, who were both drummers. Of the Mingles he wrote that "both were good fellows, not talkative but never shirking and always ready to oblige. I would have selected them from the entire drum corps for trust-worthiness of the watch-dog type. The younger one, George, could not see after dark and had to be led. He called it moonblindness, and attributed it to sleeping one night with his face toward the full moon. He was in Co. F and when we came home was transferred to the 11th Mass. Henry was in Co. A."[92]

Moon blindness, also called "mooneye," is an equine malady characterized by a recurrent inflamation of the eye that often results in blindness in horses. It is called nyctalopia when it occurs in humans. Augustus Meyers recorded an incidence of the disease that assumed epidemic proportions in his company.

About this time a singular affliction came upon nearly one-half of the garrison, which we called moonblindness. Every evening after twilight they began to lose their vision, and when it became dark they could only distinguish a bright light if very close to them. They had to be led around like blind men. In the morning they could see as well as ever. This lasted about a fortnight, and made it hard for the unafflicted who had to do double guard duty. No one seemed to know the cause for this blindness. Some had an idea that the comet was responsible for it. I was one of the fortunate who escaped this affliction.[93]

Henry Campbell is another drummer boy who left a rather complete account of his service. He too had to finagle his way into the army. He tried to enlist soon after Fort Sumter was fired upon. "All passed [the physical] but myself," he wrote, "refused on account of my age, too young. Thought I was gone sure but Captain Lilly told the Dr. that I was intended for his bugler and that 'it was essential to the interests of the service, &c.' that I be retained, which was finally done."[94]

Henry was only five feet five inches tall, and very childlike in appearance. Of slight build, it was impossible for him to pass as an eighteen-year-old. He would probably never have entered the army without the captain's intervention.

Captain Lilly treated him as a young son until 16 September 1863 when Henry assumed his independence. "Quit messing with the captain's mess. Have been messing at the captain's table for more than a year and am very thankful for the kindness and interest he has shown me by taking me to his mess and treating me more like a brother than a common soldier."[95] He moved into the mess of First Sergeant Martin J. Miller, Quartermaster Sergeant John D. Johnson, and Wagonmaster and Company Clerk, James Binford. " 'Sam' cooked for them and they thought he was 'one of the best of his profession now following the army. . . . [Sam was] a little, short, chunky darky, black as midnight with a continual grin on his sable countinance and a joke for everybody.' "[96]

Although young, Henry was a resourceful soldier in many respects: "have turned tailor for the last day or two. Been lining the cape of my overcoat with rubber so that on unbuttoning it off the collar and turning it wrong side out it becomes water proof. Finished it today."[97]

Henry Campbell's desire for maturity and independence propelled him more toward expediency than truthfulness. His basically honest character was slightly tarnished with the salts of the con artist. He also had a roving eye for the ladies.

In the evening, I went over to a respectable looking house about ½ mile from camp, thinking I would run my face for a supper. Found quite a good-looking girl, dressed in homespun, superintending the baking of "hoe cake," whose delicious fragrance filled every crack and corner of your nose and caused your mouth to water sufficiently to start a small Niagara. Wishing to make myself as agreeable and entertaining as possible, I turned the conversation to herself, remarking that I had traveled over a great deal of the South but had failed to see a good looking girl until now. "Pshaw," says she, "Yer poking fun at me." I assured her I was in sober earnest and told her that she was, emphatically, the prettiest girl in the State of Tenn. "La!" says she, "*You just oughter seen me afore I had the di-a-ree.*" A huge laugh outside the open door advised me that other ears had been listening to the conversation and I immediately vamoosed.[98]

Campbell was a good bugler with a rudimentary knowledge of music reading, and served as an instructor to buglers of nearby regiments. "The bugler of the 17 Ind. was over to day to get some calls, as they have one or two Cos. mounted. Wrote him 'Stable,' 'Water,' 'Feed,' and 'Boots and Saddles'—thats all they need at present."[99]

Both Campbell and Bardeen suffered from wanderlust and were away from their regiments a good deal. Bardeen admitted that this was tantamount to taking French leave, but continued his wanderings until Grant took command. From then on he was forced to move with his unit. Although Campbell moved about rather freely when his regiment was on the march, he was still conscientious about the performance of his duties.

Bardeen watched many battles but noted that "no drummer in his regiment played a drum on the battlefield."[100] He worked in the rear areas during combat or simply took leave and observed events from a convenient position.

Campbell, on the other hand, sounded the calls on the battlefield and performed other duties as well. His unit was on the right center of the line at Chickamauga. "It was 8 o'clock before the awful deathlike stillness that preceded this terrible battle was broken. Then there began, far away to the left, a low, distinct rumbling, gradually approaching, like a distant hail storm, as division after division became hotly engaged. . . . We did not get engaged until 10 o'clock, when the enemy charged us furiously several times, but they were rolled back with heavy losses each time. The roar was perfectly awful, as if ten million pieces of sheet iron were all shaken at once."[101]

Henry Campbell had a number of narrow escapes during his service. Outside of Chattanooga ". . . the Rebels fired a 32-pounder James rifle. . . . The shell wizzed over my head . . . striking the ground where Corp. McCorkle was lying asleep. It cut his leg entirely off below the knee."[102] At Mossy Creek, "the sharpshooters were picking off the men one after another. . . . We all were in danger of being captured if not killed."[103]

Campbell was commissioned a second lieutenant, United States Colored Infantry, on 18 November 1865. He was discharged in 1866 and returned to Crawfordsville, where he remained active in the Grand Army of the Republic.[104]

Johnnie Walker was a twelve-year-old drummer who served with the 22nd Wisconsin Infantry Regiment. Johnnie attracted a great deal of attention on dress parade when "lots of gentlemen and ladies came from the city to hear them play and see the little drummer. . . ."[105]

When we are marching Johnnie always keeps up with the big men, and is always singing and laughing but when he gets tired the big Colonel or Lieutenant Colonel or Adjutant will let Johnnie have his horse to ride. Everybody . . . likes Johnnie because he is a good little boy. . . . Johnnie used to live in Racine and he has a half brother who is corporal in our company (but he is a mean bad man, don't take care of Johnnie, who lives with the Captain of Company B).[106]

The most famous drummer boy of the war was Johnny Clem. At the age of nine he ran away from home to join the army in May 1861. John Lincoln Clem was born in Newark, Ohio, on 13 August 1851 to Roman Clem and Mary (Weaver) Clem. He first attempted to enlist as a drummer in the 3rd Ohio and

22nd Michigan Volunteer Infantry but was rejected because of his youth. He finally succeeded in enlisting as a drummer with the 22nd Michigan Infantry on 1 May 1862. He was promoted to sergeant at the battle of Chickamauga on 20 September 1863.[107]

The smashing of Johnny's drum by a shell at Pittsburg Landing won for him the sobriquet of "Johnny Shiloh." Shortly afterward he was regularly enlisted as a drummer. Subsequently he exchanged drum for musket because, as he put it, "I did not like to stand and be shot at without shooting back."

So at Chickamauga, Johnny, though still carried on the rolls as drummer, went into the fight riding an artillery cassion and carrying a musket cut down to size. When a Confederate Colonel dashed up and demanded "Surrender you damned little Yankee!" Johnny gave him a blast that knocked him from his horse. For this feat Clem, then twelve years old, was made a sergeant and became known as the drummer boy of Chickamauga . . . Johnny carried dispatches for General Thomas during the Atlanta campaign, had his pony killed under him and before the end of his service was twice wounded.[108]

Johnny Clem remained in the service after the war and was appointed second lieutenant (Infantry) on 18 December 1871. He rose through the ranks to brigader general on 13 August 1915 and was breveted a major general on 29 August 1916 when he retired from the service.

Clem participated in the battles of Shiloh, Chickamauga, Perryville, Sonte River, Resaca, Kenesaw, Atlanta, and Nashville. He died on 13 May 1937.[109]

Clem was not the only drummer boy who traded his instrument for a musket. The commander of the 52nd Ohio Infantry reported that "Charley Common, a little drummer-boy, having lost his drum, took a musket and fought manfully in the line."[110]

Elisha Carder was a drummer with the Stonewall brigade until September of 1864, "when he took a musket [and was] wounded at Fisher's Hill."[111] Charles and Ralph Perrin, two brothers, were field musicians in the same brigade. Charles died in the hospital at Charlottesville, Virginia, in August 1862, and his brother Ralph was killed at the second battle of Bull Run on 30 August 1862 at the age of sixteen.[112]

Not all of the young boys stood the test of battle. Colonel Steuart of the 1st Maryland Infantry Regiment had "organized a fine drum corps, under the peerless Hosea Pitt, and was getting up a band under Bandmaster Hubbard. . . . All day was heard in the air the doleful practising of 'Hark, I hear an Angel Sing,' the 'Mocking Bird,' and 'Maryland, My Maryland'—now becoming known."[113]

A part of the 1st Maryland was on picket duty east of Sangster's Station on 9 March 1862 where it had relieved the 13th Virginia. When relieved, the 13th moved farther forward to some open ground, where they were attacked by a small party of cavalry. About a dozen men were captured.

One of the drums was captured, or more likely thrown away by the drummer, in this affair, who made his way back to winter quarters. Assistant Surgeon Latimer told me that this drummer, on being asked what had happened, was going through a pantomime of running away and casting back a drum over his shoulder when Colonel Steuart grabbed him from behind and demanded in an awful voice, "Where is your drum!" He turned to Drum Major Hosea Pitt and said, "It's a good thing Pitt, it's a good thing that I had not yet had the Maryland flag painted on those drums!"[114]

While the drummers of the 1st Maryland were discarding their instruments in the face of the enemy, Private David Scantlon (Company C, 4th Virginia Regiment of the Stonewall Brigade) went to considerable lengths to keep his from harm. Scantlon was fifty-seven years old—old enough to be the father of the rest of the drum corps, which ranged in age from sixteen to nineteen. "At the height of the battle of First Manassas, Scantlon was ordered by Colonel James Preston to 'beat the rally' so that the regiment could be reformed. Scantlon promptly did so, after turning his back to the sound of the battle. When asked the reason for such an action, the old drummer replied, 'so you suppose I wanted the Yankees to shoot a hole through my bass drum!' "[115]

Scantlon was but one of hundreds of field musicians who served in combat. Many, like Campbell, returned safely home, but many others were captured, or worse yet, killed.

Moses Bernard was appointed chief musician of the 4th Louisiana Infantry Regiment, but led the field music for an entire corps that included musicians Morris B. Davis, Gus Heckler, and John Richarts.[116] Robert Patrick, the biographer of the regiment, was a tentmate of Davis, whom he described as "a very agreeable man. He is very well informed on almost any subject that is brought up in the course of conversation. He told me that he had kept a diary ever since he had been in the army, and being a good draughtsman he has sketches of all the places we have been, together with a plan of the battlefield of Shiloh. It was looking at his diary that first induced me to keep one."[117] Davis was indeed a very agreeable man and somewhat of a philosopher when it came to minor irritations. Patrick wrote, "I saw him the other day, and he was bareheaded."

"Hello Davis," said I, "where's your hat?" "I haven't any" he answered, "someone stole it." "Well, what are you to do for another?" I asked. "Do without I suppose," said he. He didn't seem to be at all annoyed about it and seemed to be perfectly well satisfied without a hat. . . . If I had been without a hat I should have been perfectly miserable until I could get another. Davis on the contrary made himself perfectly easy and contented until he could get another hat because as he said, "Kicking up hell would not bring him a hat any sooner."[118]

We can only hope that Davis held to his even temper when he was captured near Nashville, Tennessee, on 16 December 1864. He was exchanged on 17 February 1865.[119]

Davis' easy-going disposition was balanced by that of John Richarts, the drummer with Company A. Richarts was more a man of action. Both were hungry since neither had eaten for forty-eight hours. To remedy this they "waddled down to a farmer's house near by, to see what prospects there were of obtaining a small quantity of . . . 'grub.' "

We saw a little girl in the yard and John asked her if we could buy anything to eat. She said we could if we had gold or silver, but her ma wouldn't take any paper money. . . . The lady of the house [then] piously informed him that this was Sunday; that she had been reading that good book—holding up a Bible—and that she couldn't think for a moment of desecrating the Holy Sabbath, by selling anything whatever, at the same time recommending to get his Bible and peruse it attentively.

John, whose patience was exhausted . . . answered abruptly. "Don't talk to me about the Bible. I'm half starved, and reading the Bible will not fill my belly, and even if I did read it, I would . . . be thinking about something to eat all the time."

"Well you can't get anything here to-day" replied the old lady, "come another day and I will accomodate you. . . ."

I went to a well in the yard to wash my face and . . . John went around towards the kitchen on an exploring expedition. He returned . . . with the intelligence that he had got on the good side of the cook, and that we would have something to eat presently. . . . We accordingly waited . . . until the cook informed us that our breakfast was ready, and went into the kitchen. . . .

Just before we sat, a large, rough looking, red wiskered man came in, and when we seated ourselves at the table he took a seat also. He pitched into the bread and meat which was all we had, and . . . after eating the greater part . . . suddenly rose and left the house. When we came to settle for our breakfast the woman wanted us to pay for this red wiskered fellow but this we wouldn't begin to do. . . .

John and I acknowledged that we were sold and at first we were inclined to follow the fellow up and expose him to the first crowd we could find him in, but we finally came to the conclusion that it wasn't worth the trouble. We afterwards considered it a good joke.[120]

Richarts was captured near Columbia, Tennessee, on 16 December 1864 and was exchanged at Point Lookout, Maryland, on 17 February 1865.[121]

Many young field musicians were captured. Many others were severely wounded, or died from wounds or disease. Kate Cumming nursed a young Texas Ranger named Sloan. "He is only thirteen years of age and lost a leg in a skirmish. He is as happy as if nothing was the matter, and he was at home playing with his brothers and sisters. His father is with him, and is quite proud that his young son has distinguished himself to such a degree, and is very grateful to the ladies for the kind attention which they bestow upon him."[122]

James North, bugler with the 4th Kentucky Cavalry, was inexplicably saved from death. "In the fight at Telfords, Joe Johnson, of Trimble County, Kentucky was killed; Amos Frost was severely wounded in the head, and James North, bugler, was struck in the abdomen by a spent ball, which did not penetrate the skin, but the shock doubled him up as though he had a bad case of colic."[123]

Several of the boy musicians won the nation's highest award for gallantry in the face of the enemy: the Congressional Medal of Honor. Orion P. Howe was a drummer with the 55th Illinois Infantry. Shortly after his fourteenth birthday he was awarded the Medal of Honor for heroic service during the siege of Vicksburg. Though "severely wounded, and exposed to heavy fire from the enemy, he persistently remained upon the field of battle until he had reported to General W. T. Sherman the necessity of supplying cartridges for the use of troops under command of Colonel Malmborg."[124]

William McGee, drummer with Company C, 33rd New Jersey Infantry, was another Medal of Honor winner. He was awarded the coveted prize in December 1864 for "bravery in action at Murfreesborough, Tennessee."[125]

Two field musicians from the 9th New York Infantry Regiment (Hawkins's Zouaves), received this same award. J. C. Julius Langbein, age fifteen, was awarded the medal for gallantry at Camden, North Carolina. The unit historian wrote that

Among the drummer boys who enlisted in the Regiment at its organization was J. C. Julius Langbein. Although but thirteen years of age he was bright, intelligent and manly, but so small in stature and so feminine in looks that he could easily have passed as a girl. He at once received the sobriquet of "Jennie" from all the men, which name clung to him during his term of service and for years afterwards. . . . [During the battle at Camden], the Rebel Yell began to change its tone a little and their fire slackened up. Jennie very deliberately straightened up and looked around surveying the situation. Saying to him pretty sharp, "sit down you damned little fool, you'll get your head knocked off," he looked at me with a kind of queer expression, hitched up his trousers and with the reply, "That's what I came here for," walked off towards the left where most of the firing was.[126]

The other regimental field musician was a bugler named Horn who at Antietam, "continued, until wounded, to sound the various calls of command with as much coolness and nonchalance as though on a parade ground instead of a battle ground."[127]

An unidentified drummer of the Stonewall Brigade was another young hero. Early in March 1862 the Stonewall Brigade anchored the left of a Confederate line that extended from Fredericksburg, Virginia, on the right to a point south of Winchester on the left. The Confederate commander, General Stonewall Jackson, had divided this army into three brigades: Garnett's five regiments, three regiments and a battalion under Colonel Jesse S. Burks, and two regiments under Colonel Samuel V. Fulkerson. Jackson's 4,500 men were opposed by Union forces under General Banks that numbered at least 25,000 men.

On 9 March these two armies faced each other south of Winchester. Jack-

son sought to do battle, but Banks was reluctant to take the challenge, preferring to wait until crusty General James Shields and his 9,000 troops could join
him. After eleven days of maneuvering that carried Jackson to far south, he
received word on 21 March that General Shields was returning to Winchester
from Strasburg, and he interpreted this to mean that General Banks was leaving the valley to move against Confederate forces under General Johnston at
Manassas.

On 23 March Jackson's army was back in position at Kernstown, four miles
south of Winchester. Intelligence incorrectly informed him that a rear guard of
only four Union regiments stood between the Confederates and Winchester.
He attacked Shields with two regiments. Jackson, now certain that he was
opposed by more than four regiments, ordered Garnett's Stonewall Brigade to
assist the two regiments pinned down behind the stone fence. As Garnett
approached, the Bluecoats veered left to concentrate their fire against him.

Time was on the Federal side. Several companies of the Stonewall Brigade
ran out of ammunition, and the massed Federals forced the Confederate line to
bend dangerously. Jackson ordered Fulkerson's two reserve regiments (under
command of Colonel Bill Harman) to reinforce Garnett's beleagured troops,
but it was too late. The Stonewall Brigade had already reached a crisis.
Opposed on the front and both flanks, Garnett sent a courier to tell Harman to
stop his troops and form a secondary line on which his men could retire. He
then ordered the Stonewall Brigade to fall back. Some of the men took this
retirement as a sign that the line had collapsed and the retirement became a
general route.

At this precise moment, General Stonewall Jackson rode forward and was
startled to see his men rushing headlong towards the rear. "Where are you
going?" he shouted angrily to a running soldier. The man replied that he was
out of ammunition and did not know where to find more. Jackson, his face
flushed and trembling with rage, leaned forward and snapped, "Then go back
and give them the bayonet!"

In the tumult Old Jack hailed a nearby drummer boy, led him to a slight rise, and
shouted, "Beat the rally! Beat the rally!" The small lad began a steady rhythm on his
drum, but his efforts were drowned out by the chaos now attendant to the battle. From
his position a frustrated Jackson could see the entire Confederate line melting away as
Federals swarmed all over the scarred and littered ridge.[128]

Not all of the young boys behaved gallantly, nor even managed to adjust to
army life. William Anderson, the Eighteenth Indiana's bugler, was among
those experiencing problems:

William . . . was an introvert who had difficulty adjusting to army life mentally and
physically, and his happiest moments were those when he was away from camp in a
nearby grove reading . . . by himself. A student from Indiana Asbury University, he was

disappointed that the other soldiers showed little interest in intellectual discussions and seemed to prefer trivial and obscene subjects. Ezra Lloyd, a classmate, was the only soldier who talked with Anderson about subjects that interested him.[129]

If Anderson was somewhat aloof and withdrawn, young Finegan entered into battles with a gusto. When the Yankees tried to invade Florida with Negro soldiers they were opposed at the battle of Olustee (Ocean Pond) by Florida troops under the command of General Joseph Finegan. Finegan's young son was assigned to his staff as musician and general "go-fer." "The boy, Irish-man-like, plunged into the thick of the fray. His anxious father equally exposed, said to him: 'Go to the rear Finegan, me B'ye, go to the rear me B'ye! Ye know ye are ye mither's darlin.' "[130]

Disease and death had little respect for youth. Joseph Whitney wrote to his beloved Clara on 28 December 1862.

The Ambulances are running till eleven o'clock in the night. In the morning there was only about 20 in the hospitals and by ten at night there were 170 there. It was rather mournful a sound to hear the rumble of the ambulances, but a funeral is getting to be rather common to me now. . . . There is a good many dying. . . . There was two buried yesterday from our regiment—the drum major, James Freeman and Leroy Demmons. It is very sickly here, but I am first rate now. . . . I feel that we are doing no good here, just a tax on the government. If I ever get home, I will not enlist to lay in camp for four or five months. The camp kills off more men than the battles does.[131]

Mrs. McGuire recorded one of the most touching accounts of the death of a drummer boy whom she had tried to nurse back to health.

Spent yesterday in the hospital by the bedside of Nathan Newton, our little Alabamian. I closed his eyes last night at ten o'clock, after an illness of six weeks. His body, at his own request, will be sent to his mother. Poor little boy. He was but fifteen, and should never have left his home. It was sad to pack his knapsack, with his little gray suit, and colored shirts, so neatly stitched by his mother, of whom he often spoke, calling to us in delirium, "Mother, mother," or "Mother, come here."

He so often called me mother that I said to him one day, when his mind was clear, "Nathan, do I look like your mother?" "No ma'am, not a bit; nobody is like my mother."[132]

In addition to sounding the calls musicians served as messengers, surgical assistants, or ambulance crews. This was a grizzly business. At the tables the surgeons whacked off limb after limb. The musicians hauled the severed extremities from the hospital tents and piled them into grotesque heaps for later burial.

Sam R. Watkins, Company H, 1st Tennessee Infantry, left the line during the battle for Atlanta and went into the city.

As John and I started to go back, we thought we would visit the hospital. Great God! I get sick today [1882] when I think of the agony, and suffering, the sickening stench and odor of dead and dying; of wounds and sloughing sores, caused by the deadly gangrene; of the groaning and wailing. I cannot describe it. I remember, I went in the rear of the building, and there I saw a pile of arms and legs, rotting and decomposing; and, although I saw thousands of horrifying scenes during the war, yet today I have no recollection in my whole life, of ever seeing anything that I remember with more horror than that pile of legs and arms that had been cut off our soldiers.[133]

George T. Ulmer, a drummer with the 17th Indiana Infantry, was frequently assigned to hospital duty. With experience, he somehow managed to accommodate himself to his surroundings but found "it was a horrible task at first. My duty was to hold a sponge or 'cone" of ether to the face of the soldier who was operated on, and to stand there and see the surgeons cut and saw legs and arms as if they were cutting up swine or sheep, was an ordeal I never wish to go through again. At intervals, when the pile became large, I was obliged to take a load of legs and arms and place them in a trench nearby for burial."[134]

Henry Campbell was often assigned to a burial detail. When the Confederates evacuated their works at Resaca and the Federals moved south in pursuit, Henry was left, as a part of a burial detail, to dispose of the dead. Riding out over the field where Hooker's men had started, he was appalled at the number of casualties. "I never seen as many dead rebels on any battlefield as there were here. The ground & hillside was fairly covered with them. They were so thick that I could hardly ride through them."[135]

Following the victory at Chattanooga on 27 November General William T. Sherman attempted to relieve the pressure on Burnside's troops. Grant had ordered General Elliott to eastern Tennessee to provide cavalry support for Burnside. The 1st Brigade, under Colonel Campbell, crossed the swift flood at Caney Fork without incident on 29 November. When the 2nd Indiana crossed on 13 December the horses in one boat became unmanageable, upsetting the boat and drowning twelve troopers.[136] Henry Campbell had been visiting the Indiana regiments, and he spent December bringing the wagons and teams across the stream and burying the drowned troopers. He wrote in his diary: "I shall never forget how mournful and sad the strains from the Band sounded in that lonesome, dreary woods."[137]

J. B. Holloway, drummer with Company D, 148th Pennsylvania Infantry, was frequently assigned to the surgical tables. "I often thought that no one could place his finger on any part of the human body, but what I could say, 'I saw a man wounded there.' The largest flesh wound I saw was a man at the battle of Totopotomoy Creek. This man was shot through the buttocks with a shell or some large missile, and the flesh was laid open as if some one had plowed a furrow through it. Your two hands would not have covered the wound."[138]

Other nonmusical duties included hauling wood, corduroying roads, commanding a section of a wagon train, making headboards for graves, feeding the horses, performing picket and guard duty, cutting wood, and helping the cooks.

Nevertheless, the primary function of the musicians was musical. They announced the breaking of camp. "Before daybreak the tramp of horses reminded us that our foragers were sallying forth. The red light from countless campfires melted away as the dawn stole over the horizon. . . . while the smoke from burning pine-knots befogged the chilly morning air. Then the bugles broke the impressive stillness, and the roll of the drums was heard on all sides. Soon the scene was alive with blue coats and the hubub of roll-calling, cooking, the running for water to the nearest spring."[140]

They sounded the *general* when battle seemed imminent, which created great excitement in the camps. The men sorted through their keepsakes, discarding all but the most precious, and tried to fix their thoughts on the immediate present rather than the doubtful future. "One man in Company C [of the 16th Maine Regiment] dug a grave, and, piling in his little treasures, read service over them, and preached a sermon from the text, 'And Ephraim fed upon the east wind three days and hungered not.' A neat headboard marked the resting place of his jewels. On his return from the mud march, the grave was opened, and the numerous corpses resurrected without ceremony."[141]

Hamlin Coe thought his regiment a hotbed of rumor, but found "none that [could] be relied upon. . . . The bugle and drums sound throughout the valley, and the commotion and excitement are great . . . it will not be long before we have a fight here. The general assault must be made soon, and we shall have to charge John's Mountain which will be a greater task than it was to scale Lookout."[142]

McHenry Howard, with the 1st Maryland Regiment, recognized that the sounding of the *general* announced the impending doom of battle as he rose from his bedroll on 12 July 1863.

Slept soundly. Yankee drums were distinctly heard a while ago and more recently cannon and musketry on picket line—battle imminent.

July 13. Picket firing all day yesterday—in afternoon spent more than an hour on the picket line—had a full view of half a mile of enemy's line—moving down to our right—then drums beating and bands playing. . . . Have the benefit of their music and drums.[143]

Major Abner R. Small of the 16th Maine felt the same uneasiness as his unit prepared for Fredericksburg.

No, it could not be true; yet there lay the order, and again I read, "Headquarters, Army of the Potomac. . . . prepare for immediate action." . . . The quietness of the camp was oppressive for about five minutes. Then I heard a lone, loud yell, and then from all the men a wild whooping, and then cheer after cheer. Then there was almost silence, and down the wind came the notes of a bugle at corps headquarters. Before the last note died away, the call was repeated by the division bugler, and again repeated yet nearer at brigade headquarters, and then it was sounded clear and full, in the street outside my tent. It was the "General," the warning to pack up. I watched our boys cheerfully dismantle their homes, and separate and fold up their portable canvas houses; choose from their little treasures what lay nearest to their hearts, and destroy what remained "for want of transportation;" pack their loads and make ready to march.

"Fall in, Sixteenth!"[144]

The bugler of the 1st Wisconsin didn't limit his performances to the bivouac areas. He played on the field of battle. The 1st Wisconsin, 2nd Indiana, and 7th Kentucky Regiments were formed in front of Fort Tyler, a strong earthwork about thirty-five yards square, surrounded by a ditch twelve-feet wide and ten-feet deep. The fort was defended by two hundred sixty-five Confederates and several field pieces. The Yankee attackers "built portable bridges with lumber from nearby houses, and when the bugler sounded the charge, the three regiments rushed forward, under a scathing fire, threw their makeshift bridges across the ditch, and raced to see who would be first into the fort. The race was won by Sergeant Edward Farel of the Wisconsin Regiment."[145]

Field musicians were a significant part of the army's communications system, aiding commanders in the control of their men. Sergeant Austin Stearns, Company K, 13th Massachusetts Infantry, was proud of the professional manner in which his unit responded to these musical signals. At Martinsburg, he wrote: "Captain Hovey was as good as his word. He drilled us every day, and took great pains to go into all the details of the drill. . . . How well I remember now the drills we used to have in the field. . . . drilling the skirmish drill by the sound of the bugle. No other company could do it as well as K Company, thanks to Captain Hovey."[146]

The young field musicians were not the only ones who could behave like boys. Between battles the men sought out whatever diversions were available. Organized snowball fights were popular. John Casler described what must have been one of the most complex snowball fights ever fought, the entire battle being controlled by the calls of the field musicians.

Considerable snow fell that winter, and every time it snowed the soldiers would turn out and have sno-ball battles. One day our division challenged Rodes' Division to battle in a large field. . . . The battle raged with various success until towards evening, when a great many of our division got tired of it and went to camp. When Rodes' men saw our line weakened [they] made a charge and ran us into our quarters. It looked rather bad for us . . . so some of the boys went to General Walker and got him to . . . take command.

It was fun for Walker, so he mounted his horse, collected his staff, and sent conscript Officers all over camp and forced the men out. We had signal corps at work, took our colors out in line, had the drummers and fifers beat the long roll, had couriers carrying dispatches and everything done like in a regular engagement with the enemy.

When General Walker got everything in readiness and the line formed, he ordered us to charge up close to Rodes' men and then wheel and fall back, so as to draw them after us and away from the piles of snowballs they had made. We did so and the plan worked successfully. At the same time the Louisiana Brigade slipped around through the woods and struck them on the left flank. . . . and the route was complete. We ran them into their camps and through them. . . . We captured several stands of colors, but we had lost several in the earlier part of the fight. Officers would be captured and pulled off their horses and washed in the snow. . . . After the fight was over we went out with a flag of truce and exchanged prisoners. . . .

It was probably the greatest snow ball battle ever fought, and showed that "men are but children of larger growth."[147]

Sam Watkins had participated in a number of these contests which he described as "general knock down and drag out affair[s]."

Occasionally the soldiers would engage in a snow ball battle, in which generals, colonels, captains and privates all took part. They would usually divide off into two grand divisions, one line naturally becoming the attacking party, and the other the defensive. The snow balls would begin to fly hither and thither, with an occasional knock down, and sometimes an ugly wound, where some mean fellow had enclosed a rock in his snow ball. It was fun while it lasted, but after it was over the soldiers were wet, cold and uncomfortable. I have seen charges and attacks and routes and stampedes, etc., but before the thing was over, one side did not know one from the other.[148]

If the field musicians entered into these mock battles with glee, some of their other duties were not fit for children and were sobering for even the most battle-hardened veteran. One duty, drumming-out, involved the ceremonial disgrace of individuals—and sometimes their ritualized death. When a soldier could not adjust to army life, or was found to be a petty thief, he was drummed from the service. The more serious crime of desertion was punished by death before a firing squad. These two ceremonies were carried out in a way to discourage others from committing the same offenses. Both Henry Campbell and John Rippetoe witnessed the drumming out of a hard-looking fellow from the 75th Indiana Regiment. " 'His head was shaved and then branded on the right cheek with a red hot iron in the shape of the letter D.' Then the brigade was assembled and the culprit was marched through the lines 'with eight bayonets after him. . . . He was a bad looking spectacle after his head was shaved, how bad I should hate to be in his place,' Campbell wrote, 'He can never do any good where he is known but the laws must be enforced. . . . What would life be worth to a man disgraced in this way?' "[149]

The 1st Tennessee Regiment provided an added dimension of cruelty to the drumming-out. Sam Watkins described the punishment meted out in his regiment in 1863:

When some miserable wretch was to be whipped and branded for being absent ten days without leave, we had to see him kneel down and have his head shaved smooth and slick as a peeled onion, and then stripped to the naked skin. Then a strapping fellow with a big rawhide would make the blood flow and spurt at every lick, the wretch begging and howling like a hound, then he was branded with a red hot iron with the letter D on both hips, when he was marched through the army to the music of the "Rogue's March." It was enough![150]

Until early in the war, "the strapping fellow with a rawhide" was most likely to be a field musician. Just why the musicians were singled out for this cruelty is not clear, but musicians commonly administered punishments in the regular army, until midway through the first year of the Civil War when the practice was abandoned. Augustus Meyers was court-martialed for insubordination when he refused to take his turn with the whip.

Some soldiers who had deserted were recaptured and tried by general court-martial, which sentenced them to receive thirty-nine lashes on their bare backs, laid on with a rawhide. . . . The officer of the day read the sentence and called out the name of one of the deserters. . . . He was divested of his jacket and shirt, his wrists were bound with cords. His arms were pulled up over his head and tied to the top [of a post] while his feet were spread apart and secured to the bottom of the triangle. It had always been the custom in the army for flogging to be administered by one of the musicians. Why they were selected to do it, I never learned. When all was ready the officer of the day called one of the older boys from the ranks. He was handed the rawhide and told by the officer to strike the prisoner hard from the shoulders to the loins.
At first the blows were moderate, but increased under the officer's threats until each blow left a dark red mark and then began to cut the skin until blood flowed. . . . When the thirty-ninth blow had been struck, the officer who had kept count cried "Halt." The victim was untied. . . . and was dragged towards the guardhouse.
The second prisoner was then led forward and prepared. . . . The officer of the day turned about to select another musician to strike the blows. His glance rested on me for an instant but he passed me by and called out another by name, for which I was thankful.
When the last prisoner was ready the officer of the day called out my name; but I stood still and shook my head. He then preemptorily [sic] called me a second time, to which I replied, "I refuse." He ordered me to be placed in charge of the guard, and called on my drummer to execute the sentence which my refusal to act had delayed for a few minutes. . . . I was tried by court-martial. . . . and. . . . my sentence was promulgated. I was to be confined in the guard house for thirty days, ten of them in solitary confinement on a diet of bread and water, the remainder at hard labor, and to forfeit one month's pay. My captain tried to have my sentence commuted, but it was so glaring a refusal to obey orders. . . . that he was unsuccessful.[151]

The drummers and fifers most often provided the music for these occasions, although a band was sometimes used instead. The 1st Kentucky Cavalry, a mounted unit without a band, provided an interesting musical variation to the standard drumming-out ceremony. General Burnside had issued strict orders against marauding or committing any fraud on the downtrodden loyal citizens of eastern Tennessee. One 1st Kentucky Cavalryman bought a lot of tobacco for resale to his comrades, but paid for it in counterfeit money. "Burnside [ordered him] drummed out of the service. There being no drums belonging to the mounted forces, all the bugles in the command were summoned on duty, and he was bugled or blown out of the service."[152]

Drumming-out continued to the very end of the war. Joseph Whitney was in Nashville at the time of President Lincoln's assassination when he wrote: "A man in our brigade said he was glad that the President was killed. General Kimball ordered his head shaved and him drummed the length of the division to the tune of the rogue's march. There was quite a number of persons shot in Nashville for the same offense."[153]

If drumming-out ceremonies were grim affairs, they paled to nothingness when compared to the 240 executions ordered during the course of the war. These unfortunate soldiers were generally dispatched to their Maker one at a time, but John Casler recorded a mass execution for desertion. Shortly after he arrived at Camp Montpelier thirty men of the 1st and 3rd North Carolina Regiments deserted, taking their weapons with them. Some were killed as they attempted to cross the James River and ten were captured. The ten were court-martialed in Richmond, sentenced to death by a firing squad, and returned to their regiments for execution.

We planted ten posts in the ground, about three feet high and about fifty feet apart, all in line, boring a hole in each post near the top, and putting in a cross-piece. We dug one large grave in the edge of the woods, large enough to hold the ten coffins.

When everything was completed . . . the division was formed in a hollow square around the field, except the side the posts were on. The prisoners were then brought from the guard-house. . . . As the column entered the field they were headed by the fifers and drummers—the drums being muffled—playing the death march. They had some distance to march before arriving at the place of execution, and I noticed that they kept step and marched as precisely as if they were on drill. . . .

They were halted and the Chaplain talked to and prayed with them. Then an officer took each man, conducted him to his post, placed him on his knees, with his back to the post and his arms hooked over the crosspiece, and his hands tied together in front of his body, and then blindfolded him.

One hundred and fifty men composed the detail for the execution of the prisoners. . . . Ten marched out in front of each prisoner—making one hundred in all in the front line. . . . In the rear of each ten men there were five more soldiers with loaded guns, as a reserve to finish the execution should any of the condemned men not be killed at the first fire. At the command "Ready! Aim! Fire!" one volley was heard, all the guns in the front rank being discharged. . . . A Surgeon. . . . found two of them not dead, [then] . . . the reserve guard stepped out and fired again. When they were pronounced dead the division was marched by them in two ranks, in order that all might see them. . . . We then buried them.[154]

Not all men were killed in battle or by a firing squad. Infinitely larger numbers succumbed to disease. The 16th Maine had been issued new clothing and put into shelters prior to the battle of Fredericksburg. These improvements provided a buoyancy of spirits, but there was a darker side to their condition. Many were on the sick list and everyone knew that many would fail to return from the hospital. "In the first week in December three deaths occurred in camp; three times the remains of a soldier were borne to a grave soon to be grown over with bushes and forgotten. Those burials of men from the ranks are among the saddest that I recall," wrote Major Abner Small. "The slow march of the escort, with arms reversed, muffled drum, and piercing fife; the volleys crashing over the grave; the lively tune and the march in quick time back to camp; soon over, long remembered. We tried not to think of it, then."[155]

It was impossible for Billy Yank or Johnny Reb to escape the music of the field musicians. Their performances even extended into the prisons. When Decimus et Ultimus Barziza arrived at Sandusky, Ohio, on 3 September 1863 as a prisoner of the Union army, he and his fellow prisoners were "honored by a great turn-out of men, women and children. About twenty kettle-drums, beat by little boys, and fifes and flags in profusion, attended the jubilation of the conquerers."[156]

The music followed the captured men into the prison compounds. John Casler was imprisoned at Fort McHenry, Maryland, near the end of the war. Prison was a monotonous place. The incarcerated men invented activities to break their dull routine. They picked lice from their bodies, and threw them into anthills, betting on the results of the pitched battles that ensued. "Sometimes the aunts [sic] would drag the louse off, but often times a big louse would stand them off."[157] Music provided a welcome diversion for Casler and his fellow inmates. "We had a violin in prison and a fifer with his fife, and would have dances at night, and often had dress parade with the fife and an old camp kettle for a drum, and read out a long string of orders for the next day, and all such amusements to keep up our spirits and relieve the monotony of prison life. Rats were ready sale. The prisoners would cook and eat them."[158]

Although field musicians were the butts of many barbed judgments from their comrades, the soldiers—and even the civilians—were really quite proud of these young men. Alfred Townsend, a reporter with a cavalry unit near Hanover Court House, admitted that the bugle was his favorite military instrument.

[The Colonel shouted], "Attention! Mount!" The riders sprang to their seats; the bugles blew a lively strain; the horses pricked up their ears; and the long array moved briskly forward. . . .

If any branch of the military service is feverish, adventurous, and exciting, it is that of the cavalry. One's heart beats as fast as the hoof-falls; there is no music like the winding of the bugle, and no monotone so full of meaning as the clink of sabres rising and falling with the dashing pace. . . . We seem to be watching a joust of tournaments or following fierce Saladins and Crusaders again.[159]

Musicians were regarded as both soldiers and men, despite their often tender age, and few allowances were made for them. General Hill endorsed one Confederate bugler's request for furlough with the terse refusal: "Disapproved—shooters before tooters."[160]

The historian of the 14th New Hampshire Infantry summed up the feelings of most troopers when he wrote of his favorite drummer. "Sanborn beat the long roll as no one else could beat it, his arms playing all about him like forked lightning, his sticks rattling down upon the drum head like half a dozen magnificent hailstorms each combination of sounds welling up and flying off like . . . distant peals of thunder with no room for reverberation between the claps. The genial old drummer, gone to his rest, never dreamed of the stir he made in the bosoms of his comrades. His dinner call is sounding still."[161]

The youngest field musicians were most often honored by the romantic balladeers and composers of the war. "The Drummer Boy of Shiloh," "Little Major," and "Can I Go, Dearest Mother" are but a few of the popular songs that idolized the gallantry and valor of the boy musicians. Few were genuine heroes, the bards notwithstanding. Most were simply young boys torn from their families and loved ones by the tides of their time. They learned to cope with separation, discomfort, pain, and death when very young. They simply did their duty.

Making a living was a demanding undertaking in the nineteenth century, and male adolescence ended at an early age. Unlike today, the pursuit of education did not keep young men and women from the vicissitudes of the real world. A seventeen-year-old male was expected to pull his own weight, and unmarried young ladies of sixteen were considered to be in their early years of spinsterhood.

Even so, how so many really young boys could adjust to army life and serve honorably on the battlefield as well remains one of the mysteries of the Civil War. Although romanticized and lionized by the tunesmiths of their time, most of these lads must have crawled into their straw beds or rolled themselves in a blanket after a day of incalculable horror and pondered the text of still another drummer-boy song—"If I Sleep, Will Mother Come?"

NOTES

1. Unidentified newspaper clipping, records of the Fifth Virginia Infantry, Virginia Archives, as cited by James I. Robertson, *The Stonewall Brigade* (Baton Rouge, La.: Louisiana State University Press, 1963), pp. 12–13. *See also* Ella Lonn, *Foreigners in the Confederacy* (Chapel Hill: University of North Carolina Press, 1940), pp. 2, 16.

2. Frank R. Rossiter, *Charles Ives and His America* (New York: Liveright, 1957), p. 12. For the traditional story about the incident with General Grant, *see* "Colonel Wildman Reminiscences," *Danbury Evening Times*, 2 August 1932. A copy of the article is in scrapbook no. 3, p. 145 of the Ives Collection. George E. Ives,

Notebook 5 (UAlv) p. 34 of the Ives Collection contains his remark about his servitude. Cowell and other biographers of Charles Ives also refer to this incident.

3. For Haskell's military record *see* John Cheeves Haskell, *The Haskell Memoirs*, ed. Gilbert E. Govan and James W. Livingood (New York: G. P. Putnam's Sons, 1960), p. 80. For the observations on Bacon and Blackmer *see* Austin C. Stearns, *Three Years with Company K* (Cranbury, N.J.: Associated University Press, 1976), p. 12.

4. Bell Irvin Wiley and Herst D. Milhollen, *They Who Fought Here* (New York: MacMillan Co., 1959), p. 7.

5. Elizabeth C. Benton, "When Johnny Marched Off to War," *Selmer Bandwagon* 14, no. 5 (December 1966): 1.

6. U.S. Department of War, *General Orders*, p. 387, National Archives, Washington, D.C.

7. Augustus Meyers, *Ten Years in the Ranks, U.S. Army* (New York: Stirling Press, 1914), pp. 1–17. The discussion of the training school that follows represents a condensation of events recorded by Meyers.

8. George Bruce and Daniel Emmett, *The Drummers and Fifers Guide* (New York: Firth and Pond Co., 1862), preface.

9. Ibid.

10. *New York Times*, 18 February 1869, p. 7.

11. *New York Times*, 17 October 1911, p. 3; 25 October 1911, p. 12.

12. Bruce and Emmett, *Drummers Guide*, p. 14.

13. Ibid., p. 41.

14. Francis H. Buffum, et al., *A Memorial of the Great Rebellion . . . the Fourteenth Regiment New Hampshire Volunteers* (Boston: Franklin Press; Rand, Avery & Co., 1882), pp. 300–01.

15. Ibid.

16. Abner Ralph Small, *The Sixteenth Maine Regiment in the War of the Rebellion* (Portland, Me.: B. Thurston & Co., 1886), pp. 95–96.

17. Buffum, *Fourteenth New Hampshire*, p. 302.

18. Ibid.

19. Ibid., pp. 130–32, 303.

20. Ibid., pp. 302–03.

21. Delavan S. Miller, *Drum Taps in Dixie, Memories of a Drummer Boy, 1861–1865* (Watertown, N.Y.: Hungerford Holbrook Co., 1905), pp. 232–33.

22. Emory Upton, *Infantry Tactics*, rev. ed. (Washington, D.C.: Department of the Army, 1880), Appendix no. 1.

23. John J. Pullen, *The Twentieth Maine* (Philadelphia and New York: J. B. Lippincott Co., 1957), pp. 20–21.

24. Buffum, *Fourteenth New Hampshire*, p. 303.

25. Pullen, *Twentieth Maine*, p. 21.

26. Miller, *Drum Taps*, pp. 87–88.

27. Ibid., pp. 193–94.

28. Ibid., pp. 23–24.

29. Enos B. Vail, *Reminiscences of a Boy in the Civil War* (Brooklyn, N.Y.: privately printed, 1915), p. 94.

30. Edwin B. Houghton, *The Campaigns of the Seventeenth Maine* (Portland,

Me.: privately printed, 1866), p. 102.

31. George Dallas Mosgrove, *Kentucky Cavaliers in Dixie: Reminiscences of a Confederate Cavalryman*, ed. Bell Irvin Wiley (Jackson, Tenn.: McCowat-Mercer Press, 1957), p. 83.

32. Ibid.

33. Ibid.

34. J. W. Muffly, *The Story of Our Regiment: A History of the 148th Pennsylvania Vols* (Des Moines, Iowa: Kenyon Printing & Mfg. Co., 1904), pp. 308–311.

35. B. A. Botkin, *A Civil War Treasury of Tales, Legends, and Folklore* (New York: Random House, 1960), pp. 64–65.

36. John W. Rowell, *Yankee Artillery men...Eli Lilly's Indiana Battery* (Knoxville, Tenn.: University of Tennessee Press, 1975), p. 19. William H. Anderson's journal is in the archives of DePauw University and Indiana Methodism, Greencastle, Indiana. John W. Rowell has used this journal and the letters and diaries of sixteen other men of Eli Lilly's Indiana Battery to reconstruct the history of this unit's service.

37. Ibid., pp. 19–20.

38. Ibid., Appendix B: "1862 Volunteer Enlisted Men," compiled by Rowell from muster rolls of the 18th Indiana Battery, p. 281.

39. Mosgrove, *Kentucky Cavaliers*, p. 182.

40. Ibid., p. 194.

41. Ibid., pp. 224–25.

42. Pullen, *Twentieth Maine*, p. 2.

43. Theodore Reichardt, *Diary of Battery A, First Regiment Rhode Island Light Artillery* (Providence, R.I.: privately printed, 1865), p. 54 and appendix.

44. George Alfred Townsend, *Rustics in Rebellion* (1866; reprint ed., Chapel Hill: North Carolina University Press, 1950), p. 235.

45. Henry Campbell, "The War in Kentucky-Tennessee As Seen by a Teen-Aged Bugler," *Civil War Times Illustrated* 2, no. 7 (November 1963): 27. The Campbell journal entitled "Four Years in the Saddle" and his scrapbook are in the Wabash College Archives, Crawfordsville, Indiana. A truncated form of his journal was published in *Civil War Times Illustrated* 2, no. 7 (November 1963): 26–29; 2, no. 9 (January 1964): 42–45; 3, no. 2 (May 1964): 34–37; 3, no. 5 (August 1964): 46–48; 3, no. 6 (October 1964): 46–48; 3, no. 9 (January 1965): 36–39 (hereafter cited Campbell, *CWTI*). Campbell's journal is a primary source for Rowell's *Yankee Artillerymen*. Other Campbell letters can be found in Catherine Merrill, *The Soldiers of Indiana in the War for the Union*, 2 vols. (Indianapolis: Merrill & Co., 1866, 1869).

46. Campbell, *CWTI* 2, no. 7 (November 1963): 27.

47. Ibid., p. 28.

48. H. P. Moyer, *History of the Seventeenth Regiment Pennsylvania Volunteer Cavalry...*(Lebanon, Pa.: Sowers Printing Co., 1911), pp. 279–81.

49. Daniel B. Harris, "Personal Diary of Daniel B. Harris, Company K, Twelfth New Jersey Volunteers, December 10, 1862 to July 4, 1863." (Washington, D. C.: Smithsonian Institution). William Bufkin kindly provided a typecopy of this diary.

50. Edwin D. Bennett, *Musket and Sword, Or the Camp March and Firing Line in the Army of the Potomac* (Boston: Coburn Publishing Co., 1900), p. 13.

51. S. M. P. Fox, "Story of the 7th Kansas," *Kansas Historical Society Transactions* 7 (1902–1903): 47.

52. Muffly, *148th Pennsylvania*, pp. 317–28.

53. Meyers, *Ten Years in the Ranks*, pp. 26–27.

54. Muffly, *148th Pennsylvania*, pp. 316–17.

55. Eli R. Pickett to his wife, 29 December 1862. Minnesota Historical Society, St. Paul, Minn.

56. Susie King Taylor, *Reminiscences of My Life in Camp* (New York: Arno Press; New York Times, 1902), p. 36.

57. Meyers, *Ten Years in the Ranks*, p. 43.

58. Bell Irvin Wiley, *The Life of Billy Yank* (Indianapolis: Bobbs-Merrill Co., 1952), p. 247.

59. George T. Ulmer, *Adventures and Reminiscences of a Volunteer: or, A Drummer Boy from Maine* (Chicago: published by the author, 1892), pp. 57–58. Several young drummer boys lost their limbs when they turned implements of death into toys. Alfred Bellard was wounded in the leg at Chancellorsville and made his way to a field hospital for treatment. While he was there, "one drummer boy was brought in to be operated upon, who had both hands shattered by the explosion of a gun barrel. He had picked up a gun barrel on the field, and was holding it in the fire to have a little fun, when it exploded. His hands were shattered all to pieces, saving nothing but a thumb on one hand, and a thumb and finger on the other. When the doctors had him on the table and under the influence of cloraform, they picked out the pieces of bone with their fingers." *See* Alfred Bellard, *Gone for a Soldier*, p. 219.

60. Ulmer, *A Drummer Boy from Maine*, pp. 67–68.

61. John McElroy, *This Was Andersonville*. Reprint, ed. Roy Meredith (New York: Crown Publishers, Bonanza Books, 1957), pp. 118–19.

62. Robert J. Snetsinger, ed., *Kiss Clara for Me: The Story of Joseph Whitney and His Family*, (State College, Pa.: Carnation Press, 1969), p. 118.

63. Ibid., p. 51.

64. Ibid., p. 33.

65. Francis Trevelyn Miller, ed., *Photographic History of the Civil War*, 10 vols. (New York: Review of Reviews Co., 1911), 2:195.

66. Wiley, *Billy Yank*, p. 296.

67. Bell Irvin Wiley, *The Life of Johnny Reb* (Indianapolis: Bobbs-Merrill Co., 1943), pp. 180–85 and Wiley, *Billy Yank*, p. 274. Wiley discusses this religious revival extensively in both of these works.

68. Campbell, *CWTI*, 3, no. 9 (January 1965): 38. *See also* Rowell, *Yankee Artillerymen*, pp. 185–86.

69. Arthur H. DeRosier, Jr., ed., *Through the South with a Union Soldier* (Johnson City, Tenn.: East Tennessee State University Research Advisory Council, 1969), pp. 185–86.

70. Charles William Bardeen, *A Little Fifer's War Diary* (Syracuse, N.Y.: C. W. Bardeen, 1910), pp. 17–18.

71. Ibid.

72. Ibid.

73. Ibid., p. 19.

74. Ibid., p. 20.

75. Ibid.

76. Ibid., p. 160.

77. Ibid., p. 265.

78. Ibid., p. 275.

79. Ibid.

80. Ibid.

81. Ibid.

82. Ibid., p. 295.

83. Ibid., p. 290.

84. Ibid., p. 294.

85. Ibid.

86. Ibid., p. 314.

87. Ibid.

88. Ibid., p. 263

89. Ibid.

90. Ibid.

91. Ibid.

92. Ibid., p. 66. Young Bardeen returned home after the war and matured into one of Syracuse, New York's, outstanding citizens. He graduated from Lawrence Academy in Groton, Massachusetts, in 1865, and received a degree from Yale University four years later. He served for a number of years as editor of the *School Bulletin*, published by Columbia University. His life history is outlined in *Who's Who in America* beginning with the 1909 edition. Another autobiography is contained in *Educational Review* (vol. 22, 1869, pp. 28–39). He was honored by Nicholas Murray Butler, President of Columbia University, in an article entitled "My Schools and Schoolmasters," in the *Educational Review*. He was included in *Nutting Genealogy*, published by the Reverend Dr. Nutting in Syracuse in 1908, and was listed as an outstanding citizen of Syracuse and Onondaga Counties by the members of the county boards.

93. Meyers, *Ten Years in the Ranks*, p. 122.

94. Campbell, *CWTI* 2, no. 7 (November 1963): p. 26.

95. Campbell, *CWTI* 3, no. 2 (May 1964): p. 34.

96. Rowell, *Yankee Artillerymen*, p. 139.

97. Campbell, *CWTI* 2, no. 7 (November 1963): p. 28.

98. Ibid.

99. Rowell, *Yankee Artillerymen*, p. 61.

100. Bardeen, *A Little Fifer's War Diary*, pp. 127–28.

101. Campbell, *CWTI* 3, no. 2 (May 1964): p. 35.

102. Campbell, *CWTI* 2, no. 9 (January 1964): p. 44.

103. Campbell, *CWTI* 3, no. 6 (October 1964): p. 48.

104. Campbell, *CWTI* 3, no. 9 (January 1965): p. 39. Campbell was in the hardware business for a few years, and then took over his father's dry goods store, in partnership with his brother Stephen. He became vice-president of the First National Bank eighteen years later, and remained in that position for the rest of his life. After a prolonged illness, Henry died on 22 July 1915 at age 71. See also Rowell, *Yankee Artillerymen*, p. 272.

105. Wiley, *Billy Yank*, p. 297.

106. Ibid.

107. *Who Was Who in America*, vol. 1 (Chicago: A. N. Marquis Co., 1942), pp. 230–31.

108. Wiley, *Billy Yank*, p. 298.

109. *Who Was Who in America*, vol. 1, pp. 230–31. Other accounts of Clem are found in Benjamen F. Taylor, *Pictures of Life in Camp and Field* (Chicago: S. C. Griggs and Co., 1875), pp. 163–69; and B. A. Botkin, *A Civil War Treasury*, p. 338. *See also* "From Nursery to Battlefield," *Outlook Magazine* 107 (1914): 546–47.

110. U.S. Department of War, *Official Records of the War of the Rebellion* ser. 1, vol. 16, pt. 1 (Washington, D.C.: Government Printing Office, 1898), p. 1086.

111. John O. Casler, *Four Years in the Stonewall Brigade* (2d ed. 1906; reprint ed., Marietta, Ga.: Continental Book Co., 1951), p. 294.

112. Ibid., p. 295.

113. McHenry Howard, *Recollections of a Maryland Confederate Soldier* (1914; reprint ed., Dayton, Ohio: Morningside Bookshop, 1975), p. 65.

114. Ibid., p. 66–67.

115. Robertson, *The Stonewall Brigade*, pp. 14–15.

116. Robert Patrick, *Reluctant Rebel, . . .Secret Diary*, ed. F. Jay Taylor (Baton Rouge, La.: Louisiana State University Press, 1959), pp. 257–61.

117. Ibid., p. 46.

118. Ibid., p. 198.

119. Ibid., p. 258.

120. Ibid., p. 189–90.

121. Ibid., p. 261.

122. Kate Cummings, *Kate: The Journal of a Confederate Nurse* (1866; reprint ed., ed. Richard Barksdale Harwell, Baton Rouge, La.: Louisiana State University Press, 1959), p. 31.

123. Mosgrove, *Kentucky Cavaliers*, p. 65.

124. U.S. Department of War, *Official Records*, ser. 1, vol. 38, pt. 1, pp. 3, 192.

125. U.S. Department of War, *Official Records*, ser. 1, vol. 45, pt. 1, ,p. 645–46.

126. Matthew J. Graham, *The Ninth Regiment New York Volunteers* (New York: P. Coby & Co., 1900), p. 274. I am indebted to Edward Knob for the loan of this volume autographed by his grandfather who served with the regiment.

127. Ibid., p. 321.

128. Robertson, *The Stonewall Brigade*, p. 75.

129. Rowell, *Yankee Artillerymen*, p. 19.

130. James Cooper Nisbet, *4 Years on the Firing Line* (1914; reprint ed., ed. Bell Irvin Wiley, Jackson, Tenn.: McCowat-Mercer Press, 1963), p. 140.

131. Snetsinger, ed., *Kiss Clara for Me*, pp. 59–60.

132. Matthew Page Andrews, ed., *The Women of the South in War Times*, "Diary of Mrs. McGuire" (Baltimore: Norman Remington Co., 1920), pp. 160–61.

133. Samuel R. Watkins, *Co. Aytch*, ed. Roy P. Basler (1952; reprint ed., New York: Crowell Collier Publishing Co., 1970), p. 201.

134. Ulmer, *A Drummer Boy from Maine*, p. 59.

135. Campbell, *CWTI* 3, no. 9 (January 1965): 38.

136. U.S., Department of War, *Official Records*, ser. 1, vol. 31, pt. 3, p. 320.

137. Campbell, *CWTI* 3, no. 6 (October 1964): 46.

138. Muffly, *148th Pennsylvania*, p. 333.

139. Townsend, *Rustics in Rebellion*, p. 10.

140. Henry Steele Commager, *The Blue and the Gray* (Indianapolis: Bobbs-Merrill Co., 1950), p. 960.

141. Small, *Sixteenth Maine Regiment*, p. 90.

142. Hamlin Alexander Coe, *Mine Eyes Have Seen the Glory*, ed. David Coe (Cranbury, N.J.: Associated University Presses, 1975), pp. 128–29.

143. Howard, *Recollections of a Confederate*, p. 216.

144. Abner Ralph Small, *The Road to Richmond*, ed. Harold Adams Small (Berkeley, Calif.: University of California Press, 1939), pp. 159–60.

145. U.S. Department of War, *Official Records,* ser. 1, vol. 44, pt. 1, pp. 428–29.

146. Austen C. Stearns, *Three Years with Company K* (Cranbury, N.J.: Associated University Presses, 1976), pp. 51–52.

147. Casler, *Four Years in the Stonewall Brigade*, pp. 203–04.

148. Watkins, *Co. Aytch*, p. 130.

149. Rowell, *Yankee Artillerymen*, p. 19.

150. Watkins, *Co. Aytch*, p. 48.

151. Meyers, *Ten Years in the Ranks*, pp. 130–32.

152. E. Tarrant, *The Wild Riders of the First Kentucky Cavalry* (1894; reprint ed., Lexington, Ky.: Henry Clay Press, 1969), p. 222.

153. Snetsinger, ed., *Kiss Clara for Me*, p. 159.

154. Casler, *Four Years in the Stonewall Brigade*, pp. 189–90.

155. Small, *The Road to Richmond*, pp. 58–59.

156. Decimus et Ultimus Barziza, *Adventures of a Prisoner of War, 1863–1865* (1865; reprint ed., ed. R. Henderson Shuffler, Austin, Tex.: University of Texas Press, 1964), p. 74.

157. Casler, *Four Years in the Stonewall Brigade*, p. 283.

158. Ibid.

159. Townsend, *Rustics in Rebellion*, p. 65.

160. B. A. Botkin, *Civil War Treasury*, p. 596.

161. Buffum, *Fourteenth New Hampshire*, p. 302.

Plate 1. The band of the 3rd New Hampshire Regiment at Hiltonhead, South Carolina, during the summer of 1862. The instrumentation of the group is unusual for its inclusion of an Eb clarinet (center) and Bb clarinet (2nd from the left). The bandmaster (sixth from the left) is a commissioned officer. The young lad astraddle the snare drum is probably a Field Musician rather than a Bandsman. (Photo H-620-M-11 courtesy of the National Archives.)

Plate 2. The band of the 2nd Rhode Island Infantry Regiment photographed outside of Washington, D.C., during the winter of 1861–1862. The troop unit in the rear appears to be practicing stream fording. There is no maneuver contained in the books on tactics that would require the soldiers to hoist their weapons above their heads. (Photo H-620-6-33 courtesy of the National Archives.)

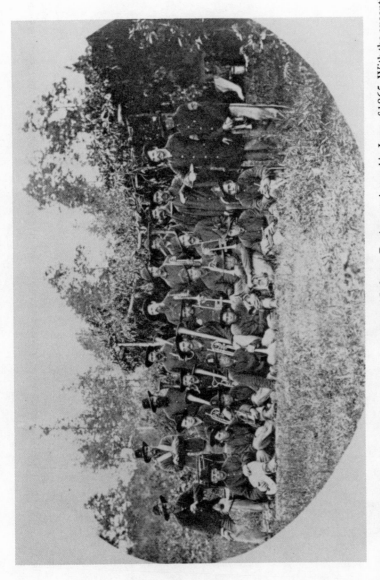

Plate 3. The band and field musicians of the 56th Mississippi Infantry Regiment pictured in June of 1865. With the exception of the cymbal player at the left, the men seated in the front row are the field musicians from the various companies of the regiment. The insignia on their hats indicate that they served with Companies "A" through "H". The sergeant at the right is the regimental bugler. The use of bugles by the field music of an infantry regiment is unusual. (Photo H-620-M-16 courtesy of the National Archives.)

Plate 4. The United States Naval Academy Hospital Band. A number of large army hospitals maintained their own musical establishments for the entertainment of the sick and wounded. (Photo courtesy of Mr. Fred Benkovic.)

Plate 5. This pseudo-Zouave unit is the East Germantown Band which served with the 12th Indiana Regiment. From left to right, the members are Jacob Harnish, cymbals; Daniel Condo, tuba; Jacob Jolliff, baritone; Amos Bear, bass drum; Jacob Spence, cornet and leader; Abraham Rummel, baritone; Theodore Laudig, snare drum; Christian Spidel, cornet and bugler; William Goldman, baritone; John H. Ruhl, tuba; Adam Rummel, baritone; William Davis (?) cornet; and John Binkley, cornet(?). F. A. Kirlin was also a member of this band but is not in the photo. The band was photographed at Scottsboro, Alabama, in August of 1862. (Photo courtesy of Mr. Fred Benkovic. The names of the bandsmen were furnished courtesy of Dr. William Bufkin.)

137

Plate 6. This splendid looking group, photographed shortly after the war, is the brass band of Elizabethtown, Kentucky. I have been unable to establish whether it served with a Kentucky regiment during the war. (Photo from a tintype recently purchased at auction in Elizabethtown, Kentucky.)

Plate 7. The brigade band of the XXIV Army Corps photographed in 1865. This is an interesting example of the photographic art of the period since the three men in the right rear have obviously been added to the photo at a later date. The bandmaster (front, center) is the only bandsman with a bell-front instrument and probably performed as a soloist with the group. (Photo courtesy of Mr. Fred Benkovic.)

Plate 8. This fine looking group is the band of the Ohio Militia taken in 1860 or early 1861. The group probably performed more for concerts than for parades since the instruments are all bell-front or upright models. The inclusion of the Kent bugle (front, 2nd from the left) was unusual for a band of this period. The instrument had gradually fallen from popularity since the introduction of valves early in the 1830s. It was generally considered to be too delicate an instrument for field duty. (Photo courtesy of Mr. Fred Benkovic.)

Plate 9. The Band of the Chicago Light Guard and the United States Zouave Cadets commanded by Colonel Elmer E. Ellsworth. Exhibitions and tours by this group did much to stimulate the revival of the militia regiments in the United States prior to the Civil War. (Photo courtesy of the Chicago Historical Society.)

141

Plate 10. The victory parade or "Last Grand Review" held on 23–24 April 1865. The band of the 1st U.S. Veteran Volunteer Infantry leads the regiment down F Street in Washington, D.C. (Photo courtesy of the Library of Congress.)

Plate 11. The United States Marine Band (Francis Scala, director) with a battalion of marines at the Navy Yard in April of 1864. This band was allowed thirty members by a special act of Congress. The instrumentation under Scala's direction was always in the French tradition and included a large woodwind section, four trombones and two French horns. The band played regular concerts on the White House lawn throughout the war. (Photo courtesy of the Library of Congress.)

143

Plate 12. The group in the bird's nest bandstand is the band of the 38th Illinois Infantry Regiment, which was stationed at Pilot Knob, Missouri. General William P. Carlin and his staff are in front of the bandstand. Carlin, who was later promoted to the command of a brigade, liked music very much and the bandstand was built by his order. The photograph was taken at Ringgold Barracks, Georgia, at an unknown time. (Photo courtesy of the Library of Congress.)

144

Plate 13. This fine looking group is the band of the 107th Colored Infantry Regiment, United States Army. Black regiments were officered by whites, and here the bandmaster is a white man. (Photo courtesy of the Library of Congress.)

Plate 14. This group with their their fancy shoulder epaulets is the band of the 8th New York State Militia of Elmira, New York. It was customary to have a young Black serve as a Band Boy. His duties were primarily to see that all of the impedimenta was loaded and unloaded when needed. He also served as a servant to some of the bandsmen and was paid for his services through the contributions of the individual band members. (Photo from the Brady Collection, courtesy of the Library of Congress.)

BANDS AT THE REAR

The *New York Times*, describing the military preparations taking place in that city, noted that "martial music resounded from everywhere."[1] War music rent the heavens above every hamlet and village, swelling to a mighty crescendo as it echoed and reverberated throughout the nation, but Washington, at the very center of mobilization, heard more of the national airs than any other single place. President Lincoln grasped the reins of government as the Marine Band played "Hail to the Chief."

Abraham Lincoln—rail splitter, circuit lawyer, preserver of the Union and emancipator of the slaves—was no musician. Yet he was extremely fond of music and as President, he probably heard more music than any other occupant of the White House. He heard the old patriotic tunes and new songs of the Civil War period. He listened to the bands, choruses, and soloists. He came to know the songs and the singers, and the bands and their leaders. He heard exuberant serenaders outside the White House and quiet singers within; he heard noisy bands in the streets of Washington and he listened to their soft strains at the evening in many of the "Hundred Circling Camps."[2]

Major Anderson's surrender at Fort Sumter was marked by a euphoric outpouring that numbed the senses for any rational evaluation of the consequences. The ever-articulate Mary Chesnut reveled in the exhilaration that gripped Orange Court House in June 1861.

Noise of drums, tramp of marching regiments all day long, rattling of artillery wagons, bands of music, friends from every quarter coming in. We ought to be miserable and anxious, and yet these are pleasant days. Perhaps we are unnaturally exhilarated and excited. . . .

A young Carolinian with queer ideas of a joke rode his horse through the barroom of this hotel. How he scattered people and things right and left! Captain Ingraham was incensed at the bad conduct of his young countryman. "He was intoxicated, of course," said Captain Ingraham. "But he was a splendid rider."[3]

James Robertson of the Stonewall Brigade, oblivious to the carnage at First Manassas and intoxicated by a Southern victory, felt that ". . . these . . . [were] happy and carefree days. Always at hand for concerts and serenades was the Fifth Regiment's 'Stonewall Brigade Band.' Organized in 1855 [they were] given their new name soon after First Manasses. . . .Jackson greatly enjoyed their music, though he confessed in private that he could not distinguish one song from another, regardless of who played it."[4]

Jackson's brigade band, and hundreds of others like it, played for anyone who would listen. Bands paraded and serenaded. They performed concerts in camps, parks, and theaters and participated in Sabbath services. They accompanied dances, balls, and picnics. They set the cadence for troops on the march. They paraded through captured cities. They drummed out the miscreants. They accompanied the condemned to their places of execution and then laid them to rest when the macabre business was done. They provided pomp and circumstance for funerals, and when not performing; the bandsmen assisted surgeons and burial details. Music did resound from everywhere.

Parades were established civilian entertainments and had long been associated with annual militia encampments. Parades continued to inspire the public after the war had begun and were an integral part of the training of every wartime regiment.

The colorful militia units were paraded before the public as soon after their federalization as possible. Wartime newspapers recount hundreds of these spirited occasions, but one of the most unusual took place in Washington on 6 July 1861. President Lincoln and the commanding general, Winfield Scott, returned the salute of twenty-six regiments passing in review, each headed by its own brass band.

One of the numerous effects of the parade is one that produced a most happy effect. As the Garibaldi Guard passed by the canopy. . .each man of the whole Regiment drew from his hat or breast, the green sprig which so strikingly ornamented them, and threw it towards, and in many instances upon, the hero of Lundy's Lane and Serro Gordo [General Scott], while from the head of each column there was a full bouquet of natural flowers thrown in his lap in the same manner. This called forth bravos from the thousands present.[5]

On 2 August 1861 the 12th Regiment of New York State Militia, commanded by Colonel Butterfield, received a tremendous ovation when it returned from its abortive attempt to reinforce Fort Sumter. "The regiment. . .emerged into the Battery-place amidst enthusiastic cheers. . . .The column finally being greeted with immense outbursts. . . .As the regiment approached St. Paul's Church, the excitement became intense. The tramp of the marching column with its own Band and Drum Corps in full play, the Band upon the balcony of Barnum's Museum playing the 'Star Spangled Banner,' the screams of the steam whistle of Engine No. 38 and the shouting of the multitude, created a scene of wild excitement which has seldom been equaled."[6]

Regiments, arriving in the virtually undefended and badly frightened city of Washington, were received with parades and thunderous ovations. But war hysteria was not limited to the capital city. Celebrations were held in many settlements as each demonstrated its pride in the troops raised from its environs. Parades increased geometically as regiment after regiment mustered into service.

When the DeKalb Regiment of New York Volunteer Militia left for the field they were accompanied by their twenty-four piece brass band. The band presented a particularly colorful appearance when the regiment paraded through Baltimore on 10 July 1861. All were attired in full Zouave uniform and each member of the band had a live kitten perched upon his shoulder. The felines did not impede their music and ". . . their appearance was the highlight of the parade."[7]

In New York and Washington newly arrived regiments were met by an escort of troops already stationed in these cities, producing a parade of considerable length. Smaller communities staged similar welcomes, not always successfully. The 13th Massachusettes Infantry paraded through Worcester in July 1861 to the deafening roar of its cheering citizens. The parade ended at Mechanics Hall where the grateful townfolk had provided a feast for the famished men.

As only a part of the Regiment could enter at a time, the right wing entered first, and from the tables bountifully supplied they made a most substantial meal. After eating all they could, they filled their haversacks and canteens. The waiters, thinking all the Regiment was in the hall, generously brought forward all they had and urged it upon them. When the left wing entered, with blank faces they confessed they had nothing but the broken food on the tables. The coffee was nothing but slops; disgusted with the fare, we went out. The rememberance of it to this day is not pleasant.[8]

Both the satisfied and the hungry left immediately for New York. They arrived the following morning and marched up to City Park. "After stacking arms, Col. Leonard dismissed the men till a certain hour in the afternoon. One of the city officials expressed surprise and offered 'a squad of police' to keep the men within certain limits, telling the Col. he never would get all of his men together again. He declined all offers. . . .At the specific time every man was in his place, and the march was resumed down Broadway in 'column by platoon,' reaching from 'curb to curb,' the band playing and the men singing 'John Brown.' "[9]

Green troops were often escorted to their camps by the "veteran regiments" that had preceded them a few days earlier.[10] Such amenities were not limited to training camps and recruiting depots. Victorious regiments were sometimes escorted into their camps following combat.

At eleven o'clock there was music along the highroad, and a general rushing from camps. The victorious regiments were returning from Hanover, under escort, and all the bands were pealing national airs. As they turned down the fields toward their old encampments, the several brigades stood under arms to welcome them, and the cheers were many and vigorous. But the solemn ambulances still followed after, and the red flag of the hospitals flaunted bloodily in the blue midnight.[11]

General Fitz John Porter received a musical escort upon his return to earth following a rather harrowing balloon ride. Porter had taken to the air to view the guns of Gloucester Point just outside of Norfolk. The balloon broke loose and gusty winds bounced it back and forth between the Confederate and Union lines.

Then as all looked agape, the air-craft plunged, and tacked, and veered, and drifted rapidly toward the Federal lines again.
    The allelujah that now went up shook the spheres, and when he regained our camp limits, the General was seen clambering up again to clutch the valve-rope. . . .This time he was successful, and the balloon fell like a stone. . . .Cavalry rode pell-mell from several different directions to reach the place of descent, and the General's personal staff galloped past me like the wind. . . .The balloon had struck a canvas tent. . .and the General unharmed, had disentangled himself from innumerable folds of oiled canvas and was now the cynosure of an immense group of people. While the officers shook his hands, the rabble bawled their satisfaction in hurrahs, and a band of music marching up directly, the throng on foot and horse gave him a vociferous escort to his quarters.[12]

Parades and training were considered synonymous by most commanders, and large portions of each day were alloted to parades. All camps contained adequate numbers of bands for this purpose, but Camp Patterson, York, Pennsylvania, must hold the record for the number of bandsmen present at a single encampment. A camp was established there on 1 September 1861 for the annual muster of the nearly defunct Enrolled Militia. Martial music filled the air as each understrength company arrived with its own band.[13]

The training day started off with a bang when, at 6:00 A.M. "all of the music collect[ed] on the parade ground, the assembly [was] beat, and the Companies drilled half an hour, concluding with the morning parade."[14] *Retreat*, held at 6:30 P.M. called for another combined concert followed by a troop of the line by all musicians. With only 336 men in the ranks, the troop must have been a short one for the 103 instrumentalists.

Militia encampments had always attracted crowds of civilians who, encumbered with picnic baskets and children, came out to view the entertainments. One civilian regarded his seat at the show as a constitutional perquisite, and wondered "why the Northern Central Railway Company. . .[did] not run an extra train from the southern part of the county. Persons arriving by the train cannot see the morning parade. . . .There is not much of a crowd of citizens here to see the sights now, but should the weather continue favorable, the latter part of the week will bring them along by the thousands."[15]

The correspondent correctly assessed Camp Patterson as a popular attraction. Several new companies arrived, bringing the total to seventeen and ten-thousand people "took the cars" to view the training. Subjects such as gunnery, tactics, or the "school of the soldier" were conspicuously absent from the training day. Most of the encampment period was consumed by a series of consecutive parades.

A General Review [was held] in the morning by General Wynkopp and the Staff Officers [and] was a very creditable affair. . . .After the review, the companies were again formed and marched through the principal streets of the town, when they were dismissed for dinner. Soon after, the Law Grays proceeded to the parade ground and went through their drill to the gratification of thousands of spectators. The manual was performed by word of command, at the tap of the drum, and at will, and their marching was pronounced excellent. This finished, the Grays preceded by the Worth Infantry Band and the Staff Officers, proceeded to the Tremont House, the Hq. of General Shaffer, and escorted him into the camp where another review took place. . . . Capt. Shaeffer's Company from Washington, and the Marine Band, attracted universal attention and admiration. . . . I have seen country towns crowded, but York today goes ahead of anything I have seen yet. To judge from the line waiting to get to dinner, the hotel keepers made a smug thing of it. The committee of arrangements will expect them to be liberal towards defraying the expenses of the camp which it is necessary for the York Citizens to bear.[16]

If large numbers of civilians invaded the encampments of the Enrolled Militia, they completely inundated the bivouacs of the regiments called to federal service. Although the men were supposedly preparing for battle, much of the training day was given over to parades which masqueraded behind such subterfuges as "regimental drill." Bands were an important part of the activities.

A division (numbering between three and four thousand men) was the smallest unit reviewed on a regular basis. While the enthralled civilians viewed the troops the soldiers viewed the ladies.

[On] Wednesday. . .I attended the review of Forney's Division. The 3 Brigades contain about 3000 men and having ten musical bands, they made it quite a nice affair.

There was an immense number of spectators, including many ladies, and some quite pretty ones among the number. I did not think the Arkansans were as nice looking as they are.

There was in particular a very pretty person with Genl. Churchill in an open carriage.[17]

The individual soldier took great pride in the performance of his unit at these affairs. One trooper beamed with satisfaction when his regiment was cited as one of the best that passed in review at Monticello on 26 September 1862.

At one o'clock P.M. we had a big review of all the army by Genl. Magruder. There were from eight to ten thousand men on the field, a good number of good musical bands, a good many Generals and handsome horsemen and all went very well. General Magruder was magnificently dressed, and wore a military look....I was very proud to learn that Mouton's [Gray's] Brigade was flatteringly complimented by the Generals for its good appearance and its military marching and that the 18th [Louisiana] in particular was singled out for its good appearance and magnificent marching. We returned from the review at 5 1/2 o'clock, covered with dust and very tired.[18]

Reviews attracted dignitaries and other civilians in proportion to the size of the parading unit. General Hooker's review of an entire army was graced by the chief executive and members of his cabinet and occupied the better part of an entire day.

Somewhere about the first of April was the grand review of the "Army of the Potomac." President Lincoln came down and Hooker, with other celebrities, looked us over. . . . After a good deal of waiting and standing in line and marching in review, which occupied all day, we arrived in camp about sundown. . . .Old Col. Wheelock of the 97th N.Y. . . .wanted a regular "Guard Mount.". . .He tried to have the men march off and then march back at the beat of the drum; the men were mad and commenced to yell, but refused to stir an inch. The old man rode up and down the line brandishing his sword and threatening dire vengeance on the first man he could catch, but when he was at one end the noise was always at the other. . .and it was getting dark, he gave the order "Right face, March." The boys obeyed with cheers for "old Butter and Cheese," as the men of his regiment called him.[19]

The Union did not outdo the Confederacy in matters of pomp and display. Captain Robert E. Lee, Jr., sat proudly beside his famous father as the white-haired general took the salute from his command, following the battle of Gettysburg. "The General was mounted on Traveller, looking very proud of his master, who had on sash and sword, which he rarely wore, a pair of new cavalry gauntlets, and, I think, a new hat. At any rate, he looked unusually fine, and sat his horse like a perfect picture of grace and power. The infantry was drawn up in columns by divisions, with their bright muskets all glittering in the sun, their battleflags standing straight out before the breeze, and their bands playing, awaiting the inspection of the General, before they broke into column by companies and marched past him in review."[20]

Division reviews were common events in both armies, but units boasting fine bands seemed to parade more often than divisions with poor music. Following Mine Run, late in November 1863, a Confederate brigade formed for review. "The men were moderately drilled and schools of instruction were ordered for the officers. The 10th Virginia was the only regiment which had a band (I think we were getting up one in the 1st North Carolina with some instruments captured in the Gettysburg Campaign), and we utilized it to the best general advantage by having daily brigade guard mounting, with as much military pomp and circumstance as we could get up."[21]

The mania for parades and reviews even extended to labor battalions. The Black Brigade of Cincinnati was a short-lived provisional unit, organized to speed the construction of defensive works, when it appeared that the city would come under attack early in the war. The Black workers organized themselves in a quasi-military manner and elected a "colonel" to command them.

The Colonel accepted the sword with a few appropriate words of acknowledgement; when the Brigade, with music playing, banners flying, with their commander at their head, marched through the streets of Covington to the pontoon bridge, and across to Cincinnati. [At Newport]. . .a handsome National Flag, presented to them by Capt. Jas. Lupton, was borne in their midst, and their march was enlivened by strains of martial music, from a band formed from the ranks, of their own motion. They were cheered on their way to their work by the good words of the citizens who lined the streets, and by the waving handkerchiefs of patriotic ladies. As they passed the different regiments in line of battle, proceeding to the fortifications, mutual cheers and greetings attested the good feeling between these co-workers in the same cause.[22]

A good band was a cause for regimental pride and a poor one provided the opportunity for a good deal of mirth. One of the poorest in the Army of the Potomac belonged to the 16th Maine Infantry. The band, without official support, met informally during the winter of 1863. Thirty-six-year-old John Shea, who had enlisted as a private in Company G when the regiment was mustered on 14 August 1862, spark-plugged its organization. By 23 April the amateur group had progressed sufficiently to attract official attention. The regimental officers raised $421 for a complete set of fine instruments. The enlisted men of the regiment contributed $250 of that sum.

Captain Waldron, a man of strong voice and opinion, contributed to the fund, but under extreme duress. He readily admitted that he had less than a remarkable ear for music and swore that he would just as soon "hear a bullet whistle or a shell explode" as to listen to the band. He regarded the arrival of the instruments as an added affliction that doomed him "to a constant succession of toots from fifteen beginners on wind instruments."

Shea's good work did not pass unnoticed by the regimental commander who rewarded him with a promotion to principal musician on 8 October 1863. Armed with his new authority he became a zealot for music, and the band made considerable progress under his chiding and leadership. By December the band played sufficiently well to lighten the tedium of a long march and the men looked forward to its performances.

On 24 December 1863 Shea "blew a blast long enough and loud enough to wake the dead." Tents were struck and in a few minutes the entire regiment was marching toward Mitchell's Station to the tune of "The Girl I Left Behind Me," but the cold was so intense that in less than five minutes the band instruments froze and the men plodded along in sullen silence.

A week later, the regiment was bivouacked in the mud, six miles north of Culpeper. Although they had arrived after sunset, the commanding general ordered the 16th Maine to fall in for a brigade review. The half-ration of whiskey that had been issued an hour before had already begun its work.

The adjutant had the bugler make the call, but there was no response from the band leader. The call was repeated, and yet no reply. The adjutant went up to the right, saw the trouble, and could not resist the temptation. "Mr. Shea, did you hear the call?" Mr. Shea was always a gentleman, and doffing his hat, managed to say, "Ashtant, I'm puty d-r-r-runk, hope you'll skuse me." "How is the B flat, Mr. Shea?" "Hesbad offsiam." "How is Locke?" " 'Slaid down—dreffultired.' " "O nonsense, Mr. Shea," said the adjutant, "there is a cold spring of water down there; send for a pailful or two, bathe your heads, and drink a quart or so, and you will be O K. Hurry up." He returned to his quarters, thinking just how it would work when the water got warm. Before he was ready for parade, the call rang out, clear and correct, as he knew it would. The band took position, and played the companies into line. Ranks were opened, then the adjutant gave the command, "Troop—Beat off!" with some misgiving. The ground seemed very uneven and full of cradle knolls to the band, and now and then the leader would lose a note, and trying to catch it, would clash into the B flat, and sandwich in between the alto and bass, and somehow the bass drum would persist in coming down heavy on the up beat, and the cymbals forgot to clang when they should, and closed with a crash when they should have been still. Countermarching, they started on quick time; but alas! the water was warm, and somehow the leader's order was misunderstood, and when half the band struck up one tune, and the other half another, it was too much! Then rang out the colonel's voice, in tones that drowned the band, "Parade is dismissed!" Well—the adjutant received a reprimand, but it was worth it. The band enjoyed it, and I think all did, from the smile which went down the line. Certainly the Sixteenth was the most jolly regiment in the brigade. They laughed so loud and so long, that the other regiments took it up, and so the good nature spread, and the adjutant was forgiven.[23]

Although Shea escaped punishment he was relieved of his responsibilities as bandmaster. On 2 January 1864 Frank Richardson, a professional musician from Maine, was engaged by the officers as bandmaster at a salary of one hundred dollars per month. The band improved rapidly under his leadership and was subsequently pronounced the best in the division by General Robinson.

On 13 January 1864 the officers purchased four more instruments at a cost of two hundred dollars and donated them to the band. By March the band had improved so much that it served the entire brigade and its costs were assessed against all of the brigade officers. Even so, the band remained the property of the 16th Maine.

The band was originally organized after regimental bands had been outlawed. To circumvent this problem, field musicians who could double on brass instruments formed the nucleus of the band. The remaining bandsmen came from the ranks of the various companies. These men were relieved from other duties when they performed with the band. Bandmaster Richardson held no military assignment whatsoever. He was simply an employee of the officers of the brigade.

Another musician got into trouble during a review of the Army of the Potomac at Stevensburg, Virginia. Since the commander in chief, President Lincoln, was present everyone was on his mettle, except for a trombonist. "The musicians of the entire division form[ed] at the head of the column, falling out and facing the reviewing officer, while the entire division pass[ed]. In the manoeuvre to face the President, an eccentric Frenchman, belonging to the division headquarters band, playing a slide trombone, took advantage of the muddle and ran his bow through the head of a drum to the chagrin and amusement of us, but of course quiet and good order prevailed."[24]

The Frenchman may well have been a superior musician, but his peculiar traits of character and lack of adaptability finally led to his desertion from the service.

The memory of the eccentric French trombonist still haunts me and sticks as close as lightning to a thunder cloud. In appearance he resembled one of Shakespeare's witches dancing around the boiling cauldron. He would get me to taste his innumerable dishes of hash made of the same ingredients only slightly varied in their proportion, and to save my life I could not tell the difference in taste, yet he was as happy as the day was long with his variety of food. The eccentricities of this individual were remarkable. In a storm of shells at Petersburg. . .he turned his back on the wicked scene, saying a living hero was worth more than a dead coward. The last thing I remember of this eccentric individual was his farewell address to the leader of the band. On this occassion he was serious. Whether he fell off the stage, leaped off or was kicked off, is mere conjecture, or transformed into a demon, or an angel, the good Lord only knows.[25]

Regiments parading through friendly cities were led by their brass bands and massed field music whenever possible. The martial airs were both reassuring and inspiriting to those citizens holding common sympathies with the troops, and their passage was marked by a sense of excitement and relief. When these same bands paced their regiments through captured communities devastated by battle, bummers, and stragglers, their stirring airs were a marked contrast to the misery of the flaming ruins all around them. In the border states Union sympathizers rejoiced over their deliverance, while citizens loyal to the Confederate cause counted the music as yet another anguish they had to endure.

When the Stonewall Brigade moved through Winchester, the citizens cheered themselves hoarse as they waved and shouted to relatives and loved ones in the ranks. "By 3 P.M. the whole army was in motion, down the dusty streets and eastward toward the brownish-green hills that rose majestically in the afternoon sun. . . . Regimental Bands began to blare out lively choruses of 'Dixie' and 'The Bonnie Blue Flag.' 'How proud a sight it was,' wrote Mrs. Cornelia McDonald, 'to witness the departing army in gallant array, with the Confederate banners waving, the bands playing, and the bayonets gleaming in the sun. . . . Many of the companies were made up of mere boys, but their earnest and joyous faces were fully as reassuring as the martial music was inspiriting.' "[26]

Winchester changed hands so many times in the course of the war that city officials became professionals in the art of surrender. In 1861 the 3rd Wisconsin Volunteer Infantry was in possession of the city. "[The skirmishers] pushed on into the town, the remainder of the regiment following closely after, and received from the mayor the formal surrender of this interesting city, which is said to have been captured and recaptured more than thirty times during the war. We found here an apparently strong Union sentiment. As our Regiment marched in with colors flying and band playing, the citizens were rejoicing everywhere over their deliverance from the Confederates. Innumerable handkerchiefs were waving to welcome us, and in some instances the stars and stripes were displayed."[27]

Somewhat later the 13th Massachusetts Infantry Band heralded the arrival of that regiment to the city. "Our stay at this place [Bunker Hill] was short," wrote one trooper. "We marched toward Winchester, halting at night within a short distance of it. Here we found the rest of Bank's Division. Early in the morning we formed a line of battle and moved across the fields to meet the enemy if they should be there. Jackson withdrew in the night further up the valley. When we found the enemy had fled, we reformed the line . . . and marched into the city with bands playing and colors flying."[28]

Early in the war a modicum of intercourse existed between Southern citizens and the conquering Union armies; Confederate ladies made a conscious effort not to offend the Union troops. "Northerners [were] not very fond of being called Yankees, but they [were] never called anything else in the South. About the commencement of the war . . . a Northern Regiment marched into some little town in Tennessee. The colonel of the regiment had out his band to perform for the edification of the townspeople and requested the lady of the house where he was quartered to choose what she would desire them to play. The lady, wishing to gratify her guest, and at the same time careful not to offend, requested that the band might play the 'Federal Doodle.' "[29]

This polite concern for delicate sensibilities was not long-lived. George Alfred Townsend, in Warrenton as a reporter for the Union press, recorded the strained fraternization between Union soldiers and Confederate belles.

There was some female society in Warrenton, but the blue-coats engrossed it all. The young women were ardent partisans, but also very pretty; and treason somehow heightened their beauty. Disloyalty is always pardonable in a woman, and these ladies appreciated the fact. They refused to walk under Federal flags, and stopped their ears when the bands played national music; but every evening they walked through the main street, arm in arm with dashing lieutenants and captains. Many flirtations ensued, and a great deal of gossip was elicited. In the end, some of the misses fell out among themselves, and hated each other more than the common enemy. I overheard a young lady talking in a low tone one evening, to a Captain in the Ninth New York Regiment.

"If you knew my brother," she said, "I am sure you would not fire upon *him*."[30]

Sergeant Matthew Woodruff was especially smitten by the combined charms of beautiful women and music when he wrote home in September 1865. "no change in the Programme only that I lay aside loosse papers and pick up a New Descriptive Book, writing out Milty. History of Co. will take me some days to finish it. take a walk in the city to settle my supper. Music greets my Ears on all corners, and lovely Females feel like possessing their charms, but resolve not to do it. have a finer Point in view."[31]

Beauty was excuse enough for treason, and the reigning belle of Richmond, Hetty Cary, used her fairness of face and figure to full advantage. Hetty and Jennie Cary arrived in Richmond early in 1861. While in Baltimore Hetty had been briefly imprisoned at Fort McHenry for wearing a white apron with red ribbons—the Confederate colors. Her imprisonment instantly elevated her to the status of a Dixie heroine. Miss Louise Wigfall, a disciple, was present at Mrs. Pegram's when Hetty triumphantly returned to the outside world.

We had a glorious time—plenty of ice cream cake and officers; the latter predominating. When the evening was a little advanced we were honored by the presence of the beautiful Miss Hetty Cary and we danced until nearly 3 o'clock. Of all the women I have met I think she was the most beautiful—and combined with great loveliness of person, a brilliancy of wit, which made her remarkable. At this time, having just come through the lines, she was dressed in the last mode, and shone resplendent in an exquisite violet moire with pink roses in her hair. This last was Titian tinted and rippled back from her fair low forehead. Her complexion was lilies and roses; and her figure magnificent. She was indeed a beauty.[32]

Miss Hetty's treason extended beyond her bicolored apron. In Baltimore she had waved a Confederate flag from an open window while Federal troops kept cadence with their band beneath her. One of the regimental officers drew her attention to his colonel and asked: "Shall I have her arrested?" The Colonel, glancing up and catching a glimpse of the vision of defiant loveliness, answered emphatically: "No! She is beautiful enough to do as she _____ pleases."[33]

The beautiful Miss Hetty was wooed and won by the dashing General John Pegram, their marriage taking place in 1863. Three weeks later to the day, the gallant Pegram fell dead in battle. Miss Wigfall was one of many who "recall[ed] those two processions up the aisle of old St. Paul's."[34]

Miss LaSalle Corbell was another celebrated Southern beauty. Her marriage to General George E. Pickett on 15 September 1863 was accompanied by the music of several Confederate bands. Miss Corbell was only eight years old in 1843 when George Pickett was widowed. LaSalle found the general fascinating and admitted that she loved him from the first day they had met. For the next twenty years she confidently prepared herself for the life of a soldier's wife, and finally—she wed her general. "The license was granted, and we were married by the Rev. Dr. Platt in dear old St. Paul's Church before congregated thousands, for soldier and civilian, rich and poor, high and low, were all made welcome by my hero. We left for Richmond on the afternoon train amidst the salute of guns, hearty cheers, and chimes and bands and bugles."[35]

They were received in Richmond by the Army of Northern Virginia with all of its bands. Of the thousands present only President Davis and his cabinet, a few ministers, and a few very old men were in civilian clothes. "The General and I greeted and welcomed them all as they came; then they passed on to the banquet and the dance—dancing as only Richmond in the Confederacy could dance. . . . The rumbling of coming earth quake struck no minor tones into her merry music. If people could not dance in the crisis of life the tragedy of existence might be even darker than it is. . . . When the last guests were going, my General and I walked out upon the veranda with them and, as they closed the outer gates, watched the stars of night fade away before the coming dawn and the morning star rise and shine gloriously upon a new happy day."[36]

Mary Boykin Chesnut, a guest at LaSalle's wedding, cheered her general, the troops, the bands, the bride, and the dancers; but by 1865 the Confederate bands broke her heart as they paraded through Chester, South Carolina. "Today," she wrote, "Stephen D. Lee's Corps marched through. The camp songs of the men were heartbreak, so sad and so stirring. I sat down as women have done before and wept. Oh, the bitterness of such weeping! There they go, the gay and gallant few; the last gathering of the flower of southern manhood. They march with as airy a tread as if they still believed the world was on their side, and that there were no Yankee bullets for the unwary."[37]

Mary Rawson, youngest daughter of the Honorable E. E. Rawson, mayor of Atlanta, succumbed to the same melancholia as Sherman's bands blared victoriously through the captured city. "On hearing the martial music, we looked up from the front porch where we were sitting to see the street filled with cavalry and infantry pack mules and army wagons and cattle crowded promiscuously together, the cavalry and infantry ensigns floating in unison together. The musicians all riding on white horses. After making the signal for the march to commence they rode silently along until they passed in front of Gen. Geary's headquarters, when simultaneously they broke into the old soul stirring 'Hail Columbia,' the suddenness of the music startled me. They then, (after finishing the piece) slowly and silently marched through the city."[38]

Mrs. Poppenhiem returned to her native Atlanta just in time to watch wave after wave of Sherman's men pass through the devastated city. She was astonished by both their number and appearance. She had recently wept at the passing of remnants of the ill-clad, underequipped, gaunt, and hungry defenders of the Confederacy. "Still they go through—hundreds and thousands—all gaiety, with bands of music, and burning houses light their march."[39]

Atlanta was not the only city victimized by Sherman's troops. When General Howard marched the XV Corps through the little village of Summertown on 29 November 1864 Sue Sample of Newbury, South Carolina, was visiting her sister-in-law, Mrs. Caleb L. Sample, on her plantation seven miles from the village. For three days the neighborhood was overrun with "bluecoats" and Sue wrote that she was "terribly excited. They camped here that night, and until 11 o'clock the camp was ringing with music, which made our hearts bleed."[40]

Miss I. D. M. listened to Sherman's bands as they marched triumphantly through Columbia on 17 February 1864. "I can best give you an idea of the vast number of the host by telling you that I counted twelve Bands of Music pass by playing at full blast, and yet they were at such a distance from each other that the music of one had died away before that of another reached my ears."[41]

An anonymous Columbian, signed "ever affectionate Mother," wrote to her daughter Gracia from her temporary quarters in the seminary. "All day Sunday they were playing the fiddle outside our window, where they were encamped and the full band was playing at General Prestons, just opposite. Such a Sabbath!"[42]

Not every Columbian found the music depressing. The city housed a large number of Union sympathizers who had been caught in the South at the outbreak of the war. They had been forced by circumstance to suppress their sentiments. Now they greeted Sherman, wildly waving their flags and handkerchiefs from the windows and balconies, while jubilant, grinning Negroes poured from cabins, their masters' houses, and their places of labor. The sympathizers and Negroes joined together in a singing, cheering, dancing, wild celebration. "The air was alive with the rousing music of regimental bands, spotted here and there along the line of march. 'Hail Columbia,' 'Yankee Doodle' and other tunes not played in the old city for years were heard by some with thrilling pleasure, by most with heartsickness, humiliation and dark foreboding."[43]

Katharine Theus Obear was the daughter of the Reverend Josiah Obear, who was conducting a school in Winnsboro when refugees from Columbia descended upon the city. The Obears graciously opened their home to the helpless and destitute, and young Katharine enjoyed the house full of company even under such trying circumstances. "By midday it looked as if we were doomed. Fire had started on every street nearby. . . . It made so hot a fire, we could not stay in the rooms on that side of the house. The army had nearly passed on and we got bold. Miss Eunice, and Maggie and Mrs. Wells were talking to an Officer, General Gary [Geary?]. . . . Evidently General Gary did not wish to leave the town in peril another night. The band, stationed at the corner, played long and loud, probably the signal for all to be on the march, for by sundown they had vanished."[44]

At least one musical instrument was saved from the flames of Winnsboro when the city was set to the torch. "While Christ Episcopal Church flamed and crashed, soldiers carried the organ outside and played popular tunes on it. In a nearby churchyard, vandals are said to have dug up a recently buried body. The casket was knocked open with an axe and stood on end so that the dead person might face the burning structure."[45]

Austin Stearns of Company K, 13th Massachusetts Infantry, marched through Cedar Mountain under the hateful gaze of its inhabitants. "As our regiment marched along with colors flying and band playing, many of the citizens (mostly female) stood in their doors or at windows. . . . none were glad to see us if we except the colored. Many were crying. . . . I shall never forget one person as she kneeled at the window with eyes and hands upturned . . . and with an expression on her face as though she was calling down . . . the most dreadful punishment . . . possible on our heads. I could not keep my eyes off from her."[46]

While the vanquished called down the wrath of God, the victorious Union soldiers and sympathizers raised prayers of thanksgiving for their deliverance. General Sherman rode out of Atlanta on 16 November 1864 headed toward Richmond. "Away off in the distance, on the McConough road, was the rear of Howard's column, the gun barrels glistening in the sun . . . and right before [him] the Fourteenth Corps, marching steadily and rapidly with a cheery look and swinging pace."[47]

The scene was still fresh in his mind years later when Sherman wrote:

Some band by accident struck up the anthem of "John Brown's Soul goes Marching on;" the men caught up the strain, and never before or since have I heard the chorus of "Glory, glory, hallelujah!" done with more spirit or in better harmony of time and place. . . . The next day we passed through the handsome town of Covington, the soldiers closing up their ranks, the color-bearers unfurling their flags, and the band striking up patriotic airs. The white people came out of their houses to behold the sight, spite of their deep hatred of the invaders, and the Negroes were simply frantic with joy. Whenever they heard my name, they clustered about my horse, shouted and prayed in their peculiar style, which had a natural eloquence that would have moved a stone. . . . [I] can now see a poor girl, in the very ecstasy of the Methodist "shout," hugging the banner of one of the regiments and jumping up to the "feet of Jesus."[48]

The "Gate City" quickly became a thing of the past. The heavens above it were one vast expanse of lurid fire, broken only by the periodic detonation of some concealed powder or exploding shells which would send sparks and flames shooting through the dense smoke. "Roaring-drunk soldiers, singing and shouting, staggered about or rode stolen animals amid the burning ruins.

While drunk and sober alike made mincemeat of 'Rally Round the Flag,' the Thirty-third Massachusetts band in another part of the city played 'John Brown's Body' over and over, reading the notes by the light of the flaming buildings. 'I have never,' averred Major Nichols, 'heard that noble anthem when it was so grand, so solemn, so inspiring.' "[49]

Sherman's troops abandoned the ashes of Atlanta and to the stirring music of the regimental bands moved on towards Milledgeville. At Madison the cavalry, well in advance of the main body of troops, set fire to the depot and in general tore up the town of two thousand souls, ". . . including an uncommonly large number of pretty women and girls who peeped at them fearfully but curiously through slightly open blinds. The apertures of these blinds widened as the band played 'Dixie,' and disappeared with a bang when it swung into 'Yankee Doodle.' "[50]

Sherman's columns moved into Georgia where they found the going much easier than their passage from Tennessee to Atlanta. At night they settled into camps and entertained themselves as best they could under the circumstances. "Regimental bands kept the martial spirit alive and furnished instrumental accompaniment for impromptu songfests. Many a Georgia community heard 'John Brown's Body' so much and so often that it would have become thoroughly sick of it even if the tune had not been extremely distasteful per se. Cockfights, card games, band concerts, songfests and woodland rendezvous with good-looking Negro women—all these and little fighting to speak of made the march through Georgia pretty much of a lark."[51]

On 15 December General Sherman returned to Cheves' rice mill, where he had left his horse two days previously. The mill, a rather tall structure, had served as an observation post during General Hazen's assault upon Fort McAllister. He mounted and rode west of Savannah about eight miles to join General Howard at his headquarters. Howard was established in a fine old plantation house owned by an uncle of the Major Anderson who had commanded the defense of Fort McAllister. "The evening was spent relating adventures. A lively campfire blazed nearby and the landscape was bright by the moon. There was group singing to the accompaniment of a soldier guitarist, and in the background an army band played popular tunes. The war had briefly lost its harsher aspects."[52]

One did not have to be a general officer to respond to the stirring martial music of a band. All of the men of the 9th Regiment (Hawkins's Zouaves) were rightly proud of theirs. It had been outfitted with new uniforms and instruments just prior to the battle of Fredericksburg, and one of the troopers proudly noted after that battle that ". . . knapsack drills were now the order of the day, but the Ninth showed they could maintain their perfect drill under any conditions. The Regimental Band had been re-organized and enlarged and the members clothed in new uniforms. Under the excellent leadership of Mr. Wallace, of New York City, their music was of a high order and their appearance decidedly attractive."[53]

The band of the 9th Regiment was a common sight on the streets of Fredericksburg and the regimental biographer was proud of their performance.

The details for picket duty on the Orange Court House, Culpepper, and other roads leading from the city into the enemy's country, consisted of entire regiments. When the Zouaves were detailed they always paraded in full dress uniforms, headed by the band with its new instruments, and led by Drum Major Wiley, who was most gorgeously arrayed; and their progress through the city which was as though marching on review, attracted universal attention. There is little doubt that the appearance of a genuine Yankee Regiment, in full dress, with colors flying, and band playing, had its effect upon the inhabitants of Fredericksburg.[54]

Wallace had been a professional bandmaster in New York prior to the war. When the membership of his popular group dwindled, due to the enlistment of his musicians, he decided to go to war himself. The 9th Regiment was delighted to receive his services, and the regimental band achieved genuine quality under his baton. The bandsmen were professionals as well and responded readily to Wallace's stimulating leadership. Even the most unlettered trooper in the regiment recognized the quality of this fine musical unit.

Another exceptionally fine band was that of the 24th Massachusetts Regiment. Patrick Gilmore, its famous director, employed a mixed instrumentation of brass and reeds, and most of the bandsmen doubled on a stringed instrument as well. Gilmore's musical contributions to the Union army were substantial. He directed several regimental bands for short periods of enlistment and organized a number of others that played under former students whom he had trained as bandmasters. The quality of his product was greatly appreciated by the men of the 24th Regiment. One trooper wrote to his girl friend, Fannie L. Partridge, in April 1862 when the regiment was marching southward down the coast of North Carolina.

I don't know what we should have done without our band. It is acknowledged by everyone to be the best in the division. Every night about sundown Gilmore gives us a splendid concert, playing selections from the operas and some very pretty marches, quicksteps, waltzes and the like, most of which are composed by himself or by Zohler, a member of his band. . . . Thus you see we get a great deal of *new* music, notwithstanding we are off here in the woods. Gilmore used to give some of the most fashionable concerts we had at home and we lack nothing but the stringed instruments now. In their place however we have five reed instruments, of which no other band can boast.[55]

When Yankee regiments marched through the rural South, Negroes would frequently team up with the bands to entertain the passing troops. A Minnesotan recounted the events of the Georgia campaign in a letter to his wife.

There were many comic occurrences on the journey. At Shady Dale a large plantation about 35 miles west of Milledgeville there were 16 young Wenches came out and danced for every Regiment that passed, the Brigade Band playing while each Brigade passed and the next one in turn taking its place. The way the[y] hoed down was caution and extremely ludicrous.... We have a couple of little darkies with the Brigade that are called Tater Boys that can beat anything in the Plan[t]ation dance I ever seen the[y] make their own music Singing the Melancholy Ya Ha all the time they are dancing.[56]

On 29 November of the same year Major James A. Connolly was camped at Shady Dale. He asked an aged black man why a place so devoid of shade trees would be called Shady Dale. The old man thoughtfully replied, "I supoz cuz theas so many of us folks heah." Connolly also recorded that the slaves at Shady Dale enjoyed the music of the bands. "The negro houses were filled with nice cleanly looking negroes of all ages and sizes.... As the head of our column came up with band playing, such a nest of negroes I never saw before; they poured out of these cabins to the road side in such numbers as to lead one to suppose they had been packed away inside like mackerel in a barrel. The music of the bands started the young niggers at dancing, and they capered around like little imps."[57]

Connolly arrived in Savannah with General Sherman on 27 December 1864. The general ordered a review of all of the troops in the city, and Connolly was assigned as a reviewing officer. "It was a magnificent spectacle. As I sat on my horse and watched the bronzed veterans as they marched by with proud firm tread, their tattered flags fluttering in the Atlantic breeze, and brass bands filling the city with inspiring music, I could scarcely refrain from shedding tears of joy."[58]

Cornelius Baker, a bugler with the 9th Pennsylvania Cavalry, wrote less ecstatically of this same affair. Sherman issued orders on 26 December for all troops to prepare for the parade to be held on the twenty-eighth. Because of almost continuous rain and cold weather the event was postponed from day to day until 12 January. Baker didn't seem to realize that he was a bronzed veteran marching with a proud firm tread. After the review he wrote in his diary: "We went to the sity and was reviewed by General Shirman and the Secretary. We were reviewed in the streats of the sity Every thing is cherishing ther in the sity We retirnd to camp at 8 o clock in the eavning."[59]

Richmond was another Southern city marked for particular musical attention by its conquerors. A black regiment was the first to reach the outskirts of the Confederate capital, but the high brass decided that the honor of initial entry into that city should be reserved for white troops, the Emancipation Proclamation notwithstanding. The black troops were pulled aside at the edge of town where they stacked their arms and ". . . watched the white soldiers pass. The Third Division continued to the heart of the city, led by a band playing patriotic airs."[60]

The black regiment followed closely upon the heels of the 3rd Division. As the Union troops poured into Richmond from one side, the Confederate army retreated rapidly from the other. Richmond slaves accompanied their masters, leaving the city at the double-quick, while former slaves, with heads erect and weapons in hand, entered under the national banner to the music of the Union. The *Richmond Gazette* found it a "... picture of humiliation and retribution on one hand, and of triumph and victory on the other."[61]

Citizens who chose to face their conquerors gaped in wonder at the splendidly equipped army marching under the old flag, and bitterly recalled better days when Confederate troops strode victoriously into Yankee cities, their regular cadence marked by the music of their bands. The spirit of victory was still alive in Sam Watkins, twenty years after the war, when he fondly recalled the advance of his regiment into Kentucky.

The unit had been thoroughly reorganized at Tupelo, Mississippi, and "took the cars" to Mobile. They crossed Mobile Bay to Montgomery, Alabama, continuing on to Chattanooga via Atlanta. Here they dismounted and scaled the mountains on foot to enter the bluegrass regions of Kentucky.

How gladly the citizens of Kentucky received us. I thought they had the prettiest girls that God ever made. . . . They had heaps and stacks of cooked rations along our route, with wine and cider everywhere, and the glad shouts of "Hurrah for our southern Boys!" greeted and welcomed us. . . . The bands played merrier and livelier tunes. It was the patient convalescing . . . the old fire was seen to illuminate his eyes . . . he felt ashamed that he had ever been "hacked," he could fight now. The bands played "Dixie" and the "Bonnie Blue Flag," the citizens cheered, and the ladies waved their handkerchiefs and threw us bouquets. Ah, those were halcyon days.[62]

Although parades and reviews were the stock in trade of both Union and Confederate bands, their performances were hardly limited to these occasions. Their music was part of a number of other ceremonies, the flag raising and color presentation being two of the most popular.

The raising of a national ensign was generally staged in conjunction with a recruiting campaign. A stand of colors was presented to units entering government service. The thrust of both was to inflame the patriotic spirit and encourage further enlistments. Sam Watkins' ardor burned white-hot when his unit received its colors, but the flame of glory flickered and died in the whirlwind of the battlefield.

Flags made by the ladies were presented to companies, and to hear the young orators tell of how they would protect that flag, and that they would come back with the flag or come not at all, and if they fell they would fall with their backs to the field and their feet to the foe, would fairly make our hair stand on end with intense patriotism, and we wanted to march right off and whip twenty Yankees. But we soon found out that the glory of war was at home among the ladies and not upon the field of blood and carnage of death, where our comrades were mutilated and torn by shot and shell. And to see the cheek blanch and to hear the fervent prayer, aye, I might say the agony of mind were very different indeed from the patriotic times at home.[63]

Back home the realities of war had planted an "agony of mind" in the head of more than one potential recruit. Major Abner Small, adjutant of the 16th Maine, was accosted by two men at his recruiting office about midway through the war.

Men were so anxious to enlist that deception was often practiced on Examining Surgeon Briggs. One morning I found waiting at the door of number nine, regimental headquarters, two anxious civilians of decided mold. Patriotism oozed from every pore, and found utterance in voices heavy with war thunder and poor whiskey. They could hardly wait the opening of the door, and growlingly said, "This Govmunt can't be so damned hard up for trupes or the boss would be round airlier in the mornin'." A close scrutiny of the embryo heroes revealed some striking peculiarities of a recent make-up. One was about forty years old. The other anywhere from twenty to eighty. Stripped of his clothing, and the mysteries of hair coloring and whisker dye, he would present a type of the resurrection.

The regulation inquiries developed the case, and the afternoon train saw the young man, with his swagger, and the old man, with his war paint and hair dye, going to the rear. The visions of large bounties and an early discharge on a comfortable pension had vanished in the mists of a new determination to aid the cause by voting "agin the war."[64]

Not all of the troops were in agreement with Watkins. Many color-bearers did die "with their feet to the foe," their only weapon the fluttering ensign they so proudly advanced at the very front of their regiments. No regiment relished the thought that their flag might fall into the hands of the enemy.

[At Gettysburg] in one of the charges on our right, a color-bearer in one of the Louisiana regiments in our division was cut off from his command and found that he would be captured, so he tore the flag from the staff, pulled off his clothes and wrapped the flag around his body, then put his clothes on over the flag. He was captured and went to prison. When he was exchanged and arrived in Richmond he took off his clothes and unfurled the flag. Soldiers love their colors with such devotion that they will die in defending them, and consider it a disgrace to have them captured and especially the color-bearers.[65]

If flag raisings fanned the patriotism of the would-be recruits and inspired feats of heroism on the field of battle, they were of equal importance to the mothers, daughters, and sweethearts who remained at home. Providing a flag gave a sense of participation to those who could not enlist for active service.

A young Wesleyan graduate was in Augusta, Georgia, at the marriage of the Empire and Palmetto States.

Never will I forget my feelings when we heard that the war had really begun. Tears, bitter tears, fell in silence, for although on a visit to gay young folks we knew not what to say or do. . . .

I was in Augusta. . . . A vast crowd was assembled to witness the scene while a band

of music pealed forth harmonious strains. Old Glory was to be placed at the top of a
lofty pole riveted on the bridge across the Savannah River, but who was brave enough to
climb that pole? No one ventured, until "a tar who ploughed the water" ran up and
taking the flag rope in his teeth climbed safely to the top amid the cheers of the crowd,
and the roar of fifteen guns for the Southern States. Triumphantly the old Revolutionary Flag waved over both states, while the people filled the sailor's pockets with bills as
he came down.[66]

While the Confederates of Augusta were having their flag raising problems,
President Lincoln was struggling with his own. Julia Taft Bayne was at the
White House to participate in the raising of the national ensign.

I went with my mother to see [the] new flag raised by President Lincoln [over the White
House], the date according to my diary, being June 29, 1861. Arriving at our destina-
tion, we went to the south portico to pay our respects to the "first lady" and were invited
to join the group by Mrs. Lincoln. . . .
    When the moment came for the flag to be raised, the Marine Band began the national
anthem and all arose, officers at salute, civilians uncovered. When the President pulled
the cord, it stuck. He pulled harder, and suddenly the upper corner of the Union tore off
and hung down. A gasp of surprise and horror at the sinister omen went around, but a
young staff officer, with great presence of mind, stepped quickly to the group of ladies
and extending his hand, hissed imploringly, "Pins! pins!"
    They were supplied at once. Women had more pins in their clothes in those days. . . .
The band had continued to play and the people on the grounds below standing at attention, did not notice anything . . . except a slight delay in raising the flag. When we
reached home and my father heard of the incident, he warned us not to mention the tearing of the stars out of the flag to anyone.
    But what do you suppose Lincoln thought when he saw nine stars torn from the flag
by his own hand, who was its chief defender?[67]

Flag raisings found renewed popularity in January 1862 when the three-
months enlistees were near the ends of their service commitments. Commanders made great efforts to encourage re-enlistment, and flag raisings and
bands were at the forefront of their exertions. A Maryland Confederate
recalled that ". . . a furlough of thirty days was offered to anyone who would reenlist for the war. . . . Randolph McKim was the first to do so. . . . Not many
followed his example, it being claimed that most were in 'for the war' . . . and
others preferring to reserve an option—many intending to change to the
cavalry or artillery."[68]
    Although flag raisings were a wartime product, concerts in the "hundred
circling camps" were a transplant from civilian life. The dime concert was
drafted into the army.
    H. P. Moyer, a bugler and historian of the 17th Pennsylvania Cavalry, noted
that bands were considered an expensive luxury by the time his regiment was
mustered into federal service. The regiment applied for a band but the idea was

not favorably received. Continued requests finally resulted in a compromise—
the musicians could be selected from the ranks to form a band without expense
to the government. However, each musician was to be trained as a cavalryman, with combat as his primary assignment. The officers provided the funds
for the purchase of instruments and provided the salary for Professor J. F.
Whittington who was hired as bandmaster. Moyer thought the band was not
only an important part of the regiment, but a rightful perquisite of every soldier
in service.

The band was a valuable adjunct to the regiment, especially for dress parade, guard
mount, and reviews, and accomplished much in relieving the monotony of camp life.
When we take into consideration how much money is spent in our large cities and towns
for concerts, balls, parades and entertainments of various kinds, I venture the opinion
that the men who exchanged all home comforts and social amusements for the hard-
ships of a soldier's life, were justly entitled to be furnished with a reasonable amount of
patriotic music to inspire their patriotism and nerve them for the sterner music of
cannon, musketry, minnie balls and bursting shells.[69]

Officers and enlisted men of both armies were moved to melancholia by the
nostalgic strains of sentimental airs, wafted through the night by a brass band
indistinct in the dim twilight. Some were more sensitive to the arts than others,
but none were completely immune.

To Alburtus Dunham, assigned on 31 August 1864 to a camp two miles
north of the Chattahoochee River in Georgia, the music of the band brought a
little bit of America to a strange land. "Our Briggade is strung out a Co. in a
place. I think our corps will be strung out on the railroad this winter for thare
has got to be a very heavy guard for the rebs ar doing the best they can to cut off
our cracker line. . . . Our Briggade band is a playing and it sounds very nice.
Sems a good deal like America once again."[70]

Felix Pierre Poché was assigned to the commissary department as a volunteer on the staff of Brigadier General Henry Gray. The music of the band
turned his thoughts to his beloved wife Selima. "This evening the brass bands
from the Texas regiments played some very lively and sweet music, and I
enjoyed it delightfully, being at about ½ miles distance, the proper distance for
good effect of brass band music."[71]

Alburtus Dunham appreciated music no matter what its distance. On 23
October 1864 he awoke in Marietta, Georgia, to the sound of the regimental
band. "It is most a splendid morning this morning," he wrote. "Our Briggade
band is a playing and it sounds tip top."[72]

Bugler Campbell was with Sherman's troops when General Johnston evacuated his position on Kennesaw Mountain. The Yankees spent the night at
Sweetwater Creek, and Campbell was ". . . awakened by the Brig. Band playing the National airs. Learned from that, that it was the 4th of July."[73]

Sergeant Matthew Woodruff, of the 21st Missouri Volunteers, wrote his mother: "I was awakened last night and quite enchanted at hearing a Band discou[r]sing a lovely Serenade in the city, they were playing one of those lively Enchanting Melodies that never fails to arouse the warmest sympathy of the Soul."[74]

Major Charles B. Fox lay just outside of Richmond when he recorded the band's program in a letter to his wife. He must have enjoyed music for he readily recognized all of the tunes.

The band are just now playing "Love Not." It is a sweet air but the words are rather heathenish. . . . They must be playing a medley of airs, for they have just passed to "Katy Darling" and are even now changing to "Annie Laurie." . . . At this point they suddenly started off into "Ain't you glad to get out of the Wilderness." . . . Here comes "Pop Goes the Weasel." . . . They are winding up with "The Lancers."[75]

Major Connolly was one of the most sensitive of men, and his articulate and polished letters and diary reveal a predisposition towards music. On 3 October 1862 he was just outside Taylorsville, Kentucky, when he wrote, "As far as the eye can reach the camp fires of our army can be seen, and the hum of thousands of voices mingled with the strains of martial music, comes up to our camp and serves to inspire the weary soldier, laying upon the ground, wrapped in his blanket, and without any shelter save perhaps a tree."[76]

On 28 April 1864 he wrote to his wife from Ringgold, Georgia, while he enjoyed the music of the brigade band. "This is a beautiful starlit night, and a splendid brass band is serenading General [Baird] next door. I have been sitting here idle, for an hour, listening to the music."[77]

On 9 June of the same year he was at Acworth, Georgia, intoxicated by the music and the wonders of nature. "I am sitting in the door yard of a 'Georgia Planter,' under the shade of his mulberry trees, the ripe fruit hanging above me. . . . Brass bands are playing in every direction and the mocking bird is making the leafy shade vocal with his attempts to imitate the brass music of 'Dixie,' 'Star Spangled Banner,' etc."[78]

On 13 October he was in the company of Hanes, a fellow devotee of the arts and somewhat of a maudlin mind.

While waiting for the distribution of rations, the General and Staff stopped at Mr. Hanes near where our tents had been pitched. Capt. Acheson astonished the ladies by playing finely on the piano. Colonel Gleason's Band came up in front of the house, and played several pieces very finely. I had been talking with the old gentleman while the band was playing and he was expressing his regrets to me that he was not in a condition to treat us as hospitable as he could have done before the war; suddenly the band commenced playing the "Star Spangled Banner," the old man became silent, tears came into his eyes and rolled down his cheeks, his head bent forward and his thoughts were evidently busy with the distant past, recalling to him the days when those same patriotic strains stirred the impulses of his young heart.[79]

The music of the Yankee bands was, for the most part, the property of the Confederates as well. The thoughts of Confederate Lieutenant L. D. Young of Kentucky's "Orphan Brigade" verged upon treason as he listened to the music of the Union bands. His regiment retired to Dalton following the battle of Chattanooga, where it established winter quarters within sight and sound of the Union army.

We . . . took position in the gap on the mountain, from which we could see extending for miles [Sherman's] grand encampment of infantry and artillery, the stars and stripes floating from every regimental, brigade, division and corps headquarters and presenting the greatest panorama I ever beheld. Softly and sweetly the music from their bands as they played the national airs were wafted up and over the summit of the mountain. Somehow, some way, in some inexplicable and unseen manner, "Hail Columbia," "America" and the "Star Spangled Banner" sounded sweeter than I had ever before heard them, and filled my soul with feelings that I could not describe or forget. It haunted me for days, but never shook my loyalty to the Stars and Bars or relaxed my efforts in behalf of our cause.[80]

Camp concerts were frequently linked with some other patriotic celebration such as the Fourth of July. Hamlin Coe of the 19th Michigan Infantry wrote to his wife of such an occasion. "This afternoon there was a brigade celebration in honor of Washington. We were addressed by the Colonel of the several regiments. There was music by the brass band of the 22nd Indiana. We also passed several resolutions and had a good time. Thus passed the aniversary of Washington."[81]

George Townsend noted that the Blacks organized their own celebrations when a band was available. He was with the 9th New York Regiment at Warrenton when he wrote of both the bands and his own prejudice. "The Negroes remained in Warrenton in great numbers and held carnival of evenings when the bands played. Contrabands were coming daily into town, and idleness and vice soon characterized the mass of them. They were ignorant, degraded, animal beings, and many of them loved rum; it was the last link that bound them to human kind."[82]

Early in the war the more pious commanders banished music from the Sabbath unless it was a part of the divine service. The ban was soon lifted in most regiments, and a pious private complained of this bedevilment in a letter to his folks. "It is sunday," he wrote, "but if you was heare I dont believe you would think it was sunday for the fidles and other kinds of music are ratteling away, some singing, some a little of everything."[83]

Another not-so-pious Yank was stuck in Bristol, Tennessee, on Sunday 15 March 1863 but would have preferred a locale more suited to his larcenous intent.

We have remained here all day simply because the Colonel in charge of us is religious, and it is against his principles to transact business on the Sabbath; but he can bet, drink and fight without smiting his conscience a bit.

I have amused myself as I did at Chattanooga but did not make it pay as well, for the pies I stole I could not eat, and I am hungry enough to eat almost anything. . . . It has commenced raining again tonight, but I have slipped the guard and got into a box car, where I will be secure from the storm one night more.[84]

Regimental bands composed of professional musicians could also perform as a string orchestra since many of the wind players doubled on other instruments. Polignac's Brigade had enlisted just such a band, and the musicians filled the night air with the chamber music of Mozart, Haydn, and Beethoven. Felix Poché enjoyed the orchestra and the music always renewed, refreshed, and intensified his longing for his beloved wife, Selima.

This morning I crossed the river [at Natchitoches] and assisted at mass. I brought two Methodist ministers with me who behaved very well. At the pressing invitation of my friend Julien Charlesville, I had dinner at the home of his brother-in-law Abel Sus. I had the pleasure of meeting two young and interesting widows Mrs. Levasseur and Mrs. Hyams, the young lovely widow, and so fresh-looking, of an old man of seventy who died under the weight of happiness of possessing such a lovely young wife.

After dinner I returned to camp 3 miles from Cloutierville. . . . Tonight we had some very good music by an orchestra from Polignac's Brigade. The good music gave me still greater pleasure as it awakened such tender memories of my beloved Selima.[85]

The 19th Michigan Infantry Regiment also had the benefit of professional musicians, and Alexander Coe enjoyed the music of the string orchestra. "Another pleasant and beautiful day has passed, and we have been blessed with the presence of the Paymaster. I received $43.50, and tonight I have listened to a string band playing their music and many a thought did it bring to my mind of the pleasant past."[86]

General J. E. B. Stuart included other forms of musical activities in camp. One of his staff officers noted that ". . . Stuart's camp is always one of the jolliest; as the General is very fond of music and singing, and is always gay and in good spirits himself, and when he laughs heartily, as frequently happens, he winds up with a shout very cheering to hear. One of his couriers, Grant, has a magnificent voice."[87]

General McClellan was assigned to Stuart's command prior to the Chambersburg raid. During the lull following Sharpsburg the cavalry headquarters was located under the magnificent oaks that graced the lawn of The Bower, the elegant residence of Mr. A. S. Dandridge, near Charleston. McClellan wrote that "on the afternoon of the 8th, Stuart ordered his acting adjutant, Lieutenant R. Channing Price, to prepare all official papers which required his attention. The evening, until eleven o'clock was spent in the society of the ladies of 'The Bower.' Retiring to his tent Stuart then consumed two hours in closing up the business of his office. This done, the banjo, fiddle, and bones were awakened, and a parting serenade was given to his friends."[88]

Fitzgerald Ross was invited to spend Christmas at General Stuart's headquarters then located near Orange Courthouse. He was received by "... Stuart and the officers of his staff [who] gave us a hearty welcome, and before long we were seated around a roaring fire in the General's tent. The two Sweenies [Sweeneys] played the banjo and violin; a quartet of young fellows, couriers of the General, sang some capital songs, in the choruses of which we all joined; V ... who is a great favorite of the General's told some of his best stories; and altogether we passed as merry a Christmas Eve as we could desire."[89]

The two Sweeneys were Sam and Dick, musical brothers assigned to Stuart's camp. Colonel W. W. Blackford wrote that by the fall of 1861,

... Stuart had ... organized the band of stringed instruments and singers which afterwards became so well known and so associated with him. Sween[e]y who had brought the banjo into European notice by his skill upon it, was one of the band; he played the banjo and sang. . . . [Stuart] collected around him a number of experts, not only in music, but in theatricals and tricks of various kinds, and they added much to the pleasure of camp life. Sween[e]y and his banjo and his negro melodies were the favorites; and Sween[e]y always carried his instrument slung at his back on marches, and often in long night marches the life of the men was restored by its tinkle.[90]

General Stuart made a determined effort to recruit artistically talented individuals as a part of his headquarter's retinue.

Almost at the beginning of the war he managed to surround himself with a number of persons whose principal qualification for membership of his military household was their ability to make fun. One of these was a noted banjo-player and ex-negro minstrel. He played the banjo and sang comic songs to perfection, and *therefore* Stuart wanted him. I have known him to ride with his banjo, playing and singing, even on a march which might be changed at any moment into a battle; and Stuart's laughter on such occasions was sure to be heard as an accompaniment as far as the minstrel's voice could reach. He had another queer character about him whose chief recommendation was his grotesque fierceness of appearance. This was Corporal Hagan, a very giant in frame, with an abnormal tendency to develop hair. His face was heavily bearded almost to his eyes, and his voice was as hoarse as distant thunder, which indeed it closely resembled. Stuart, seeing him in the ranks, fell in love with his peculiarities of person at once, and had him detailed for duty at head-quarters, where he made him a corporal and gave him charge of the stables. Hagan, whose greatness was bodily only, was much elated by the attention shown him, and his person seemed to swell and his voice to grow deeper than ever under the influence of the newly acquired dignity of chevrons. All this was amusing, of course, and Stuart's delight was unbounded. The man remained with him till the time of his death, though not always as a corporal. In a mad freak of fun one day, the chief recommended his corporal for promotion, to see, he said, if the giant was capable of further swelling, and so the corporal became a lieutenant upon the staff.[91]

Of all the musicians who entertained at Stuart's headquarters, Sweeney was by far the general's favorite, and Stuart felt a deep personal loss when his banjo player succumbed to pneumonia in 1863.

Although most military musical and theatrical productions were accomplished through the efforts of the men in the ranks, they were sometimes augmented by civilians with established stage reputations. These public-spirited artists moved into the camps and hospitals to cheer the troops, establishing what, in later wars, would be called the USO.

Union troops went into quarters following Vicksburg, and the opening of water communications to the north brought an influx of civilians to their camps. Sanitary and Christian Commission agents (civil war equivalents of Red Cross workers) arrived with clothing and hospital supplies. Each soldier was made to feel that he was important to the war effort as governors vied with the lowliest citizens in expressions of gratitude and concern for the welfare of the troops. An army of artists from the civilian stage came with them.

The Lombard Brothers of Chicago [Julius and Frank] had acquired more than merely local fame in concert singing; and were employed and sent to the army in front of Vicksburg to visit all headquarters and hospitals (and all regiments so far as practicable), to give free concerts to enliven the monotony of camp life, and to cheer and inspire the troops by their excellent singing. The lines and Camps were made vocal at night for several weeks, and the uproarious encoring and applauding which was always given them, proved how heartily and deeply the soldiers appreciated the entertainment. "Old Shady," "Dixie," "The Battle Cry of Freedom," "Old John Brown," "The Star Spangled Banner," "Columbia," "Home Sweet Home," "The Mocking Bird," and dozens of other patriotic and sentimental songs were excellently-exquisitely-rendered, interspersed with comic songs, such as the "Irishman's Shanty," & "Widow Machree," which had the run of popular favor in those days. Occasionally operatic selections and solos were artistically rendered. But the ballads and home songs of the nation were the standing favorites, and thousands on thousands were alternately convulsed with weeping and laughter. These songs were better than rations or medicine to many a poor homesick private, and brought healthy sentiments and inspirations in place of morbid unhealthy ones.[92]

General Stuart was not the only commander who promoted the arts. Many others encouraged the enlisted men to produce their own theatrical and musical entertainments. Since both armies contained scores of professional actors, minstrels, and musicians many of these homegrown performances displayed a decidedly professional quality.

No public worship was held in the place. The Sundays were busy as other days; trains came and went, teams made dust in the streets, cavalry passed through the village, music arose from all the outlying camps; parades and inspections were made, and all preparations for killing men were relentlessly forwarded. A pleasant entertainment occurred one evening, when a plot of ground adjoining the Warrenton Inn was appropriated for a camp theatre. Candle footlights were arranged, and the stage was canopied with national flags. The citizens congregated, and the performers deferred to their prejudices by singing no Federal songs. The Negroes climbed the trees to listen, and their gratified guffaws made the night quiver. The war lost half its bitterness at such times; but I thought with a shudder of Stuart's thundering horsemen, charging into the village, and closing the nights mimicry with a horrible tragedy.[93]

John O. Casler was with the Stonewall Brigade in winter quarters near Orange Courthouse, where it joined forces with a Louisiana brigade to organize a theatrical troop.

[They] built a large log house, covered it with clapboards, erected a stage, organized a theatrical troupe of negro minstrels and gave performances nearly every night to a crowded audience. "Admission one dollar—net proceeds to be given to widows and orphans of Confederate soldiers."

Nobel T. Johnson, of the 5th Virginia, was one of the end men, handled the bones, and was one of the most comical characters I ever saw. He could keep the house in a roar of applause all the time. Miller, of the 1st Louisiana was banjoist, and a splendid performer. They would write some of their own plays, suitable to the times and occasion. . . .

Many such pieces . . . were acted—burlesques on the Officers, quartermasters and commissaries, or whatever was interesting and amusing. Taking it all together we had splendid performances. I have never seen better since the war, as we had amongst us professional actors and musicians; and the theatre became a great place of resort to while away the dull winter nights.[94]

These professional thespians were supported by the excellent brass band of the Stonewall Brigade. The band was originally organized at Staunton, Virginia, in 1855 as the "Mountain Saxhorn Band" and enlisted with the 5th Virginia Regiment. It was designated the official band for the entire brigade a short time later and adopted the "Stonewall" sobriquet when the brigade assumed that title.

The band served during the entire four years of strife, and the members were often exposed to great danger, as they acted as assistant surgeon, and helped to bear the dead and wounded from the field. They also did hospital duty, and several of them could, in war times, amputate a leg or an arm as well as a regular surgeon. Only two were killed in battle.

At Appomattox General Grant issued an order to allow the members of the band to take their instruments home with them, and they are now [1906] on exhibition in their band hall.

The band occupied a post of honor at the funeral of General Grant, in New York, and has attended nearly all the famous military events in this country. The organization was incorporated in 1874 under the laws of Virginia.[95]

The band's instruments, still on display in Staunton, are probably the only complete set that survived the war. The band provided music for all social

occasions in addition to the usual parades and services. During the winter of
1863 "some of the boys would get up parties and dances in the country, and
have a houseful of ladies. We would take the musicians from camp and, altogether, spent a pleasant time that winter."[96]

Scores of regimental bands were of sufficient quality to provide this service,
but it is difficult to determine whether they performed as string orchestras or as
brass bands. Ignoring all subtleties of orchestration, regimental biographers
displayed a lamentable tendency to label any group of instrumentalists a band.

Some dances were held within the camps, but generally the band was trans-
ported to more elegant surroundings. An Englishman covering the war for the
British press was invited to join a rather distinguished party hosted by the
Governor of Alabama.

We went down [Mobile] . . . bay to visit the outer defenses in a magnificent river-
steamer. The Governor, . . . Admiral Buchanan, General Maury, and other gentlemen
and ladies were of the party. A very good band of music from one of the regiments of the
garrison played, and dancing was soon got up in the splendid saloon. They dance the
"finale" of the quadrille here with all sorts of figures—one of them like the last figure in
the Lancers, walking around and giving the right and left hand alternately. Admiral
Buchanan, who was looking on, joined in this, and naturally by doing so created a great
deal of confusion and merriment. . . . He is immensely popular, and the young ladies all
call him a charming old gentleman, although he is at least ten years too young to be an
admiral in England.[97]

Mary Chesnut, an inveterate partygoer, wallowed in the social swirl of the
Confederacy, but preferred conversation and dinner to dancing. As a warm-up
for the social season she joined the festivities aboard another river steamer.
She thought that "Preston Hampton was the handsomest man on board, and as
lazy and as sleepy as ever. At dinner he stood behind my chair, a great hungry
six-foot-two boy. I asked for everything on the table, and passed it over my
shoulder to Preston, who stood at ease and ate at his leisure. So now I am in
fine condition for Hetty Cary's starvation party, where they will give thirty
dollars for the music, and not a cent for a morsel to eat."[98]

Matthew Woodruff may have been an earlier incarnation of Fred Astaire,
but he lacked a young man's tolerance for the latest dance steps. He must have
been the wet blanket of the party on 30 August 1865: "was up Town last night
to a dance, took no part. got up by the Officers of 96 U. S. C. I. was much
diverted by the *Stiles* such agony, & so ignorant of dancing, perfectly dis-
gusting. our Musicians played for them all night and did not even get their
suppers."[99]

As might be expected, the success of a dance was proportional to the quality
of the music. If a good band was not to be had the celebrants had to make do
with whatever was available. Felix Poché was a handsome, sensitive, well-
educated, bilingual man of the world who loved the arts almost as much as he

loved dancing and the company of beautiful women, but his delicate ear could not tolerate a poor musical performance. While he was at the Sicily Island camp ". . . a dance was given at the home of Dr. Lovelace in honor of Genl Gray's general staff. . . . There were about a dozen young ladies of whom five were named Lovelace. Miss Florence Lovelace was the belle of the ball. The dance consisted of cotillions without order or cadence, to the sound of an atrocious violin squeakily played by a miserable negro. It was dull and no one seemed to be enjoying themselves."[100]

Dances were not limited to metropolitan centers. Although large cities reaped the benefits of greater cultural munificence, even the most remote military posts offered limited social and musical entertainments. Fort Ripley was the center citadel in a chain of forts running diagonally across central Minnesota. Fort Snelling anchored the line in the southeast and Fort Abercrombie provided its western mooring. Fort Ripley was on the western bank of the Mississippi, opposite the mouth of the Nokaysippi River and seven miles north of its confluence with the Crow Wing River. Through treaties, ratified in 1846, the Winnebago Indians had been moved into this area to serve as a buffer between the warring Sioux and Chippewa. The fort, constructed in 1848, was positioned at the confluence of these tribal boundaries.

Fort Ripley is one hundred miles northwest of St. Paul and in 1848 represented the last civilized outpost north of that city. The Crow Wing settlement, located a few miles north of the fort, had its beginning in 1843 when Alexander Morrison opened a trading post. Donald MacDonald entered into partnership with Morrison in 1845. These two entrepreneurs, living within the hunting grounds of the Chippewa, were the only white men between St. Paul and Fort Garry in Winnipeg.

Fort Ripley was completed in 1849 and garrisoned by the 6th United States Infantry Regiment, a unit of the Regular Army. On 13 June 1859 the headquarters of the 2nd Infantry Regiment replaced the 6th at Fort Ripley. The garrison included the regimental headquarters and staff, Company K, and the regimental band.[101] Still at the post in January 1861 the band helped ring in the New Year at a dance for the garrison complement. The *Saint Paul Democrat* informed its readers that "A large ball came off at Fort Ripley. We are informed that eighty couples were present and that excellent order was preserved, not one drunken person in the room."[102]

The entire area regretted the loss of the regimental band when the 2nd Regiment was relieved by Company A of the 1st Minnesota Volunteers on 4 June 1861. Several volunteer regiments rotated through the post during the war. Company A of the 1st Minnesota was replaced by Company A of the 2nd Minnesota on 9 July 1861.

Social life at the post was nonexistent until Company F of the 4th Minnesota arrived with its regimental band in October. The musicians were immediately put to good use. "On Christmas night 1861 the boys had one of the large dining rooms at the Fort decorated with flags, evergreens and pictures and after a good supper finished the night with a dance. Over thirty ladies were present, quite a number of them being from Crow Wing and Little Falls."[103]

Crow Wing had grown a little by 1861. Its residents included Indian Agent George Fuller, his wife Abby, and Samuel, their son. The Fullers had been assigned at Crow Wing when the post was first garrisoned by the Regular Army. In a letter to a customer named Trotwood, Samuel Fuller expressed his admiration for the professionalism of the regulars, but was appalled by the conduct of the volunteers. His jaundiced appraisal of the volunteers was unusual for the time, but perhaps not for the place. Isolated in this cultural and military backwater, the Fullers were untouched by the flames of patriotism that licked the souls of those citizens closer to the conflagration in Charleston. "We are very quiet on the War question," he wrote, "and I am happy to inform you that they have not as yet got the first recruit from this Burg. We have a Company of Home Guards at the Fort and they are home guards to a dead certainty. Every man has his wife and family with him and a small sprinkling of Aunts, Sisters &c., &c. The Rank and File occupy the officers quarters in common with the officers and all mess together."[104]

Company C of the 5th Regiment of Minnesota Volunteers arrived on 1 April 1862 and was replaced in turn by elements of the 8th Regiment on 4 October of the same year. Since neither had a band, the garrison hired the Anoka Brass Band (which traveled nearly one hundred miles through the deep snow of a frigid Minnesota winter) to play a concert at the fort on 18 February 1863.[105] Private Edison Washburn wrote excitedly of the concert and dance that followed but could find little to record in his diary once the band returned home. He sadly noted their departure on 19 February. Social life immediately settled into a routine of numbing dullness, and on 20 February he tersely recorded the only excitement that he encountered that day. "Skunk killed in guard house—guard house removed to new quarters owing to stink."[106]

Washburn's social life did not improve until 2 March 1863 when he noted that "the boys had a dance in Co. 'B' quarters."[107] The field musicians must have provided the music since there was no band at the post.

Private Fearing and Sergeant Lambrey were court-martialed on 4 March and two days later the field musicians helped execute the verdict of the court. "Fearing was dressed up in women's skirts and marched around the parade ground with a guard and the musicians playing the Rogue's March."[108] Private Fearing must have been treated to more than a "march around the parade," for Washburn recorded his death at "six-and-one-fourth o'clock on the 27th of March."[109]

It appears that the field musicians did not please their dancing public. On 22 January 1864 Washburn excitedly reported that "the boys met for to organize a dance."

23 January—Jim D. starts for Monticello for the girls for the dance.
24 January—Ells and Lieut. Tollington got to clearwater after more ladies. Dave to go
        to Fair Haven also.
25 January—Russell (John) goes to Sauk Centre after the musicians. Ells and Lieut.
        and Dave arrive without any ladies.
26 January—Time arrives with 4 girls. Some of the boys go to Manonosok - get 5
        ladies. They have a joyful old breakdown in the evening.

Manonosok was an Indian agency and in all probability the five ladies were Indian
maidens. Even so, Washburn regretfully recorded: 27 January—Most of the girls go
home!"[110]

Various companies of the 6th and 8th Regiments of Minnesota Volunteers
and units of the 2nd Minnesota Cavalry successively occupied the post to the
end of the war but none had bands. After Appomattox the post was garrisoned
by regular troops who continued to protect the frontier until 5 September 1876
when Commissary Sergeant Thomas Stanley was the only man left on duty—
and he was awaiting reassignment.[111] After his departure the post was gradually dismantled by a stream of settlers in need of building materials. By 1940
the stone powder magazine was all that remained.

If the dances at Fort Ripley lacked the more subtle social graces, at least
they were fêtes accompli. Not all such affairs came off as planned. Mary Chesnut was in Richmond, Virginia, in 1863 when General John Bell Hood invited
her to a picnic at Drury's Bluff. "The Naval heroes were to receive us, and then
we were to dine at the Texan's camp. We were to have bands of music, dances,
turkeys, chickens, buffalo's tongues. But next morning, just as my foot was on
the carriage step. . .up rode John Darby in red hot haste. . . .'Stop! It's all up.
We are ordered back to the Rappahannock. The brigade is marching through
Richmond now!' So we unpacked, unloaded, dismissed our hacks and sat down
with a sigh."[112]

A Scotsman with an eye toward earning a little extra money for himself
planned an entertainment at Fort Lookout early in the war. It started off in
grand style, but the musicians' heavy imbibing reduced an otherwise nice affair
to a shambles.

Sandy. . .was an excellent cook and a born caterer. During the winter he proposed to get
up a dinner to be followed by dancing in the company's mess-room. Permission was obtained for "Sandy's ball," Sandy shrewdly collected the cash and gave no credit, then
he sent to St. Paul for stone china dishes. . . .He ordered hams, tongues, sardines,
pickles, preserves, lemons, etc., not forgetting a few dozen bottles of American champagne. . . .We helped him put up a few decorations and a lot of candles round the walls.
    All was ready. . . .The dinner was to be at eight o'clock, followed by dancing until
midnight with two fiddlers and a flute player to furnish the music. A half dozen soldiers'

wives were the only ladies present; but we had as many more of the younger men dressed up in borrowed female clothes. The dinner was voted a great success. . . .Then the tables and benches were moved into a corner. . .and the dancing commenced.

Everything went well for a while and we had lots of fun, until trouble started between the fiddlers. One of them, Mike Burns, had partaken of too much punch and wanted to play an Irish jig, while his German partner held out for a waltz. This enraged Mike so that he explained, "Oi despises no nation, but damn the Dutch!" and smashed his fiddle over his partner's head. The combatants were separated, Mike was put out, order restored and the dancing resumed. While the dance went on, Sandy had been busy in the kitchen selling Ohio champagne to the soldiers at steep prices. This, together with liberal quantities of whiskey punch began to show its effects and the fun became fast and furious until near midnight a fight started in one end of the room and in a moment a dozen or more of the soldiers were in the midst of it. Bottles and dishes were thrown about the room; the women screamed and rushed for the door; Sandy was up on a table waving his arms shouting, "Quit yer fechting! dinna be breaking me dishes, I'm a puir mon," when the table upset and he went down to the floor among his broken dishes. . . .

Sandy's ball had a sad sequel for him. He was a canny Scot and took good care of his bawbees (pence), saving much of his pay.[113]

The bands of the military units performed duties similar to those carried out by the field musicians: attending drummings-out, executions, and funerals; serving as surgical assistants; providing for entertainment and inspiration, both patriotic and religious. The musicians of the 8th Minnesota Volunteers were not the only ones to accompany the drumming-out of goldbricks and assorted miscreants. The main event always included a parade through the assembled command to the accompaniment of the "Rogues March." Mary Chesnut, who witnessed a drumming-out in 1864, questioned its effect upon the morale of the soldiers.

Three men of our Foreign Legion have been taken up for an attempt at garroting. They were heavily manacled and driven with bayonets pointed at their backs up and down the line. They had put the barrel shirt on some others, and they had to march to the tune of "Rogues March." I could not bear to look. . . .Another man was bucked, and another was made to ride the wooden horse. When the other men refused to hoot at these poor things as they were driven along, an officer struck several of them with the flat of his sword. Yet these dumb driven cattle are expected to be heroes in the strife. . . .We have shut all the windows on the house on that side.[114]

We can gain an idea of the frequency of the event from John Casler. While assigned to the 23rd Virginia, John was tried for a long list of minor offenses and promptly sent to prison where he "found two or three hundred in the guard house, and the court martial in full blast. Punishments of all kinds were being inflicted on the prisoners, such as shot to death, whipped, heads shaved and drummed out of service, riding wooden horses, wearing barrel shirts, and all other punishments in the catalogue of court martials."[115]

The precise order of the ritual of death varied from regiment to regiment, but all had two elements in common. The condemned man marched to his place of execution accompanied by the band, and all executions were conducted in front of as large a troop unit as possible. This discouraged others from duplicating the offense.

Desertion was the most common crime warranting death. Four deserters were returned to the Stonewall Brigade for trial and punishment prior to the brigade's departure from Gordonsville in 1862.[116] All were found guilty. The mournful cadence of the "Rogues March" paced their shuffle to the execution site.

The division was assembled in a three-sided formation, the Stonewall Brigade facing the open end. Into the center of the hollow square came the condemned men under heavy guard. Each man was blindfolded and then placed in a kneeling position beside an open grave. Twenty paces away twelve riflemen stood at attention, half the rifles loaded with balls, the other half with blanks. After the death sentences were read to the condemned, a lieutenant barked out commands, the crack of musketry split the still air, and the deserters toppled backward into the pits. Officers then marched their regiments past the graves, to impress indelibly upon them the awful consequences of desertion.[117]

The instigation of the draft made bounty-jumping a commonplace event, and the army brass decided that a wholesale shooting would be most beneficial in curbing the desertions that were depleting the ranks. The implementation of this ill-conceived deterrent produced one of the most morbidly impressive spectacles of the war. Five Philadelphia recruits deserted enroute to their assignments with the Corn Exchange Regiment. Their speedy apprehension conveniently coincided with the army's personnel requirements and provided an object lesson in military conduct.

The entire V Corps was selected to witness the event. Newspaper reporters and sketch artists from several illustrated magazines were called in to record the grizzly business.

The gruesome affair took place in an immense field on August 29, a bright cool day with the air clear and still. . . .The formation when completed made a vast and silent array around three sides of a hollow square. On the open side were five newly dug graves. The. . .men stood and looked at the graves, while the silence. . .grew deeper and deeper. . . .The corps stood still as death. It was all very much like an elaborate funeral, with the added depression of realizing that the corpses were to be manufactured on the spot.

Presently they heard sad music—a dirge—and the procession of doomed men came into view. . . .First came the band, playing its doleful music, marching with a slow, measured pace. Then the Provost Marshall with his firing party of fifty men with reversed arms, keeping time to the slow beat of the *Dead March*. Then the procession of coffins, each borne by four men and followed by a manacled prisoner. Another party from the Provost Guard brought up the rear.

Slowly the procession moved around three sides of the hollow square and then halted by the graves. The five coffins were placed beside the five graves. The five deserters sat upon the coffins. . . .The firing party now separated into five groups, ten men to a deserter. The Provost Marshall read the order of execution. The rabbi, priest and minister stepped forward to administer their final consolations. . . .The rabbi, priest and minister were praying earnestly. Their ghostly ministrations were taking too long. . . The men heard a shrill voice rising in protest in front of the division. It was General Charles Griffin. . . who was mindful of the fact that the order for the men's execution had fixed the time between 12 noon and 4 P.M., and it was now after 3:45. "Shoot those men," he yelled, "or after ten minutes it will be murder!"

The clergy stood aside. The deserters' eyes were bandaged. The Provost Marshall called, "Attention, guard! Shoulder Arms! Forward! Guide right—march!" The firing party moved to within six paces of the condemned men. "Halt! Ready. . .aim. . .fire!" The volley shocked the still air, and was followed by a note of insupportable horror. Four of the five men had fallen back upon their coffins. But the fifth man remained sitting! Frantically, the Provost Marshall called, "Inspection arms!" All fifty ramrods, when dropped into the bores and "sprung," rang with tones showing that the muskets had all been fired. The Provost Marshall drew his pistol and moved to the side of figure still sitting erect on the coffin, where it was discovered that there was no need of a final shot. . . .The man was sufficiently dead.

The band struck up a lively air—"The Girl I Left Behind Me." The [men]. . .marched briskly away, but march as far as [they]. . .would, [they]. . .would never forget. Wrote one of the Maine men. . ."it is a very solemn thing to see human beings led forth to be shot like dogs."[118]

Julius A. Leinbach who played Eb tuba (later, second cornet) with the band of the 26th North Carolina Regiment, recorded an execution with an unusual ending. A deserter was condemned to death by musketry in their camp at Magnolia, North Carolina, on 26 January 1863. The bandsmen were assigned the task of loading the muskets for the squad. Half were armed. Half contained blanks. When the task was completed "the brigade was formed on three sides of a hollow square, the prisoner being placed on the open side with the firing squad a short distance in front of him. . . .The assistant adjutant general stepped forward and read the sentence of the court martial . . . which condemned him to be shot to death. Then, to [Leinbach's] . . . intense relief . . . another paper was read, being a full pardon, and he was permitted to rejoin his company. He declared that he would never desert again nor did he, but was a good soldier and was killed bravely fighting at Gettysburg."[119]

Regimental bands provided the music for funerals. Some were carried out with pomp and flamboyant display while others were simple, if not rustic. All were accompanied, when possible, by the music of a band. Bands were in the funeral business long before the first battle, since many soldiers succumbed to illness shortly after their enlistments. Samuel Merrill was immersed in a sea of depression as "Company after Company formed with reversed arms and followed the wailing band and muffled drum as the wild melody of 'Pleyel's

Hymn' or some other equally solemn tune, quivered on the air. When the order came, no more funeral dirges, no more volleys over the sleeping dust, because of the depressing effect on those who tremblingly trod the border line of life and death, all began to learn the stern nature of war."[120]

Mrs. D. Giraud Wright pondered the "stern nature of war" as she tearfully followed the passing cortege of the "gallant Pelham." Only one week had passed since, in the full flower of manhood, he rode proudly from his wedding bed to his death at Kellysville. In a short seven days, his radiant young bride traded white for widow's weeds, and tremblingly followed her hero to his final rest.

Far down the street. . .we heard the tramp, tramp, of many feet and the unearthly, mournful sound of the dead march. We knew what it was. They were bearing to his last resting place the "gallant Pelham," the young Alabama hero, who had commanded Stuart's Horse Artillery and laid down his life. . .in the first great Cavalry battle of the war. We watched the sad procession file past the door and the music floated to our ears like the wail of a human voice. We wept in sympathy—for one so brave, so young, so fair. Such scenes were now frequent and we were soon called upon to bear the heaviest grief yet laid upon the people, who were to be whelmed in sorrow before the end should come.[121]

Although Pelham's funeral service and procession were rather ornate, they paled to unpretentiousness when compared to the services for men of still higher rank. General Stonewall Jackson's procession included the band of the 19th Virginia Regiment and several others that were unidentified. The parade was formed and "the mournful cortege moved on in silence. . .broken by the solemn strains of music and the discharge of artillery at intervals of half an hour. Tears rolled down many cheeks, and hundreds. . .wept as though mourning a brother."[122]

Sometimes the common soldier was buried with more than simple ceremony because of the circumstances of his death.

The intensity of the religious revival of 1863 was reflected in the frequency of divine services held in the camps. Soldiers grew serious on the subject of salvation, and divines waxed eloquent on the evils of sin. Sam Watkins was one of many Confederates who questioned the well-being of his eternal soul. His was not an idle curiosity and he attended all of the services preached by the Reverend J. C. Bolton, chaplain of the 15th Tennessee Regiment. During the policing up of the area in which the meetings had been held an old tree had been set afire and left smoking and burning for several days. Services were held under this burned-out hulk, and a makeshift altar was backed nearly against it.

As it was the custom to "call up mourners, " a long bench had been placed in proper position for them to kneel down at. Ten of them were kneeling at this mourners' bench, pouring out their souls in prayer to God, asking Him for the forgiveness of their sins. . .

when the burning tree, without any warning, fell with a crash right across the ten mourners, crushing and killing them instantly. God heard their prayers. . .they had joined the army of the hosts of heaven.

By order of the General, they were buried with great pomp and splendor, that is, for those times. Every one of them was buried in a coffin. Brass bands followed, playing the "Dead March," and platoons fired over their graves. It was a soldier's funeral. The beautiful burial service of the Episcopal church was read by Rev. Allen Tribble. A hymn was sung, and prayer offered, and then their graves were filled as we marched sadly back to camp.[123]

Death is an expected concomitant of war, but the rivalry between the volunteers and the regulars produced a wasteful expenditure of life. On 7 December 1862 Privates John Greathous, George N. Longcor, and William H. Holcomb, all combat veterans of the 21st Missouri Volunteer Infantry, were still full of fight and decided to substitute the troops of the 15th U.S. Infantry for the Rebels. Mathew Woodruff recalled the results. "[They]...go to the city on a Bum comeing back pas some regulars on the cor[ner] one in number begin singing 'I'll never jump the bounty any more' regs take it as an insult & make a fight. Are getting the better of them & about to use them up when speckled Dick 'Mounted Orderly' comes along & instead of stoping to help them out, put spurs to his horse & gave the alarm in the camp."[124]

A general riot resulted from Speckled Dick's alarm when several companies entered the fray, armed with brickbats, knives, and anything else available. Officers rushed to the site of the melee and temporarily quelled the disturbance before anyone was seriously injured. But on the following night "Sergt. Baker Co. 'C' & Sergt. Matlick Co. 'D' go to the city, get intoxicated & come back quite excited. Baker has a severe wound in right arm, & Matlick bruised up in the face. Say they got in a [fight]...off down the street to try to settle the riot."[125] This was sufficient incentive to involve nearly all of the men of both regiments. The results of the second round were more unfortunate. "Three of the 15 [injured]...died of the Effects of the riot. I heard the dead march played once today in their camp."[126]

Civilians soon became as familiar with the solemn strains of the "Dead March" as any battlefield veteran. Mary Chesnut, Judge Nisbett, "and others were grieving over Georgia's loss in Bartow, saying everything that was good of him, when a military funeral passed the hotel. As the march came wailing nearer, Mrs. Bartow fainted. The empty saddle and the led war horse; we saw and heard it all. Now it seems we are never out of the sound of the Dead March in Saul. It comes and it comes until I feel inclined to close my ears and scream."[127] One wag, in a more jocular spirit, observed that even the "mockingbirds...learned to whistle the 'Dead March from Saul.' "[128]

Bands not only played for the dead, they attended the dying. Hospital concerts were common fare for the regimental bands, while several of the larger hospitals had their own instrumental establishments. The most famous of these was the Finley Hospital band. The Harwood Hospital band of Washington, D. C., entertained a civilian audience at the patent office to celebrate the fall of Richmond.[129] A typical hospital performance by a regimental band was recorded by the biographer of the 9th New York Volunteers.

> Lieutenant Colonel Kimball marched the Regimental Band all the way from camp one Sunday to play for the sick boys. They gave their best selections of marching tunes and other music and devoted several hours to alternately playing and visiting from bed to bed, or to be more correct, from man to man, as there were no beds, all the men lying on the ground or on such makeshift protection from direct contact with mother earth as the soldier nurses could improvise out of the materials within reach. Lt. Col. Kimball and several commissioned officers, together with a number of enlisted men accompanied the band on this occasion.[130]

Colonel Kimball again ordered the band to "give its best selections"[131] at a concert for the wounded from the battlefield at Antietam.

The bandsmen, as did the field musicians, ministered to the wounded in still another way. During battles they were routinely assigned as stretcher-bearers, and they assisted the surgeons after recovering the wounded from the field. Many musicians received rudimentary training in first aid, and they administered what help they could to the wounded on the field. They then transported the maimed to the hospitals, where they helped the surgeons by holding limbs for amputation, providing a water supply, and burying the remains of the surgery. Their work did not go unnoticed. General W. B. Hazen applauded their efforts "at Resaca, [where] the removal of the wounded from the firing line was much more promptly and efficiently performed by Musicians than the ambulance corps. This was due to the training of the Musicians...and the low morale of Infantrymen who...would have preferred serving with their units."[132]

Hazen's plaudits did not represent the views of all commanders in this matter. An assistant surgeon at Seven Pines wrote that "the bands. . .proved utterly worthless in bringing off the wounded, behaving with utmost cowardice, and required more persons to watch and see that they did their duty than their services were worth. As a natural consequence of this, whenever a man fell out of the ranks wounded, four and sometimes six of his comrades would fall out for the purpose of carrying him away, thus seriously depleting the ranks and affording opportunity to the skulkers and cowards to sneak away."[133]

George Hicks was with the 96th Regiment on 17 September 1863 when it passed through Chattanooga into Georgia. "The distant cannonading indicated that the expected battle had begun. . . .During the day [the]. . .regiment was ordered to prepare for action. The sick and those disabled by the long march were left at Rossville with the tents and luggage; our musicians left their drums and fifes so that they might be free to assist the wounded."[134]

At Gettysburg the 1st Minnesota Regiment fought near Little Round Top. The 150th New York Infantry rushed to the aid of the embattled Minnesotans, and the New York band pitched in to aid the wounded. "It was the wounded from [Minnesota] which they worked so late in carrying off the field that night, for our own regiment did not lose any men there. A group of the band men were so busy...that they did not know when the regiment was recalled."[135]

The band of the 114th Pennsylvania Zouaves organized a small hospital just to the rear of Big Round Top. It moved to a new position when the Rebels nearly overran it, and the band continued to assist the surgeons and wounded under the direction of Bandmaster Frank Rauscher. "The wounded could be counted by the thousands. . . . To and from our hospital the ambulances were running all day...and even during the night....Surgeons were amputating limbs....Frequently the severed arms and legs reached the level of the tables [and]...under the intense heat of July...the peculiar stench became unbearable."[136]

The bandsmen of the 20th Maine aided the surgeons at the rear of Little Round Top. They may well have shared the tables with the band of the 114th Pennsylvania, for one of the Maine musicians described the scene in nearly the same terms. "Frequently the severed arms and legs reached level with the tables, in ghastly heaps, when a detail of men would dig long trenches and bury them....All this, too, taking place under the intense heat of a July sun! The second day around the tables, the peculiar stench became unbearable."[137]

The band of the 10th Massachusetts Infantry was assigned to Eustis' Brigade, 2nd Division, VI Army Corps in 1862 when many other regimental bands were mustered from the service. It worked in the rear areas during a number of major engagements, but in the Wilderness engagement the band was "ordered from the extreme front to assist the surgeons at the division hospital."[138]

The bandsmen of the 2nd Minnesota served as stretcher-bearers at Chickamauga. "During the first fighting our bandsmen...were busy with the stretchers, picking up the wounded and carrying them back up the slope of the ridge.... Some of these men were shot a second time [and]...carrying was suspended until the firing should cease."[139]

Frank M. Flinn regretted that during the siege of Port Hudson the medical services performed by his band did not allow much time for musical performance. "The ambulance corps is made up largely of the musicians; but music, we never hear it now, not even the drum and fife. It is too stern a time for that."[140]

Although field hospitals were places of incalculable suffering, prisons ran a close second by any measure of man's inhumanity to man. Even here, the musicians improvised entertainments to help while away the enforced idleness of troops incarcerated in prison. McHenry Howard, captured at Spotsylvania, encountered a Union band on his way to the prison camp. "I followed Generals Johnson and Steuart on foot," he wrote. "I next remember our being at the head of our column of prisoners and being guarded by infantry....We passed some fresh troops in new uniforms, coming from the North to the front, and the band or drums of one regiment which had halted on the roadside to let us go by, struck up the 'Rogues March.' But the veterans who were guarding us called out angrily, 'Stop that—smash those instruments,' and the music abruptly ceased....They were of Burnside's Corps, I think. I felt some gratification in reading in the newspapers afterwards that these uncivil new troops suffered heavy loss in their first battle."[141]

The "uncivil new troops" were with the 11th Vermont Infantry, assigned to General Horatio G. Wright's VI Corps. George E. Chamberlin, a Vermont officer, thought Howard and his fellow prisoners were "resolute looking," and provided a different account of the incident with the band.[142]

Members of military bands were themselves subject to capture, like the unidentified Rebel band taken at the battle of Sailors Creek in 1864. Contrary to general practice, the band was allowed to retain its instruments. The Rebel prisoners were formed in column and "marched along the roadside...headed by the band, playing their national air of Dixie."

The scene was an impressive one. They were prisoners of war, bleeding from wounds, faint and famished, ragged and nearly barefoot and their last hope gone, but as the familiar strains of the music floated back over the line their faces brightened, their steps quickened and they marched as they had marched many a time behind their beloved leader, General Lee.

Our men had too much respect for these brave men to jeer at them. The brave invariably respect the brave, and as the soldiers of the "Lost Cause" passed the veterans of the second corps all were silent and respectful, except for an occasional burst of applause which manifested itself by the clapping of hands.[143]

Instruments were generally confiscated when a band was captured, but the bands of their captors often played near the prison camps. John Ransom, in Libby Prison, enjoyed the music of a Confederate band but remained proudly pro-Union. He looked beyond the "dead line" one morning to find that "a brass band was over...giving us a tune. Looks more like a wandering tribe of vagabonds than musicians. Discoursed sweet music, such as 'Bonnie Blue Flag,' 'The Girl I Left Behind Me,' and for their pains got three groans from their enemies in limbo."[144] On 9 February 1863 he recorded that "Brass Bands [were]...playing their best to encourage the broken down Confederacy."[145]

On 14 May of the same year Ransom heard a Confederate band performing at a picnic. He enjoyed the music but the merriment of the picnickers stood in stark contrast to his own despondency and squalid surroundings. "A band of music [came] from Macon yesterday to attend the picnic. A large crowd of women were present to grace the occasion. The grounds on which the festivities were held, lay a mile off in sight of all. In the evening a Bowery Dance was one of the pleasures enjoyed. 'The Girl I Left Behind Me' was about all they could play and that very poorly."[146]

Fort Delaware, on Pea Patch Island in the Delaware River, was a Union prison. Confederate troops from General Archer's brigade, captured during the first day's fighting at Gettysburg, were imprisoned here. Troops from the 19th Delaware Infantry were assigned as guards. This detachment was accompanied by the regimental band under the direction of Major H. E. Turner. Sergeant Joseph H. Enos described the band and its vocal soloists as first-rate professionals. The 19th Regimental Band had twenty members, but the garrison band assigned at the fort was still larger and included a male chorus. Enos rated his own duty as pleasant, but decribed the plight of the prisoners as a "living hell."[147]

Since prison performances by bands were few, prisoners improvised their own entertainments, including music. Singing with or without accompaniment was popular, but if it was of a defiant character retaliation resulted.

Captain Willard Worcester Glazier, a Federal cavalryman, was captured near Charlotte, North Carolina, in 1863. Under heavy guard he was marched to the commons of that city on 13 May where he thought an issue of rations would be forthcoming.

On learning that there were Yankee prisoners in town, the citizens came out in large numbers. Many approached the guard line, and endeavored to converse with us, but were forced back at the point of the bayonet. Finding that we could not converse with them, we concluded to entertain them with some music; accordingly we struck up the "Star Spangled Banner," "Rally Round the Flag, Boys," etc. In each interlude, we could see white handkerchiefs waving in the breeze, showing that we were among loyal people who hailed again their countries [sic] stirring songs. These demonstrations so exasperated the Virginia guard that they sent a detail to drive the "d . . . d tar-heels," as they style the North Carolinians, off the field.[148]

Glazier was incarcerated on Belle Isle where his health took an immediate turn for the worse, but this did not diminish his musical expressions of patriotism.

Jan. 24, 1864. It has all along been our custom to go down to the cook-room occasionally for a promenade, there being better opportunities for exercise there. . . . Accordingly, I went down last evening for a walk, and there found about sixty comrades marching around the room at double-quick, in column of fours. I fell in with them and all commenced singing "Star Spangled Banner," "Rally Round the Flag Boys," etc.

This had continued for some time, when the door leading into the street suddenly opened, and a squad of armed rebels filed in. Turner was at their head, and quickly . . . placing himself at the door . . . he began, "Now then, you d_____d boisterous scoundrels, I'll teach you to begin your cursed howling in this building again. . . . You mus'n't drive people crazy . . . with your villanious "Yankee Songs." Then, turning to the guards—"Take your stations about these d_____d rascals, and shoot the first man that dares to stir out of his tracks.". . . So much for singing national songs. But patriotism will find vent somehow, in spite of Rebel vengeance.[149]

National holidays were welcome excuses for celebrations by the prisoners of both armies. Impromptu formats included speeches, songs, and, when possible, instrumental music. Captain Glazier had been moved from Belle Isle to a prison in Columbia, South Carolina, where on 4 July 1864 his fellow prisoner,

Captain Todd [of the] Eighth New Jersey Infantry, displayed a small silk flag four by six inches, which had been presented to him by Miss. Paradise, of Jersey City and which thus far escaped the vigilance of southern relic seekers. The miniature "Star Spangled Banner" was hailed with rounds of cheers, which showed that they came from loyal hearts. We then adjourned to the large building occupied by the general and field officers, where Chaplain Dixon, Sixteenth Connecticut Volunteers, opened the exercises with prayer. . . . [Several others] then followed with speeches and toasts, interspersed with national songs, while far above our heads, attached to a long pole was the emblem of freedom, the "Red, White, and Blue."[150]

The most prevalent form of musical entertainment in both Union and Confederate prisons was a cappella singing. Glazier was deeply touched by the singing of the Blacks imprisoned with him.

At the close of day the [Negro] prisoners made a practice of getting together in the jail, and singing their plaintive melodies till late in the evening. The character of their songs was usually mournful; and it was often affecting to listen to them—always embodying, as they did, those simple, child-like emotions and sentiments for which the negro is so justly celebrated. The harmony and rich melody of their voices are rarely surpassed. Indeed, this seems a special gift to them. This very fact gives the surest promise of their future elevation and refinement. No race so delicately sensitive to the emotional can be essentially coarse and barbarous.[151]

Sometimes the conflict begun on the battlefield was carried into the prisons where it continued on a purely musical level. John McElroy was tormented by the songs of the Confederate guards at Andersonville, but he managed to get in a few retaliatory licks of his own. "We heard these songs with tiresome iteration, daily and nightly, during our stay in the Southern Confederacy. Some one of the guards seemed to be perpetually beguiling the weariness of his watch by singing in all keys, in every sort of voice and with the wildest latitude as to air and time. They became so terribly irritating to us that to this day the remembrance of those soul-lacerating lyrics abides with me as one of the chief minor torments of our situation. They were, in fact, nearly as bad as the lice. We revenged ourselves as best we could by constructing fearfully wicked, obscene and insulting parodies on these and by singing them with irritating effusiveness in the hearing of the guards who were inflicting these nuisances upon us."[152]

Singing, either a cappella or to the accompaniment of a brass band, was a popular pastime for all of the troops in the field. The soldiers paraphrased popular lyrics, adapting them to the moment. If a good vocalist was present to lead the singing so much the better.

Amongst the subs was a Frenchman who was a sweet singer and many were the nights we used to sit and hear him sing; he always sang in French. . . . The Marseillaise Hymn was a great favorite with us, and Frenchy could sing it in a way that only a Frenchman can. . . . Before he could finish one verse the regiment began to gather around and as he proceeded the men from other reg'ts came, and soon we had nearly the entire brigade around our little fire. After his singing a song or two, the Col. sent for him to come to headquarters, and Frenchy was then singing when I went to sleep.[153]

Frenchy's patriotism was not as strong as his voice, and he deserted at the first opportunity.[154]

James Nisbet recorded a songfest by the 21st Georgia Regiment. Following the battle of McDowell on 8 May 1862 the regiment "remained in camp in Swift Run about two weeks, [the] . . . boys enjoyed the company of the mountaineer families; it was so homelike. They visited, had dances and 'Singings.' The 'Square note' hymn books were popular. These books were borrowed from the country girls, and thumbed around the camp-fires, thousands of soldiers joining in the songs. And many a fellow was off in a bee-line for Kite's apple brandy distillery, when chance offered."[155]

Mary Ann Loughborough, hiding in a cave during the siege of Vicksburg, recorded a sterling vocal performance under trying circumstances. "It was astonishing how the young officers kept up their spirits, frequently singing quartets and glees amid the pattering of Minié balls; and I often heard gay peals of laughter from headquarters, as the officers that had spent the day, and perhaps the night, previous in the rifle pits, would collect to make our reports. This evening a gentleman visited us, and, among other songs, sang words to the air of the 'Mocking Bird. . . .' "[156]

The serenade was the most popular musical outlet for both armies. Serenading was particularly, though not exclusively, the property of the volunteer regiments where it represented a transplanted civilian tradition. Almost any event or circumstance could spark a serenade, and men of military rank looked forward to this honor with enthusiasm. General Kershaw, a friend of Mary Chesnut, and a man of boundless ambition, "was told that he was to have a serenade. He gathered together the sleepy ladies at the hotel. 'Keep awake, there is to be a serenade tonight for me!' He made ready his fiery eloquence. But alas, none came to serenade him."[157]

Knowledge of the forthcoming discharge of the regimental bands in 1862 prompted thousands of serenades in a very short time. George Townsend was with General McDowell's headquarters at Warrenton Springs when the separation order for the bands was promulgated. "We rode southward over a picturesque turnpike, under a clear moonlight. The distance was seven miles, and a part of this route was enlivened by the fires, halloos, and the music of

camps. Volunteers are fond of serenading their officers; and this particular
evening was the occasion of much merry-making, since a majority of the brass
bands were to be mustered out of the service tomorrow. We could hear the roll
of drums from imperceptible localities, and the sharp winding of bugles broke
upon the silence like the trumpet of the Archangel."[158]

Mrs. W. D. Phillips was the recipient of an emotion-packed serenade when
she returned to the "Orphan Brigade" (Hanson's Brigade of Breckinridge's
Division). Mrs. Phillips accompanied her husband into service when he was
assigned as quartermaster of the 4th Kentucky Regiment. She remained for
two years, nursing the casualties of the regiment. When her own health failed
she set out for her home in Morganfield, Kentucky, but was arrested as a spy
when she tried to pass through Nashville. She was tried in Louisville and exon-
erated of all charges. Her captors took her back through the lines and abandoned her in a lonely forest in Tennessee. After wandering for days, with no
food and little water, she was finally found by a passing woodsman who took
her to the nearest railroad station. Disheveled, haggard, weeping, and ill, she
stumbled into the camp of the Orphan Brigade. "Every man in the command
begged the honor of shaking her hand; the band played 'Home Again,' and
strong men wept. At last, this sorely tried but dauntless little woman felt herself
under the protecting care of the grand old 'Orphan Brigade,' than whom braver
men never fought or fell. With them Mrs. Phillips remained until the end of the
war."[159]

Concerts were nearly as commonplace as serenades. These military mani-
festations of civilian dime concerts were one of the most popular entertainments among the soldiers. Concerts, played in Union camps and friendly
communities, were always well received, but performances in occupied Confederate cities met with only limited audience appeal. Phoebe Yates Pember
was in Richmond following its capture by the despised Yankees. Regimental
bands, as a gesture towards reconciliation, organized a series of concerts on
the capital square. Miss Pember traced the progress of the faltering series of
entertainments with great satisfaction.

In the daily newspaper a notice had appeared that the military bands would play in the
beautiful capital grounds every afternoon, but when the appointed hour arrived, except
for the Federal Officers, musicians and soldiers, not a white face was to be seen. The
negroes crowded every bench and path. The next week another notice was issued that
the colored population would not be admitted; and then the absence of everything and
anything feminine was appalling. The entertainers went along to their own entertainment. The third week still another notice appeared: "Colored nurses were to be
admitted with their white charges," and lo! each fortunate white baby received the
cherished care of a dozen finely-dressed black ladies, the only drawback being that in
two or three days the music ceased altogether, the entertainers feeling at last the ingrati-
tude of the subjugated people.[160]

Serenades and concerts were common vehicles for the bands of both armies, but divine services occasionally conscripted the musicians into the army of the Lord. The music for Sabbath celebrations most often assumed the form of a capella singing, but an occasionally inspired divine recruited his regimental band for this purpose.

Sam Watkins rather irreverently recorded the details of an unusually fine field worship service. An eloquent and able preacher had been imported from Nashville to preach from God's Holy Word, "and as he was one of the 'big ones,' the whole army was formed in close column and stacked their arms."

The cannon were parked, all pointing back toward Chattanooga. . . . It was in a dark wilderness of woods and vines and overhanging limbs. In fact, it seemed but the home of the owl and the bat, and other varmints that turn night into day. Everything looked solemn. The trees looked solemn, the scene looked solemn, the men looked solemn, even the horses looked solemn. You may be sure, reader, that we felt solemn.

The reverend LL.D. had prepared a regular war sermon before he left home, and of course had to preach it, appropriate or not appropriate; it was in him and had to come out. He opened the service with a song. I did remember the piece that was sung, but right now I cannot recall it to memory; but as near as I can now recollect here is his prayer, verbatim et literatim:

"Oh, Thou immaculate, invisible, eternal and holy Being, the exudations of whose effulgence illuminates this terrestrial sphere, we approach Thy presence, being covered all over with wounds and bruises and putrifying sores, from the crowns of our heads to the soles of our feet. And Thou, O Lord, art our dernier resort. The whole world is one great machine, managed by Thy puissance. The beautific splendors of Thy face irradiate the celestial region and felicitate the saints. They are most exuberant profusions of Thy grace and the sempiternal effux of Thy glory. God is an abyss of light, a circle whose center is everywhere and His circumference nowhere. . . ."

When the old fellow got this far, I lost the further run of his prayer, but regret very much that I did so, because it was so grand and fine . . . but they will have to get the balance of it from the eminent LL.D. In fact, he was so "high larnt" that I don't think anyone understood him but the generals. The colonels might every now and then have understood a word, and maybe a few of the captains and lieutenants, because Lieutenant Lansdown told me he understood every word the preacher said, and further informed me that it was none of your one-horse, old-fashioned country prayers that privates knew anything about, but was bang-up, first rate, orthodox.

Well, after singing and praying, he took his text. . . . "Blessed be the Lord God, who teaches my hands to war and my fingers to fight." Now . . . that was the very subject we boys did not want to hear preached — on that occasion at least. We felt like some other subject would have suited us better. . . . I remember that after he got warmed up a little, he began to pitch in on the Yankee nation, and gave them particular fits as to their geneology. . . . He was warm on this subject, and waked up the echoes of the forest. He said that he and his brethren would fight the Yankees in this world, and if God permit, chase their frightened ghosts in the next, through fire and brimstone.

About this time we heard the awfullest racket . . . "Look Out! Look Out! Hooie! Hooie! Hooie! Look Out!" and there came running right through our midst a wild bull, mad with terror and fright, running right over and knocking down the divine, and scattering Bibles and hymn books in every direction. The services were brought to a close without the doxology.[161]

Although Sam poked fun at the learned servant of God, he nonetheless remembered the prayer, so the service was not totally wasted on him.

A Sabbath service left a lasting impression upon Mrs. Maria Lydig Daly of New York City. She was acutely conscious of her social position as the wife of a judge, and doted upon her recognition as a social gadfly. She was much enamored with Colonel Corcoran of the 69th New York Regiment, while most other citizens regarded him as moderately treasonous for his refusal to obey the lawful command of his superior officer when ordered to parade his regiment to receive the Prince of Wales. At that time Corcoran was the keeper of what was known in vernacular as a "three cent grog shop" (Hibernia Hall) in New York's Prince Street. He led his regiment to the front in response to the call for three-months troops, was taken prisoner at Bull Run, and was confined for a time in Libby Prison. Paroled by his captors, he was later appointed brigadier general and served for a short time as commander of the Corcoran Legion. He was killed when he fell from his horse on a night ride escorting a group of visitors, citizens, and soldiers of his unit.

Corcoran attracted the attention of Mrs. Daly when he was appointed brigadier in 1861, and she used her position to help raise funds for his regiment. On 19 October 1862 she attended Sabbath services with the regiment as a personal guest of the commander.

We went to Staten Island to witness the ceremony of confirmation. Corcoran sent an Officer to escort me there as the Judge could not go. . . . I have never saw anything in my life that impressed me so much. There were five thousand men present with bared heads and bended knees. Corcoran, who knelt near us, was at their head. The Archbishop (John Hughes), his golden crozier in his hand, and his venerable benevolent countenance, was supported by Father Hares in a deacon's dress, a black cassock and a short white surplice. Another deacon was on the other side, the banner was flying, the fine band was performing the music for the mass. It was a picture such as I never saw equaled. Four thousand men were confirmed and as many more took the sacrament. I could scarcely restrain my tears, for I felt it was like a mass for the dead.[162]

Colonel Corcoran was a genuinely religious man, in spite of his three cent grog shop background, and he established divine services as a regular part of each duty day. He "introduced singing into his regiment, in which all of the men and officers [were] . . . expected to take part, and . . . established daily religious services through the regimental chaplain. 'John Brown's Soul is Marching On,' chorused by a thousand men at evening parade, [gave] . . . a Cromwellian earnestness to this war, in at least one camp."[163]

Lucius L. Shattuck was with the 24th Michigan Infantry. The regiment was part of the famous Iron Brigade which had been assigned as rear guard during the battle of Chancellorsville and thus had sustained no casualties. Lucius wrote to his brother on the day that Confederate General Robert E. Lee renewed his attack against the Union forces. "The bugle has sounded the church call and the band have commenced playing. . . . It would seem strange to you to have a full brass band to play for a service. But I assure you it is excellent and it is very appropriate."[164]

A Rhode Island regiment also made evening vespers a regular part of dress parade, and the combined ceremonies were one of the best-attended entertainments in Washington. The entire city is "one stirring drama," wrote John Sullivan Dwight,

but the "thing to see" among the daily sights, is the evening parade and vespers of the Rhode Island Regiment. . . . Amid one of the most beautiful of sunsets . . . we found a large representation of the society of the capitol already on the ground—the band playing and the men under review by their colonel. . . . The Poetic part of it is the prayer. The grounding of arms, the sudden silence of the drums, the stepping forward of the chaplain, and the well-chosen words of the invocation and blessing, left scarce a dry eye among the spectators. . . . I can scarcely imagine a righteous battle better prepared for, than by the closing hymn that was sung after the prayer, accompanied with the music of the military band. The voices of the men swelled up like that trained tumult of an advancing host, through an atmosphere that was all aglow with red and gold of a magnificent sunset, and the smoke of the camp fires among the trees seemed to pause and tremble with the reverberations.[165]

Although Mrs. Daly was impressed by the music and pomp of the mass and John Dwight by the thundering hymns, the bands were most appreciated by the men in the ranks when their music relieved the tedium of their everyday camp experiences. Whether the musicians played concerts or serenades, played at the outposts or in the hospitals, played on the march or on dress parade the music lightened the burdens of the line trooper. He truly appreciated their efforts, but rarely articulated his feelings. The biographer of the 14th Regiment of New Hampshire Volunteers spoke on behalf of every soldier who tried to swallow the lump in his throat as he watched the massed ensigns of an entire division advance to the color line. All were stunned into silence by the magnificent array of masses of men moving as one giant machine, with a potential for destruction and death that exceeded the mere sum of its individual parts. "But the surpassing charm of those parades . . . lay in the drum-corps and band music of the hour. We were proud of that band. It was not a first-class musical organization, but it was the best we knew of then; and its playing was excellent. We were fond of the burly, whole-souled leader; and we became attached to the physiognomy of every member. Yes, the high private who tailed the bass drum, and boasted (when away) that he played in the band; his ramrod erectness and solemn tread,—became a cherished feature of the programme."[166]

NOTES

1. *New York Times*, 14 June 1861, p. 1.
2. Kenneth A. Bernard, *Lincoln and the Music of the Civil War* (Caldwell, Idaho: Caxton Printers, 1966), Dustcover and pp. xvii–xviii.
3. Mary Boykin Chesnut, *A Diary From Dixie*, 2d ed., ed. Ben Ames Williams (Boston: Houghton Mifflin Co., Riverside Press, 1949), p. 75.
4. James I. Robertson, *The Stonewall Brigade* (Baton Rouge, La.: Louisiana State University Press, 1963), p. 47.
5. *New York Times*, 6 July 1861, p. 3.
6. *New York Herald*, 2 August 1861, p. 1.
7. *Baltimore Sun*, 11 July 1861, p. 1.
8. Austen C. Stearns, *Three Years With Company K* (Cranbury, N.J.: Associated University Presses, 1976), p. 13.
9. Ibid.
10. Ibid., p. 39.
11. George Alfred Townsend, *Rustics in Rebellion* (1866; reprint ed., Chapel Hill: North Carolina University Press, 1950), p. 89.
12. Ibid., p. 95.
13. *Baltimore Sun*, 1 September 1861, p. 2.

> The camp is on the commons at the southern limits of the town, and comprises four hundred tents, and the following companies—Worth Infantry of York, Capt. Zeigh, 70 men and a band of 16 men; Hanover Infantry, Capt. Baughman, 40 men, band 18 men; Gettysburg Blues, Capt. Buehler, 25 men and a band of 10 men; Independent Riflemen of Hanover, Pa., Capt. H. G. Meyers, 31 men and martial music; York (Pa.) Riflemen, Lieut. John Schall Commander, 50 men and a Band of 17 men; Allentown (Pa.) Riflemen, Capt. Good, 36 men and martial music; Washington Guards of Newberry York county, Pa., Capt. Krall, 21 men and martial music; Philadelphia Greys, Capt. Rusch, 32 men and Musicians; National Riflemen of Washington, D.C., Schaefer, Capt., 31 men and the Marine Band.

Captain Schaefer possessed considerable political clout, since the Marine Band was already considered "The President's Own" by 1861. The band boasted thirty members—just one man less than the entire company's size. Nearly one-third of all the men in the camp were musicians.

14. Ibid.
15. Ibid., p. 8.
16. *Baltimore Sun*, 7 September 1861, p. 2. Only the Enrolled Militia rested upon this shaky financial foundation. A remnant of the revolutionary period, the Enrolled Militia was at best militarily unsound and without question tactically ineffective. Nonetheless, one Enrolled Militia unit did participate in the Civil War—with predictable results. At the battle of Griswoldville, in November 1863, three thousand Georgia militiamen (mostly old men and boys) charged Walcutt's entrenched infantry, not just once—but seven times, sustaining 523 casualties in the process. During the battle, Walcutt was seriously though not mortally wounded, and lost 92 men of his command.

17. Felix Pierre Poché, *A Louisiana Confederate*, ed. Edwin C. Bearss, trans. Eugenie Watson Somdal (Natchitoches, La.: Louisiana Studies Institute, Northwestern State University, 1972), pp. 165–66.

18. Ibid., p. 166–67.

19. Stearns, *Three Years With Company K*, p. 159.

20. Robert E. Lee, Jr., *Recollections and Letters of General Robert E. Lee* (New York: Doubleday, Page & Co., 1904), pp. 106–07.

21. McHenry Howard, *Recollections of a Maryland Confederate Soldier . . .* (1914; reprint ed., Dayton, Ohio: Morningside Bookshop, 1975), p. 249. The 1st North Carolina Regiment had a band at its muster in 1861, but it was disbanded sometime later in the year. The band was reorganized in the fall of 1863. *See* Manarin, *North Carolina Troops*, 3, pp. 143, 158, and 161. The captured instruments could have been those of the 1st Minnesota Volunteer Infantry Regiment which lost or discarded its instruments at Gettysburg.

22. Peter H. Clark, *The Black Brigade of Cincinnati* (New York: Arno Press, New York Times, 1969), pp. 13, 19.

23. Abner Ralph Small, *The Sixteenth Maine in the War of the Rebellion* (Portland, Me.: B. Thurston & Co., 1886). Information on the band has been assembled from pp. 99, 159–65, 167, 171, and the statistical tables on pp. 252–313. The bandsmen were assigned as follows:

    Frank Richardson (Bandmaster).
    John Shea (1st Eb Cornet) Musician, Company G.
    Peletiah Cooltroth (2nd Eb Cornet) Musician, Company G.
    Charles A. Locke (1st Bb Cornet) Musician, Company D.
    Harston W. McKenney (2nd Bb Cornet) Musician, Company C.
    Benjamin W. Johnson (1st Alto) Private, Company E (Promoted to Musician).
    Wesley Webber (2nd Alto) Private, Company B.
    David H. Thorpe (1st Tenor) Private, Company F.
    Samuel B. Geary (2nd Tenor) Musician, Company H.
    Charles H. Gould (Baritone) Private, Company H (Conscript).
    Frank Jones (Bass) Private, Company E.
    Eben Curtis (Bass) Corporal, Company E.
    James A. Barrows (Tenor Drum) Musician, Company E.
    Robert C. Brann (Bass Drum) Private, Company E.
    William A. Follett (Cymbals) Musician, Company F.

Since Johnson and Gould were drafted into the service on 3 August 1863 and 15 September 1863 respectively, they were transferred to the 20th Maine Infantry when the other bandsmen were mustered out, having completed their terms of service on 4 June 1865.

24. J. W. Muffly, *The Story of Our Regiment, the 148th Pennsylvania* (Des Moines, Iowa: Kenyon Printing & Mfg. Co., 1904), p. 324.

25. Ibid., p. 328.

26. Robertson, *The Stonewall Brigade*, p. 34.

27. Julian Wisner Hinkley, *A Narrative of Service With the Third Wisconsin Infantry*, Original Papers no. 7, September 1912, p. 17, Archive Division, State Historical Society of Wisconsin, Madison, Wis.

28. Stearns, *Three Years with Company K*, p. 57–58.

29. Fitzgerald Ross, *Cities and Camps of the Confederate States*, ed. Richard B. Harwell (Urbana, Ill.: University of Illinois Press, 1958), p. 87.

30. Townsend, *Rustics in Rebellion*, p. 197.

31. Matthew Woodruff, *A Union Soldier in the Land of the Vanquished*, Southern Historical Publications no. 15 (Tuscalousa, Ala.: University of Alabama Press, 1969), p. 40.

32. Mrs. D. Giraud Wright, *A Southern Girl in '61* (New York: Doubleday, Page & Co., 1905), p. 119. Jennie Cary had set to music the poem that became the song "Maryland, My Maryland" and Hetty sang it first in Baltimore and then many times throughout the war. Their cousin, Constance Cary, wrote one of the fine social records of the war with her *Recollections Grave and Gay*. *See* Chesnut, *Diary*, p. 311.

33. Mrs. D. Giraud Wright, *A Southern Girl in '61*, p. 120.

34. Ibid.

35. Katharine M. Jones, ed., *Heroines of Dixie, Winter of Desperation* (New York: Ballantine Books, 1975), p. 33.

36. Ibid., p. 34.

37. Chesnut, *Diary*, p. 509–10.

38. Jones, *Heroines of Dixie*, p. 150.

39. Matthew Page Andrews, ed., *The Women of the South in War Times* (Baltimore: Norman Remington Co., 1920), pp. 244–45.

40. Katharine M. Jones, *When Sherman Came: Southern Women and the "Great March"* (Indianapolis: Bobbs-Merrill Co., 1964), p. 44.

41. Ibid., p. 163.

42. Ibid., p. 198.

43. John M. Gibson, *Those 163 Days . . . Sherman's March* (New York: Clarkson N. Potter, Bramhall House, 1961), p. 152.

44. Jones, *When Sherman Came*, p. 225.

45. Gibson, *Those 163 Days*, p. 172.

46. Stearns, *Three Years With Company K*, p. 86.

47. Henry Steele Commager, *The Blue and The Gray* (Indianapolis: Bobbs-Merrill Co., 1950), p. 948.

48. Ibid., pp. 949–50. Commager has taken this from General Sherman's *Memoirs*.

49. Gibson, *Those 163 Days*, p. 31.

50. Ibid., p. 39.

51. Ibid., p. 64.

52. Ibid., p. 103.

53. Matthew J. Graham, *The Ninth Regiment New York Volunteers* (New York: P. Coby & Co., 1900), p. 244.

54. Ibid., p. 245.

55. John (last name unknown) to Fannie L. Partridge 19 April 1862, manuscript in the Chicago Historical Society, as cited by Bell Irvin Wiley, *The Life of Billy Yank* (Indianapolis: Bobbs-Merrill Co., 1952), p. 158.

56. Michall R. Dresbach to his wife 14 December 1864, Minnesota Historical Society, St. Paul, Minn.

57. James A. Connolly, *Three Years in the Army of the Cumberland*, ed. Paul M. Angle (Bloomington, Ind.: Civil War Centennial Series, Indiana University Press, 1959), p. 312.

58. Ibid., p. 369.

59. John W. Rowell, *Yankee Cavalrymen . . . the Ninth Pennsylvania* (Knoxville, Tenn.: University of Tennessee Press, 1971), p. 218.

60. Rembert W. Patrick, *The Fall of Richmond* (Baton Rouge, La.: Louisiana State University Press, 1960), p. 36.

61. *Richmond Daily Gazette*, 4 April 1865, p. 2.

62. Sam R. Watkins, *Co. Aytch*, Roy P. Basler, ed. (1952; reprint ed., New York: Crowell Collier Publishing Co., 1970), pp. 59–60.

63. Ibid., p. 21.

64. Small, *The Sixteenth Maine*, p. 12.

65. John O. Casler, *Four Years in the Stonewall Brigade* (2d ed. 1906; reprinted., Marietta, Ga.: Continental Book Co., 1951), p. 182.

66. Andrews, ed., *Women of the South*, pp. 191–92.

67. Julia Taft Bayne, *Tad Lincoln's Father* (Boston: Little, Brown & Co., 1931), pp. 114–17.

68. Howard, *Recollections of a Maryland Confederate*, p. 65.

69. Henry P. Moyer, *History of the Seventeenth Regiment Pennsylvania Volunteer Cavalry* (Lebanon, Pa.: Sowers Printing Co., 1911), p. 303.

70. Arthur H. DeRosier, Jr., ed., *Through the South with a Union Soldier* (Johnson City, Tenn.: East Tennessee State University Research Advisory Council, 1969), p. 143.

71. Poché, *A Louisiana Confederate*, p. 12.

72. DeRosier, ed., *Through the South*, p. 157.

73. Campbell, *Diary*, as cited by John W. Rowell, *Yankee Artillerymen . . . Eli Lilly's Indiana Battery* (Knoxville, Tenn.: University of Tennessee Press, 1975), p. 208.

74. Woodruff, *A Union Soldier in the Land of the Vanquished* (Tuscalousa, Ala.: University of Alabama Press, 1969), p. 41.

75. Journal of Major Charles B. Fox, 7 November 1863, as cited by Wiley, *Billy Yank*, p. 158.

76. Connolly, *Three Years in the Army*, p. 19.

77. Ibid., p. 199.

78. Ibid., p. 217.

79. Ibid., p. 276.

80. L. D. Young, *Reminiscences of a Soldier of the Orphan Brigade* (Paris, Ky.: privately printed, n.d.), pp. 75–76.

81. Hamlin Alexander Coe, *Mine Eyes Have Seen the Glory*, ed. David Coe (Cranbury, N.J.: Associated University Presses, 1975), pp. 56–57.

82. Townsend, *Rustics in Rebellion*, p. 199.

83. DeRosier, ed., *Through the South*, p. 90.

84. Coe, *Mine Eyes Have Seen the Glory*, p. 62.

85. Poché, *A Louisiana Confederate*, pp. 100–01.

86. Coe, *Mine Eyes Have Seen the Glory*, p. 93.

87. Ross, *Cities and Camps*, p. 168.

88. H. B. McClellan, *I Rode With Jeb Stuart.* (Bloomington, Ind.: Civil War Centennial Series, Indiana University Press, 1958), p. 136.

89. Ross, *Cities and Camps*, p. 167.

90. William Willis Blackford, *War Years With Jeb Stuart* (New York: Charles Scribner's Sons, 1945), pp. 50–51. *See also* "Band Joe Sweeney and His Banjo," *Virginia Cavalcade* 2 (Summer 1952): 34–35.

91. George Cary Eggleston, *A Rebel's Recollections* (New York: Hurd and Houghton, 1875), pp. 127–28.

92. Sylvanus Cadwallader, *Three Years With Grant*, ed. Benjamin P. Thomas (New York: Alfred A. Knopf, 1956), pp. 96–97.

93. Townsend, *Rustics in Rebellion*, p. 199.

94. Casler, *Four Years in the Stonewall Brigade*, pp. 204–05.

95. Ibid., p. 48–49.

96. Ibid., p. 201.

97. Ross, *Cities and Camps*, p. 196.

98. Chesnut, *Diary*, p. 229.

99. Woodruff, *A Union Soldier*, pp. 31–32.

100. Poché, *A Louisiana Confederate*, p. 158.

101. "Special Order No. 57, Hq., U.S. Army" 13 June 1859 *Post Returns, Fort Ripley, Minnesota*, June, August 1859. Minnesota Historical Society, St. Paul, Minn.

102. *Saint Paul* (Minn.) *Democrat*, 2 January 1861.

103. Alonzo L. Brown, *History of the Fourth Regiment of Minnesota Infantry Volunteers* (St. Paul, Minn.: Pioneer Press Co., 1892), pp. 32–33.

104. Samuel Fuller to George Fuller, 12 December 1861. The Abby Abbe Fuller and Family Papers, Minnesota Historical Society, St. Paul, Minn.

105. Edson D. Washburn Diary, 18 February 1863. Minnesota Historical Society, St. Paul, Minn. Washburn was stationed at the fort with the 8th Regiment.

106. Ibid., 19, 20 February 1863.

107. Ibid., 2 March 1863.

108. Ibid., 4, 6 March 1863.

109. Ibid., 27 March 1863.

110. Ibid., 22–27 January 1864.

111. U.S. Department of War, "Special Order No. 84," *General Orders* (Washington, D.C.: Government Printing Office, 1876).

112. Chesnut, *Diary*, p. 297.

113. Augustus Meyers, *Ten Years in the Ranks* (New York: Stirling Press, 1914), pp. 167–70.

114. Chesnut, *Diary*, p. 297.

115. Casler, *Four Years With the Stonewall Brigade*, p. 206.

116. Edward Moore recorded that three men were shot and Mercer Otey recorded that five men were killed. Both were present at the execution. See Edward Moore, *The Study of a Cannoneer under Stonewall Jackson*, pp. 262–63; and Mercer Otey, "Letters," *Confederate Veteran* 7, No. 9 (September 1899): 99–100.

117. Casler, *Four Years with the Stonewall Brigade*, p. 164.

118. John J. Pullen, *The Twentieth Maine* (Philadelphia and New York: J. B. Lippincott Co., 1957), pp. 155–57.

119. Harry Hobart Hall, *A Johnny Reb Band from Salem: The Pride of Tarheelia* (Raleigh, N.C.: North Carolina Confederate Centennial Committee, 1963), p. 25.

120. Samuel Merrill, *The Seventeenth Indiana Volunteer Infantry in the War of the Rebellion* (Indianapolis: Bower-Merrill Co., 1900), p. 160.

121. Wright, *A Southern Girl in '61*, pp. 125–26.

122. Casler, *Four Years With the Stonewall Brigade*, p. 157.

123. Samuel R. Watkins, *Company Aytch*, ed. Roy P. Basler (1952; reprint ed., New York: Crowell Collier Publishing Co., 1970), p. 131.

124. Woodruff, *A Union Soldier*, pp. 72–73.

125. Ibid., p. 78.

126. Ibid.

127. Chesnut, *Diary*, p. 87.

128. Matthew John Graham, *The Ninth regiment, New York volunteers (Hawkins' Zouaves) . . . from 1860 to 1900*. (New York: E. P. Coby & Co., 1900), p. 108.

129. This celebration was attended by a large number of bands and is recorded in all of the Washington and New York newspapers.

130. Graham, *The Ninth New York*, p. 349.

131. Ibid., p. 148.

132. U.S., Department of War. *Official Records of the War of the Rebellion. Medical and Surgical History*, Medical Volume, pt. 1 (Washington, D.C.: Government Printing Office, 1898), pp. 70–78.

133. Ibid.

134. Robert J. Snetsinger, ed., *Kiss Clara for Me: The Story of Joseph Whitney* (State College, Pa.: Carnation Press, 1969), p. 107.

135. Edward O. Bartlett, *The "Dutchess County Regiment" (150th Regiment of New York State Volunteer Infantry) in the Civil War*, ed. S. G. Cook, M.D. and Charles E. Benton (Danbury, Conn.: Danbury Medical Printing Co., 1907), p. 180.

136. Frank Rauscher, *Music on the march, 1862–1865, with the Army of the Potomac. 114th regt. P. V. Collis Zouaves*. (Philadelphia: W. F. Fell & Co., 1892), p. 94–95.

137. Pullen, *The Twentieth Maine*, p. 136.

138. Alfred S. Roe, *The Tenth Regiment Massachusetts Volunteer Infantry 1861–1864* (Springfield, Mass.: Tenth Regiment Veteran Association, 1909), p. 344.

139. Judson W. Bishop, *The Story of a Regiment . . . Second Minnesota* (St. Paul, Minn.: n.p., 1890), p. 101.

140. Frank M. Flinn, *Campaigning With Banks and Sheridan in Louisiana, '63 and '64* (Lynn, Mass.: Thomas P. Nicholas, 1887), p. 85.

141. Howard, *Recollections of a Maryland Confederate*, pp. 303–04.

142. George Ephraim Chamberlin, *Letters of George E. Chamberlin*, ed. Caroline Chamberlin Lutz (Springfield, Ill.: H. W. Rokker, 1883), pp. 315–16.

143. Delavan S. Miller, *Drum Taps in Dixie* (Watertown, N.Y.: Hungerford Holbrook Co., 1905), p. 175.

144. John Ransom, *John Ramson's Diary* (1881; reprint ed., New York: Paul S. Erickson, 1963), p. 25.

145. Ibid., p. 38.

146. Ibid., p. 70.

147. W. Emerson Wilson, "Band Membership Good Duty at Prison." Mr. Wilson, president of the Wilmington Civil War Round Table, prepared a brief of the activities described by Enos's letters and provided Bufkin with a single photographed copy. My comments here are taken from a lengthy discussion of the bands at Fort Delaware that

Bufkin prepared from these materials. *See* William F. Bufkin, "Union Bands of the Civil War" (Ph.D. diss., Louisiana State University, 1973), pp. 143–44.

148. Willard Worcester Glazier, *The Capture, the Prison Pen, and the Escape* (New York: R. H. Ferguson and Co., 1870), pp. 108–09.

149. Ibid., pp. 77–78.

150. Ibid., pp. 127–28.

151. Ibid., pp. 151–52.

152. John McElroy, *This Was Andersonville*. Reprint, ed. Roy Meredith (New York: Crown Publishers, Bonanza Books, 1957), p. 135.

153. Stearns, *Three Years With Company K*, p. 219.

154. Ibid., p. 223.

155. James Cooper Nisbet, *4 Years on the Firing Line* (1914; reprint ed., ed. Bell Irvin Wiley, Jackson, Tenn.: McCowat-Mercer Press, 1963), p. 33.

156. Jones, ed., *Heroines of Dixie*, pp. 16–17.

157. Chesnut, *Diary*, p. 182.

158. Townsend, *Rustics in Rebellion*, p. 205.

159. Andrews, ed., *Women of the South*, pp. 122–24.

160. Phoebe Yates Pember, *A Southern Woman's Story, Life in Confederate Richmond*, ed. Bell I. Wiley (Jackson, Tenn.: McCowat-Mercer Press, 1959), pp. 96–97.

161. Watkins, *Co. Aytch*, pp. 101–02.

162. Harold Earl Hammond, ed., *Diary of a Union Lady 1861–65* (New York: Funk and Wagnalls, 1962), p. 60.

163. *DJM* 20, no. 16 (18 January 1862): 335.

164. Lucius L. Shattuck to his brother (24th Michigan Infantry at Camp Isabella) 3 May 1863, as cited by Bufkin, "Union Bands," p. 78.

165. *DJM* 19, no. 17 (27 July 1861): 135.

166. Francis H. Buffum et al., *A Memorial of the Great Rebellion . . . the Fourteenth New Hampshire Volunteers* (Boston: Franklin Press, Rand, Avery & Co., 1882), p. 134.

BANDS AT THE FRONT

With the single exception of the monuments in Fort Sumter, no Civil War battlefield visited by this author records the presence of a brass band. In spite of this oversight on the part of the veterans' organizations, sufficient evidence is available to establish the presence of a band on every major battlefield of the war. If the molders of bronze and chiselers of marble and granite overlooked these embattled musicians, the soldiers, diarists, and regimental historians did not. Although few bands influenced the course of battle, their presence on the field was of sufficient importance to be recorded by the combatants of both armies. There were ten bands on the field at Gettysburg, including the bandsmen of the 12th New Jersey who traded their instruments for weapons and fought as soldiers on the Union left flank.[1]

It is sometimes difficult to differentiate between battlefield and nonbattlefield performances. Shelling was not limited to the point where combatant armies faced each other, and rear areas could quickly turn into combat zones. Nor did major engagements erupt full-blown. They convulsed spasmodically as the leading elements of the attacking regiments drove the defending pickets from their posts while larger units jockeyed for position. The noise and killing increased as major commands were committed, and the carnage continued unabated until darkness mercifully covered the field. The horrendous cacophony of shot and shell, mingled with the yells and curses of the gladiators, gradually evaporated into the night, followed by the pitiful pleas of the wounded and dying. Those who survived—sound in body and mind—slept fitfully on their arms awaiting the dawn and the resumption of the slaughter. Finally one army, forced from its position, would fall back and regroup, providing a brief respite for all of the combatants. The temporarily vanquished now assumed the aggressor's role and their counterattack renewed the struggle. The contest continued to seesaw until the decimated and depleted regiments of one side surrendered the field, and both armies retired to lick their wounds.

A major battle was not a sudden event, nor did it continue without interruption until the issue was decided. It evolved slowly, grew in intensity, and was sometimes interrupted by truces, only some of which were sanctioned by authority. The bands were active participants at all levels of this process.

Concerts in the staging areas were commonplace. Confederate and Union commanders recognized the psychological benefits inherent in a good band, and musicians frequently performed within easy reach of enemy artillery.

Mrs. McGuire served as an unwilling hostess to several Union cavalry regiments that selected her plantation as their staging area. Music, enhanced by "heavy waters," swelled the courage of the young troopers awaiting the Confederate Army, while their despairing hostess tearfully watched them gradually dismantle her property. "Not a fence is left except mutilated garden enclosures. The fields [are] . . . as free from vegetation . . . as the Arabian Desert; the very roots seemed eradicated from the earth. . . . Ten thousand cavalry were drawn up in line of battle for two days on the two plantations, expecting the approach of the Confederates; bands of music were constantly playing martial airs in all parts of the premises; and whiskey flowed freely."[2]

Bandsmen were such common habitues of staging areas that Sergeant E. Tarrant, of the 1st Kentucky Cavalry, was able to enjoy the benefits of music on a regular basis during the siege of Knoxville. "While camped on the north side of Holston, we were enlivened every night by soul-stirring and patriotic airs of the band of the One Hundred and Twelfth Illinois. 'Yankee Doodle' was a favorite with Col. Wolford, and it was often played in their own peculiar style for his benefit."[3]

James Nisbet was with General Jackson's division as it moved toward Front Royal during the valley campaign of 1861. To allow the passage of another brigade, Timbe's brigade, at the head of the column, was brought to a halt fronting the pike road on the edge of town. Jackson's troops assembled on both sides of the road and snapped to attention as "General Dick Taylor's Louisiana Brigade [passed between them] over three thousand strong. Each man, every inch a soldier, was perfectly uniformed, wearing white gaiters and leggings, marching quick-step, with his rifle at 'right-shoulder-shift,' while the band in front played 'The Girl I Left Behind Me.' The blue-gray uniforms of the officers were brilliant with gold lace, their rakish slouch hats adorned with tassels and plumes. Behold a military pageant, beautiful and memorable. We stood at 'present arms' as they passed."[4]

General Jackson's fondness for music was reflected in the quality of the splendid band of the Stonewall Brigade. Although most of the brigade was held in reserve during the battle of Chantilly on 1 September 1862 the men were still nervous and tired from a long period of marching and fighting and their encampments were rather uneasy. A few men were detailed to bury the dead that lay around the rail cut, but most of the troopers had little to do. Then on 4 September the command left the Manassas plain and moved northwestward.

"Passing through Leesburg on the fifth, the men crossed the Potomac at White's Ford. The brigade waded across the river in columns of four, laughing, shouting and singing as the Stonewall Brigade Band up front filled the air with strains of 'Maryland, My Maryland.' "[5] The brigade continued westward over the rolling hills of Boonsboro. Then, to the surprise of every man in the ranks, the command turned southward and recrossed the Potomac at Williamsport. "In spite of their bewilderment at this change of march, the troops were so happy at returning to the valley that chorus after chorus of 'Carry Me Back to Old Virginny' rang across the hillsides."[6]

The Stonewall Brigade was easily given to singing and if the band was not present to lead they performed a cappella. At Fredericksburg on 13 December 1862 the brigade bivouacked near the railroad at Hamilton's Crossing. The night was extremely cold, but the men constructed new earthworks and then gathered around their campfires where they "told jokes, and related incidents in the day's fighting. As the hour grew late, several choruses of 'Annie Laurie' rang out across the Fredericksburg plain, covered with thousands of Union dead and dying."[7]

The brigade's finest a cappella performance occurred just before the battle of Fredericksburg, as they marched down the pike road, across the Blue Ridge, to Madison Court House. An issue of brandy took the chill off the cold November afternoon and the entire brigade was in a hilarious mood. "They sang corn-shucking songs. One of [the] . . . men, Riley Thurman, who had a remarkably fine voice, led. The whole brigade joined in the chorus, which they could do well, as the leading regiment was often close to the rear of the Brigade, on account of the windings of the road."[8]

Following Fredericksburg, Jackson moved into winter quarters where the troops evidenced their happy feelings with wild choruses of Rebel yells at all hours of the day or night. "At night the popular Stonewall Brigade Band entertained with concerts. Until the weather grew unbearable, the men often passed the early evening hours singing 'Lorena,' 'Home Sweet Home,' 'Her Bright Smile Haunts Me Still,' 'Ever of Thee,' and other camp favorites."[9]

General Johnston's army enjoyed the music of the Union bands as they wintered at Dalton after the fall of Chattanooga. Furloughs were the order of the day, and the men applied all of the powers of their intellect and imagination to the formulation of applications for leave that would soften the hearts of the officers charged with granting them. "Sergeant Major Maxfield sent up his application, based upon Deuteronomy, twentieth chapter, seventh verse: 'And what man is there that hath betrothed a wife, and hath not taken her? Let him go and return unto his house, lest he die in battle and another man take her.' "[10] If his application was approved he planned on basing his request for an extension of leave upon Deuteronomy, twenty-fifth chapter, fifth verse: "When a man hath taken a new wife, he shall not go out to war, neither shall he be charged with any business; but he shall be free at home one year, and shall cheer up his wife which he hath taken."[11] Much to his surprise, his leave application was approved while those of two officers were passed over.

Those less fortunate than Sergeant Major Maxfield were left to entertain themselves as best they could. One rather pious Yank wrote of the wide range of possible entertainments beckoning him towards everlasting salvation or eternal damnation. "Let me tell you what is going on within eight hundred yards of my tent at nine P.M., Sabbath evening. A sutler selling whisky, a prayer-meeting, boys playing poker, band playing 'Johnnie, Fill up the Bowl,' four hundred men at work on fortifications, stimulated by half-ration of government whisky, profanity in all directions, violin and banjo quicksteps, and five horns sounding tattoo."[12]

One Confederate whiled away his idle hours listening to the music of the Union bands as Steuarts' brigade formed a line of battle north of Hagerstown, Maryland, on 12 July 1863. On the 13th, he was assigned to picket duty where he had "a full view of half a mile of the enemy's line—moving to [the] . . . right—then drums beating and bands playing. . . . Sharp firing and pickets on [the] . . . right . . . driven back a little. . . . Have the benefit of their music and drums."[13]

Following the battle of the Wilderness on 5–6 May 1864 the Yanks remained behind their breastworks wondering about the outcome. May seventh was fair and warm. "Not a great deal of fighting today. Various reports flying around. Is this a victory? Bands were playing, and there was cheering in different parts of the line."[14]

Union and Confederate bands were often in close proximity. When this happened the opposing musicians waged their own musical war, struggling to establish their superiority in a sort of one-upmanship battle of the bands. This semifriendly rivalry was in evidence as the Yanks approached the outposts of Richmond. "In the outlaying defenses of the city, Confederate bands covered the retreat with a military concert. Federal musicians responded to Confederate tunes with national airs until the night was filled with melody."[15]

As the siege preparations continued, Confederate wagons and men were shuffled hither and yon until their numbers were reduced to a minimum at the most exposed positions. "Bands ceased their serenades in the outlying defense works. Silence brooded over the contending battle lines. Confederate musicians joined their fellows in retreat. Only picket guards remained within the battlements."[16]

Most concerts within staging areas were for psychological or entertainment purposes, but at least one time a band was used to fool the enemy. Stuart had so successfully screened Lee's army, as it moved northward from Culpeper Court House, that General Meade was unaware that it had left the village. Late in the afternoon Meade countermarched the II, V, and VI Corps and Buford's division of cavalry, intending to do battle with Lee at Culpeper. Meade's advance struck Rosser's regiment about 2 P.M., forcing him to fall back in a delaying action. Rosser accomplished this so skillfully that it was nearly dark before Meade reached the wooded ridge, Slaughter's Hill, north of Culpeper. In the meantime Colonel Young rushed his brigade from James City to reinforce Rosser along his thinly spread defensive line. Every trooper in Young's command was ordered to light a campfire, even though all were within sight of Meade's army. "Fortunately Young had with him a regimental band. This was moved rapidly from point to point in the rear, and by its music tended to exaggerate, in the enemy's estimation, the force at his disposal. Young however, passed an anxious night...which could not fail to disclose his real weaknesses. But during the night Meade was made aware of events which had transpired that afternoon at Warrenton Springs, and hurriedly recalled his army to meet Lee's advance upon the Orange and Alexandria Railroad."[17]

The fact that Meade's intelligence finally pinpointed Lee's movements does not detract from the credit due Rosser and Young. Their management of a small force and the band caused Meade to move with caution against their position.

General Hancock used his bands to overcome the depressing effects that the sight of the dead and wounded had upon the living at Chancellorsville. "Seeing the unfavorable impression that the ghastly remains of humanity had on the troops, and being close to the enemy, he ordered every band and drum corps to play 'Rally Round the Flag,' and in a moment, had the enemy made their appearance, they would have met with a warm reception."[18]

At Malvern Hill a Regular Army band nerved the troops for combat in their staging area and then accompanied them into battle.

The morning of July first broke bright and clear, and gave promise of a hot day. The Union Army seemed in excellent spirits; bands could be heard playing patriotic airs in the early morning on various parts of our line; our own band played for a time with a most cheering effect. Our gigantic and genial Drum Major Lovell whirled his baton joyously and showed no disappointment because his daily prayer to the Lord to send him a million dollars remained unanswered. He hoped, as he explained to us, that some day He would get tired and say, "Let the poor devil have it and not bother me any longer."

Suddenly we received orders to form ranks and my regiment marched off by the Quaker Road in the direction of Crew House, near the center of our line and about a mile away. Our band, led by the drum-major, was at the head and, by orders of Captain Poland, began playing. It was the first and only time during the war that I heard a band play, while a battle was on. We marched as if on parade; the music was inspiring and drew cheers from the troops among which we passed. This was kept up until we turned off the road and some spent balls began to drop among us, when the band ceased playing and fell in behind.[19]

Although most bandsmen faced shot and shell as bravely as any infantry trooper, the bandsmen of the 2nd Minnesota Regiment were less anxious to participate in actual combat. The band had enrolled for three-months service, and their enlistment drew to a close as the regiment marched to Gettysburg. As the infantrymen stared into the muzzles of the enemy's artillery, the bandsmen "unceremoniously dumped their instruments in the woods before leaving for home."[20] The band was later reorganized with new members and outfitted with fine German silver instruments paid for through private subscription. This second band served with distinction to the end of the war.

As wounds, sickness, death, and desertion stripped regiments, reducing some to company size, commanders called upon the bandsmen and musicians for a different type of combat service. When Colonel William Terry was promoted to brigadier of his brigade, he sought to bring his old command, the 4th Virginia Regiment, to full strength. This was partially accomplished "by putting in ranks some of the musicians, the wagoners and pioneers that belonged to the brigade, and calling in nearly all that were on different details."[21]

At Gettysburg, while the 20th Maine was engaged around Little Round Top, "every pioneer and musician who could carry a musket went into the ranks. Even the sick and footsore, who could not keep up in the march, came up as soon as they could find their regiments, and took their places in line of battle."[22]

The assignment of bandsmen to the line was considered standard operating procedure by many regimental commanders, and large numbers of musicians doubled on the musket. Many regiments had enlisted bandsmen as line soldiers to circumvent the orders that outlawed bands. Once enlisted, the musicians were in no position to quibble about their military occupational specialty, and most never questioned the priority of their combat assignments.

All of the bandsmen of the 148th Pennsylvania had enlisted as infantrymen. They came together as musicians whenever they could and frequently performed in the rear areas. Band music always attracted the attention of enemy artillerists and more than one concert was given under battle conditions. When the right wing of Oliver Wendell Holmes's regiment was pushed back, "the enemy opened with a section [of artillery], taking [them]...almost if not quite in reverse and rather bothering [their]...headquarters. There was much stampeding of wagons, bands, hospital men and other noncombatants."[23]

Rear area shelling was so common that noncombatants routinely dug foxholes and erected bombproofs whenever time permitted. When the Stonewall Brigade prepared for Spotsylvania, "the artillery was posted behind the works...and the horses were all taken to the rear. The cannoneers themselves had pits dug to shield them. The ambulance corps, the bands and musicians, with the pioneers, all had pits to get into, as at times the shells would fairly rain...[in]."[24]

A West Virginia band decided skedaddling was the better part of valor when they were shelled at Cedar Mountain on 9 August 1862. It was nearly dark and the troops were bedding down for the night when Colonel Samuel S. Carroll's

"West Virginia Brigade came up with a band playing their favorite tune, which was 'West Virginia is Union Still.' When the band was about up to where we were...a shell came shrieking along and exploded just over our heads, quickly followed by another, and another; the music ceased on the instant and the members quickly beat a retreat, followed by the bummers and the officers' servants."[25]

Alfred Bellard was a private with the 5th New Jersey Infantry Regiment during the winter of 1862. General McClellan, with a bad case of "the slows" as Lincoln later observed, had allowed the Confederates to erect batteries at Cockpit Point and at other strategic locations commanding a thirty-mile stretch of the Potomac River south of Washington. General McClellan reluctantly dispatched troops, including Bellard's regiment and the 7th New Jersey Infantry, to the Maryland shore opposite the Confederate batteries. The opposing artillery would occasionally fire across the Potomac to test the range and sighting of their guns. The exchange rarely resulted in injury but this was not always the case. "On one occasion as the 7th N. J. was forming for dress parade, a shell came screching across the river and dropped close to the band, who were playing at the time. That tune was cut shorter than usual, and coat-tails was about all that could be seen as they disappeared behind the tents."[26]

Missiles and music were regularly combined in a kind of eighteenth-century chamber music entertainment when John Haskell's regiment was stationed at Washington, North Carolina. Following the skirmish at New Bern, his unit moved back, placing its batteries at Fort Hill, on Hill's Point, across the river and downstream from Washington. Washington is situated on the Tar River just before it enters the Pamlico. "There the enemy fleet in the Pamlico River had the first calliope I had ever heard. Every day after dinner they would play it for a while and then shell our position for an hour or two. They never did any real harm; it was almost as if it were done for an evening's entertainment."[27] The calliope concert began with the siege of Washington on 30 March 1863 and continued nightly until the Confederates withdrew on 29 April.

While most commanders recognized the signal effect of good music on troop morale, some of the more enterprising carried the concept to rather absurd extremes. Their unfortunate bandsmen were placed in the front ranks with nothing more to defend themselves than their instruments.

Phil Sheridan was fond of music and took a personal interest in the bands of his command. His special attention was manifest in the equipment, mounts, and privileges of the bandsmen who were resplendently uniformed and mounted on spirited steeds of a uniform gray color. They were exempt from stretcher duty during battles, but paid dearly for this privilege. "They were brought out to the front and made to play the liveliest airs in their repertory. . . . After having several of their instruments pierced by bullets, however, and the drums crushed by shells, as often happened, it must be admitted that the music...was open to adverse criticism."[28] At least one engraving depicts Sheridan's bands mounted upon their snorting chargers, doing their best to play while moving at a full gallop.[29]

General Horace Porter enjoyed the music of another of Sheridan's bands at Five Forks. "Hearing heavy firing in the direction of the Five Forks road, I hurried on in that direction. I saw a portion of our cavalry moving eastward, pressed by a heavy force of the enemy....[They] were falling back toward Boydton plank road....I turned the corner of the Brooks cross-road and the Five Forks road...and encountered one of Sheridan's bands, under a heavy fire, playing 'Nellie Bly' as cheerily as if it were furnishing music for a country picnic."[30]

Performances under fire were the norm in Sheridan's command. At Dinwiddie Court House, he rounded up all of his musicians and massed them on the firing line with the order to "play the gayest tunes in their books. . . . Play them loud and keep on playing them, and never mind if a bullet goes through a trombone, or even a trombonist, now and then."[31]

As might be expected, the flamboyant general, George Armstrong Custer, was another commander who took his bands into combat. A pencil sketch shows his mounted band leading the troops. His famous cavalry charge at Columbia Furnace was spearheaded by his stalwart corps of musicians. "As usual there are the bright brazen instruments of the band near him, the men not much of players perhaps, but what is better, capable of sticking to their parts under fire and playing 'Yankee Doodle,' 'Gary Owen,' and other enlivening pieces to the shrill accompaniment of whistling lead."[32]

The Stonewall Brigade Band, frequently under Yankee guns, evened the score at Chancellorsville where it treated the band of the 14th Connecticut Infantry to a scathing fire. On the second day of the fight Jackson flanked the XI Corps, the parent unit of the Connecticut regiment. The Band of the 14th was ordered to the Union right to stabilize the line with their music. "With shot and shell crashing all about them...[they] played 'The Star-Spangled Banner,' 'The Red, White, and Blue,' and 'Yankee Doodle' and repeated them for fully twenty minutes....The effect on the men was magical. It was a remarkable circumstance that none of them were killed. I think one or two of them were slightly wounded by pieces of exploding shells."[33]

The performance of the band of the 14th Regiment inspired the nearby band of the 12th New Jersey. They joined in the battle (musically speaking) until "some of the shells, attracted, no doubt by the sweet music, came whistling through [the] treetops...and the band, which was playing 'Yankee Doodle' stopped right in the middle of the tune, played 'Yankee' but missed the 'Doodle.' "[34]

When the Confederates evacuated Yorktown they fell back to a secondary line of defense and erected the formidable Fort Magruder astride the road from Yorktown. The approaches to the fort were protected with an abatis of felled trees, ditches, and rifle pits. After maneuvering through the abatis Bellard's regiment was posted on the right of the road in support of a Regular Army battery, and the 6th, 7th, and 8th New Jersey Regiments held the right side of the road. The celebrated Louisiana Tigers, carrying the Stars and Stripes in hopes of being mistaken for Federal troops, mounted a furious charge against the advancing 6th, 7th, and 8th Regiments. The Tigers were repulsed as was their second charge against the 5th Regiment. By afternoon the fighting had generalized along the entire front and the Confederates captured the Regular Army battery and immediately turned the guns against the 5th Regiment, forcing them to gradually and grudgingly fall back. The regiment fought for every inch of ground, but "as the fight was going against us and the men being about used up, the regimental bands were ordered to consolidate and play. On wanting to know what they should play, [General Hooker]...answered Toot, Toot, Toot something, and Toot they did. And as soon as the bands struck up, three cheers for the red, white, and blue, two guns were run out on the road. A shower of grape and cannister was sent into the advancing rebels who were seen comming down the road. And as cheer upon cheer rent the air, the infantry, who had a few moments before been on the skedadle, now rushed in with renewed vigor, as did also the stragglers who had previously been got together as a sort of forlorn hope."[35]

Lookout Mountain was another engagement accompanied by music. Sheridan's troops were on the field and his bands were in the thick of the fight. Sylvanus Cadwallader, a correspondent covering Grant's army, had an excellent view of the unfolding panorama as the Union troops maneuvered into position during the preliminary stages of the battle. "As the echoes of the signal guns [from Orchard Knob] died away, the Union army filed out through selected and prepared places and took their position in line of battle. . . . The men whooping, yelling and hurrahing...bugles sounding commands on the flanks in the distance....With bands playing, flags flying, soldiers cheering and yelling, our men three lines deep in perfect alignment, poured out through the young cottonwood timber, swept the rebel skirmishers out of the underbrush...and pursued them on the run."[36]

Major John Connolly, an active participant in the "Battle in the Clouds," wrote of the struggle and resulting victory.

Dear Wife:..On Monday, Nov. 23rd our Division was ordered to move out just in front of the fortifications...and rebels, as they looked down on us...no doubt thought we had come out for a review. But Sheridan's Division followed and formed in line with us...yet not a gun fired. All was peace in Chattanooga valley that day. The sun shone brightly, the bands played stirring airs; tattered banners that had waved on battlefields... streamed out gaily....

But three o'clock came, and a solitary shot way over on our left . . . made every fellow think. Wood's line moved forward, and Sheridan's started forward....Two important hills were gained....Cheer after cheer rang out in the valley....The bands commenced playing and the valley was again peaceful, but we all knew there was "something up."...

On Tuesday, Nov 24...after hours of anxious suspense I see a single rebel winding his way back from the firing and around to our side...but look! look! Here comes a crowd of stragglers....The mountain is covered with them!...There comes our flag around the point of the mountain!...Oh such a cheer as then went up in the valley! Manly cheeks were wet with tears of joy, our bands played "Hail to the Chief," and 50 brazen throated cannon...thundered out from the fortifications of Chattanooga, a salute to the old flag. The work was done. Lookout was ours.[37]

Another officer, nearly overwhelmed by the emotion of the moment, watched as "around the curving slope came rank after rank of Hooker's men.... Victory achieved in plain view of everybody...regimental bands spontaneously began to play from one end of the line to the other....An emotional officer on the plain confessed that 'The pealing of all the bands was as if all the harps of Heaven were filling the dome with triumphant music.' "[38]

The initial assault at Franklin, Tennessee, resembled nothing more than a dress parade. General Hood had allowed the Union columns to slip through his fingers, and in a fit of pique decided to confront them at Franklin. In spite of their entrenched positions, Hood ordered a frontal attack, and centered the colors and the band well forward of the advancing line of battle.

S. A. Cunningham was the right guide of the 41st Tennessee Infantry. Marching four paces to the front of his regiment, he could see a substantial segment of the line and noted "the look of determination that was on every face. [The troops] had an unbounded faith in Gen. Hood, whom they believed would achieve a victory that would give them Nashville....Our generals were ready, and some of them rode in front of our main line. With a quick step we moved forward to the sound of stirring music. This is the only battle that I was in...where bands of music were used."[39]

S. C. Trigg of Company C, 3rd Missouri Infantry, Cockrell's Brigade, underestimated the difficulties involved in the assault, and cheerfully moved forward with the line as it marched in perfect alignment toward the entrenched Yankees.

When we arrived on the hill in sight of Franklin on the Columbia Pike, we were filed to the right and halted in a skirt of woods and ordered to rest at will....About this time Col. Elija Gates rode up and called our attention to two lines of infantry in front of us, the same time saying: "Boys, look in your front; we won't get a smell." When we saw this, we too thought we would have a walkover.

Seeing the nice, smooth field between us and the enemy's works...many...called on the Colonel for music and for a brigade drill. To this he readily consented....As soon as we started the band began to play, and continued until the enemy's batteries began to rake our lines. One man was killed (Taliaferro) and one wounded (G. A. Ewing, of my company) before the music ceased.[40]

Joseph Boyce, also with Cockrell's Brigade, recorded the unusual circumstances that took this famous band into the very mouths of the Union guns.

General Cockrell gave orders to march straight for the position, and not to fire a shot until we gained the top of the works; then when the decisive moment arrived, in clear, ringing tones gave the final commands, "Shoulder arms!" "Right shoulder shift arms!" "Brigade forward!" "Guide Center!" "Music!" "Quick Time!" "March!" and this array of hardened veterans, every eye straight to the front in actual perfection of drill and discipline, moved forward to our last and bloodiest charge.

Our brigade...had one of the best brass bands in the army. It went up with us, starting off with "The Bonnie Blue Flag," changing to "Dixie" as we reached the deadly point.

As it was an unusual thing for the "Tooters" to go up in a charge with the "Shooters," I give the names of the veterans composing this band....They were Prof. John O'Neil (leader), John and Chris O'Neil, James and Thad Doyle, Charles Ketchum, Samuel Lyon, James Young, Shelby Jones, James Roboinet, and Simeon Phillips.[41]

Although Yates claimed the band for the 28th Tennessee Infantry, all other sources identify it as Cockrell's Brigade Band. C. E. St. Clair of the 6th Missouri confirms this identification. "I do know that Crockrell's Brigade did go into the Battle of Franklin with a band playing....Cockrell's Brigade generally went as far as any other troops. It lost one hundred and thirty in that battle, when it didn't number more than a full regiment."[42]

A band of music was nearly the cause of failure for the entire military expedition at Fredericksburg. For two days the Union left poured across two hastily constructed pontoon bridges at Franklin Crossing on the Rappahannock. All was going well until a regimental commander decided to relieve the monotony of the march with a little music. "The Colonel of one of the Regiments of General Devens' Division ordered his band to 'strike up a tune.' Just as the head of the column swept onto the flimsy planking, the band began to play. Before the Regiment was halfway across, the men had unconsciously fallen into step and the whole fabric was swaying to the cadenced feet. Vibrating like a great fiddle string, the whole thing would have parted and sunk had not a keen eyed officer seen the danger. The staff officer spurred his horse through the men shouting 'stop that music.'...He finally reached the head of the column and the blundering music stopped."[43]

The band of the 114th Pennsylvania Volunteers found itself abandoned during the same engagement. The band had sought shelter in a deep railroad cut during the first day's fighting and failed to receive the order when the Army of the Potomac retreated across the Rappahannock during the night. By morning they were completely surrounded by Rebels and meekly surrendered. An unidentified Confederate band liberated their instruments and the bandsmen were incarcerated in Libby Prison for the next three weeks. General Grant had not yet forbidden prisoner exchange and they were soon reunited with their unit. They received a new set of instruments, paid for through popular subscription by friends at home, "in honor of their gallantry and good service."[44]

The band of the 114th Pennsylvania included an unusual, nonmusical member named Marie. This fair young damsel had unofficially attached herself to the band as a vivandiere. Her duties included housekeeping, laundry, cooking, and caring for the wounded. She served with distinction to the end of the war and her photo is included in the regimental history authored by bandmaster Frank Rauscher. Not all vivandiere were as pure in heart as the fair Marie. The unofficial ministrations of a vivandiere attached to a New York regiment eventually got the generous lady into trouble. She was given the option of leaving the area quietly or being drummed from the camp. She elected the easy way out.

The Army had regiments of female camp followers. The hard facts of economics prompted them to attach themselves to regimental or larger commands rather than to small units—let alone to a single band. William Howard Russell found little to admire in the women who followed the army as vivandieres. "In the luggage vans there were three foolish young women with slop-dress imitation clothes of the vivandiere type, who, with dishevelled hair, dirty faces, and dusty hats and jackets, looked sad, sorry and absurd. Their notions of propriety did not justify them in adopting straps, boots and trousers, and the rest of the tawdry illmade costume looked very bad indeed."[45]

Not all women associated with the army practiced the "tawdry trade." Most remained at home aiding whatever regiments marched within their reach. They turned out in large numbers to tend the wounded of major engagements, and were frequent camp visitors. George Eggleston appreciated their ministrations and applauded the efforts of a truly determined group who brought a USO show to his camp at Petersburg.

The women carried their efforts to cheer and help the troops into every act of their lives. Along the lines of march they came out with water or coffee or tea....A bevy of girls stood under a sharp fire from the enemy's lines at Petersburg one day, while they sang Bayard Taylor's Song of the Camp, responding to an encore with the stanza:
"Ah! soldiers, to your honored rest,
    Your truth and valor bearing,
The bravest are the tenderest,
    The loving are the daring!"[46]

The war was a bloody affair, and battles were fiercely contested, but combatants themselves displayed little personal animosity toward one another. Men performed the duties expected of them. They clubbed, maimed, and killed at close quarters but, like General Rommel, most could have entitled their memoirs *Krieg ohne Hass* (War Without Hate). When the firing ceased men from both armies came out to bury the dead and assist the wounded, regardless of the color of their uniforms. Individual soldiers crossed over the lines to exchange small talk, coffee, tobacco, newspapers, or some sweet that they had secreted away in their odorous knapsacks.

The Sabbath quiet of 3 July 1864 was only occasionally interrupted by a shot on the skirmish line and the occasional booming of a sixty-four pounder away up on the right of the 16th Marine's position.

The First Corps and the rebel troops in its front suspended hostilities as if by mutual consent. Guns were stacked, and many of the men lay around on the works, talking with the enemy just across the way. Occasionally a Yankee and a rebel would meet between the lines and exhange coffee and tobacco, and offer an "Enquirer" for a "Herald." The Johnnies were careful to cut out the "news," and the Yanks, equally cautious, passed over a mutilated paper. When a rebel battery was about to open upon us, the skirmishers would shout, "Down Yanks!" One day the range was low and our kitchen department was knocked up, and the rations distributed broadcast. When the Union batteries were to open, "Down, Reb!" went the cry, and not a grey-back was seen during the artillery duel which followed. The band was with the regiment, and for an hour in the morning, and just before sunset, would play some of its best selections, generally closing with some national air. Often would the enemy crowd up to their works and listen to "America," or the "Battle Cry of Freedom." None of the rebel bands had been heard since we left the North Anna. Sunday evenings, "Old Hundred," and "Pleyal's Hymn" would come rolling in over the works, from a thousand throats, to mingle harmoniously with thoughts of home and a better life. And this was war![47]

A tacit agreement between the pickets of both armies precluded their shooting at one another unless their skirmish was part of a larger engagement. All seemed agreed that the loss of a single picket would have little effect on the outcome of the war. Although discouraged by the officers, pickets would often negotiate a local truce and rendezvous in the no-man's-land separating the lines. A Rebel soldier wrote of such a furtive meeting at Mulvern Hill. On "the 4th of July, we lay in line all day, my regiment being on picket; but not a shot was fired. The post I was on was in the woods, and in front of us was an open field; beyond the field were woods, and the enemy was on picket there. This field was full of blackberries; so our boys and the 'Yanks' made a bargain not to fire at each other, and went out in the field, leaving one man on each post with the arms, and gathered berries together and talked over the fight, traded tobacco and coffee and exchanged newspapers as peacefully and kindly as if they had not been engaged for the past seven days in butchering one another."[48]

The bands frequently took part in these unauthorized fraternizations and their music was enjoyed by the soldiers of both armies, even though the concerts often had a strong partisan flavor. The historian of the 1st Minnesota told of pushing a Rebel soldier in a makeshift swing, improvised on a convenient limb, while both enjoyed the music of the Union and Confederate bands playing on opposite sides of the river.

The officers felt that these gatherings undermined the men's morale and their will to fight, but they were ineffective in preventing them. They may even have lent their tacit approval. "Before Fredericksburg a band went down to the banks of the Rappahannock River. Rebels left their defenses to listen and ventured out onto the remains of a bridge, whose center section was missing. [When the music stopped] . . . the rebels returned to their side to construct additional rifle pits."[49]

Impromptu concerts were sometimes extensions of the larger conflict as combatant bands sought support from the claques of their constituencies. "One fine evening a band...mounted the parapets of Fort Wood, and were playing national tunes. After becoming wearied, their music died away on the night air, and immediately a band in the camp of the enemy struck up 'Dixie,' continuing for some time, and when they ceased a cheer went up from their lines. Instantly our own musicians took up the same tune, and when it was finished, a yell went up from our lines, followed by a 'bah' from the rebels."[50]

Most battles of the bands ended on such a relatively peaceful note, but not always. "The tedium of life in the trenches was sometimes relieved in the evening by bringing up the regimental bands, and the Confederates doing the same....There was the same rivalry among the musicians as among the sharpshooters, each trying to outdo the other. Usually arms were silent while the bands played. Each side would cheer its national airs....Once when 'Old John Brown' was being given with much vigor and snap, the rival concert ceased and twenty cannon thundered an answer to the insolent song."[51]

A concert in the earthworks before Atlanta, prior to the battle of Peachtree Creek, featured competing soloists from the rival armies.

The officers and most of the men of Shoaff's Battalion were from Savannah. They had a splendid brass band; their cornet player was the best I have ever heard. In the evening after supper he would come to our salient and play solos. Sometimes when the firing was brisk he wouldn't come. Then the Yanks would call out: "Oh Johnnie, we want to hear that cornet player."

We would answer: "He would play, but he's afraid you will spoil his horn!"

The Yanks would call out; "We will stop shooting."

"All right, Yanks," we would reply. The cornet player would mount our works and play solos from the operas and sing "Come Where My Love Lies Dreaming" or "I Dreamt that I Dwelt in Marble Halls" and other familiar airs. He had an exquisite tenor voice. How the Yanks would applaud! They had a good cornet player who would alternate with our man.[52]

During a lull in the battle of Spotsylvania a Confederate band moved to a small hill off the line and played "Nearer My God to Thee." A Federal band responded with "The Dead March" from *Saul*. The Rebs continued the concert with "The Bonnie Blue Flag" and the Federals grew more partisan with "The Star-Spangled Banner." "From the responsive yell which greeted this last selection, it seemed as if every man in the Army of the Potomac had been listening. The Southern band then played 'Home Sweet Home,' and a united yell from both sides went up such a one as was never heard among the hills of Spotsylvania County before or since."[53]

Of all Civil War authors, Bruce Catton has probably been most successful in capturing the essence of the Civil War soldier's being. In simple but eloquent prose he caught the emotion of the moment as the soldiers listened to the sentimental songs and national airs that were the common property of both armies. Following Fredericksburg, the Blue and the Gray were drawn up on opposite sides of the Rappahannock where they struggled against a common enemy—a bitterly cold winter—while preparing for the next major engagement of the war. By tacit consent, neither side shot at the other and mid-morning found "the boys on the opposing picket posts daily swapping coffee for tobacco and comparing notes on their Generals, their rations, and other matters...."

With each camp in full sight and hearing of the other, one evening massed Union Bands came down to the riverbank to play "John Brown's Body," "The Battle Cry of Freedom" and "Tramp, Tramp, Tramp." Northerners and Southerners, the soldiers sang those songs or sat and listened to them massed in their thousands on the hillsides, while the darkness came down to fill the river valley and the light of the camp fires glinted off the black water. Finally the southerners called across, "Now play some of ours," so without pause the Yankee Bands played "Home Sweet Home," and 150,000 fighting men tried to sing it and choked up and just sat there, silent, staring off into the darkness; and at last the music died away and the bandsmen put up their instruments and both armies went to bed. A few weeks later they were tearing each other apart in the lonely thickets around Chancellorsville.[54]

Truly music was a common ground for both armies where the soldiers of the Blue and the soldiers of the Gray could meet in brotherhood.

NOTES

1. William F. Bufkin, "Union Bands of the Civil War" (Ph.D. diss., Louisiana State University, 1973), pp. 91–92.

2. Matthew Page Andrews, ed., *The Women of the South in War Times* (Baltimore: Norman Remington Co., 1920), pp. 379–80.

3. E. Tarrant, *The Wild Riders of the First Kentucky Cavalry* (1894; reprint ed., Lexington, Ky.: Henry Clay Press, 1969) p. 253.

4. James Cooper Nisbet, *4 Years on the Firing Line* (1914; reprint ed., ed. Bell Irvin Wiley, Jackson, Tenn.: McCowat-Mercer Press, 1963), pp. 40–41.

5. James J. Robertson, Jr., *The Stonewall Brigade* (Baton Rouge, La.: Louisiana State University Press, 1963), p. 153.

6. Ibid., p. 154.

7. Ibid., p. 174. *See also* Henry Kyd Douglas, *I Rode with Stonewall...*(Chapel Hill, N.C.: The University of North Carolina Press, 1949), pp. 203–04, and *The Land We Love* 1 (1866): p. 116.

8. Nisbet, *4 Years on the Firing Line*, p. 118.

9. Robertson, Jr., *The Stonewall Brigade*, p. 177. *See also Confederate Veteran*, 20 (1912): p. 25.

10. Abner Ralph Small, *The Sixteenth Maine* (Portland, Me.: B. Thurston & Co., 1886), p. 159.

11. Ibid.

12. Ibid., p. 194.

13. McHenry Howard, *Recollections of a Maryland Confederate Soldier . . .* (1914; reprint ed., Dayton, Ohio: Morningside Bookshop, 1975), pp. 216–17.

14. Austen C. Stearns, *Three Years With Company K* (Cranbury, N.J.: Associated University Presses, 1976), p. 261.

15. Rembert W. Patrick, *The Fall of Richmond* (Baton Rouge, La.: Louisiana State University Press, 1960), p. 36.

16. Ibid., p. 38.

17. H. B. McClellen, *I Rode With Jeb Stuart.* (Bloomington, Ind.: Civil War Centennial Series, Indiana University Press, 1958), pp. 383–84.

18. J. W. Muffly, *The Story of Our Regiment, the 148th Pennsylvania* (Des Moines, Iowa: Kenyon Printing & Mfg. Co., 1904), p. 322.

19. Augustus Meyers, *Ten Years in the Ranks* (New York: Stirling Press, 1914), pp. 246, 428.

20. Judson W. Bishop *The Story of a Regiment...Second Minnesota* (St. Paul, Minn.: n.p., 1890), p. 61.

21. John O. Casler, *Four Years With the Stonewall Brigade* (2d ed. 1906; reprint ed., Marietta, Ga.: Continental Book Co., 1951), pp. 218–19.

22. John J. Pullen, *The Twentieth Maine* (Philadelphia and New York: J.B. Lippincott Co., 1957), p. 126.

23. Oliver Wendell Holmes, Jr., *Touched With Fire*, ed. Mark de Wolfe Howe (Cambridge, Mass.: Harvard University Press, 1947), p. 141.

24. Casler, *Four Years With the Stonewall Brigade*, p. 210.

25. Stearns, *Three Years With Company K*, pp. 87–88.

26. Alfred Bellard, *Gone For a Soldier,... Civil War Memoirs*, ed. David Herbert Donald (Boston: Little, Brown & Co., 1975), p. 43.

27. John Cheves Haskell, *The Haskell Memoirs*, ed. Gilbert E. Govan and James W. Livingood (New York: J. P. Putnam's Sons, 1960), p. 43.

28. Horace Porter, *Campaigning With Grant*, ed. Wayne C. Temple (Bloomington, Ind.: Indiana University Press, 1961), p. 431.

29. Robert Johnson and Clarence Buel, eds., *Battles and Leaders of the Civil War*, 4 vols. (1887; reprint ed., New York: Castle Books, Thomas Yoseloff, 1956), 4, p. 708.

30. Ibid., 4: 710–11.

31. Bruce Catton, *A Stillness at Appomattox* (Garden City, N.Y.: Doubleday & Co., 1954), p. 347.

32. J. E. Taylor, "Custer Charging Near Columbia Furnace" (pencil sketch). Regimental Papers, part 12, container 35, folder 3, pp. 426–27. (Cleveland, Ohio: Western Reserve Historical Society, n.p., 1864). I am indebted to William Bufkin who kindly supplied a copy of this material.

33. Charles D. Page, *History of the Fourteenth Regiment Connecticut Volunteer Infantry* (Meriden, Conn.: Horton Printing Co., 1906), pp. 120–21.

34. Daniel B. Harris, "Personal Diary," 10 December 1862 to 4 July 1863. Original manuscript in the Smithsonian Institution, Washington, D. C. Typescript p. 19. Harris was with Company K, 12th New Jersey Volunteers. William Bufkin kindly provided a copy of this material.

35. Bellard, *Gone for a Soldier*, p. 67.

36. Sylvanus Cadwallader, *Three Years With Grant*, ed. Benjamin P. Thomas (New York: Alfred A. Knopf, 1956), p. 150.

37. Henry Steele Commanger, *The Blue and the Gray* (Indianapolis: Bobbs-Merrill Co., 1950), pp. 908–10.

38. Bruce Catton, *Grant Takes Command* (Garden City, N.Y.: Doubleday & Co., 1951), p. 74.

39. S. A. Cummingham, "Letter," *Confederate Veteran* 1, no. 4 (April 1893): 101–102.

40. S. C. Trigg, "Why the Band Played at Franklin," *Confederate Veteran* 19 no. 1 (1911): 32.

41. Joseph Boyce, "Cockrell's Brigade Band at Franklin," *Confederate Veteran*, 19, No. 6 (June, 1911): 271.

42. C. E. St. Clair, "Letter," *Confederate Veteran* 19 no. 6 (June 1911): 271.

43. Francis Trevelyn Miller, ed., *Photographic History of the Civil War*, 10 Vols. (New York: Review of Reviews Co., 1911), 2, p. 91.

44. Frank Rauscher, *Music on the March, 1862–65...*(Philadelphia: W. F. Fell & Co., 1892), p. 39.

45. William Howard Russell, *My Diary North and South*, ed. Fletcher Pratt (New York: Harper and Brothers, 1954), p. 177.

46. George Cary Eggleston, *A Rebel's Recollections* (New York: Hurd and Houghton, 1875), p. 72.

47. Small, *The Sixteenth Maine*, pp. 193–94.

48. Casler, *Four Years With the Stonewall Brigade*, p. 95.

49. Edward J. Stackpole, *Drama on the Rappahannock, The Fredericksburg Campaign* (Harrisburg, Pa.: Military Service Publishing Co., 1957), p. 119.

50. Asbury L. Kerwood, *Annals of the Fifty-seventh Regiment Indiana Volunteers* (Dayton, Ohio: W. J. Shuey, 1868), p. 216.

51. George A. Bruce, *The Twentieth Regiment of Massachusetts Volunteer Infantry, 1861–1865* (Boston: Houghton Mifflin Co., 1906), p. 396.

52. Nisbet, *4 Years on the Firing Line*, p. 204.

53. Francis A. Lord and Arthur Wise, *Bands and Drummer Boys of the Civil War* (New York: Thomas Yoseloff, 1966), p. 206.

54. Bruce Catton, *The Army of the Potomac: Mr. Lincoln's Army* (Garden City, N.Y.: Doubleday & Co., 1951), p. 174. Allen Hall in *Center of Conflict* (Paducah, Ky.: *Sun Democrat*, 1961), p. 159, also records this incident but presents a variation of the ending of the story.

BANDS ON THE
HOME FRONT

It is curious to note how youth will extract gaiety and pleasure out of adverse surroundings....In spite of gnawing anxieties which were weighing down the hearts of all serious people, sundry delightful parties were organized to partake of strawberries and ice cream at "Pizzini's," the famous confectioners of the day in Richmond. Expeditions were planned to Drewry's Bluff with a band of music in attendance, and, of course, with the ususal accompaniment of the delightful officer, who, equally of course, was either halt, lame or blind, as all whole men were at their posts in the field in June of 1863. Serenades, too, were in order, and I find that on our return from one of the aforesaid strawberry feasts, about twelve o'clock in the same night Ella_____had a charming serenade of a *full brass band* from one of her admirers. This combination of serenade, with strawberries and ice cream, seemed to fill the cup of joy to the brim.[1]

Louise Wigfall was in her late teens when she made this entry in her diary; but for one so young, she was shapely, poised, bilingual, articulate, sophisticated, intelligent, coquettish—and the daughter of a Confederate senator. These obvious attributes made her a much sought-after Southern belle who demurely dominated the hub of the Richmond social whirl. An ardent patriot for the Confederate cause, she regarded Richmond as the center of the universe. War was exciting—even exhilarating—and her life was a series of genteel entertainments characterized by rustling crinoline and polite conversation.

Not everyone shared Miss Wigfall's advantages of position and beauty. Social encounters on the lower rungs were of a different kind—less elegant, more bawdy—and with the advancement of time and the war the bawdiness approached degradation.

Colonel Nisbet, furloughed to Richmond following the battle of the Wilderness, found—not a genteel city—but a "wide-open town. The theaters played 'broad vaudeville' and operated a bar and gambling table upstairs, the demimonde mixing freely with the soldiers."[2]

Many of the soldiers, as they have in all wars, attracted vice to Northern and Sothern cities alike. People who were part of Miss Wigfall's world, as well as the less fortunate, sought respite from war and pursued pleasures. Kate Cumming caught the spirit of Miss Wigfall's Confederacy while in Mobile, where life was "gayer than ever[.] It seems as if the people have become reckless. I have just returned from paying a visit to Bienville Square; a very fine band of music plays there some two or three times a week, and makes it a very pleasant place to resort."[3]

Mrs. J. Henry Smith, a lady of Greensboro who led a life of gaiety and abandon, stressed the importance of music in these civilian entertainments. "Our old Southern songs kept alive the precious heritage of the past, while all braced themselves for the coming terrors of which we then had little conception."[4]

The Yankees could afford to be even more carefree and reckless in their pursuit of pleasure. They did not have to contend with invading troops, burning cities, bummers from both armies, and the violence and destruction that gradually impoverished the South. Having witnessed the miseries heaped upon the Confederacy, Decimus et Ultimus Barziza was repelled by the general well-being of the Yankees, as he sought his escape to Canada through an enemy land. "I was struck at the seeming state of prosperity of every class of industry. . . . No one would have supposed that this people was engaged in a most stupendous and exhausting war, had he not been so constantly reminded of it by gay uniforms, the display of banners, and martial music."[5]

He too sampled the Northern counterpart of Colonel Nisbet's Richmond. Wide-open Southern cities were certainly no pace-setters when it came to vice and lewdness. Northern cities could match them sin for sin.

Prostitution was most rampant in the cities frequented by soldiers. The raising of the Northern armies was paralleled by informal mobilization for active service of a vast horde of loose women anxious to capitalize on the sexual longings of the men who donned the blue. In every Northern metropolis these unsavory characters set up shop and peddled their tawdry wares. A Cincinnati newspaper complained in January of 1864 that *femmes du monde* had "nearly succeeded in elbowing all decent women from the public promenade" of that city, and in Chicago in 1864 and 1865 an estimated 2,000 lewd women thronged the streets and filled the bawdy houses. Boston was said to have swarmed with strumpets and in New York loose females doubling as waitresses in "concert saloons" became such a nuisance that a state law was passed in 1862 closing these dens of debauchery; but the dispensers of sin evaded the prohibition by simply dropping the concerts, and by 1864 houses in the Broadway area specializing in liquor and lewdness were more numerous and active than ever before.[6]

Next to the camps themselves, Washington had the greatest concentration of military men and consequently the largest population of whores of any Northern city. A war correspondent, departing from the capital in 1862, found Washington to be "the most pestiferous hole since the days of Sodom and

Gomorrah . . . every possible form of human vice and crime, dregs, offscourings and scum . . . flowed into the capitol and made it a national catchbasin of indescribable foulness."[7]

The "concert saloons" of New York offered primarily prostitution and pornography, but most musical endeavors did not. Music was the principal emotional release and entertainment for all citizens. Another Yankee reporter, equally negative in his appraisal of Washington, appreciated the concerts presented by the United States Marine Band in that city. "The Marine Band (in red coats), played twice a week in the Capital grounds, and Senators, Cyprians, Ethiops, and children rallied to enjoy; a theatre or two played time-honored dramas with Thespian companies; a couple of scholars lectured in the sombre Smithsonian Institution; an intrigue and a duel filled some most doleful hiatus; and a clerk absconded with half a million, or an Indian agent robbed the red men and fell back to the protection of his 'party.' A very dismal, a very dirty, and a very Democratic settlement was the American Capital."[8] The Marine Band was continuing the summer concert series that had been inaugurated by President Polk.

The war increased the number of bands performing at concerts, picnics, theaters, excursions, weddings, public celebrations, serenades and divine services. Eastern cities were privileged to hear performances by professionals, while more provincial villages relied upon amateur musicians. These homegrown presentations were augmented by the regimental bands that performed for the civilian populations as often as duty allowed. Additional programs were presented through the joint efforts of civilian and military musicians, and thousands of other entertainments were staged by other civilians whose only talents were burning desires to contribute to the war effort.

Regimental bands served as training schools for musicians, and bandsmen became a glut on the civilian market when so many were mustered out in 1862. Their return in such large numbers created an unstable financial environment, and job competition became so intense that professional New York musicians sought relief through the organization of the Musical Mutual Protection Union. New York newspapers from April through June of 1863 recorded the progress of the organization.

Prior to the formation of this union, there was no such thing as an established pay scale for musicians outside of the military. Wages fluctuated wildly according to the time of year and availability of bandsmen. The Lenten season always found an excess of musicians seeking a paucity of jobs, producing a predictable, if not inevitable, drop in wages. Underbidding of one band by another was commonplace and this cutthroat practice often erupted into violence.

The members of the Boston Brass Band planned a "special reception," promising to "fix their lips" and "batter their instruments," when Patrick Gilmore's fine Salem Brass Band contracted several jobs in Boston. Gilmore found out about the plot and added to his musical forces a group of sturdy dock-hands and roustabouts. When the whistle blew, the thugs were to come running. The Boston Brass Band appeared, the whistle blew, the dockhands came, and after a short skirmish the Boston Brass Band was put to flight. The Salem Band "remained sober as usual" following the events of the day, but the body-guards got "gloriously drunk."[9]

The formation of the Musical Mutual Protective Union eliminated such confrontations and improved the standard of living for all New York musicians. In spite of its success, there is nothing to indicate that the practice spread to other locales.

Smaller communities were not similarly affected by the returning bands-men. They were welcomed home with open arms since little towns seldom produced enough accomplished musicians to meet the demands for their services.

The best professional civilian bands had two things in common. First, each was organized under a charter to which all members agreed. Band charters followed traditions established by German Vereins which were frequent visitors to the United States during the nineteenth century. Second, profes-sional military bands were all-brass, but the most successful also employed musicians who could double on a number of instruments. These bands could provide string groups for dances and balls, mixed woodwind and brass groups for concerts, and an all-brass group for military purposes.

Choice of instrumentation was a commercial rather than an artistic con-sideration. A profitable outdoor performance was one where the greatest volume of sound was generated by the fewest possible musicians. A corre-spondent for Dwight's venerable Journal stated the matter succinctly.

Allow me to draw on your patience and good nature while I refer once more to the sub-ject of military music. I have been told that other, and more practical reasons, exist for the degenerate condition of our street bands, than those suggested in my communica-tion of last week. And a principal one is, that, in most cities possessing abundant ma-terial for the purpose, there is not sufficient occupation for a band of proper construc-tion and dimensions, to warrant the trouble and expense of keeping it up; in other words, *it don't pay.*

This is . . . the true and plain statement of the case. On the ordinary occasions for street music, a few pieces only are engaged, for the very good reason that the price of more cannot well be afforded. Consequently, those few must be of the ear-splitting order, that lack of numbers and variety may be made up in noise. And I see no present probability of change in this state of things, in our own city.

There appears, then, to my mind, but one way in which we can hope to obtain a prop-erly organized force for out-door music, with a full complement of instruments, and that is to enlist the patronage of the city in its support. Let an association be formed, which shall be called the Municipal or Metropolitan Band, if you please, with the stipulation that it shall be employed on all occasions of city celebrations, and the like, and to play for the benefit of the music-loving public two or three times a week, or oftener, upon the Common, in the pleasant evenings of summer.

No injustice would be done by this plan to any of the organizations for street music that now exist; for on all occasions of public demonstrations, the whole resident force, and more, will be called into requisition besides. Nor do I mean any disparagement, by this proposition, to the various bands we already possess. They are excellent of their kind, and will, I venture to say, vie in superiority with those of any other city in the Union, as far as they go. But to produce the intended effect of a full instrumental band, in the open air, requires . . . a combination of instruments, differing in kind and far ex-ceeding in numbers any that, at present, exist among us.[10]

Ideas like these led eventually to the establishment of the municipal band as an American institution. However, this same visionary deplored the growing all-brass instrumentation, regarding the valve as an instrumental improve-ment gone berserk.

But the love of new things becomes a passion with men. All at once the idea of a Brass Band shot forth; and from this prolific germ sprang up a multitude of its kind in every part of the land, like the crop of iron men from the infernal seed of the dragon's teeth. And as if the invention of new and deadlier implements of war . . . had hardened men's hearts, all the softer companions of the savage science were banished. The wood winds were first, bassoons, serpents, oboes, clarinets, flutes—a sad, complaining train. Next, all that mollified and tended to harmonize the fierce clangor of what was left; the mellow bugles gave way to valve trumpets and angry cornets, and in place of the contralto and tenor trombones, came the tuba and ophiclyde. Last and most deplored, the gentle horns retired, and noise and clamor and cracking brass had full possession of the field. What matter now, if it finds its sphere in the thoroughfares and crowded ways of the city. What are the shoutings of men and the rattle and clatter of paved streets, but a fit-ting accompaniment to the braying brass?

Nor did the work of innovation rest here. Latest and worse still, if possible, came into being the whole tribe of cornet bands so called, being an assemblage of instruments all of one and the same kind essentially, differing only in size, like a register of metallic pipes in an organ.

One very natural result of this transformation . . . was their gradual decrease in num-bers, till at length, from being composed of twenty-five and thirty pieces, they have dwindled down to about seventeen, cymbals and drums included. At the same time, the sum total of bands has largely increased. . . . It is not always the greatest noise that reaches farthest, or produces most effect. . . . But a well balanced band should and does have undue prominence of no particular instrument or class of instruments. . . . It is thus with the splendid bands in the Prussian service; it is so, in a great degree, in the effective music of the English troops at Montreal; and it is so too, (may we be thankful) with the most excellent band attached to the 7th Regiment of National Guards in New York.[11]

A third element common to most professional bands was its attachment to a militia regiment. Nearly all bands had contractual agreements with militia units, but, with few exceptions, the bandsmen themselves were not members of the regiments. The attachment of Grafulla's Band exclusively to the 7th New

York was unusual. Most bands were contracted to several different military organizations.

These militia units were more social than military. Franklin Aretas Haskell, who joined the Governor's Guard when it was organized in Wisconsin on 30 January 1858, stated his reason for membership: "I go in for a reasonable amount of fun, and [the] military has some little fun together with some nonsense in it. . . . The company's many military balls . . . were a favorite with the little city's social leaders."[12]

If the militia units were ill-prepared for their ultimate purpose—war, their bands were admirably suited to the musical requirements of their day. The band business was competitive. Only those groups with a clear grasp of their market could survive and prosper.

All the bands are of brass. Shall we sing with Handel: "Let us break our *bands* asunder"? This is partly fashion—of a bustling age—partly economy, the bands depending for their support mainly on their military engagements. Some of them are very good brass bands, but brass bands are not good for every kind of music, and they are ambitious to attempt all kinds. They are the people's music and have much to do with forming the taste for better or for worse. Now it is natural that in this competition for the public ear and admiration they should bait the hook with novelties, strive to outstrip each other in offering "the last thing out," to keep up with the fashions, like the miliners and drygoods dealers; for these they watch the Opera as sharply as the miliners watch Paris. Bands deal chiefly in the musical fashions, as do the music shops; the first principle in the selection of their repertoires is to secure whatever "has a run," and serve it up as piquantly as possible, but by all means lose no time in getting it. . . . It makes a vast difference what kind of music the popular bands select. Just now the frothy, vulgar Offerbach [Offenbach] tunes rule the hour. These, with absurd potpourris or medleys of the most tragical with the most light and brilliant moments of the graver operas, chowders of national airs (very rank with onions)—gouty solos upon burly tubas, or rapid, senseless variations *double-tongued* upon the cornet—with now and then a Mendelssohn part—song, or some other classical "arrangement" just to save character with "the appreciative few," commonly make up the programmes.

. . . .

We certainly remember seasons when our bands, if not so brilliant, so expert in solo execution, gave us better music on the whole. . . . But with the brass bands as they are, there may be much improvement made by taste and care in the selections. And in this connexion we may pay a passing compliment to the *Germania Band*, which in the matter of its selections seems more shy of clap-trap than some of its rivals, . . . with musician-like arrangement, tasteful, effective, not extravagant or vulgar in the rendering, and (what is one of the last virtues in a brass band) playing together in *tune*. . . . *Brown's Brigade Band*, our oldest and one of the best, announce a series of promenade concerts in the Music Hall, from which we hope good things,—provided it be not *all* brass.[13]

The conflict between the litterati (represented by Dwight and his followers) and the lovers of popular band music has a surprisingly modern ring. Profes-

sional bandmasters possessed a grasp of the public taste that evaded the
Dwights of the music world, and editorial harangues did little to undermine the
financial success of the bands. Bands were the undisputed favorites of the
common people.

Large eastern cities offered employment for many bandsmen who provided
music for parades, regimental reviews, picnics, excursions, dances, balls,
concerts in the parks, and serenades.

Mr. Weber's Cotillion and Military Band, although small in number, was
one of the most popular in Washington. Each bandsman was an accomplished
performer on one stringed instrument as well as upon a brass and a woodwind.
"The group is provided with the newest music, will execute to the best satisfaction all dances for balls, parties, and soirees. Mr. Weber has just returned
from New York with the latest and most fashionable music, which he is prepared to furnish. A pianoforte performer can be furnished if required. Please
leave orders at the Music Depot, corner of Eleventh Street and Pennsylvania
Avenue, Ganier's Resturant; or at Mr. Weber's residence, No. 509 7th Street
between G and I streets, Navy Yard."[14] A strong and imaginative public relations campaign combined with a vigorous adherence to the latest trends in
fashionable music insured Mr. Weber's musicians of a good income and constant employment. The sun rarely set on a Washington day that did not include
a performance by Mr. Weber's Band.

The Germania Band was more versatile in its instrumentation. It originally
toured the United States as a symphony orchestra but was reorganized in 1858
to compete commercially. In spite of its superior musical qualities it did not
fare as well financially as others of lesser ability. It could not seem to escape
its classical roots and the new management did not understand that educating
the public is never a profitable undertaking.

A rumor has somehow obtained that the *Germania Band* was dissolved, the members
having mostly enlisted in the various regimental bands for the war. Nothing could be
farther from the truth, as the band was never in a healthier condition than at present,
though we are sorry to say, it does not now, nor has it ever received the share of patronage its superior qualities merit. The fault however, has not been entirely with the public.
The members being one and all professional musicians, have not that natural business
capacity which in this land of go aheaditiveness must characterize the man who will
succeed pecuniarily. Relying too much on the fact of which they were aware, that they
could and did furnish better music than any band in New England, they have waited for
business to come to them, not remembering that one half the public do not know how a
brass or reed band should be formed, or how the musicians should play after being
formed into a band. Many people who would have engaged the *Germania Band* did not
know where to find it, and we have frequently spoken privately of the lack of system in
its business arrangements. But a change has recently taken place, and now, with Sig. De
Ribas, well known as one of the first musicians in the country, at the head of the bureau
of engagement, we hope to see the band rise like a Phoenix from its ashes. With
Heinicke for a leader, and with such musicians as the brothers Eichler, Regestein,

Pinter, Ribas, Faulwasser, and other well known players, we see no reason why the *Germania Band* should not at once take the position it ought rightfully to occupy.[15]

Promoting a successful musical operation required a good sense of organization and public relations: the ability to quickly turn out arrangements of popular medleys; a public identity as a performer and as a conductor; a reputation for financial success and consistent employment for participating musicians; and an unfailing sense of the public taste. Succcessful professional bandmasters possessed these qualities, as Patrick Gilmore's career demonstrates.

Patrick Gilmore was born in the army town of Athlone, Ireland, in 1829. Athlone housed three regiments, each complete with its own band, and it was there that Gilmore at the age of sixteen caught band fever. He applied to Mr. Keating for cornet lessons and within three months became a soloist with Keating's Regimental Band. In 1847 he went to Canada with the regiment. After a short stay he migrated to Boston where he accepted a position with Ordway Brothers Music Store and promptly organized a minstrel company featuring himself as cornet soloist. The minstrel troupe presented regular concerts and his playing soon attracted the attention of Boston's Charlestown Militia Company. He was asked to organize a militia band for them and was so successful in this undertaking that he was offered in 1852 the position of bandmaster with the already famous Boston Brass Band.

The Boston Brass Band, more familiarly known as Flagg's Brass Band, had been organized in 1843 by the famous keyed bugle player, Edward Kendall. Kendall was followed by Eben Flagg as conductor. *Gleason's Pictorial Drawing-Room Companion* noted in 1851 that "its present head is Eben Flagg, who had led the band for some eight years or more, sustaining an excellent reputation, no less for his professional skill than for his manly and sociable qualities. The members of the Boston Brass Band are composed mainly of professors, musical composers and artists, each one highly accomplished in the use of his particular instrument."[16] Within a few months of this article Gilmore was pictured in the same publication as bandmaster. The entire group used the over-the-shoulder instruments common to militia bands, except for Gilmore, who played a bell-front cornet. Gilmore remained with the Boston Brass Band for three years. Feeling the need to branch out, he joined Joseph M. Russell of Boston in the music publishing business. The firm of Gilmore and Russell quickly established itself as the most respected publishing house in Boston. In addition to publishing, the business included a retail outlet for sheet music and instruments and served as a base of operations for Gilmore and the band.

About the same time Jerome Smith, director of the Salem Brass Band, was seeking a successor. He had held the post since 1846 when he succeeded Francis Morse, but was compelled by ill health to relinquish his baton. He had met Gilmore and was acquainted with the Boston band. Smith recommended

Gilmore to the officers of the Salem Light Infantry Regiment. Gilmore was offered, according to H. W. Schartz's *Bands of America*, "one thousand a year and all he [could] . . . make" to accept the post. This was a substantial salary for a bandmaster. The average government bureaucrat in 1855 earned less that $600 annually. Gilmore accepted the post and set out to fulfill that part of his contract that read "and all you can make."

Pat Gilmore was a diligent and imaginative promoter. In December 1865 he advertised a musical duel between himself and the great Edward "Ned" Kendall, each to play the same passage on their respective instruments. Kendall, a supreme egotist internationally known as a bugle virtuoso, found to his dismay that the technically awkward bugle was not a match for the cornet when it came to rapid execution. Gilmore was clearly the winner.

The fame and reputation of the Salem band increased with each performance and it was sought for the most prestigious events. One of its more notable appearances was the inaugural parade for President Buchanan. The New England Guards Militia Company of Charleston hired the Salem Brass Band to lead the parade. The *Washington Post* wrote that the band "made an excellent appearance and were sober and well disciplined all during their stay in Washington."[17]

As the Salem band attracted more and more attention—and its leader more personal fame—the old Boston Brigade Band took an interest in Gilmore. With his reputation firmly established he agreed in 1859 to accept the position of bandmaster in Boston, but only if he could assume all expenses for the band, and, further, that the name of the group be changed to the "Gilmore Band." Once hired, he increased the size, scope, and quality of the ensemble so that he could provide music of professional caliber for any social or civic occasion. His concerts on the Boston Common were the highlight of the summer season. During the winter he played successful engagements in the Boston Music Hall where the seats were removed from the auditorium to provide for a promenade.

Gilmore tried to carry on business as usual in 1861, but when Sumter was fired upon he and his band gave their full support to the war effort. The Gilmore Band escorted regiment after regiment to their training camps. Finally, fearing that his band might break up due to individual enlistments, he enlisted the entire group with the 24th Massachusetts Volunteer Regiment. When the 24th marched off to its training camp Gilmore's band was escorted through Washington by the famous Dodworth Band. After a short stay in the capital city, they were assigned to General Burnside's corps which was already fighting in Virginia.

Gilmore's band was one of those discharged in 1862. Returning to Boston he continued to serve the war effort until, in 1863, Governor Andrew of Massachusetts asked him to reorganize completely all of the state militia bands. In this capacity he organized and trained military bands for other Massachusetts regiments entering federal service.

At the same time Dodworth was leading the 13th New York Regimental

Band and operating a school for bandsmen in that state. By the end of the war Dodworth had trained fifty bandmasters and over five hundred musicians for the Union forces.

Shortly after Gilmore assumed the leadership of the Boston Brass Band he had the opportunity to hear Jullien and his orchestra. After seeing "The Mons" in action, he conceived the idea for the monster concerts that he staged during the next tour of active duty as well as later in his career.

Gilmore served with two other bands that he had organized for federal service. The first was assigned to the command of General Banks in New Orleans. Banks asked that he prepare appropriate music for the inauguration of Governor Michael Hahn of the "Freed and Restored Louisiana" on 4 March 1864. Gilmore felt that the occasion called for execution on a Jullienesque scale. He received permission to form a chorus of 5,000 school children. He massed all regimental bands in the city to provide a suitable accompaniment, forming an ensemble of 500 instrumentalists. This monumental force included 120 cornets, Eb and Bb, 90 alto horns, 30 baritone horns, 60 tenor horns, 60 bass horns, Eb and Bb, 60 snare drums and 30 bass drums. After rigorous rehearsal he staged the extravaganza in Lafayette Square.

The program opened with the "Star-Spangled Banner," enthusiastically chorused by the 5,000 children waving American flags. The concert unfolded, heaping splendor upon splendor, climaxing with the last few bars of the final number, "Hail Columbia," when 36 cannon were fired in time with the music. Simultaneously every church bell in the city pealed out in a wild frenzy. Jullien would have been proud as the maestro acknowledged the prolonged applause of the audience.

Gilmore possessed a sixth sense about coming events. He had already penned several hit war songs, and it was his band arrangement of "John Brown's Body" that made that song, by James Greenleaf, so popular. Greenleaf had borrowed the melody from an old camp tune entitled "Say, Brethren, Will You Meet With Us?" but it was Gilmore's arrangement that attracted the attention of Julia Ward Howe who supplied the text that transformed it into "The Battle Hymn of the Republic."

Sensing the end of the conflict, Gilmore wrote the words and music to "When Johnny Comes Marching Home," and published it in 1864 under the pseudonym Louis Lambert. It was soon second in popularity only to "John Brown's Body." Selling in the tens of thousands as sheet music, it expressed the weariness of war common to both the North and the South. The timeless quality of the lyric assured its revival during both world wars.

When the conflict ended, Gilmore returned to Boston where, like a later Bostonian, Arthur Fiedler, he was gradually enshrined as a local folk hero. He remained musically productive until the day of his death in 1892, and his influences are still felt by America's present-day bands. His impact upon the band music of the Civil War was profound and far-reaching.[18]

Gilmore's groups typified the professional bands of his day in both their quality and their attention to public taste. The Boston band, under his baton, received the plaudits of the public and the snobbish Dwight from its first performance, although Dwight only bestowed his tacit blessing by reprinting an article from the *Courier*.

The appearance of Mr. Gilmore's new band last Saturday evening gave assurance of much success in its future operations. The audience was immense, and the applause abundant, compelling many encores not anticipated. The formation of a thorough and complete military band has been the object of Mr. Gilmore's efforts and he has done better and gone farther in this direction than any of his predecessors. Hitherto we have had only brass bands regularly organized, all attempts to combine a well balanced body of brass and reed instruments having failed. Mr. Gilmore seems to have affected this arrangement, and declares himself determined to perpetuate it. His military band consists of some thirty-five members, among whom are the proper proportions of players upon reed instruments.... In the disposition of the brass department, some thought has been given to more harmonious, and less noisy, combinations than are common among us.... The performances last Saturday night were good, and will undoubtedly be better as the band grows older. The Drum Corps, thirteen in number, deported themselves vigorously. The effect of their united exertions suggested the Rolling of the Spheres. Their performance was certainly very remarkable, and in many ways calculated to inspire profound respect. There was not the variation of a second's fraction in their movements, and we are confident we never before heard so much noise so well made. Mr. Mariani with his staff of office, looked every inch a Drum Major, and as Nature has supplied him with a great many inches, to which he adds a considerable number by a towering hat and plume, he is aggregately, about the most imposing human creature that ever astonished the eyes of a Boston audience. Mr. Gilmore's orchestra also performed some pieces very well, and the concert, altogether, was received with so much favor that it is to be repeated next Saturday evening at the Music Hall.[19]

Although Dwight's initial comments were secondhand, his wartime support of Gilmore was both active and unrestrained. He chronicled each benefit performance by the indefatigable bandmaster, and heaped praise upon his person and his music.

Mr. Gilmore's Patriotic Concerts for the benefit of the Sanitary Department of six Boston regiments, (with one of which, the 24th, Mr. Gilmore and his excellent Band served during the first year of the war), have been given with faithful adherence to programme, and with good success apparently, every afternoon and evening of this week. The usual place has been the Tremont Temple, but on the evening of Fast Day, Faneuil Hall resounded to the stirring strains of orchestra, and reed band....The selections have been mostly light and popular, but good of their kind, and the execution has left little to be desired. Mr. Gilmore enters with real patriotic fervor and enthusiasm into his work; and so does his most active and obliging agent, Mr. Blake. The spirit and purpose of these concerts certainly commends them. ... We trust that the material results will fully equal the large sums he anticipated; it will be a noble gift of one man's heart and energy to the defenders of the sacred cause.[20]

Unquestionably Gilmore's band was a first-rate organization, enjoying more than a regional reputation, but it had to be in order to survive and prosper. However, the quality and musicianship of his competition makes it doubtful that he represented the pinnacle of band music in America in his day. Other conductors also assembled some pretty formidable musical organizations.

Brass bands of the Regular Army did not amount to much, so it was left to the citizen-soldiers, the Organized Militia, to set the standards for martial music. Their models were the bands of the European regiments, many of which contained the finest solo performers on the continent.

The band of the 7th Regiment of New York was considered a pace-setter, not just for military music but for popular music in general. Originally organized in 1853 by two immigrant Germans, Kroll and Reitsel, the direction of this mixed wind ensemble passed to Claudio S. Grafulla in 1860, when it merged with the famous Shelton Band which had been organized in 1854. Grafulla, like Gilmore, named the band after himself when he assumed its leadership, but it continued to be popularly known as the band of the 7th Regiment because of its long and successful association with that group.

William R. Bayley, who had played with the State Fencibles Band of Philadelphia early in the 1840s, accounted for Grafulla's success as a bandmaster.

One of the most accomplished musicians of these days was Grafulla of the New York Seventh Regiment Band. His particular talent was in arranging band music. At this he was very rapid and accurate. On one occasion my band was playing for the day in New York City. One of the members was engaged in the Chestnut Street Theatre, where they were to produce Frye's new opera "Leonora". . . .This man whistled from memory some of the popular airs to Grafulla, who wrote them down, and before we left he handed me a completely arranged potpourri, which we played in Philadelphia that night while marching past the Chestnut Street Theatre. This off-hand arrangement with trifling corrections, became very popular with the bands shortly afterwards. The New York Seventh Band then, as now, was deservedly popular and made up of first class performers.

A considerable amount of the music used by my band was arranged to order by Grafulla and two other composers well known in those days, Thomas Coates, of this city, (later of Easton) and E. K. Eaton, of Groversville, New York. These latter gentlemen were Americans, and composed some of the finest band music that has ever been written.[21]

The band of the 7th Regiment was recognized as one of the finest in the country, but Dwight seriously questioned any attempt to label it as *the* best military band in America. In 1860 he strongly refuted this assertion on the part of the music critic of the *Herald*.

Shortly after the recent concert of this band at the Academy of Music, some quid nunc gave it the benefit of a very stupid article...in which he rejoiced over the artistic skill of the members and strongly intimated that we had at last a military band worthy of some notice.

Now we do not wish to disparage the merits of this really fine band, but we do not hesitate to assert that when the subject is brought to a strict criticism, there is no military band in this country that will compare with the Dodworth's. The latter is composed of veterans, led by veterans, as strict in military tactics and discipline as in their fidelity to the highest standards of their art; and who have done more for the improvement of military music in this country than all the other bands...put together.

The present Dodworth's Band was organized in the year 1825, by Mr. William Peterschen (conductor) and Mr. Thomas Dilks (leader). In its fourth year (1828) Messrs. Thomas and Allen Dodworth—father and son—became members and in 1836 they succeeded to the management, which has been retained in their family every since. Originally composed of the best instrumental performers in the country, and managed by men thoroughly acquainted with the best European models, the band soon achieved prominence among military men, and took the lead of all others. Shelton's Band was the strongest rival it ever had. Its subsequent enlargement was attributable to the princely magnificence of the unrivalled company, the New York Light Guard, who secured Dodworth's for all the parades...and to the example of that company the credit of the enlargement of military bands generally is solely due.

In the course of their long and brilliant career, Dodworth's Band have made great improvements in the plans and machinery of brass instruments generally. The Nova Ebor Corno (New York Horn) was invented and used by them twenty-three years ago, to supply the important desideratum of a medium harmony in brass-band music. They also invented those curious instruments composed of bells turned backward, and first used them in 1841.

But the gentlemen composing this famous constellation of artistic talents do not confine their efforts to military music alone, though they are, de facto, a military band. The public is aware of their great success in concerts at Castle Garden, at Tripler Hall, where they were associated with Mr. Fry, in the rendition of the overture to "William Tell," and other compositions of the highest and most difficult nature—at the opera house, at the Crystal Palace, and more recently in the Central Park. The talented Harvey B. Dodworth may be proud of a band like this, and can afford to smile at the efforts of imitators and the imbecility of cheap bombast.[22]

All of the Dodworths were entrepreneurs in the finest American tradition. Not only did they run the most successful band in New York, they ran a school for bandsmen. They designed, manufactured, and sold brass instruments, arranged music for other groups, published and printed several successful collections of brass band music, ran a dancing academy at two New York locations[23], and provided music for every conceivable type of celebration. The inclusion of the Dodworth Band on any program insured the financial success of the entertainment. His Central Park summer concert series was always well attended.

A select audience enjoyed the admirable strains of Dodworth's Band and, according to the old way, made up in enthusiasm what was lacking in numbers. The programme contained some of the most popular military pieces of the day, and was interpreted with that precision and elegance for which the Band is justly famous. It is to be hoped that the liberal patrons who furnish us with this agreeable weekly treat, will find it desirable to continue them during the coming days of autumn. When the weather is reasonably fine, nothing can be conceived more charming than listening to soft music surrounded by youth and beauty, in the Central Park.[24]

Professional bands were in great demand, and Dodworth's musicians were both talented and proficient upon several different instruments, allowing him to contract for any entertainment requiring music. In May of 1854 the Dodworth Band performed for a series of concerts and parades in Boston where Dwight attested to the caliber of their musicianship and their sense of ensemble.

The visit to our city of this model band from New York...had charmed our multitudes of eager and delighted listeners in street and concert room. . . .
    Their playing was admirable, really reminding one, in point of brilliant sonority, unity and precision, of Jullien. The band numbered nearly forty instruments, and played sometimes as cornet band, sometimes as reed and brass band, and sometimes with violins and double basses as orchestra. . . .In this latter form the overture to Oberon, quadrilles, accompaniments to the highly finished solos by the brothers Dodworth etc., were finely performed. The grotesque quadrille, in which the sounds of the barn yard were mimicked, was quite worthy of Jullien.[25]

With the outbreak of hostilities Dodworth freely donated his time and talent in support of the war effort. New York newspapers record large numbers of his charitable performances such as that for the Ball of the National Cadets (66th Regiment of New York Militia), held on 15 January 1861. The proceeds were equally divided between the house, under the charge of the Sisters of Mercy, and the Catholic Orphan Asylum.[26] Other performances were given for the relief of the widows and orphans of the strife.

Dodworth took his band to war with the 71st New York Militia Regiment, and the bandsmen served the wounded on the field of First Manassas (Bull Run). When their three-months enlistment expired, they returned to New York to continue their charitable work.

Thomas and Allen Dodworth's reputations as performers and teachers attracted large numbers of aspiring students. Thomas approached instrumental pedagogy in a systematic manner and was one of the earliest to employ group-instructional methods. His band school was continued by his grandson, Harvey B. Dodworth, and its success assured New York of more than its share of excellent regimental bands during the war years. It was Harvey B. Dodworth who led the band throughout the Civil War.

Harvey Dodworth gave the same thoughtful consideration to the organization and training of drum-and-fife corps. Early in his career he associated himself with Ned Lothian who had established a modest reputation as leader of a semi-professional corps. Lothian's group frequently marched with Dodworth's Band as a single unit. The two men collaborated on publications for the drum-and-fife corps that complemented those published by Dodworth for the military band.

In 1834 Thomas Dodworth added keyed bugles to his band to provide more volume for outdoor concerts. In 1842, when the leadership passed to Harvey Dodworth, the bugles were discarded in favor of the over-the-shoulder instruments that he had designed. Although Dodworth claimed a patent for this invention, the United States Patent Office has no such record.

Each successive generation of Dodworths increased the fame and influence of the band and their music school—so much so that other groups sought to cash in on their success by adopting similar instrumentations, instruments, and techniques.

Harvey Dodworth enjoyed national recognition as a cornet soloist, designing and constructing a four-valved instrument for his own use that had a written range to small c. His reputation as a manufacturer and performer attracted many aspiring young cornetists who sought his aid in the selection of suitable instruments. Unscrupulous music dealers tried to cash in on his fame by claiming that the instruments they stocked had all been tried and approved by Dodworth. This became such a vexing problem that Dodworth finally engraved the instruments that he had approved for the use of his students.

Dodworth's Band was very popular but other professional bands vied with it for public approval. Of these, the band of the 7th Regiment and Shelton's Band provided Dodworth with his only serious competition.

Shelton's Brass Band was composed of professional musicians, most of whom were German immigrants. Shelton's group and the New York City Guard Band were two of several from out-of-town that presented a series of concerts in Boston during June 1855. The Boston Brigade Band was the most distinguished local group to participate. They had only recently converted to a brass instrumentation. One listener found that the New York City Guard Band "though numbering no more than our Brigade Band. . .performed in such superior style, as to give rise to comparisons not altogether favorable to our musicians."[27] He, like Dwight, lamented the passing of the woodwinds from the Boston bands and concluded that this had occurred because "the cornets are much more simple in their construction, and consequently did not require such good performers."[28] "Still, [Shelton's] Band had no reed instruments, and yet how superior their music was to ours! We noticed this particularly on the last day of their sojourn among us when they passed up State Street; the music of Shelton's Band was deep, full and smooth; that of our musicians noisy, discordant and shrill. Can there be no reform in this respect! If money be a consideration, the various military corps of this city would willingly pay an additional price for the sake of better music."[29]

Bond's Brass Band was another early professional group active on the eastern seaboard. Although, early in its career, it had attached itself to Colonel Chickering's Regiment of New York State Militia, it did not enter federal service during the Civil War. In July 1855 it performed a series of concerts on the Boston Common. "When walking across the Common, our ears were greeted by unwonted sounds, fraught with the memory of good old times, when bands were not all brass. Verily we caught the sound of reeds, of clarinets and on closer observation we even recognized the mello blending influence of French horns! It was battalion parade...and for the occasion Bond's excellent Cornet Band had been strengthened by extra instruments to the number of forty-two. There were not far from a dozen reeds, and we will venture to say, what no one within hearing that time will dispute, that never for years has our city heard such satisfactory music in the open air."[30]

There were a number of other professional bands active in 1860 that enjoyed at least regional acclaim. Felton's Brass Band was organized in June 1852 under the direction of G. W. Felton. J. S. Jacobus (a bugle soloist with a national reputation) assumed its leadership in 1853 when the group adopted the name of the Bay State Band. This excellent musical unit was reorganized in 1856 under the leadership of Isaac W. Wales and performed many concerts in behalf of the war effort.

One of the earliest New York bands was organized in 1810 under the direction of Thomas Brown. It immediately allied itself with the 11th Regiment of New York State Militia and saw service with this group during the War of 1812 when it was stationed on Bedloe's Island. Its concerts, from the present site of the Statue of Liberty, attracted large crowds to Battery Park on the southern tip of Manhattan island.

Philadelphia was home to several professional bands in 1860. Of these, Johnson's Band, the Liberty Band, Beck's Band, and Hazzard's Band are mentioned most often in wartime newspapers. Johnson's Band, comprised entirely of Black musicians, enjoyed an excellent musical reputation. Johnson was one of the finest bugle soloists of his day. His band was frequently employed by the Philadelphia State Fencibles even though "race feeling was then pronounced and bitter, and although Johnson had a fine band which few could equal, he often suffered from this foolish and illnatured prejudice."[31]

Beck's Band used different uniforms to complement the character of the functions for which it was hired. Their costuming costs attest to their commercial success and musical excellence.

The Newburg Brass Band was a New York wartime favorite. Originally organized in 1839 by Frederick Lockwood it merged in 1867 with another New York band led by C. W. Moscow. Moscow's group had been known as the Hughes Band, but assumed the name of Professor Moscow's Band after the merger. It enjoyed commercial and social success until 1884 when it was disbanded due to Professor Moscow's retirement.

Another fine wartime band was originally organized in 1809 at Bethlehem, Pennsylvania, for religious purposes. This Moravian organization represented a compromise between a long musical tradition based upon their religious beliefs and a state militia requirement affecting men between the ages of eighteen and forty-five. "As this [Moravian] society has been offered to the Brigade Inspector and Colonel of the Regiment to furnish military music on occasion of Battalion parades, the said musical society shall not be subject to any military fines, and as said society has accepted this offer, they agree to be bound by the following constitution."[32] Adopting "The Columbian Band" as their name, they continued to support the 95th Pennsylvania Militia until the Civil War. The band was reorganized in 1839 under John Singley, and its leadership passed to Lewis F. Beckel in 1845. Beckel held the post to the end of the war. The band did not enlist for service as a unit, but a number of its musicians volunteered to serve with other regimental bands for the duration of the war.

The Moravian settlement at Salem did provide a band for the 26th North Carolina Regiment which served with that unit to the end of the war. Although composed of only eight men, each was an accomplished artist, and the band was one of the best in the service.[33]

There were a number of other professional bands that confined their service to the home front.[34] Professional bands, donating their services, frequently joined forces with regimental musicians to present vocal and instrumental concerts. These were generally charitable undertakings in support of relief organizations or specific regiments. Dodworth's Band was a favorite for this kind of activity since its reputation insured an excellent attendance.

Our troops in the Federal City, beside giving proofs of their expertness as mechanics of every sort, show that there are not a few among them possessed of not little skill in the divine art of music. . . .The following program [is]. . .to be given, May 9th, by the Light Guard, Company A, 71st Regiment, New York, at the Navy Yard Barracks at Washington. . . .With Harrison Millard (a private in the regiment) for conductor, and Dodworth's famous band for orchestra, our readers will readily believe that the concert [is]. . .well worth attending.[35]

Professional bands were most often found in large metropolitan centers. Chicago boasted a fine organization in the "Great Western Band," and St. Louis enjoyed the music of "Bohci's Band" which numbered over one hundred instrumentalists. Both of these groups were asked to participate in the cortege of the assassinated President Lincoln in 1865.[36] Quality and professionalism diminished as one moved farther west. As late as 1857, a Cincinnati correspondent for *Dwight's Journal* lamented that "many very able German musicians, when emigrating to this country, seem to remain in New York, and there to be lost in the crowd and among the many temptations of a great metropolis; whereas, should they come to the Western cities, we doubt not they would in a short time secure a much better position and find more solid friends than in the Broadway beer saloons."[37]

Bands from small communities had less ability and in an effort to improve their quality professional bandmasters were hired to organize and direct them. Sometimes a self-styled professor—an early manifestation of the "Music Man"—would take it upon himself to do the job. Some professors were knowledgeable musicians, and some surprisingly good bands were organized and instructed by these men. The limiting element was the amateur quality of the instrumentalists.

Bands that were less than models of musicianship nevertheless served the needs of and were loved and supported by citizens. Small communities felt fortunate to secure the services of a trained bandmaster, and a really good man could command a substantial salary when several potential employers bid for his services.

Securing a good bandmaster was not easy. The musical world was filled with fakes, quacks, and charlatans.

A foreigner looking through the directory of this, or any other American city, would be apt to conclude us to be a remarkable musical people, judging from the innumerable "Professors of Music" whose addresses are to be found inserted in the cumbrous volume. Indeed, even we have often been surprised at the scores of persons claiming this distinctive title, while in fact, they have no right so to dupe themselves, and while no reason exists for their being so termed by others. "Artist" and "Professor" are rapidly becoming meaningless words....We have professors of dancing, professors of boxing, of magic, and of almost everything that one can call to mind....We...who live in the midst of these so styled Professors, know a great majority of them to be as unworthy of the designation as the magicians, fencing masters and the rest....As a general rule the less a man knows about the business the more he parades the "Professor," and we used to believe that the public would at length perceive the impositions perpetually practiced upon them, so that the evil would work its own cure....We are mistaken; there are more "Professors" than ever, and the few who are really such, now sensibly style themselves Teachers of Harmony, Composition, Instrumental or Vocal Music as they may chance to be.[38]

Some of these scoundrels could make a reasonable living hoodwinking the civilians, but they were quickly shown up if they joined the military. Several self-styled professors of music were discharged from the regimental bands and returned to the ranks as privates or sent home when their incompetence was discovered.

Professional bands set the musical pace on the home front but, professional or amateur, they all supported the war effort. National holidays had always called for band music. The war intensified expressions of patriotism by the North and the South, especially on the Fourth of July. While the armies celebrated with artillery salutes, the civilians called out their bands for parades, concerts, and dances.

Lewis and Henry Turk wrote to Joseph Whitney, in July of 1865, to tell of the celebration that had taken place in their community. "Lewis and I spent the 4th of July at McHenry and had a pleasant time....Mr. Twombly delivered the oration, which I believe was excellent. We were charged $1.05 per couple for dinner at the tavern. We then were conducted to a spacious ballroom where numerous toasts were delivered. This was accompanied by soul stirring martial music. The whole thing lasted from 10 o'clock til 5 PM. Lewis wants me to tell you that he is a first rate boy, fat, ragged, and saucy and thinks of getting married soon."[39]

James Newton celebrated the same Fourth of July in occupied Confederate territory where Southern orators drawled out their love for the Union to the accompaniment of the bands.

I spent the poorest "fourth" this year that I ever expect to spend....In the first place the Regt was "fell in" at daylight & fired three rounds of blank cartridges. At 8 o'cl'ck we fell in again and had a Brigade Review. After that every man went where he pleased. Ryan, Beattie & myself went down to the city to witness the performance which was to take place there, but 'twas nearly over before we got there.

The citizens & military formed a procession, marched thro' the streets, & out to a little grove where they were regaled with "music by the band" & speeches from prominent men: you know there is hardly a prominent man here in the south who has not been an active secessionist, & it was highly ludicrous to hear them bluster & blow about their "undying devotion to the Union," "living and dying under the good old flag"..."let the fires of patriotism burn upon the altars of our hearts to the end of all time," &c &c &c all this from the mouths of men...who, but a few short weeks ago did not scruple to use every vile epithet they could think of to express the contempt they felt for the Gov. but especially for us "Lincoln hirelings."...After this grand farce...every one went "on his own hook." Our crowd...went out to the race course...after we got out there we found everyone drunk as fools, fighting, quarreling, & "raising Cain" generally, so we got into a carriage & came back to camp in disgust.[40]

For fifteen-year-old Margaret Kinnear, the Fourth of July was a delightful family affair. She bubbled with excitement and enthusiasm as she described the day's events in a letter to her young soldier uncle.

There were 20 folks to our house for dinner...and we all had a good time. I tell you now in the forenoon a company of soldiers was out. Oh! I never saw anthing so handsome in my life as they were. Father was one of them too. Oh! How I wished that you could be there too....There was drums, a brass band and what music there was. There was a cannon and all sorts of guns in the world, fire crackers and so forth. In the afternoon there was a great celebration in a little grove near the town....There were five speeches and 15 cheers for the Independence Day, and flags waving and a drum as large as a barrel and more too. The most and best music I ever heard from a brass band. There was a great dinner too....This was all in the day time and in the night time the fire works would make you think that the world was going to burn up. The balls of fire were as large as a bowl. They seemed to almost touch the sky and burst and be seen no more and then to fire in every which way.[41]

The lovely Misses Hettie and Jennie Cary celebrated 4 July 1861 at Orange Court House, Virginia, where they were received as heroines, having just run the blockade from Baltimore. The festive spirit was somewhat dampened by the deaths of First Manassas which were only now being made known to them. The celebration spilled into the bivouacs of some Maryland regiments when General Beauregard sent passes and an escort to conduct the Carys and their friends to the camp to visit relatives. Captain Sterret who had recently been in charge of the Manassas fortifications was appointed as an aide to the Cary sisters, with instructions to provide them with shelter and entertainment.

The visitors received a royal welcome from the homesick soldiers. On the evening of their arrival they were given a serenade by the "Washington Artillery Band," aided by the best voices of the camp. When the serenade was over, Captain Sterret expressed the thanks of the ladies, asking, for them, if there were any service they might render in return. At once a shout went up: "Let us hear a woman's voice."

In response, Miss Jennie Cary came forward and, standing in the door of the tent, sang "Maryland, My Maryland." The enthusiasm of the soldiers was unbounded. The refrain was caught up and carried by hundreds of voices, until, "as the last note died away...there surged from the throng a wild shout." There was not a dry eye in the tent and...not a cap [left] with a rim on it in camp.[42]

The song "Maryland, My Maryland" was closely associated with the Cary sisters who sang it frequently after its publication. The lyrics, written in April 1861 by James Ryder Randall, appeared first as a broadside in Baltimore, Randall's hometown, on May 31. The two Carys immediately adapted the text to the music of "Lauriger Horatius," and presented it in public performance. The new tune was quickly adopted as a theme song by the Monument Street Girls of Baltimore, an enthusiastic group of Southern sympathizers. This was tantamount to treason, since General Butler had ordered the arrest of all women wearing Southern colors and had outlawed all Rebel songs. In spite of his ban the song was published by Rebecca Nicholson, a granddaughter of Judge Joseph Hopper Nicholson who had helped adapt Francis Scott Key's text to the music of "Anacreon in Heaven," producing the "Star-Spangled Banner."

The serenade extended to the Carys represents a long-standing civilian tradition. Almost anyone of consequence was granted this courtesy, and President Lincoln was the object of a great many of them. The first took place on 28 February 1861 just after his arrival from Springfield. The president had attended a dinner (described as very elegant and highly intellectual) at the National Hotel, given in his honor by Eldbridge G. Spaulding, a congressman from New York. While the president lunched, the Republican Association of Washington held its regular meeting elsewhere in the city. New members were admitted and one prospective member was blackballed because of his color. The chairman then announced that a serenade for Lincoln, originally planned for his arrival in the city, would take place immediately after adjournment. The Marine Band was ready, but refused to play until it received its thirty dollar fee in cash. A collection from the party faithful netted only twelve dollars. A second passing of the hat provided an additional five dollars. After considerable debate it was resolved to take the remaining thirteen dollars from the treasury. The meeting adjourned. The band was paid and the members, headed by the musicians in their scarlet coats, started for Willard's Hotel, where Lincoln had retired following the dinner. They accumulated a horde of well-wishers and job-seekers enroute as the band played "Ever of Thee I'm Fondly Dreaming." "Hail to the Chief" announced their arrival at the hotel. After sustained cheering, Lincoln appeared at the window and closed his brief remarks with a request for more music. "I again return my thanks for this compliment," he said, tipping his stovepipe hat to the crowd, "and expressing my desire to hear a little more of your good music, I bid you good night."[43]

Lincoln frequently called upon the Marine Band during his administration, and it quickly became a favorite of the president and his family. The Marine Band provided the music for all White House functions, but the most popular, from the public's point of view, were the Grand Levees given by Mary Todd Lincoln.

These soirees opened with an afternoon concert on the White House lawn. The gates were thrown open to the general public, and thousands of citizens passed through the presidential receiving line. The evening dinner and gala ball which followed were by invitation only. The Marine Band furnished the music for both events although Weber's Military and Cotillion Band and Professor Moscow's Band also participated upon occasion. The levees were the highlight of the Washington social season and were colorful affairs, the war notwithstanding. The Prince of Wales who arrived on 4 October 1861 was the honored guest at the first Grand Levee sponsored by the presidential family. "The East Room presented one of the most brilliant assemblages ever witnessed therein—there were members of the cabinet and their wives, Officers of the Army and Navy in full uniform...ladies and gentlemen from Georgetown, Alexandria, Prince George and Montgomery counties...some of the oldest and most influential citizens....At noon, admission was given, and the hall was soon filled. The Marine Band of music performing several popular airs, and the police in full uniform at the doors and windows."[44]

The prince was treated to another levee at the New York Academy of Music where "exactly 500 more than the house could hold" had been invited. "This...crushed [the guests'] toilettes into one indistinguishable mass of splendor. The hall was decked out in all types of flowers...and all that music could do to enchant an aromatic atmosphere with melody, the most superb bands procurable in America abundantly did."[45]

Civic celebrations always required band music. The opening of Druid Hall Park in Baltimore in October 1861 was typical. The program included a prayer by the Reverend Dr. Cummings, music by the bands, an address by Thomas Swann, Esq., music by the bands, an ode by children of the public schools, music by the bands, and a benediction. The formal program concluded with a salute fired by the students, while an artillery unit performed drill. The crowd moved into the streets to observe the parade which followed. "Bands included were the Maryland Guard Band, the Band and Drum Corps (10 drums and 20 wind instruments) of the newly formed Chasseur-Zouave Regiment which wore a uniform that included about all of the basic colors with fringes, buttons, and braid spread over it liberally. The Independent Blues Band was also present, but the one that caught most attention was that of the Chasseur-Zouaves."[46]

Bands were hired by well-to-do families to add a festive or solemn note to celebrations marking important events in their lives. May Whitney Rockenbach remembered that her friends and relatives filled the two enormous parlors and the dining room of her father's house on her wedding day in 1862. "She descended the wide staircase, slim and elegant in a pink silk taffeta gown. She and Orman Rockenbach were married in the big parlour. A five-piece brass band played all afternoon and evening. The guests feasted on wedding cake, chicken, lemonade, and homemade ice cream. When she was preparing to leave, she threw her bouquet of roses from the top of the stairs."[47]

Graduation was another event calling for band music. On 20 August 1861 Felix Poché traveled by mule from his camp to Grand Coteau, Louisiana, to attend a day of commencement. He found the elegant school exhibition hall "well finished," with scenery at one end. "We got there too late for the first piece, which was in French, but saw the last drama in English, and found that the boys acted very well. The audience was composed mostly of ladies whom I cannot praise for their beauty. The brass band was very good and the music sweet and lively. The whole was followed by the distribution of premiums, consisting of books and certificates."[48]

Music for civilian consumption was offered in different ways. Robert Patrick, a Confederate officer, frequently walked several miles from his camp to Mobile to attend theatrical performances presented there in the fall of 1863. On 12 September he and a group of his comrades "attended a concert of negro minstrels at Odd Fellows Hall. The music was poor, the songs and jokes were stale, and altogether it was a miserable affair. After the performance we had an oyster supper and then paid a visit to St. Michael Street."[49]

He and his friends traveled to New Orleans on 5 December 1862 for a potpourri concert presented by some of the most distinguished musicians of that city. Although a band was present under the direction of Mr. Cain, it was the other performers who most impressed the cultured Lieutenant Patrick.

I attended the concert on Friday evening and liked it very much. Miss Jane Stoke devoted herself entirely to the piano, playing only accompaniments to songs. Sure it was a charming sight to see her led out by the handsome Mr. Cain of the band. How graceful she looked while sitting at the piano, her beautiful neck about as long as my arm and as large as a broomstick; her charming auburn locks about the color of carrots; her beautiful rounded, snow-white arms, which look like the leg bones of a turkey after all the flesh has been taken off, or a well-rope with a knot tied in it; her heaving bosom and swelling bust were exhibited to the greatest advantage on this momentous occasion. Taking her altogether, she looked like the devil as she was led out to the piano and her back seemed as though it would break in two, she was so long and limber. Mrs. Hardesty looked a little seedy, like the tail end of better times. I suppose she cannot obtain the thousand and one little articles from the millionaires now that she had before the war and consequently, cannot bolster herself up and look as well as she used to when cash was more abundant than it is now. Miss Hannah Roach looked tolerably well but seemed to be a little embarrassed on first coming out, but she soon recovered herself and sang a song in very good style.

Mrs. Comstock next attracted my attention. She looked as ugly as ever. She sang in opera style and piled on some of the most excruciating agonies, but she sang so much better than that of the others.

Mrs. Ball thought she sang very well and evidently appreciated her own music if no one else did. Her mouth shut and opened like a rat-trap. Garnell Crocket made a short and appropriate speech which broke up the concert much to my satisfaction.[50]

Concerts combined vocal and instrumental soloists with other features: tableaux, speakers, or more exotic entertainments. Theaters in the poorer districts of large cities played down to the taste of their clientele. Gouging contests (a form of wrestling in which the loser could save his sight by shouting "king's cross"), and horse-breaking by Mr. Rarey were popular offerings. Mr. Rarey's advertisements encouraged his patrons to bring unbroken horses to the theater. He concluded his demonstration by riding the animal, now docile and domesticated, across the stage and down the theater aisle, exiting to the applause of the multitudes.

Military bands joined with civilian groups to present smorgasbörd programs for all sorts of causes. In December 1864 the ladies of Calvary Baptist Church prepared a series of entertainments "of the most delightful sort" at Odd Fellows Hall in Washington. "The fair will be all that the skill and taste of the ladies can make it. Much labor and expense have been bestowed upon preparations for this tableau. In procuring suitable costumes, etc., and we can safely affirm that this portion of the entertainment will exceed anything of the kind theretofore attempted in Washington. . . .The whole [fair] to conclude with a Grand Vocal and Instrumental Concert Saturday night January 7th, 1865. The Finley Hospital Band, under the direction of Mr. Lillie, will be in attendance for this concert."[51]

Programs were as varied as imagination could make them. Ford's Theater presented a "grand vocal and instrumental concert" on 20 February 1865 which concluded with a "complete program for dance etc. with one hundred canaries and two bands."[52] One month later Grover's Theater in New York, playing to a more sophisticated clientele, presented a series of ten operas. An instrumental soloist and a band were added as a gesture to popular taste. "The great trombone soloist, Mr. Burnstein, will appear on the first and sixth nights. A military band will play prior to the opera on Thursday."[53]

When the temperature in the Northern states dropped below freezing, ice skating rinks became one of the principal places of amusement for entire families. Many were simply ponds or sections of streams that had been cleared, but metropolitan centers constructed elaborate indoor rinks. These rather extensive buildings were illuminated by gas lights and were fitted for the comfort and convenience of the patrons. Decimus et Ultimus Barziza encountered such a rink on his way to the Canadian border. "Hundreds of skaters, of all ages and sexes, glided like spectres along the smooth surface. I have seen polkas, cotillions, and other dances performed by the skaters, which to me, appeared wonderful. . . . A band of music added to the hilarity of the scene, and the night . . . was spent in joyousness and gaiety. . . . I think a rink filled with a hundred skaters, lighted by the soft beams from gas, enlivened by strains of music, presents one of the most beautiful and attractive scenes I ever beheld."[54]

Confederate cities occupied by Northern troops were more somber and austere than other communities in the North or South. The theaters and places of entertainment remained closed, for there were few participants for merrymaking save perhaps the Yankee soldiers. Most Confederate citizens gathered in their churches to seek relief for the spirit if not for the flesh.

Mrs. Burton Harrison was in Richmond on 4 April 1865 and described the scenes accompanying the occupation of this once gay, lighthearted city.

The ending of the first day of occupation was truly horrible. . . .One gang of drunken rioters dragged coffins sacked from undertakers, filled with spoils from the speculators' shops, howling so madly one expected to hear them break into the Carmagnole. . . . Dr. Minnegerode has been allowed to continue his daily services. . . .When the rector prayed for the sick and wounded soldiers and "all in distress of mind or body," there was a brief pause, filled with a sound of weeping all over the church. He then gave out the hymn: "When gathering clouds around I view." There was no organ and a voice that started the hymn broke down. Another took it up, and failed likewise. I, then, with a tremendous struggle for self-control, stood up in the corner of the pew and sang alone. At the words, "Thou Saviour see'st the tears I shed," there was again a great burst of crying and sobbing all over the church, many people came up and squeezed my hand and tried to speak, but could not. Just then a splendid military band was passing, the like of which we had not heard in years. The great swell of its triumphant music seemed to mock the shabby broken-spirited congregation defiling out of the gray old church buried in shadows, where in early Richmond days a theatre with many well-known citizens was burned! That was one of the tremendous moments of feeling I experienced that week.[55]

Mrs. McGuire confessed kindred emotions as she walked through Alexandria, Virginia, in 1862.

The Confederate flag waved. . .from the Marshall House, the Market-house and the several barracks. The peaceful, quiet old town looks quite warlike. I feel sometimes, when walking on King's Street, meeting men in uniform, passing companies of Cavalry, hearing martial music, etc. that I must be in a dream. . . .

Everything is so sad around us! We went to the Chapel on Sunday as usual, but it was grievous to see the change—the organ mute, the organist gone, the seats of the students of both institutions empty;—Tucker Conrad, one of the few students who is still here raised the tunes; his voice seemed unusually sweet because it was so sad. He was feebly supported by all who were not in tears.[56]

Tucker Conrad's small, sweet voice was stilled at Manassas less than three months after he had "raised the tunes" in Alexandria.

In unoccupied communities Confederate citizens sought entertainment where they could find it. Mary Chesnut was enjoying what Richmond had to offer in 1864. "The Foreign Battalion drills now fairly at my front steps. We sat on the porch or at our windows, near enough to catch the eye of the officers as they step about. We can see their white teeth as they smile in passing us. This is enlivening, even if it is a dangerous proximity for the too-young ladies. Also, they have a capital band of music, which plays every afternoon, and is another distraction. We need all that we can get of that."[57]

Music on the home front was not limited to public displays by professional musicians. The nation was filled with amateurs and dilettantes who took great pride in the pianos that stood in their parlors. The ballads and war songs were taken into their hearts and their homes. The success of a popular tune was measured by the total sales of sheet music purchased for home consumption. Whether performed by accomplished musicians or dabblers, music occupied a central position in many households.

Some of General Sherman's troops encountered a music lover, Mrs. Shepherd, at the Boteler home on 19 July 1864. Captain Martindale, commander of a company of cavalry, had been instructed to burn the house and its contents. Since pleading for the house was to no avail Mrs. Shepherd and Miss Boteler begged the captain to spare the contents and personal effects of the inhabitants and servants. This too was denied by Martindale who had been instructed to consign everything to the flames.

In the midst of this work of destruction, Miss Boteler, a devoted student of music, pleaded for her piano. This was denied and while the flames were bursting out in other rooms, she went into the parlor, and seating herself for the last time before the instrument, began to sing Charlotte Elliott's hymn. . . .A soldier seized her to lead her out of the house, but she pulled away from him and sang again. In amazement, the cavalry men thought the girl was crazed with grief; but as the flames came nearer, Miss Boteler calmly shut down the lid of the piano, locked it, and went out under the trees,—the only shelter left for herself, her sick sister, and the frightened little children.[58]

Music was not the exclusive property of whites. Hamlin Coe in Nashville in

March 1865 witnessed what could well be a precursor of the freedom marches of the 1960s. He wrote in his diary that the "day [had]. . .been celebrated by the negroes of the city. A large number paraded the streets with music, badges and banners. On the latter were several mottoes. Among them were, 'we can forget and forgive the past.'. . .I only saw the procession pass through the street, and, to give my opinion, the nigger is getting mighty saucy, but I give them credit for good organization and order."[59]

The national airs were the most popular songs on the home front. These tunes, played in the North or South, invariably awakened feelings of patriotism. A Louisiana correspondent for *Dwight's Journal* wrote to claim these popular songs, poor as they might be intrinsically, as the rightful property of the Confederacy. Although proclaiming Southern ownership of this simple music, he really voiced the emotions of Yankee and Rebel alike.

I sincerely believe I never could learn to get entirely over a certain moisture of the eyelids that always comes to me listening to the sweet and stately melody of the Star Spangled Banner, whether issuing from a company of mimic soldiers in the broad glare of day, or whether at nightfall, gently swelling over moonlit waves from a far-off line-of-battle ship. Nor do I think I could easily conquer a certain tingling of the finger-ends, and a peculiar combative tendency which will creep over my usually quiet nature, when the soul-strring notes of Hail Columbia, marching onward like an army to the field, suddenly breaks upon my ear. Much less, in view of the fact that even Yankee Doodle, played on a two stringed fiddle by a negro boy, seated upon a cotton bale, will cause emotions patriotic in character, would I guarantee to nerve my heart to utter forgetfulness of any other of our national melodies, endeared to us by so many recollections of bravely-fought fields and hard-earned victories.

These tunes and anthems of right belong to the South; and as they are glorious tunes and anthems, we should cherish and perpetuate them, instead of throwing them back into the possession of those who have causelessly and wantonly become our enemies. These magnificent compositions first burst upon the world when the whole country was a slave-holding country; and like nearly everything great in war, peace, intellect and science, which made our forefathers illustrious, sprung from one general source. Instead of abandoning, let us claim them as our own legitimate property. Our whole people have listened to their swelling strains with unalloyed delight; and tens of thousands would almost as soon fight for their retention as they would for the protection of their section—so strong is their reverence for, and powerful their attachment to, the grand old tunes they have admired and loved from earliest boyhood to the present moment.[60]

This anonymous Confederate stated a paradox. The music that was the product of a century of struggle to establish an independent union for all states was the self-same music that intensified the combative tendencies of both armies—one of which now sought to dissolve that union. Southerners rightfully claimed this music as their own—but so did Billy Yank. The eminent John Dwight stated the case for future generations when, in 1861, he eloquently pleaded for the time when these songs would "be a part of the common birthright of *all* Americans."[61] And now—it has come to pass.

NOTES

1. Mrs. D. Giraud Wright, *A Southern Girl in '61* (New York: Doubleday, Page & Co., 1905), pp. 135–36.

2. James Cooper Nisbet, *4 Years on the Firing Line* (1914, reprint ed., ed. Bell Irvin Wiley, Jackson, Tenn.: McCowat–Mercer Press, 1963), p. 81.

3. Kate Cumming, *Kate: The Journal of a Confederate Nurse* (1866; reprint ed., ed. Richard Barksdale Harwell, Baton Rouge, La.: Louisiana State University Press, 1959), pp. 248–250.

4. Matthew Page Andrews, ed., *The Women of the South in War Times* (Baltimore: Norman Remington Co., 1920), p. 236.

5. Decimus et Ultimus Barziza, *Adventures of a Prisoner of War, 1863–65* (1865; reprint ed., ed. R. Henderson Shuffler, Austin, Tex.: University of Texas Press, 1964), p. 65.

6. Bell Irvin Wiley, *The Life of Billy Yank* (Indianapolis: Bobbs-Merrill Co., 1952), p. 257.

7. Ibid.

8. George Alfred Townsend, *Rustics in Rebellion* (1866; reprint ed., Chapel Hill: North Carolina University Press, 1950), p. 189.

9. H. W. Schwartz, *Bands of America* (Garden City, N.Y.: Doubleday & Company, 1957), p. 44.

10. *DJM* 3, no. 3 (23 April 1853): 18.

11. *DJM* 3, no. 2 (16 April 1853): 9–10.

12. Frank L. Byrne and Andrew T. Weaver, eds., *Haskell of Gettysburg* (Madison, Wis.: State Historical Society of Wisconsin, 1970), p. 12.

13. *DJM* 27, no. 10 (1 August 1868): 287.

14. *New York Times*, 28 December 1861, p. 9.

15. *DJM* 20, no. 7 (16 November 1861): 262.

16. *Gleason's Pictorial Drawing-Room Companion* ,September 1851, p. 28.

17. *Washington Post*, 4 March 1851, p. 28.

18. Marwood Darlington, *Irish Orpheus* (Philadelphia: Oliver-Maney-Klein Co., 1950), chaps. 1, 2, 3, 4, 5, 14 & 16. *See also* Schwartz, *Bands of America*, chaps. 2–6, passim.

19. *DJM* 15, no. 1 (16 April 1859): 21.

20. *DJM* 23, no. 1 (4 April 1863): 6–7.

21. The article, written by William R. Bayley for The *Philadelphia Evening Star* in 1893 but never published, covers the period around 1830 to 1890. Quote as cited by White, *A History of Military Music*, pp. 59–60.

22. *DJM* 16, no. 26 (24 March 1860): 412–13 (reprint from the *New York Sunday Mercury*). William Fry was an enterprising composer whom some called "The Beethoven of America." Fry had a flair for the dramatic and collaborated with Jullien in the performance of some of his symphonies. Of questionable quality, his works achieved a wide hearing primarily because of his public relations program and the volatile journalism that accompanied the premier of each new work.

23. *"Advertisement,"* *New York Times*, 15 January 1861, p. 8.

24. *New York Times*, 19 August 1861, p. 2.

25. *DJM* 5, no. 8 (27 May 1854): 63.

26. *New York Times*, 15 January 1861, p. 8.

27. *DJM* 7, no. 13 (30 June 1855): 102.

28. Ibid.

29. Ibid.

30. *DJM* 7, no. 17 (28 July 1855): 134.

31. White, *A History of Military Music*, p. 60.

32. Preamble, *The Constitution of the Musical Society of the 95th Pennsylvania Militia* as cited by Willaim C. White, *A History of Military Music in America* (New York: Exposition Press, 1944), p. 56.

33. Hall has traced the history of the band of the 26th North Carolina Regiment as well as several others from the Moravian settlements. *See* Harry Hobart Hall, *A Johnny Reb Band from Salem* (Raleigh, N. C.: North Carolina Confederate Centennial Committee, 1963).

34. The Worth Infantry Band, Professor Charles's Military and Cotillion Band, Volandt's Band and Drum Corps, Mentor's Band, the New Haven City Band, the Jamestown Cornet Band (which did enter service with the 72nd New York Infantry Regiment near the end of the war), the City Cornet Band (which served the Maryland Guard during its three-months tour of duty), and a host of others performed for military and civilian entertainments in their areas. In October 1861 the City Cornet Band numbered forty pieces and appeared in Baltimore "in their Zouave Uniforms [to] perform some choice operatic Merceaux [sic] before the commencement of the opera and between the acts." (*Baltimore Sun*, 18 October 1861.)

35. *DJM* 19, no. 7 (18 May 1861): 55.

36. *New York Times*, 26 April 1865, p. 3.

37. *DJM* 11, no. 6 (9 November 1875): 44.

38. *DJM* 9, no. 26 (27 September 1856): 44.

39. Robert J. Snetsinger, ed., *Kiss Clara for Me: The Story of Joseph Whitney* (State College, Pa.: Carnation Press, 1969), p. 17.

40. James to one of his sisters 5 July 1865 as cited in James K. Newton, *A Wisconsin Boy in Dixie, The Selected Letters of James K. Newton*, ed. Stephen E. Ambrose (Madison, Wisc.: University of Wisconsin Press, 1961), p. 164.

41. Margaret Kinnear to Joseph Whitney as cited by Snetsinger, ed., *Kiss Clara for Me*, p. 25.

42. Andrews, ed., *Women of the South*, pp. 68–69. *See also* "Songs of the Civil War," *Century Magazine* (August 1886), p. 32.

43. *Washington Evening Star*, 25 February, 1 March 1861; *New York Herald*, 1 March 1861; *New York Times*, 1 March 1861.

44. *National Intelligencer*, 4 October 1861, pp. 1, 3.

45. *Baltimore Sun*, 15 October 1861, p. 1.

46. *Baltimore Sun*, 18 October 1861, p. 1.

47. Snetsinger, ed., *Kiss Clara for Me*, p. 167.

48. Felix Pierre Poché, *Louisiana Confederate*, ed. Edwin C. Bearss, translated by Eugenie Watson Somdal (Natchitoches, La.: Louisiana Studies Institute, 1972), p. 21.

49. Robert Patrick, *Reluctant Rebel . . . Secret Diary*, ed. F. Jay Taylor (Baton Rouge, La.: Louisiana State University Press, 1959), p. 127.

50. Ibid., pp. 61–62.

51. *New York Times*, 31 December 1864, p. 8.

52. *Washington Post*, 20 February 1865, p. 4.

53. *New York Times*, 1 March 1865, p. 8.

54. Barziza, *Adventures of a Prisoner*, p. 110.

55. Mrs. Burton Harrison, *Recollections Grave and Gay*, as cited in Henry Steele Commager, *The Blue and the Gray* (Indianapolis: Bobbs-Merrill Co., 1950), pp. 1127–29.

56. Andrews, ed., *Women of the South*, pp. 77–79.

57. Mary Boykin Chesnut, *A Diary from Dixie*, 2d ed., ed. Ben Ames Williams (Boston: Houghton Mifflin Co., Riverside Press, 1949), p. 460.

58. Andrews, ed., *Women of the South*, pp. 197–99.

59. Hamlin Alexander Coe, *Mine Eyes Have Seen the Glory*, ed. David Coe (Cranbury, N. J.: Associated University Presses, 1975), p. 219.

60. *DJM* 17, no. 15 (12 January 1861): 335.

61. Ibid.

APPOMATTOX, JOHNSTON'S SURRENDER, AND THE LAST GRAND REVIEW

On 7 April 1865 General Ulysses S. Grant established his headquarters in Farmville, Virginia, taking up residence in the village hotel. Simultaneously Crook's cavalry, on the north side of the Appomattox River, was engaged in a rather desperate struggle with Rebel cavalry forces commanded by General Fitzhugh Lee. Crook's troops were supporting Federal infantry commanded by General Humphreys, and the combined force opposed a large portion of the remains of General Lee's Army of Northern Virginia.

When these dispositions were made known to General Grant in Farmville he ordered General Wright's corps to cross the river and support the infantry and cavalry units which were already engaged in battle. Wright's troops responded instantly, even though they were bone-weary from the long, fatiguing march they had already completed that day, and his columns swung down Farmville's main street as darkness closed around them. As the troops passed the torch-lit hotel piazza, they could make out the three-starred shoulder straps and beaming features of the commanding general, and his obvious pride added a smartness to their step. "Then was witnessed one of the most inspiring scenes of the campaign. Bonfires were lighted on the sides of the street, the men seized straw and pineknots, and improvised torches; cheers arose from throats already hoarse with shouts of victory, bands played, banners waved, arms were tossed high in the air and caught again. The night march had become a grand review, with Grant as the reviewing officer."[1]

The remnant of Lee's army was camped in and around the village of Appomattox Court House, twenty miles to the northwest of Grant's headquarters, and their advance guard held a breastworks about a half-mile west of the village. The Confederate positions grew steadily more untenable as Yankee troops maneuvered around them.

By the ninth of April, Palm Sunday, the Federals occupied positions on three sides of Lee's army. The Yankee cavalry was drawn up on the Confederate west and Blue lines of infantry opposed any movement to the south. The north side of the square was open, but Lee could neither escape nor receive supplies if he moved in that direction. General Meade, commanding the II and VI Corps, moved rapidly from the east to threaten the Confederate rear and close the trap. Lee's only salvation lay to the west down the Lynchburg road and through the Yankee cavalry.

General Sheridan, commanding the Yankee cavalry, had established his headquarters in a small house near the railroad. There he met with Generals Ord and Gibbon, commanders respectively of the lead elements of the Army of the James and the V Corps, both of which were moving rapidly across the fields to close behind the Yankee cavalry on the west. Sheridan predicted that Lee would attempt a westward passage of the Lynchburg Road. Skirmish firing soon confirmed his assessment and he quickly moved the rest of his cavalry onto line, ordering Ord and Gibbon to press forward with the infantry as rapidly as possible.

Lee's troops, fighting desperately westward, easily scattered Sheridan's cavalry, and for a brief moment it appeared that they would make good their escape. But the Federal infantry had crossed the Lynchburg Road and swung into a battle line facing east. Rank after rank closed the gap—there was no going any farther. Sheridan regrouped his cavalry on the infantry right, and when the bugles sounded his brigades wheeled onto line. All was in readiness for a final killing.

As the troops of both armies tensed for the certainty of battle, a lone Confederate officer spurred his mount and galloped headlong toward Chamberlain's infantry. A white flag fluttered from the staff in his hand. Firing ceased abruptly and the unbelieving Federals watched as the Rebel troops moved their artillery to the rear and stacked their muskets. The correspondence that Grant had initiated with Lee, from his headquarters in Farmville, had borne fruit. The killing was nearly over.

Lee was already at the McLean house in Appomattox Court House and Union Generals Sheridan, Ord, Custer, Merritt, Parker, and some other officers waited just outside of the village to herald the arrival of their commanding general, U. S. Grant. Grant soon joined them and the little knot of officers trotted up the dusty road to the village while both armies sat in silent wonder. "A Yankee band near the town struck up *Auld Lang Syne*"[2] as the bevy of generals neared the house where Lee waited.

Salutes were fired from several points when the news of the surrender reached the Union lines, but Grant sent orders at once to have them stopped. "The war is over, the rebels are our countrymen again, and the best sign of rejoicing after the victory will be to abstain from all demonstrations in the field."[3] Submitting to their commanders' wills, the Union army and the Army of Northern Virginia silently turned their backs toward each other for the first time in four years.

But the war was not over yet and final celebrations had to wait. Confederate General Johnston was attempting to reach Danville with the remnant of his army, and General Sherman sought to make him stand and fight. Sherman's columns entered Smithfield on the morning of the eleventh of April, after fighting their way through several hastily erected Confederate roadblocks, only to find that Johnston had retreated across the Neuse River two days earlier, burning the bridges behind him. General Slocum's engineers pontooned the river, and Sherman's troops prepared to pursue the fleeing Confederates.

Mid-morning on the twelfth of April two officers rode into Smithfield carrying the details of Lee's surrender. Slocum's troops heard the news first as they marched through the village enroute to the pontooned Neuse River. "Billows of tumultuous cheering. . .rolled down the line like a tidal wave. Regimental bands made the old town echo with music as beautiful as it was patriotic."[4]

When the news spread, the entire Union army went wild with excitement. Every command mounted its own celebration. When Sergeant Upson posted the guard at General Wood's headquarters, the general ordered him to dismiss the troops and to come into his tent where "there was a giant bowl of potent beverage. . . .Everybody drank. Brimming cups and glasses were carried to those unable to get inside. . . .A band appeared and started playing and drinking, stopping the former to do the latter. Some of them could not wait till they got through with a tune till they had to pledge Grant and his gallant army, also Lee and his gallant fighters. . . .The band finally got so they were trying to play two or three tunes at once."[5]

The commotion attracted officers from other units who came to see what the music and singing were all about. As the pandemonium increased Colonel Johnson ushered Sergeant Upson through the crowd to General Woods. Upson recalled:

The General again shook my hand, and said he would promote me, that I could consider myself a Lieutenant. After a little more talk from Colonel Johnson he made me a Captain, and I might have gone higher if the General had not noticed that the band was not playing. Going out to see about it, he found the members seated on the ground or anything they could find, several on the big bass drum. Then he realized that they were tired, very tired, and he would relieve them. He got the big drum, other officers took the various horns and started on a tour through the camps—every fellow blowing his horn to suit himself and the jolly old General pounding the bass drum for all it was worth. Of course we all followed and some sang, or tried to sing, but [several tunes were] . . . all sung together . . . so I don't really think the singing was a grand success from an artistic standpoint at least. . . . The parade kept on and on, but along toward daylight the tired marchers began drifting back to their tents. A day or two later General Woods recognized Sergeant Upson and spoke, but the Sergeant's rapid promotion had apparently vanished with the festivities.[6]

On the eleventh of April General Johnston's bedraggled army marched through Raleigh, North Carolina. The citizens received the troops with pride but not with joy, for all knew that their passing marked the certain arrival of the dreaded Bluecoats. As Johnston led his troops into the city, the "bands played 'Dixie' and other patriotic and popular songs. There were jestful exchanges between spectators and men. Everybody made a brave pretense of being cheerful, and everybody made a failure of it."[7]

The beleaguered Confederates left Raleigh with the Federals close on their heels. On the day prior to the Union arrival in the city Governor Zebulon B. Vance of North Carolina conferred with two of his predecessors, Davis L. Swain and W. A. Graham, about a plan to end the war. He proposed calling a special session of the North Carolina legislature to adopt a resolution expressing their desire to terminate hostilities. Other Southern states would be invited to take similar action. The results would then be reported to Washington by a commission of deputies. The governor proposed to arrange a truce with General Sherman until such time as Washington could take appropriate action on these resolutions.

Governor Vance left Raleigh by the Smithfield highway to present his proposal to General Johnston who advised him to stay in Raleigh and cooperate with Sherman.

Ignoring Johnston's advice, Vance, Graham, and Swain framed a letter to Sherman. Armed with a safe-conduct pass signed by General Hardee (in temporary command at Raleigh during Johnston's absence), the latter two men left Raleigh aboard a special train to meet with the Union general. They were soon captured by Federal cavalry but were ultimately taken to Sherman's headquarters. It was nearly dusk when they arrived and the general, fearing for the safety of their return to Raleigh, insisted that they spend the night as his guests. "He treated them royally, feeding them choice viands and serenading them with music by a regimental band."[8]

When Vance's plan ultimately failed, the governor instructed Mayor Harrison to arrange for the surrender of Raleigh. Meanwhile, Graham and Swain returned to the city. Swain walked to the capitol building which had been closed and locked. He obtained the keys from a faithful Negro servant, who had run errands for the governor's office for many years, and opened the edifice. As he gazed across the village square from a window, he saw Wheeler's cavalry systematically sacking the businesses facing the building. When Swain shouted that he had just seen the head of Kilpatrick's cavalry, they ran to their horses, except for a Texan named Walsh, and galloped away from the city. "Kilpatrick's advanced units moved smartly up the wide thoroughfare. . . . The air was alive with flags, and regimental bands were playing victory marches. The parade ground atmosphere subsided quickly, however, [when Walsh], the lone Confederate cavalryman [,] rode his black horse down the middle of the street in front of the Federals, shouting 'God damn 'em!' and 'Hurrah for the Southern Confederacy!' He fired five pistol shots at the approaching columns, then reeled his horse about and galloped away. . . . He . . . probably would have escaped if his horse hand not stumbled and fallen."[9]

Fourteen days later Generals Johnston and Sherman met at Bennett's house near Durham's Station, North Carolina. On the twenty-seventh of April 1865 both men agreed to the terms of a military convention that brought the war to a close. Sherman arrived at the governor's mansion early that evening where he was met by several officers eager for any news. "An army band was playing in the front yard. . . . Pulling his copy of the agreement from a pocket, Sherman handed it to Grant and asked him to sign it as evidence of his approval. Grant read it carefully, then took a pen and wrote 'Approved: U. S. Grant, Lieutenant General.' . . . The news spread rapidly. The troops received it jubilantly. Band concerts burst forth all over town, and torchlight processions gave a carnival air. This went on for two days."[10]

So the long bloody war finally ended at Durham's Station—just as it had begun at Fort Sumter—with a band of music present. The bands at Durham's Station performed the final wartime concert, but the bands in Washington, on the twenty-third and twenty-fourth of April, presented the penultimate parade. On those two days the capital city witnessed one of the longest military reviews in history. Division after division passed by President Andrew Johnson and the other dignitaries. It took six and one-half hours for the Army of the West alone to pass by the reviewing stand. The steadiness and firmness of tread, the careful dress on the guides, the uniform intervals between the regiments (all eyes directly to the front), and the tattered and bullet-riven flags festooned with flowers all attracted attention.

Some scenes calling for laughter and cheers from the crowd enlivened the day. Each division was followed by six ambulances as representatives of its baggage train. Some division commanders had added, by way of variety, goats, milk cows, and pack mules whose loads consisted of game cocks, poultry of other types, hams, and sundry foodstuffs. Some included the families of freed slaves—with women leading their children. Each division was preceded by its corps of Black pioneers with their picks and spades at right shoulder shift. They marched abreast in double ranks, keeping perfect dress and step, and added "much to the interest of the occasion. On the whole, the Grand Review was a splendid success and was a fitting conclusion to the campaigns of the war."[11]

Each brigade, division, or regiment proudly displayed its band if it had one. The limiting acts, passed by Congress in 1862, and the reduction of the remaining brigade bands through discharge, French leave, and death all combined to make a complete brass band a scarce item. All available civilian bands were pressed into service and regimental and brigade bands that had survived the slaughter marched proudly at the heads of their columns. Units that could not engage civilian bands turned to their field music as a substitute. All field musicians within a division or brigade were massed into a single marching unit. But even these measures were inadequate, and not all commands were headed by music.

Colonel Charles S. Wainwright, whose unit was served by an amateur corps of field musicians, recorded some of the sadness and much of the splendor of the last Grand Review. In his brigade,

the cannoneers were mounted on the boxes, all had good clothes, sacks, and sabre belts, with letters and numbers on their caps. I regretted more than ever not having a trained Corps of Buglers, but as I had none, I directed them not to play at all.

My own get up was rather shabby, I not having a decent full-dress coat; I was obliged to appear in a double breasted sack. But I was overshadowed by the handsomest flag in the Army. . . . So we ended the two Grand Reviews without a single accident or drawback. I have never seen anything of the kind in Europe, but judge from the pictures that they understand making much more of a show of it than we do.

All the ornamenting of the streets and buildings was very crude. Nor could we show the variety, style, and showiness of uniforms to be seen in a European Army. Still, it was a grand sight; 130,000 citizen soldiers, with everything for service and not a particle for appearance. Had it been more like a European Review, it would have been less American.[12]

Obviously Colonel Wainwright regarded the Grand Review as a fitting conclusion to the protracted struggle, but not all officers agreed with him. Major Abner Small, adjutant of the 16th Maine, regarded it as unnecessary and, indeed, as the height of military folly. The command of the regiment had devolved upon him when Colonel Tildon was granted fifteen days leave to attend his seriously ill wife on 21 April 1865. The regiment had left Appomattox Court House on 15 April and moved into camp at Black and White Station where it remained until the twenty-first of April. It then made a forced march to Washington, D.C. to participate in the last Grand Review on the twenty-third of April. The 16th Maine had fought in most of the important battles of the war and had made a number of long marches, but "of all of the marches made by the 16th, for rapidity and length, without rest, none could compare with that most inhuman tramp for display at the 'Grand Review.' It was the last ounce of suffering needed to break the health of thousands of veterans. It was indeed a magnificent spectacle. The vanity of that prince of military humbugs, Halleck, as well as that of President Johnson was fully gratified."[13]

When the last unit had passed the reviewing stand on the twenty-fourth of April the troops marched into the hundreds of camps that surrounded Washington to await their separation from Federal service. On the twenty-fifth of May an incident took place in the bivouac of the II and V Corps that cannot possibly be imagined in a modern army.

An issue of candles had been made. As darkness settled, it was noticed that the camps of the Second Corps had been illuminated. Not to be outdone, Fifth Corps soldiers placed lighted candles in rifle muzzles and in the sockets of their bayonets.

Individual soldiers began attempting the manual of arms and other antics. . . . Then groups formed and moved—one in the shape of a giant revolving Catherine wheel.

Soon, perhaps from habit, the candle-bearers assembled in military formations—companies; then regiments, brigades and divisions—a vast sparkling parade growing spontaneously and forming under the command of enlisted men who had promoted themselves to temporary officers. . . . The little flames burned steadily . . . and here in this group of battle-hardened veterans was something that very much resembled a candle ceremony at a Boy Scout Jamboree. . . .

Bands and drum corps struck up a cadence. The troops marched to salute their generals. A headquarters clerk described the approach of Chamberlain's division as "an immense column . . . a line of living fire." . . . And when the division had formed around the headquarters tents . . . "the place was so illuminated that the smallest print could have been easily read."

There were cries of "Speech! Speech!" and Chamberlain, with his background in Oratory and Rhetoric at Bowdoin College, was able to mount a cracker box and produce an appropriate flight of eloquence. The band played and there were patriotic songs and cheers for the generals and the Army. The demonstration went on until, as one soldier-historian put it, "the oratory and exercises . . . were cut short by the ration of candles burning out, leaving all in the dark."[14]

The darkness that settled over the camp and this ultimate wartime parade also enveloped the Golden Age of the Brass Band. The Civil War was its last grand hurrah. Veteran musicians returned home to become a part of a civilian band tradition that was taking its cue from Gilmore and others by adopting a mixed instrumentation.

Militia units were too grim a reminder of the recent death and devastation to assume an immediate importance in the postwar scheme of military reorganization. Eventually the old militia was replaced by the National Guard, characterized by sound military structures that substantially reduced the requirements for music. Regular Army bands were reduced in number by assigning one to each division rather than to each brigade. Never again would an American army be accompanied by so much music.

Bandsmen and musicians had served with courage and distinction. Although both governments had been compelled to draft their soldiers, all bandsmen served as volunteers. Since they were volunteers, musicians retained much of the romantic spirit so prevalent at the beginning of the war. If a musician's outlook was now more realistic, it was nonetheless idealistic. Patriotism was still the basic emotion that propelled a bandsman into service. If an occasional musician was drunk on duty, or if some went over the hill, none could be classed with the shirks, bummers, sneaks, and thieves that populated many of the regiments because of an inequitable application of the draft laws and the unscrupulous draft brokers who grew rich at the expense of the combat effectiveness of both armies.

But by 1865 war had worn thin—even for the bandsmen. During the four years of intense deprivation and combat, ruby-cheeked boy musicians had matured into thoughtful young men. The entire nation was exhausted by the destruction, suffering, and slaughter. Nearly every home, as the wartime song had predicted, had its "Vacant Chair." Soldiers and civilians alike grew tired of the songs of bravado, of sadness, of superpatriotism, and of those that found humor in pathos. The national airs lost their popularity—except on Decoration Day and at the encampments of the Grand Army of the Republic where old soldiers reminisced. John Sullivan Dwight finally got his wish. As the national airs faded into the mists of history the brass bands faded with them.

The bandsmen and musicians, who were such a vital part of both armies, have never been eulogized as individuals, although a few of the outstanding bandmasters have been recorded in the footnotes of music history. Most were not remembered beyond their own generations, but their accomplishments and service will long be a cherished part of our national heritage.

A number of factors contributed to the demise of the brass band in America. Most bandsmen took their instruments home with them, but as they turned to civilian pursuits few kept up with their music. All were proud of their service but few were anxious to continue membership in any sort of military organization, with the exception of the veterans' groups. Militia units were no longer popular. Military units that did experience a resurrection were organized with an eye toward military practicality. Parades, drills, serenades, and bands seemed superfluous.

The Regular Army was also subjected to critical study, analysis, and revamping. Units were restructured to reflect the requirements of a frontier force. Infantry regiments were replaced by the more mobile cavalry. Surviving musical units were assigned at division or higher levels of command, where they remain to this day. Company musicians were replaced by a single bugler assigned to each regiment, but even this lone survivor of the drummer-boy heritage faded into history at the end of World War I. Buglers of World War II were simply decorative—not essential, nor even useful.

Most postwar professional civilian bands confined their activities to civilian pursuits. The military associations, so essential to their previous financial success, no longer required them. Militia patronage was replaced by that of large and small companies and corporations. Herbert Clarke, for example, directed the Anglo-Canadian Leather Company Band of Huntsville, Ontario, well into the twentieth century. John Sullivan Dwight lived long enough to see yet another of his dreams materialize as municipal bands, supported by public funds, tootled in the bandstands and public parks of America.

Bands continued to march through the cities and hamlets of the nation, but occasions demanding parades were gradually reduced in number. Serenades were abandoned as an anachronism and civic celebrations were limited to major holidays like Decoration Day and the Fourth of July. Veterans' organizations paraded with their music, but these grand occasions were slowly eroded by the passage of time until only a handful of tottering, dotty, gray-bearded veterans awaited the call to their eternal encampments.

Concerts became the mainstay of the postwar wind ensembles; and the requirements of the bandstand relegated the over-the-shoulder instruments to the family attic, in favor of the bell-front and upright models. The more demanding concert repertoire required a band of varied instrumental colors. Woodwinds became a part of their standard instrumentation. The Eb cornet succumbed to the astounding technique of barnstorming Bb cornet virtuosi. Every amateur hoped to become another Arban. The Eb cornets were replaced by the clarinets, oboes, and flutes, while the Bb cornet assumed leadership of the brass section. The robust and versatile trombone replaced the voice of the tenor horn and the French horns welded the reeds and brass together. The transformation was complete.

Gilmore, Scala, Grafulla, and Dodworth had always used a mixed instrumentation, but it was Gilmore's band that provided the postwar model. He was imitated by bandmasters all over America. John Phillip Sousa and John Duss of the next generation of bandmasters sought a flexibility of musical expression through greater expansion of their instrumental resources. Their bands finally included all wind and percussion instruments—even the new-fangled saxophone. There are few instruments left for the contemporary bandmaster to add to the list.

It is always sad to witness the end of one tradition and its replacement by another, but the passing of the regimental brass band was not only accepted by the Civil War musicians, it was viewed as an inevitability. By the turn of the century hordes of veterans had mustered before the archangel of death. Those who remained mellowed with age. Though they reflected upon the past, they lived very much in the present and even anticipated the future. Musical changes merely reflected the reorganization of society as a whole, and the veterans were a vital force in shaping that new society. By 1900 most Union and Confederate veterans probably would have agreed with the irrepressible Sam Watkins of Company H, 1st Tennessee Infantry Regiment.

Sam had been in all of the major battles of the war. Of the one hundred twenty men who had enlisted with him in 1861 only seven were alive when General Joseph E. Johnston surrendered the last major unit of the Confederate Army at Greensboro, North Carolina. Of the whole Army of Tennessee, which totaled three thousand two hundred men, only sixty-five remained to be paroled that day. In spite of the battles he fought, the suffering he endured, and the deaths he recorded, he was able to write, only fifteen years after the end of the struggle that "the United States has no North, no South, no East, no West. *We are one and undivided!*"[15] Sam provided the italics.

NOTES

1. Robert Johnson and Clarence Buel, eds., *Battles and Leaders of the Civil War*, 4 vols. (1887; reprint., New York: Castle Books, Thomas Yoseloff, 1956), 4:729–30.

2. E. M. Woodward, *History of the One Hundred and Ninety-eighth Pennsylvania Volunteers* (Trenton, N.J.: MacCrellish & Quigley, 1884), p. 58. *See also* Catton, *A Stillness at Appomattox*, p. 380.

3. Johnson and Buel, eds., *Battles and Leaders*, 4. p. 743.

4. John M. Gibson, *Those 163 Days, A Southern Account of Sherman's March from Atlanta to Raleigh* (New York: Clarkson N. Potter, Bramhall House, 1961), p. 239.

5. Ibid., pp. 240–41.

6. Ibid.

7. Ibid., p. 242.

8. Ibid., p. 246.

9. Ibid., p. 249.

10. Ibid., p. 289.

11. *New York Times*, 25 April 1865, p. 4.

12. Charles S. Wainwright, *A Diary of Battle*, ed. Allan Nevins (New York: Harcourt, Brace and World, 1962), p. 530.

13. Abner Ralph Small, *The SAixteenth Maine in the War of the Rebellion* (Portland, Me.: B. Thurston & Co., 1886), p. 218.

14. John J. Pullen, *The Twentieth Maine* (Philadelphia and New York: J. B. Lippincott Co., 1957), pp. 287–88.

15. Samuel R. Watkins, Co. *Aytch*, ed. Roy P. Basler (1952; reprint ed., New York: Crowell Collier Publishing Co., 1970), pp. 244–45.

THE INSTRUMENTS
AND THE MUSIC

Information on the construction and manufacture of nineteenth-century wind instruments is abundant. A summary of this material will help provide an assessment of the quality of the regimental bands during the Civil War period.[1]

Although a number of regimental and brigade bands used instruments of European manufacture, at least thirty-five American companies produced brass instruments equal in quality to those made on the Continent. A much larger number of American companies manufactured woodwind and percussion instruments. All enjoyed a brisk business long before 1860, but these companies must have appreciated the increased sales generated by the proliferation of wartime bands. Most manufacturers were located in eastern cities, with Boston serving as a modest center for the trade, but some firms established major outlets as far west as Chicago.

The Federal and Confederate governments assumed the costs of the instruments used by the field music, but military band instruments were purchased with monies provided by the regimental officers, the regimental funds, civic donations, or in some instances by the musicians themselves. The first proposal for sealed bids for Union army equipment, issued in September 1861, was to provide musical instruments and accoutrements for the field music. It included:

> 150 bugles with extra mouthpieces.
> 150 trumpets with extra mouthpieces.
> 200 fifes (B and C).
> 80 drums complete (Artillery).
> 80 drums complete (Infantry).
> 800 drum heads, batter.

800 drum heads, snare.

200 drum snare sets.

200 pairs of sticks.

200 drum cords of Italian hemp.

100 drum slings.

5000 brass bugle insignia (to be issued to Musicians).

200 swords (Musicians).[2]

The inclusion of one hundred fifty trumpets is puzzling since none of the bands nor field musicians used them. Since the list includes bugles the bureaucrats obviously knew the difference between the two instruments. Perhaps this is simply an example of inefficiency in supplying material—a trait common to all armies. The short musician's sword was meant to dress up the uniform. Of little value as a weapon, instrumentalists found them handy for skewering fowl over an open fire when that delicate bird was available.

The bewildering list of brass instruments offered for sale included a multitude of colorfully named creations in addition to the more common types still in use today. Alt horns, neo cors, ophicleides, bombardones, trombacellos, post horns, ebor cornos, clavicors, tenorhorns, burdons, saxotrombas, saxtubas, cornophones and sudrephones all vied with the saxhorns for public approval. Trumpets, trombones, and French horns had fallen out of favor while post horns and the keyed brass family were considered rather old-fashioned.

Conically bored instruments were generally preferred over those with a cylindrical bore, and the eminent Dodworth did not hesitate to speak of the superiority of their mellifluous sounds. "I have always, in my own mind, classed trumpets, post horns, trombones and French horns, as supernumeraries; for, since the introduction of bugles, cornets, ebor cornos and sax horns, they are no longer depended upon for the principal parts."[3] In a chart showing the proper instrumentation for bands of various sizes the first fourteen instruments should be "nothing but sax horns, ebor cornos and cornets, or instruments of like character...that is valve instruments of large calibre."[4] Dodworth recommended the inclusion of an alto, a tenor, and a bass trombone in ensembles exceeding sixteen brass parts, and suggested the addition of two post horns as the twentieth and twenty-first instruments. He eliminated the cylindrically bored instruments completely when he published his *Journal for Brass Bands* a few years later. Whether he set the pace or reflected the taste of his time one thing is certain: regimental and brigade bands used the mellow, conically bored instruments almost exclusively.

Their selection may have resulted from considerations other than those related to musical aesthetics or public taste. Brass instruments were manufactured in bell-front, upright, and over-the-shoulder models, but the latter was the favored style for bands serving militia units. "In selection of the instruments, attention should be paid to the use intended. If for military purposes only, those with bells being over the shoulder, are preferable, as they throw all the tone to those who are marching to it, but for any other purpose are not so good. These were first introduced by the Dodworth family in the year 1838. For general purposes, those with the bells upward...are most convenient, and should be adopted by all whose business is not exclusively military; care should be taken to have all the bells one way."[5] Wartime bands were intimately associated with the military and, heeding Dodsworth's advice, adopted the over-the-shoulder models. Since only conically bored instruments were manufactured in this shape, regimental and brigade bands became saxhorn bands by default.

The over-the-shoulder design raises the interesting question of how the instrumentalists were arranged during concert performances. Period photographs do not provide an answer, since they were either posed or showed bands on the march. Of several hundred in my posession not one pictures a band in a concert setting. Professional ensembles probably used two different sets of instruments, but no army band operated on that kind of a budget. Present-day revivals, employing period instruments, have adopted the simple expedient of seating the instrumentalists with their backs to their audience. This creates a nearly insurmountable problem for the conductor since the sound he hears is radically different from that heard by the audience. Since wartime bands played most of their concerts in the field they may have sat in a circle, letting the sound fan out in all directions. The unsophisticated trooper in the audience certainly didn't clutter his mind with analytical criticisms of blend and balance, and even the musicians probably regarded such concerns as trivial, if, indeed, they thought of them at all.

Musical subtleties like blend and balance appeared to be only minor irritations when compared to problems of intonation. Instruments with as many as five valves were available to correct the intonation of individual fingering combinations, but most army bands opted for the cheaper three-valved models. Intonation problems were compounded by the amateur caliber of many bandsmen and the lack of a standard pitch acceptable to all instrument manufacturers. Bands comprised of instruments purchased from several different companies must have suffered from a certain vagrancy of pitch.

If the intonation of the average Civil War band would fall short of modern day expectations, their mellifluous timbre would be a welcome surprise to contemporary audiences. The naturally mellow tone of the cylindrically bored instruments was intensified through the use of mouthpieces with deep V-shaped cups, much like those found on contemporary French horns. The tulip-shaped mouthpieces, so popular today, were not used during the Civil War. Period mouthpieces are further characterized by sharp inner rims that did little to extend the endurance of the average player.

A few larger post bands included two or three clarinets. During the first half of the nineteenth century, the clarinet had progressed from a five or six-keyed model to the thirteen-keyed system developed by Mueller. He had unveiled his new clarinet in 1812, and his boxwood instruments offered obvious mechanical and intonational improvements over earlier models.

The Boehm system, patented in 1844, was far superior to that offered by Mueller, as was the Albert system that preceded it by a few years, but both required such radical changes in fingering technique that the Mueller model remained as the standard Civil War instrument.

Nineteenth-century experiments produced clarinets in a number of keys and sizes, but only the Eb and Bb soprano instruments found their way into Civil War bands. It is presumed that they either doubled or replaced the Eb and Bb cornets.

The flute, although not used in regimental and brigade bands, was probably the single most popular instrument for the musical amateur during the first quarter of the nineteenth century. Thousands were manufactured with from four to eight keys, the eight-keyed model being the most popular. London became a flute center of sorts, and here the instrument, when not played incessantly, was constantly written about and discussed. It was equally popular in the United States as an amateur instrument for the home, and was used by professionals in cotillion and theater orchestras. More than one soldier carried a flute in his knapsack and used it to relieve the more monotonous periods of his service.

Eighteenth-century flutes were conically bored but those that survived into the nineteenth century were less cone-shaped than those of earlier periods. Theobald Boehm came to London in 1831 when flute playing was at its height. Trained as a jeweler and possessing a scientific bent of mind, he set about to perfect the existing, rather rudimentary, flute. In 1832 he introduced a conically bored instrument with an improved evenness of tone throughout all registers. In spite of its superiority, it was not readily accepted until the early 1840s. By then Boehm had discarded the conical bore in favor of a cylindrical one. He patented this improvement in 1847. All of these models were readily available in 1860, and the selection of an instrument was a matter of individual preference.

The history of the piccolo is similar to that of the flute. The two foot-keys and the cylindrical bore of the Boehm flute were not applied to the piccolo, although it does use the Boehm fingering system. Nineteenth-century piccolos can be found with one, four, or six keys, corresponding to the one, four, and eight-keyed flutes.

The piccolo was accepted as a standard European military instrument during the final decade of the eighteenth century, but it was only occasionally used by large post bands and civilian bands in America during the Civil War period. The Eb flute was an even greater rarity, replacing or doubling the Eb cornets in large bands using a mixed instrumentation. Neither of these instruments was used by the average regimental band.

Nineteenth-century flutes and piccolos wallow in a confusion of nomenclature. Since the fundamental scale of the piccolo (minus foot keys of the flute) was D, it was said to be in D, but even so it was treated as a non-transposing instrument. The higher piccolos and flutes (a semitone or a minor third above) were then said to be in Eb and F. Today's flute with the two added foot keys has a fundamental scale of C and is treated as a nontransposing instrument. The corresponding higher instruments are now more correctly described as being in Db and Eb. It was this Db piccolo (in the twentieth-century contemporary sense) that was used by the Civil War bands even when the score called for a D instrument. Whether it was considered to be in the key of D or Db was of little importance since it was always treated as a nontransposing C instrument that happened to be missing the necessary length and key mechanisms to allow it to sound its fundamental. The Eb/F flute, on the other hand, was treated as a transposing instrument and the parts for it were always written a minor third lower than they sounded. Matters of nomenclature were still badly muddled in 1860, but the nontransposing D/Db instrument was the most commonly used piccolo during the Civil War. Large professional bands occasionally doubled the Eb cornet parts with an Eb/F flute. Of course, the normal octave displacement of the piccolo is presumed.

Civil War percussion instruments differ little in basic structure from those of today although they lack contemporary refinements. Field musicians used the regulation wooden models supplied by the government and bandsmen adopted the same instruments for their use. An occasional brass or silver-plated snare drum can be found but these were probably presentation models awarded for outstanding service. All were single-tension instruments with ropes threaded through the edges of the beater and snare heads in a zigzag fashion. Heads were of sheepskin. The four to six snares were made of gut. Civil War snare drums had a deep timbre and lacked the crisp response of today's instruments. The rather rudimentary tension system could not stretch the heavy heads enough to provide today's brilliant tone.

Bass drums of similar construction were much larger than the present-day models. The term "barrel drum" was aptly applied to their bulk. Most measured about 24″ X 24″ and period photographs show the unfortunate bass drummer struggling with the size and weight of his load.

Cymbals have changed in size only during the past 120 years, wartime cymbals being generally much smaller than those in use today. A pair in the Fort Ward Museum in Washington measures only twelve inches in diameter and the Ford Museum displays an eleven-inch set. An advertisement in the *Brass Band School* offered cymbals measuring from eleven to fifteen inches, but the larger sizes found little acceptance. Most were attached to the bass drum and played by the drummer. Wooden grips and pads were as common to the period as they are today.

Wartime bass drum sticks had heavy wooden shafts topped with leather-covered cotton balls, and snare drum sticks were much heavier than those used today.

Drum technique included thirty-six basic rudiments which are similar to the twenty-six presently recognized by the National Association of Rudimental Drumming. Nine of the thirty-six are rhythmic variations or compounds of two or more present-day rudiments.[6] Twenty-six of the remaining twenty-seven rudiments are still in use, but several were named differently than they are today. The Civil War drummer did not have to master the single-stroke roll but Bruce included a "tap ruff" that consisted of two sixteenth notes followed by an eighth note. The sixteenths were double-stroked on the upbeat. Although Bruce included the tap ruff, he noted that it had already fallen into disuse. The basic twenty-six rudiments were already well established prior to 1860, and any good Civil War drummer could have passed the NARD examinations for membership in that association.

Not many complete sets of period band music have survived but some conclusions can be drawn from the few that remain. Parts were written for first and second Eb cornets, first and second Bb cornets, first and second Eb altos, first and second Bb tenors, baritone and Bb and Eb bass horns. Small bands adapted this basic scoring to the instruments at hand.

The Eb cornet was the work horse of the group. It carried the melody line which was usually doubled at the unison or octave by the first Bb cornet. The first Eb alto received an occasional melodic fragment, but this was not a common practice. The basic harmony line, supplied by the second Eb and Bb cornets, occasionally provided a modest counterpoint to the melody. The Eb altos, Bb tenors and baritone shared the duties of a three-part rhythmic/harmonic accompaniment. The baritone was not treated as an obbligato instrument as it is today. The two bass horns, sometimes at the unison and sometimes in octaves, supplied a fundamental bass line to the entire ensemble.

Clarinets and flutes, if used at all, substituted for the Eb cornets or played in unison with them. Harmonizations were simple, utilizing the basic tonic, subdominant, and dominant triads of the major modes. Minor modes were rare and secondary tiads almost nonexistent. Modulations, if present, were generally to the dominant. Dominant sevenths were infrequent, and altered chords occurred only in the harmonizations of opera arias, supplied by the original composers rather than by the tunesmiths of the day. Arias were not the common fare of the average regimental band. These works were the property of the professional ensembles composed of accomplished instrumentalists.

Bb, Eb and Ab concert were favorite keys, but a few bands pressed their luck with arrangements in Db concert. Sharp keys were usually avoided. Most regimental band music was in the popular vein and the simple harmonizations and straightforward presentations are what one would expect for this type of music.

The music itself was available in three forms. Several collections of popular airs had been published prior to the war in arrangements that allowed performance by as few as eight or as many as twenty musicians. These publications were compiled by the best-known band directors of the day, and a great many of them were included in the repertoires of the average regimental bands.

Professional bands like Grafulla's 7th Regimental Band of New York used arrangements written especially for them.

Most bands increased their libraries from whatever sources were available. Each musician carried his music in a small pouch, suspended over one hip by a strap across the opposite shoulder. The pouch contained published arrangements and blank manuscript books which were used to copy parts from scores acquired by the bandmaster or from the music of other bands. Manuscript books have been found that contain as few as fifteen and as many as one hundred compositions. These provided enough music for three or four hours of performance time.

Since the music was the property of each individual, bandsmen took their pouches home with them when they received their discharges. This unfortunate practice has severely limited the amount of music available for present-day study. Quantities of music must still be lying about in hundreds of family attics. Even more has probably fallen victim to fire or some other catastrophe. However, complete sets of hand-copied parts from a few wartime bands have been discovered in several libraries during the past decade, and others will no doubt be unearthed. The published collections are currently the largest source of period music. (The bibliography contains a list of all collections presently known to the author.)

Although period music is a scarce item, printed programs survive in quantity. These indicate that 1860 audiences demanded potpourri entertainments that included several different performance media. It was a rare concert that featured only a band or an orchestra. Programs included bands, instrumental and vocal solos, small ensembles, keyboard performances, glee clubs, banjo selections, and even orations—on a wide range of topics. Regimental concerts presented in formal settings followed this tradition while informal camp entertainments included whatever talent was at hand. Spontaneous evening concerts after a hard day of campaigning were probably limited to the band.

Programs consisted of popular medleys, dancing tunes, and the national airs. This last group included all of the hundreds of patriotic war songs sung by Confederates and Yankees alike. In addition to this popular fare professional bands always included transcriptions of opera arias—a practice that severely questions the contemporary assumption that most nineteenth-century Americans were completely lacking in any sort of musical sophistication.

On the surface there seems little reason to believe that the average concert-goer of the past century, who took such delight in these popular presentations, would know any more about opera than his twentieth-century cousin. There is even less reason to believe that the average soldier could tell an aria from an air. Yet the length of these opera transcriptions makes it obvious that they were intended as the centerpiece of any program. Perhaps historians have underestimated the musical sophistication of nineteenth-century America. Since full opera productions were limited to the largest cities the bands were probably the most popular media through which this music was made known to the general public. Bands kept the old favorites alive and introduced the newest hits from the European opera houses. The nineteenth-century band was not a peripheral organization. It was an important and popular medium of performance.

The wind band played a significant part in the social development of our nation and was tremendously important to Billy Yank and Johnny Reb. Robert Patrick, a Confederate soldier, spoke for many of his fellow soldiers who carried a flute or a shaped-note songbook in their knapsacks: "I sit down sometimes and picture to myself the joys of home with all its blessings, when I passed my time honorably and profitably. There is one thing I miss more than anything else and that is my music. I had become so attached to my old violin that it had become, as I might say, a part and parcel of myself. I have a fine collection of music at home, if I ever get back home to practice it again."[7]

When camped in the woods south of the Chattahoochee River near Camp Wilderness on 25 May 1864 Patrick, reflecting on the significance of the music of the brass bands, spoke for all of the inarticulate and lonely-in-spirit when he wrote:

I feel rather sad and low spirited this evening and I get so very often and I cannot help it. I wonder if it is so with everyone....There is a brass band along with our [supply] train and they are playing "Shells of Ocean" and as the familiar notes of this sweet air are gently wafted in delightful cadences over the woody hills and dewy fields of the quiet forest, numberless visions of home in happier hours and sweet reminiscences of the past crowd thick and fast upon my soul and bring to view a green spot on memory's wide waste.

There is nothing in the world that reminds me more of home than those old familiar airs that I heard when life had brighter appearances than it does at present, and causes me to feel more keenly my present position and to long the more earnestly for peace. But alas! There is no peace for the end is not yet."[8]

Even budget-minded bureaucrats were compelled to admit that the elimination of the bands was a cheeseparing economy. Following the battle of Balls Bluff J. H. Douglas was asked to investigate the usefulness and effectiveness of the regimental bands and to report his findings to the Sanitary Commission. His report is a resounding endorsement of army bands that would quicken the heart of any Civil War musician. "I am convinced that music in a camp after a battle, whether it is a successful engagement or not is of great importance, especially so after defeat. One of the soldiers said to me, 'I can fight with ten-fold more spirits, hearing the national airs, than I can without music.' Others of the wounded said they wished the bands would play more frequently."[9]

The bands did play, and Johnny and Billy did fight with "tenfold more spirits" for the cause they each felt was right until the Confederacy was ground into nothingness. "Auld Lang Syne" echoing across the hills of Appomattox sounded the death knell for an era of American history. The exhausted and ragged soldiers of the line furled their battle flags, stacked their arms, and marched home with all the other Billys and Johnnys. The generals and lesser luminaries refought the war through decades of articles, books, and papers— all detailing their brilliant tactics and leadership and conveniently overlooking the mortality figures and their errors. The musicians took their music and their instruments to their homes where they lovingly relegated them to the attic.

For the next nine decades the ranks of the veterans of the Blue and the Gray were gradually reduced in numbers as each responded in turn to the long roll of eternity. Finally on 17 December 1959 Walter W. Williams, age 117, a Confederate infantryman and the last surviving veteran of the Civil War, was laid to rest at Franklin, Texas. Soldiers, nearly a century younger than Williams, stood at rigid attention as they stretched the Confederate Stars and Bars over his steel gray coffin. A color guard snapped to attention. Their rifles barked a unison salute. Babies whimpered briefly and then were still. Then, somewhere over the hill, a lone musician winded the final bugle of the war. The familiar sounds of "Dan, Dan, Dan; Butterfield; Butterfield, Butterfield, Butterfield," echoed and reverberated through the Texas hills and finally evaporated into the mists of the valley. "General" Walter W. Williams and an era of American history were slowly lowered into the earth where their dust has become one with the everlasting hills. But the brass band in America—why its ghost still haunts all of those attics.

NOTES

1. See the following for information on the construction of nineteenth-century winds and their manufacturers:

a. Robert E. Eliason, *Keyed Bugles in the United States* (Washington, D.C.: Smithsonian Institution Press, 1972).

b. Robert E. Eliason, "Brass Instrument Key and Valve Mechanisms Made in America before 1875" (D. M. A. diss., University of Missouri at Kansas City, 1968).

c. Martin Kirvin, "A Century of Wind Instrument Manufacturing in the United States" (Ph.D. diss. State University of Iowa, 1962).

d. William F. Bufkin, "Union Bands of the Civil War (1862–1865): Instrumentation and Score Analysis" (Ph.D. diss., Louisiana State University, 1973).

e. Kenneth E. Olson, "Yankee Bands of the Civil War" (Ph.D. diss., University of Minnesota, 1971).

2. *Baltimore Sun*, 5 September 1861, p. 1.

3. Allen Dodworth, *Dodworth's Brass Band School* (New York: H. B. Dodworth, 1853), p. 11.

4. Ibid., p. 12.

5. Ibid.

6. George B. Bruce and Daniel D. Emmett, *The Drummers and Fifers Guide* (New York: Firth and Pond Co., 1862), pp. 4–12.

7. Robert Patrick, *Reluctant Rebel...Secret Diary*, ed. F. Jay Taylor (Baton Rouge, La.: Louisiana State University Press, 1959), p. 177.

8. Ibid., pp. 172–73.

9. U.S. Sanitary Commission, "Report: To Secretary of War: Operation of the Sanitary Commission on the Volunteer Army - months of September and October," *Documents, U.S. Sanitary Commission* (New York: U.S. Sanitary Commission, 1866), doc. 11, nos. 1–40 (1861), pp. 41, 42.

BIBLIOGRAPHY

GENERAL WORKS

Altenburg, Johann Ernest. *Essay on an Introduction to the Heroic and Musical Trumpeters' and Kettledrummers' Art, For the Sake of a Wider Acceptance of the Same. Described Historically, Theoretically, and Practically and Illustrated with Examples.* Translated by Edward H. Tarr. Nashville, Tenn.: Brass Press, 1974.

Andrews,Matthew Page. *Virginia, The Old Dominion.* Garden City, N.Y.: Doubleday, Doran & Co., 1937.

———. *The Women of the South in War Times.* Baltimore: Norman Remington Co., 1920.

Baines, Anthoney. *Woodwind Instruments and Their History.* New York: W. W. Norton, 1957.

Barrett, John G. *Sherman's March Through the Carolinas.* Chapel Hill: University of North Carolina Press, 1956.

Bayne, Julia Taft. *Tad Lincoln's Father.* Boston: Little, Brown & Co., 1931.

Bernard, Kenneth A. *Lincoln and the Music of the Civil War.* Caldwell, Idaho: Caxton Printers, 1966.

Botkin, B. A. *A Civil War Treasury of Tales, Legends and Folklore.* New York: Random House, 1960.

Brooks, Noah. *Washington In Lincoln's Time.* New York: Century Co., 1896.

Camus, Raoul F. *Military Music of the American Revolution.* Chapel Hill: University of North Carolina Press, 1976.

Carse, Adam. *Musical Wind Instruments.* Reprint. Introduction by Himie Voxman. New York: Da Capo Press, 1965.

Catton, Bruce. *The Army of the Potomac: Mr. Lincoln's Army.* Garden City, N.Y.: Doubleday & Co., 1951.

———. *The Coming Fury.* Garden City, N.Y.: Doubleday & Co., 1961.

———. *Grant Takes Command.* Garden City, N.Y.: Doubleday & Co., 1951.

———. *Never Call Retreat.* Garden City, N.Y.: Doubleday & Co., 1965.

———. *A Stillness at Appomattox.* Garden City, N.Y.: Doubleday & Co., 1954.

——. *Terrible Swift Sword*. Garden City, N.Y.: Doubleday & Co., 1963.

Commager, Henry Steele. *The Blue and The Gray*. Indianapolis: Bobbs-Merrill Co., 1950.

Cotton, John. *Singing of Psalmes, a Gospel Ordinance: or a Treatise, Wherein Are Handled these Foure Particulars. 1. Touching the Duty it Selfe. 2. Touching the Matter to be Sung. 3. Touching the Singers. 4. Touching the Manner of Singing*. London: Printed for Hannah Allen at the Crowne in Popes-Head Alley and John Rothwell at the Sunne and Fountaine in Pauls Churchyard: by M.S., 1647.

Darlington, Marwood. *Irish Orpheus: The Life of Patrick S. Gilmore, Bandmaster Extraordinary*. Philadelphia: Oliver-Maney-Klein Co., 1950.

Dieck, Alfred. *Die Wandermusikanten von Salzgitter*. Gottingen, BRD: Heinz Reise Verlag, 1962.

Dixon, Norman F. *On the Psychology of Military Incompetence*. New York: Basic Books, 1976.

Dornbusch, C. E., comp. *Military Bibliography of the Civil War*. 3 vols. New York: New York Public Library (Astor, Lenox, and Tilden Foundations), 1972.

Dyer, Frederick. *A Compendium of the War of the Rebellion*. 3d ed. New York: Thomas Yoseloff, 1959.

Edwards, George Thornton. *Music and Musicians of Maine*. Portland, Me.: Southworth Press, 1928.

Eliason, Robert E. *Keyed Bugles in the United States*. Washington, D.C.: Smithsonian Institute Press, 1972.

Elson, Louis C. *The History of American Music*. New York: Macmillan Co., 1915.

——. *The National Music of America and its Sources*. 1899. Reprint. Boston: Colonial Press, 1915.

Ernst, Robert. *Immigrant Life in New York City, 1825–1863*. New York: Columbia University, 1949.

Farmer, Henry G. *Handel's Kettledrums and Other Papers on Military Music*. London: Hinrichsen, 1950.

——. *History of the Royal Artillery Band*. London: Royal Artillery Institute, 1954.

——. *Memoirs of the Royal Artillery Band*. London: Boosey & Co., 1904.

——. *Military Music*. New York: Chanticlear Press, 1950.

——. *The Rise & Development of Military Music*. London: Wm. Reeves, 1912.

Fisher, William Arms. *One Hundred and Fifty Years of Music Publishing in the United States, 1783–1922*. Boston: Oliver Ditson Co., 1933.

Fitzpatrick, John C., ed. *The Writings of George Washington from Manuscript Sources, 1745–1797*. 26 vols. George Washington Bicentennial Commission. Washington, D.C.: Government Printing Office, 1931–1944.

Foote, Henry Wilder. "Musical Life in Boston in the Eighteenth Century." Reprinted from the Proceedings of the American Antiquarian Society for October 1939. *American Antiquarian Society, Worcester, Massachusetts, Proceedings*. Worcester, Mass., 1940. Vol. 49, pp. 293–313.

Gardner, Charles K. *Compend of the United States System of Infantry Exercise and Manoeuvres*. New York: William W. Merclin, 1819.

Gibson, John M. *Those 163 Days, A Southern Account of Sherman's March from Atlanta to Raleigh*. New York: Bramhall House, 1961.

University Microfilms, 1967. UM no. 67–13, 308.

rick, Rembert W. *The Fall of Richmond*. Baton Rouge: Louisiana State University Press, 1960.

rin, Albert Antoine. *Military Bands*. Translated by Arthur Matthison. London: Hodson, 1863.

isterer, Frederick, comp. *New York in the War of the Rebellion, 1861–1865*. 3d ed. Albany, N.Y.: F. B. Lyon Co., 1912.

iiner, E. B. *Military History of Wisconsin*. Chicago: Clarke and Co., 1866.

eves, D. W., comp. "Reeves' Grand Benefit Concert," *History of the American Brass Band*, n.p., 1896.

ollinson, T. H. *Treatise on Harmony, Counterpoint, Instrumentation and Orchestration with Appendix Treating Upon the Instrumentation of Military Bands*. Philadelphia: J. W. Pepper Co., 1886.

oss, Fitzgerald. *Cities and Camps of the Confederate States*. Edited by Richard B. Harwell. Urbana: University of Illinois Press, 1958.

ossiter, Frank R. *Charles Ives and His America*. New York: Liveright, 1957.

chnapper, Edith B. *The British Union-Catalogue of Early Music*. 2 vols. London: Butterworths Scientific Publications, 1957.

chwartz, H. W. *Bands of America*. Garden City, N.Y.: Doubleday & Co., 1957.

mes, Thomas. *Military Guide For the Young Officer*. Vol. 1. 1772. Reprint. Philadelphia: J. Humphres, R. Bell & R. Aitken, 1776.

onneck, Oscar George Theodore. *A Bibliography of Early Secular American Music*. 1945. Reprint. New York: Da Capo Press, 1964.

———. *Early Concert-Life in America (1731–1800)*. Leipzig: Breitkopf and Haertel, 1907.

———. *Early Opera in America*. New York: G. Schirmer, 1915.

oaeth, Sigmund. *A History of Popular Music in America*. New York: Random House, 1948.

tackpole, Edward J. *Drama on the Rappahannock: The Fredericksburg Campaign*. Harrisburg, Pa.: Military Service Publishing Co., 1957.

tern, Philip Van Doren, ed. *Soldier Life in the Union and Confederate Armies*. New York: Bonanza Books, 1961.

toutamire, Albert. *Music of the Old South: Colony to Confederacy*. Cranbury, N.J.: Associated University Presses, 1972.

wanberg, W. A. *First Blood: The Story of Fort Sumter*. New York: Charles Scribner's Sons, 1951.

Upton, Emory. *Infantry Tactics*. 1880. rev. ed. Washington, D.C.: Department of the Army, 1867.

Vard, Christopher. *The War of the Revolution*. Vol. 1. New York: Macmillan Co., 1952.

Varner, Thomas E. *An Annotated Bibliography of Woodwind Instruction Books, 1600–1830*. Detroit: Information Coordinators, 1967.

Vetzel, Richard D. *Frontier Musicians on the Connoquenessing, Wabash, and Ohio: A History of the Music and Musicians of George Rapp's Harmony Society (1805–1906)*. Athens, Ohio: Ohio University Press, 1976.

White, William C. *A History of Military Music in America*. New York: Exposition Press, 1944.

Gilman, Samuel. *Memoirs of a New England Village Ch*
 tions. By a Member. Boston: S. G. Goodrich and
Griffiths, Samuel Charles. *The Military Band.* London: F
Hall, Allen. *Center of Conflict.* Paducah, Ky.: *Sun Demc*
Helbig, Otto H. *A History of Music in the U.S. Armed Force*
 adelphia: M. W. Lads, 1966.
Hill, Jim Dan. *The Minute Man in Peace and War; A History*
 Harrisburg, Pa.: Stackpole Co., 1964.
Hind, Robert. *Discipline of the Light Horse.* London: W. Ov
Johnson, Robert, and Buel, Clarence, eds. *Battles and Lead*
 4 vols. 1887. Reprint. New York: Thomas Yoseloff, 19
Jones, Katharine M., ed. *Heroines of Dixie, Winter of Desperat*
 lantine Books, 1975.
Jones, Katharine M. *When Sherman Came: Southern Wome*
 March." Indianapolis: Bobbs-Merrill Co., 1964.
Koch, Adrienne. *The Life and Selected Writings of Thomas Jeffe*
 with an introduction by A. Koch and Willien Piden. Nev
 Library, 1944.
Lawrence, Vera Brodsky. *Music for Patriots, Politicians, and Preside*
 and Discords of the First Hundred Years. New York: Macmil
Lonn, Ella. *Foreigners in the Confederacy.* Chapel Hill: University o
 lina Press, 1940.
———. *Foreigners in the Union Army and Navy.* Binghamington: Vail-I
 1951.
Lord, Francis A., and Wise, Arthur. *Bands and Drummer Boys of the Civi*
 York: Thomas Yoseloff, 1966.
Lowens, Irving. *Music and Musicians in Early America.* New York: W. W
 Co., 1964.
Mandel, Charles. *A Treatise on the Instrumentation of Military Bands.*
 Boosey & Sons, 186?.
Mason, George W. *Minute Men of '61.* Boston: Smith and McCance, 1910
Meredith, Roy. *Storm Over Sumter: The Opening Engagement of the Civil Wa*
 York: Simon and Schuster, 1957.
Merrill, Catherine. *The Soldiers of Indiana in the War for the Union.* 2 vols. I
 napolis: Merrill & Co., 1866–1869.
Miller, Francis Trevelyn, ed. *Photographic History of the Civil War.* 10 vols. I
 York: Review of Reviews Co., 1911.
Moore, Frank. *The Civil War in Song and Story,* 2d ed. New York: O. F. Colli
 1889.
Morley-Pegge, Reginald. "Valves," *Grove's Dictionary of Music and Musicians*
 Edited by Erick Blom. 10 vols. 5th ed. New York: St. Martin's Press, 1955.
Nevins, Allan, et al. *Civil War Books: A Critical Bibliography.* 2 vols. Baton Rouge,
 La.: Louisiana State University Press, 1967.
"Orderly Book of General Putnam's Regiment." *Proceedings of the Bunker Hill*
 Monument Association. Boston: Bunker Hill Monument Association, June
 1878.
Paige, Paul Eric. *Musical Organizations in Boston, 1830–1850.* Ann Arbor, Mich.:

Who Was Who in America, 1897–1942. Vol. 1. Chicago: A. N. Marquis Co., 1942.

Wiley, Bell Irvin. *The Life of Billy Yank.* Indianapolis: Bobbs-Merrill Co., 1952.

———. *The Life of Johnny Reb.* Indianapolis: Bobbs-Merrill Co., 1942.

Wiley, Bell Irvin, and Milhollen, Herst D. *They Who Fought Here.* New York: Macmillan Co., 1959.

Willard, George Owen. *History of the Providence State, 1762–1891.* Providence, R.I.: Rhode Island News Co., 1891.

Wilson, W. Emerson. "Band Membership Good Duty at Prison." A paper presented to the Civil War Round Table, Wilmington, Del., 1970. A copy was kindly provided to the author by William Bufkin.

Wolfe, Richard J. *Secular Music in America, 1801–1825.* 3 vols. New York: New York Public Library, 1964.

Wright, Mrs. D. Giraud. *A Southern Girl in '61.* New York: Doubleday, Page & Co., 1905.

UNIT HISTORIES, DIARIES, JOURNALS, LETTERS, AND RELATED PAPERS

Balch, Thomas. *Papers Relating to the Maryland Line During the Revolution.* Philadelphia: Seventy-Six Society, 1857.

Bardeen, Charles William. *A Little Fifer's War Diary.* Syracuse, N.Y.: C. W. Bardeen, 1910.

Bartlett, Edward O.; Cooke, S. G.; and Benton, Charles E., eds. *The "Dutchess County Regiment" (150th Regiment of New York State Volunteer Infantry) in the Civil War.* Danbury, Conn.: Danbury Medical Printing Co., 1907.

Barziza, Decimus et Ultimus. *The Adventures of a Prisoner of War and Life and Scenes in Federal Prisons: Johnson's Island, Fort Delaware, and Point Lookout by an Escaped Prisoner of Hood's Texas Brigade.* 1865. Reprint titled *The Adventures of a Prisoner of War, 1863–65.* Edited by R. Henderson Shuffler. Austin, Tex.: University of Texas Press, 1964.

The Battle of Fort Sumter, and First Victory of Southern Troops. Charleston, S.C.: [n. p.], 1861.

Bellard, Alfred. *Gone for a Soldier, The Civil War Memoirs of Private Alfred Bellard.* Edited by David Herbert Donald. Boston: Little, Brown & Co., 1975.

Bennett, Edwin D. *Musket and Sword: or the Camp, March and Firing Line in the Army of the Potomac.* Boston: Coburn Publishing Co., 1900.

Bering, John A., and Montgomery, Thomas. *History of the Forty-Eighth Ohio Veteran Volunteer Infantry.* Hillsboro, Ohio: Highland News Office, 1880.

Billings, John D. *Hard Tack and Coffee or the Unwritten Story of Army Life, Including Chapters on Enlisting, Life in Tents and Log Huts, Jonahs and Beats, Offences and Punishments, Raw Recruits, Foraging, Corps and Corps Badges, the Wagon Trains, the Army Mule, the Engineer Corps, the Signal Corps etc.* 1887. Reprint. Williamstown, Mass.: Corner House Publishers, 1973.

Bircher, William. *A Drummer-Boy's Diary: Comprising Four Years of Service with the Second Regiment Minnesota Volunteers, 1861–1865.* St. Paul Minn.: St. Paul Book and Stationery Co., 1889.

Birkheimer, William E. *Historical Sketch of the Organization, Administration, Material and Tactics of the Artillery, United States Army.* Washington, D.C.: J. J. Chapman, 1884.

Bishop, Judson Wade. *The Story of a Regiment Being a Narrative of the Service of the Second Regiment, Minnesota Veteran Volunteer Infantry, In the Civil War of 1861–1865.* St. Paul, Minn.: Written for, and by Request of the Surviving Members of the Regiment, 1890.

Blackford, William Willis. *War Years with Jeb Stuart.* New York: Charles Scribner's Sons, 1945.

Brainerd, Mary Genevive Green, comp. *Campaigns of the One-Hundred and Forty-Sixth Regiment New York State Volunteers.* New York: Knickerbocker Press, 1915.

Brown, Alonzo L. *History of the Fourth Regiment of Minnesota Infantry Volunteers.* St. Paul, Minn.: Pioneer Press Co., 1892.

Bruce, George A. *The Twentieth Regiment of Massachusetts Volunteer Infantry, 1861–1865.* Boston: Houghton Mifflin Co., 1906.

Buffum, Francis H. et al. *A Memorial of the Great Rebellion Being a History of the Fourteenth Regiment New-Hampshire Volunteers, Covering Its Three Years of Service, with Original Sketches of Army Life.* Boston: Franklin Press, Rand, Avery & Co., 1882.

Byrne, Frank L., and Weaver, Andrew T., eds. *Haskell of Gettysburg.* Madison, Wis.: State Historical Society of Wisconsin, 1970.

Cadwallader, Sylvanus. *Three Years with Grant.* Edited by Benjamin P. Thomas. New York: Alfred A. Knopf, 1956.

Casler, John O. *Four Years in the Stonewall Brigade, Containing the daily experiences of four years' service in the ranks from a Diary kept at the time.* 2d ed. 1906. Reprint. Marietta, Ga.: Continental Book Co., 1951.

Chamberlin, George Ephraim. *Letters of George E. Chamberlin, Who Fell in the service of his country near Charles Town, Va., August 21, 1864.* Edited by Caroline Chamberlin Lutz. Springfield, Ill.: H. W. Rokker, 1883.

Chesnut, Mary Boykin. *A Diary From Dixie.* Edited by Ben Ames Williams. 2d ed. Boston: Houghton Mifflin Co., Riverside Press, 1949.

"Chronology [of the history of the United States Marine Band]." An unpublished typewritten manuscript in the Marine Band Office, Marine Barracks, Washington, D.C.

Clark, Emmons. *History of the Seventh Regiment of New York.* 2 vols. Published by the Seventh Regiment, 1890.

Clark, Peter H. *The Black Brigade of Cincinnati.* New York: Arno Press, New York Times, 1969.

Coe, Hamlin Alexander. *Mine Eyes Have Seen the Glory.* Edited by David Coe. Cranbury, N.J.: Associated University Presses, 1975.

Cogswell, Leander Winslow. *A History of the Eleventh New Hampshire Regiment Volunteer Infantry in the Rebellion War.* Concord, N.H.: Republican Press Association, 1891.

Cole, Jacob H. *Under Five Commanders: or A Boy's Experience With the Army of the Potomac.* Paterson, N.J.: News Printing Co., 1906.

Connolly, James A. *Three Years in the Army of the Cumberland, the Letters and*

Diary of a JAG. Edited by Paul M. Angle. Civil War Centennial Series. Bloomington, Ind.: Indiana University Press, 1959.

Crawford, Samuel Wylie. *The Genesis of the Civil War; the Story of Fort Sumter 1860–61.* New York: Charles L. Webster & Co., 1887.

Cumming, Kate. *A Journal of Hospital Life in the Confederate Army of Tennessee.* 1866. Reprint titled *Kate: The Journal of a Confederate Nurse.* Edited by Richard Barksdale Harwell. Baton Rouge: Louisiana State University Press, 1959.

Curtis, O. B. *History of the Twenty-Fourth Michigan of the Iron Brigade.* Detroit: Winn and Hammond, 1891.

Dana, Charles A. *Recollections of the Civil War.* New York: D. Appleton and Co., 1902.

Davis, Charles E., Jr., *Three Years in the Army, The Story of the Thirteenth Massachusetts Volunteers.* Boston: Estes and Lauriat, 1894.

Davis, W. W. H. *History of the 104th Pennsylvania Regiment (Ringgold Regiment) August 22, 1861, to September 30, 1864.* Philadelphia: James B. Rodgers, 1866.

Day, David L. *My Diary of Rambles With the 25th Mass. volunteer infantry, with Burnside's coast division; 18th army corps, and Army of the James.* Milford, Mass.: King and Billings, 1884.

DeRosier, Arthur H., Jr., ed. *Through the South with a Union Soldier. The Letters of Alburtus A. and Charles Laforest Dunham.* Johnson City, Tenn.: East Tennessee State University Research Advisory Council, 1969.

Dodge, William Sumner. *A Waif of the War, The History of the Seventy-fifth Illinois infantry, embracing the entire campaigns of the Army of the Cumberland.* Chicago: Church and Goodman, 1866.

———. *Robert Henry Hendershot; or, the brave drummer boy of the Rappahannock.* Chicago: Church and Goodman, 1867.

Doubleday, Abner. *Reminiscences of Fort Sumter and Fort Moultrie 1860–61.* New York: Harper and Brothers, 1876.

Douglas, Henry Kyd. *I Rode with Stonewall, being chiefly the war experiences of the youngest member of Jackson's staff from the John Brown raid to the hanging of Mrs. Surratt.* Chapel Hill: The University of North Carolina Press, 1949.

Dresbach, Michall R. See Archives Materials.

Dudley, William Wade. *The Iron Brigade at Gettysburg.* Cincinnati: Price Printers, 1879.

Eggleston, George Cary. *A Rebel's Recollections.* New York: Hurd and Houghton, 1875.

Emilio, Louis F. *History of the Fifty-Fourth Regiment of Massachusetts Volunteer Infantry, 1863–1865.* 1894. Reprint titled *A Brave Black Regiment, History of the Fifty-Fourth Regiment of Massachusetts Volunteer Infantry, 1863–1865.* New York: Arno Press, New York Times, 1969.

Emmerton, James A. *A Record of the Twenty-Third Regiment Massachusetts Volunteer Infantry in the War of the Rebellion, 1861–1865 with Alphabetical Roster; Company Rolls . . . etc.* Boston: W. Ware & Co., 1866.

Ewer, James K. *The Third Massachusetts Cavalry in the War for the Union.* Maplewood, Mass.: Wm. G. J. Perry Press, 1903.

Fletcher, A. *Within Fort Sumter, or, A View of Major Anderson's Garrison Family for One Hundred and Ten Days*. Widows' and Orphans' edition. New York: N. Tibbals & Co., 1861.

Flinn, Frank M. *Campaigning with Banks and Sheridan in Louisiana, '63 and '64*. Lynn, Mass.: Thomas P. Nicholas, 1887.

Fuller, Stephen. *See* Archives Materials.

Gamble, Robert. *See* Archives Materials.

Glazier, Willard Worcester. *The Capture, the Prison Pen, and the Escape, giving a complete History of Prison Life in the South*. New York: R. H. Ferguson and Co., 1870.

Graham, Matthew J. *The Ninth Regiment New York Volunteers (Hawkin's Zouaves), Being a History of the Regiment and Veteran Association from 1860–1900*. New York: P. Coby & Co., 1900.

Hall, Harry Hobart. *A Johnny Reb Band from Salem, The Pride of Tarheelia*. Raleigh, N.C.: North Carolina Confederate Centennial Committee, 1963.

Hammond, Harold Earl, ed. *Diary of a Union Lady 1861–65*. New York: Funk and Wagnalls, 1962.

Harris, Daniel B. *See* Archives Materials.

Harris, W. A., comp. *The Record of Fort Sumter from the Occupation by Major Anderson to Its Reduction by South Carolina Troops During the Administration of Governor Pickens*. Columbia, S.C.: South Carolina Steam Job Printing Office, 1862.

Harrison, Mrs. Burton. *Recollections Grave and Gay*. New York: Charles Scribner's Sons, 1911.

Haskell, John Cheves. *The Haskell Memoirs*. Edited by Gilbert E. Govan and James W. Livingood. New York: G. P. Putnam's Sons, 1960.

Haydon, Charles B. *See* Archives Materials.

Heg, Hans Christian. *The Civil War Letters of Colonel Hans Christian Heg*. Edited by Theodore C. Blegen. Northfield, Minn.: Norwegian-American Historical Association, 1936.

Heth, William. "Orderly Book of Major William Heth." *Collections of the Virginia Historical Society*. R. A. Brock, ed. New Series vol. 11. Richmond, Va.: Published by the Society, 1892.

Higginson, Thomas Wentworth. *Army Life in a Black Regiment*. Williamstown, Mass.: Corner House Publishers, 1971.

Hinkley, Julian Wisner. *A Narrative of Service with the Third Wisconsin Infantry*. Madison, Wis.: Wisconsin History Commission, Original Papers no. 7, September, 1912.

Holmes, Oliver Wendell, Jr. *Touched With Fire*. Edited by Mark de Wolfe Howe. Cambridge, Mass.: Harvard University Press, 1947.

Houghton, Edwin B. *The Campaigns of the Seventeenth Maine*. Portland, Me.: privately printed, 1866.

Howard, McHenry. *Recollections of a Maryland Confederate Soldier and Staff Officer under Johnston, Jackson and Lee*. 1914. Reprint. Dayton, Ohio: Morningside Bookshop, 1975.

Ingraham, Charles A. *Elmer E. Ellsworth and the Zouaves of '61*. Chicago: Published for the Chicago Historical Society by the University of Chicago Press, 1925.

Kerwood, Asbury L. *Annals of the Fifty-Seventh Regiment Indiana Volunteeers.* Dayton, Ohio: W. J. Shuey, 1868.

Kimberly, E. O. *See* Archives Materials.

Lapham, William B. *My Recollections of the War of the Rebellion.* Augusta, Me.: privately printed, Burleigh & Flynt, 1892.

Lawton, Eba Anderson. *Major Robert Anderson and Fort Sumter 1861.* New York: The Knickerbocker Press, 1911.

Lee, Robert E., Jr. *Recollections and Letters of General Robert E. Lee.* New York: Doubleday, Page & Co., 1904.

Lufkin, Edward B. *The Story of the Maine Thirteenth.* Bridgeton, Me.: H. S. Shoney and Son, 1898.

Manarin, Louis H. *North Carolina Troops 1861–1865.* Raleigh, N.C.: The State Department of Archives and History, 4 Vols. (1966–   ).

McClellan, H. B. *I Rode with Jeb Stuart, the Life and Campaigns of Major General J. E. B. Stuart.* Bloomington, Ind.: Civil War Centennial Series. Indiana University Press, 1958.

McDonald, Cornelia A. *A Diary with Reminiscences of the War and Refugee Life in the Shenandoah Valley 1860–1865.* Nashville, Tenn.: Cullom & Ghertner Co., 1935.

McElroy, John. *This Was Andersonville. The True Story of Andersonville Military Prison As Told in the Personal Recollections of John McElroy, Sometimes Private, Co. I, 16th Illinois Cavalry.* Edited by Roy Meredith. Reprint. New York: Bonanza Books, 1957.

Merrill, Samuel. *The Seventeenth Indiana Volunteer Infantry in the War of the Rebellion.* Indianapolis: Bowen Merrill Co., 1900.

Meyers, Augustus. *Tenn Years in the Ranks, U.S. Army.* New York: Stirling Press, 1914.

Miller, Delavan S. *Drum Taps in Dixie, memories of a drummer boy, 1861–1865.* Watertown, N.Y.: Hungerford Holbrook Co., 1905.

Moore, Edward A. *The Story of a Cannoneer under Stonewall Jackson, in which is told the part taken by the Rockbridge Artillery in the Army of Northern Virginia.* N.Y. and Washington: Heale Publishing Co., 1907.

Mosgrove, George Dallas. *Kentucky Cavaliers in Dixie: Reminiscences of a Confederate Cavalryman.* Edited by Bell Irvin Wiley. Jackson, Tenn.: McCowat-Mercer Press, 1957.

Moyer, Henry P. *History of the Seventeenth regiment Pennsylvania volunteer cavalry, or one hundred and sixty-second in the line of Pennsylvania volunteer regiments, war to suppress the rebellion, 1861–1865; comp. from records of the rebellion, official reports, recollections, reminiscences, incidents, diaries and company rosters, with an appendix, by H. P. Moyer, formerly bugler Co. E, 17th Regt., Pa. Vol. cavalry.* Lebanon, Pa.: Sowers Printing Co., 1911.

Muffly, J. W., ed. *The Story of Our Regiment, A History of the 148th Pennsylvania Vols., written by the Comrades.* Des Moines, Iowa: Kenyon Printing & Mfg. Co., 1904.

Newton, James K. *A Wisconsin Boy in Dixie, The Selected Letters of James K. Newton.* Edited by Stephen E. Ambrose. Madison, Wis.: University of Wisconsin Press, 1961.

Nisbet, James Cooper. *4 Years on the Firing Line.* 1914. Reprint. Edited by Bell Irvin Wiley. Jackson, Tenn.: McCowat-Mercer Press, 1963.

Page, Charles D. *History of the Fourteenth Regiment Connecticut Volunteer Infantry.* Meriden, Conn.: Horton Printing Co., 1906.

Patrick, Robert. *Reluctant Rebel, The Secret Diary of Robert Patrick 1861–65.* Edited by F. Jay Taylor. Baton Rouge: Louisiana State University Press, 1959.

Pember, Phoebe Yates. *A Southern Woman's Story, Life in Confederate Richmond.* Edited by Bell Irvin Wiley. Jackson, Tenn.: McCowat-Mercer Press, 1959.

Pickett, Eli R. *See* Archives Materials.

Poague, William Thomas. *Gunner with Stonewall.* Edited by Monroe F. Cockrell. Jackson, Tenn.: McCowat-Mercer Press, 1957.

Poché, Felix Pierre. *A Louisiana Confederate.* Edited by Edwin C. Bearss. Translated by Eugenie Watson Somdal. Natchitoches, La.: Louisiana Studies Institute. Northwestern State University, 1972.

Porter, Horace. *Campaigning with Grant.* Edited by Wayne C. Temple. Bloomington, Ind.: Indiana University Press, 1961.

Prowell, George R. *History of the Eighty-Seventh Regiment Pennsylvania Volunteers.* York, Pa.: Press of the York Daily, 1901.

Pullen, John J. *The Twentieth Maine.* Philadelphia and New York: J. B. Lippincott Co., 1957.

Putnam, Charles. *See* Archives Materials.

Ransom, John. *Andersonville.* 1881. Reprint titled *John Ransom's Diary.* New York: Paul S. Erickson, 1963.

Rauscher, Frank. *Music on the march, 1862–65, with the Army of the Potomac. 114th regt. P. V., Collis' Zouaves.* Philadelphia: W. F. Fell & Co., 1892.

Reichardt, Theodore. *Diary of Battery A, First Regiment Rhode Island Light Artillery.* Providence, R.I.: privately printed, 1865.

Report of the Proceedings of the Society of the Army of the Tennessee, at the Second Annual Meeting, held at St. Louis, Missouri, November 13 and 15, 1867. Cincinnati, Ohio: published by the Society, 1877.

Riling, Joseph R. *Baron Von Steuben and His Regulations.* Philadelphia: Roy Riling Arms Books Co., 1966.

Robertson, James I. *The Stonewall Brigade.* Baton Rouge: Louisiana State University Press, 1963.

Roe, Alfred S. *The Tenth Regiment Massachusetts Volunteer Infantry 1861–1864.* Springfield, Mass.: Tenth Regiment Veteran Association, 1909.

———. *The Twenty-Fourth Regiment Massachusetts Volunteers.* Worcester, Mass.: Twenty-Fourth Veteran's Association, 1907.

Rowell, John W. *Yankee Artillerymen, Through the Civil War with Eli Lilly's Indiana Battery.* Knoxville, Tenn.: University of Tennessee Press, 1975.

———. *Yankee Cavalrymen, Through the Civil War with the Ninth Pennsylvania Cavalry.* Knoxville, Tenn.: University of Tennessee Press, 1971.

Russell, William Howard. *My Diary North and South.* Edited by Fletcher Pratt. New York: Harper and Brothers, 1954.

Small, Abner Ralph. *The Road to Richmond, the civil war memoirs of Major Abner R. Small of the Sixteenth Maine volunteers. Together with the diary which he kept when he was a prisoner of war.* Edited by Harold Adams Small. Berkeley, Calif.: University of California Press, 1939.

————. *The Sixteenth Maine regiment in the war of the rebellion, 1861–1865, by Major A. R. Small; with an introduction written by Gen. James A. Hall.* Portland, Me.: B. Thurston & Co., 1886.

Smith, Donald L. *The Twenty-Fourth Michigan of the Iron Brigade.* Harrisburg, Pa.: Stackpole Co., 1962.

Snetsinger, Robert J., ed. *Kiss Clara for Me, The Story of Joseph Whitney and his family, early days in the midwest, and soldiering in the American Civil War. (A Collection of Letters).* State College, Pa.: Carnation Press, 1969.

Stearns, Austen C. *Three Years with Company K.* Cranbury, N.J.: Associated University Presses, 1976.

Stubblefield, George. *See* Archives Material.

Steuben, Friedrich, Baron von. *See* Archives Material, United States. Inspector General's Office.

Sweeny, Leonora Higginbotham. "The First Rifle Company," *Amherst County, Virginia in the Revolution.* Lynchburg, Va.: J. P. Bell Co., 1951.

Swinton, William. *History of the Seventh regiment, National guard, state of New York, during the war of the rebellion; with a preliminary chapter on the origin and early history of the regiment, a summary of its history since the war, and a roll of honor, comprising brief sketches of the services rendered by members of the regiment in the army and navy of the United States.* Illustrated by Thomas Nast. New York and Boston: Fields, Osgood & Co., 1870.

Tarrant, Sergeant E. *The Wild Riders of the First Kentucky Cavalry, A History of the Regiment, in the Great War of the Rebellion, 1861–65.* 1894. Reprint. Lexington, Ky.: Henry Clay Press, 1969.

Taylor, Benjamen F. *Pictures of Life in Camp and Field.* Chicago: S. C. Griggs and Co., 1875.

Taylor, J. E. *See* Archives Materials.

Taylor, Susie King. *Reminiscences of My Life in Camp.* New York: Arno Press; New York Times, 1902.

Townsend, George Alfred. *Campaigns of a Non-Combatant.* 1866. Reprint titled *Rustics in Rebellion, A Yankee Reporter on the Road to Richmond, 1861–65.* Chapel Hill: North Carolina University Press, 1950.

Ulmer, George T. *Adventures & Reminiscences of a Volunteer, or a Drummer Boy from Maine.* [Chicago]: [Published by the author], 1892.

Underwood, Adin B. *The Three Years' Service of the Thirty-Third Massachusetts Infantry Regiment 1862–1865.* Boston: A Williams and Co., 1881.

Vail, Enos B. *Reminiscences of a Boy in the Civil War.* Brooklyn, N.Y.: privately printed, 1915.

Wainwright, Charles S. *A Diary of Battle.* Edited by Allan Nevins. New York: Harcourt, Brace and World, 1962.

Washburn, Edson D. *See* Archives Materials.

Watkins, Sam R. *"Co. Aytch," Maury Grays, First Tennessee Regiment; or A side show of the big show.* 1952. Reprint titled *Co. Aytch, a Confederate Soldier's Memoirs.* Edited by Roy P. Basler. New York: Crowell Collier Publishing Co., 1970.

Within Fort Sumter by one of the Company. New York: N. Tibbals & Co., 1861.

Woodward, Evan Morrison. *History of the One Hundred and Ninty-Eighth Pennsylvania Volunteers, being a complete record of the regiment with its camps, marches and battles together with the personal records of every Officer and man during his term of service.* Trenton, N.J.: MacCrellish & Quigley, 1884.

Wright, T. J. *History of the Eighth Regiment Kentucky Vol. Inf. during its three years campaigns embracing Organization, Marches, Skirmishes, and Battles of the Command with much of the history of the Old Reliable Third Brigade Commanded by Hon. Stanley Matthews and containing interesting and amusing incidents of Army Life.* St. Joseph, Mo.: St. Joseph Steam Printing Co., 1880.

Young, L. D. *Reminiscences of a Soldier of the Orphan Brigade.* Paris, Ky.: privately printed, n.d.

GOVERNMENT PUBLICATIONS

Compiled Military Service Records in the National Archives. National Archives Publication no. 63–3. Washington, D.C. Government Printing Office, 1965. A pamphlet explaining service records and how to order them.

Egle, William H., ed. "Associated Battalions and Militia 1776–1777," *Pennsylvania Archives.* 2d ser., vol. 13. Harrisburg: E. K. Meyers, State Printer, 1887.

———. "Journals & Diaries of the War of the Revolution with Lists of Officers and Soldiers 1775–1783," *Pennsylvania Archives.* 2d ser., vol. 15. Harrisburg: E. K. Meyers, State Printer, 1890.

Linn, John B., & Wm. H. Egle, eds. "Officers and Men of the Pennsylvania Navy 1775–1781." *Pennsylvania Archives.* 2d ser., vol. 1. Harrisburg, Penn.: Benjamin Simgerlay, State Printer, 1874.

Munden, K. W. and Peers, H. P. *Guide to Federal Archives Relating to the Civil War.* National Archives Publication, no. 63–1. Washington, D.C.: Government Printing Office, 1962.

"Muster Rolls and other Records." *Pennsylvania Archives.* ser. 1, vol. 10; ser. 2, vols. 1, 2, 11–17; series 5, vol. 1. Harrisburg, Pa.: Benjamin Simgerlay, State Printer, 1874.

"Muster Rolls and Other Records of Service of Maryland Troops in the American Revolution, 1775–1783." *Archives of Maryland,* 17. Baltimore: Maryland Historical Society, 1900.

Stafford, Frederick H. *Medals of Honor awarded for distinguished Service during the War of the Rebellion. Compiled under the direction of Brigadier General Richard C. Drum, Adjutant General, U.S. Army, by Frederick H. Stafford.* Washington, D.C.: Government Printing Office, 1886.

State of Massachusetts. *Laws for Regulating and Governing the Militia of the Commonwealth of Massachusetts.* Section 14. Boston: Young and Minns, 1800.

State of New York. "An Act further to amend the Laws respecting the Militia of the State." *Laws of the State of New York.* Vol. 344. New York: Printed for J. Tiebut by Southwick and Pelsue, 1810.

———. "An act to organize the militia of the State of New-York. Passed March 29, 1809." *Laws, Statutes, etc.* New York: Printed for J. Tiebut by Southwick and Pelsue, 1809. With this is "An act to ammend [sic] the act entitled: 'An act to organize the militia of this state.'" n.p., 1810.

———. "An act to organize the militia of the State of New-York, . . . with the acts amending the same." *Laws, Statutes, etc.* Albany, N.Y.: Websters & Skinners, 1821.

U.S., Department of War. "Circular." *Medals of Honor Issued by the War Depart-ment, Up to and Including September 1, 1904. An Alphabetical List With Date of Issue, Place and Date of Action and Citation.* Published by the direc-tion of the Secretary of War. Washington, D.C.: Government Printing Office, 1904.

———. "General Order No. 15." *General Orders Affecting the Volunteer Force, 1861.* Adjutant General's Office. Washington, D.C.: Government Printing Office, 1862.

———. *General Regulations of the Army.* Washington, D.C.: Davis and Force, 1825.

———. "Medals of Honor awarded for distinguished services under resolution of Congress, No. 43, approved July 12, 1862 and section 6 of Act of Congress approved March 3, 1863." *Official Records of the War of the Rebellion.* ser. 1, vol. 45, pt. 1, p. 645. Washington, D.C.: Government Printing Office, 1898.

———. *Medical and Surgical History of the War of the Rebellion.* 6 vols. Washing-ton, D.C.: Surgeon General's Office, 1870–1886.

———. *Official Records of the War of the Rebellion.* 128 vols. Washington, D.C.: Government Printing Office, 1898.

———. *Official Records of the War of the Rebellion. Medical and Surgical History.* Medical vol., pt. 1. Washington, D.C.: Government Printing Office, 1898.

———. *Report of the Paymaster General 5 Dec. 1861.* Washington, D.C.: Govern-ment Printing Office, 1862.

———. "Special Order No. 84," *General Orders.* Washington, D.C.: Government Printing Office, 1876.

U.S., Inspector General's Office. *Regulations for the Order and Discipline of the Troops of the United States.* Philadelphia: Styner and Cist, 1779. [Note: These are universally known as "Steuben's Regulations." Reprint available Philadel-phia: Roy Riling Arms Books Co., 1966.]

U.S. Sanitary Commission, Documents. 2 vols. New York: U.S. Sanitary Commis-sion, 1866.

U.S. *Statutes at Large.* "An Act for the Better Organization of the Marine Corps." Vol. 19. Washington, D.C.: Government Printing Office. 1861.

ARCHIVES MATERIALS

Ann Arbor, Mich. Michigan Historical Collections, Bentley Historical Library. "Per-sonal Diary of Charles B. Haydon, Co. I, Second Michigan Volunteer Infantry 1861–1862."

Barre, Vt. Barre Historical Society. Property of Mildred Phelps, Director. "Diary and Journal of Charles Putnum of the Brigade Band attached to the First Vermont Brigade, 1863–65." [by Charles Putnum]. (Microfilm copy courtesy of Ver-mont Historical Society.)

Cleveland, Ohio. Western Reserve Historical Society. "Regimental Papers." pt. 12, container 35, folder 3. n.p., 1864.

Cleveland, Ohio. Western Reserve Historical Society. "Regimental Papers," pt. 12, container 35, folder 3. "Custer Charging Near Columbia Furnace." [pencil sketch by J. E. Taylor].

"General Order No. 12" July 1803 from *General Wilkinson's Order Book*, p. 404. Washington, D.C. National Archives. Record Group 94, microfilm M-645, roll

3, as cited by Raoul Camus, "The Military Band in the United States Army Prior to 1834." Ph.D. dissertation, New York University, 1969, p. 429.

Madison, Wis. Archive Division, State Historical Society of Wisconsin. 1861–65 series. Letters of E. O. Kimberly.

Richmond, Va. Virginia Historical Society. Collections 1887, vol. 6. "Orderly Book of the Company of George Stubblefield, 1776" [by George Stubblefield].

Richmond, Va. Virginia Historical Society. Collections, 1892, new ser., vol. 11. "Orderly Book of Captain Robert Gamble." [edited by R. A. Brock].

St. Paul, Minn. Minnesota Historical Society. Abby Abbe Fuller and Family Papers. Stephen Fuller to Trotwood 12 December 1861.

St. Paul, Minn. Minnesota Historical Society. Diary of Edson D. Washburn.

St. Paul, Minnesota Historical Society. Diary of Elmer E. Ellsworth.

St. Paul, Minn. Minnesota Historical Society. Eli R. Pickett to his wife 29 December 1862.

St. Paul, Minn. Minnesota Historical Society. Michael R. Dresbach Papers. Michael R. Dresbach to his wife 4 December 1864.

St. Paul, Minn. Minnesota Historical Society. "Special Order No. 57, Hq., U.S. Army," 13 June 1859. *Post Returns, Fort Ripley, Minnesota*, June and August, 1859.

Washington, D.C. Library of Congress, Music Division. Scala Collection. "Letter from the Commandant of the Marine Corps to Congressman Frothingham, House of Representatives," 27 July 1927.

Washington, D.C. National Archives. "Account Book of the Unit Fund, 44th Massachusetts Infantry," 1861.

Washington, D.C. National Archives. "General Index to the Pension Files 1861–1924." Peter Rice, no. W0379987.

Washington, D.C. National Archives. "General Index to the Pension Files 1861–1934." John Urquart, no. SC200773.

Washington, D.C. National Archives. "General Returns of Officers, Non Commissioned Officers, Musicians, Privates of the United States Marine Corps, January, 1854–February, 1867.

Washington, D.C. National Archives. "Muster Roll of the Field, Staff and Band, First Regiment of Artillery, January, 1860."

Washington, D.C. National Archives. Record Group 127 old, 1859–65. "Letterbooks 7 through 17, Commandant's Office, U.S.M.C.," Records of the United States Marine Corps.

Washington, D.C. National Archives. Record Group 127 old, 1860–63. "Letter Boxes 33-41, Commandant's Office, U.S.M.C.," Records of the United States Marine Corps.

Washington, D.C. National Archives. U.S., Department of War. "General Orders Affecting the Volunteer Force, 1862." *General Orders and Records of the Adjutant General*.

Washington, D.C. National Archives. U.S., Department of War. "General Orders Affecting the Volunteer Force, 1863." *General Orders and Records of the Adjutant General.*

Washington, D.C. National Archives. Record Group 94. U.S. Department of War.

"General Order No. 31." 5 April 1832. *General Orders and Records of the Adjutant General.*

Washington, D.C. National Archives. Record Group 94. U.S., Department of War. "General Order No. 48–1, 31 July, 1861," contained in "An Act Determining the Organization of Infantry, Cavalry and Artillery Regiments." *General Orders and Records of the Adjutant General.*

Washington, D.C. National Archives. Record Group 94. U.S., Department of War. "General Order No. 58," 29 October 1821. *General Orders and Records of the Adjutant General.*

Washington, D.C. National Archives. Record Group 94. U.S., Department of War. "General Order No. 91," 26 October 1861." *General Orders and Records of the Adjutant General.*

Washington, D.C. National Archives. "Tri-Monthly Return, Muster Roll of the Field, Staff and Band, First Regiment of Artillery, from 28th day of February to 30th day of April, 1861" from Fort Hamilton, New York.

Washington, D.C. National Archives. "Tri-Monthly Return, Muster Roll of the Field, Staff and Band, First Regiment of Artillery, from 31st day of October 1861 to 31st day of December, 1861." from Fort Warren, Mass.

Washington, D.C. Smithsonian Institution. "Personal Diary of Daniel B. Harris, Co. K, Twelfth New Jersey Volunteers, December 10, 1862 to July 4, 1863." (Typescript copy courtesy William Bufkin.)

DISSERTATIONS

Allwardt, Anton Paul. "Sacred Music in New York, 1800–1850." D.S.M. dissertation, Union Theological Seminary, 1950.

Anderson, Simon Vance. "American Music During the War for Independence." Ph.D. dissertation, University of Michigan, 1965.

Baltzer, Kenneth R. "American Instrumental Music of the Revolutionary War Period." Master's thesis, University of Minnesota, 1969.

Betterton, William F. "A History of Music in Davenport, Iowa, Before 1900." Ph.D. dissertation, State University of Iowa, 1962.

Bruner, Robert Russell. "A History of Music in Cedar Rapids, Iowa, Before 1900." Ph.D. dissertation, State University of Iowa, 1964.

Bufkin, William F. "Union Bands of the Civil War (1862–1865): Instrumentation and Score Analysis." Ph.D. dissertation, Louisiana State University, 1973.

Camus, Raoul F. "The Military Band in the United States Army Prior to 1834." Ph.D. dissertation, New York University, 1969.

Carpenter, Kenneth William. "A History of the United States Marine Band." Ph.D. dissertation. University of Iowa, 1970.

Dudley, Walter S., Jr. "Orchestration in the *Musique D' Harmonie* of the French Revolution." Ph.D. dissertation, University of California at Berkley, 1968.

Eliason, Robert E. "Brass Instrument Key and Valve Mechanisms Made in America before 1875." D.M.A. dissertation, University of Missouri at Kansas City, 1968.

Fouts, Gordon E. "Music Instruction in America to Around 1830 as Suggested by the

Hartzler Collection of Early Protestant American Tune Books." Ph.D. dissertation, University of Iowa, 1968.

Hall, Harry Hobart. "The Moravian Wind Ensemble: Distinctive Chapter in America's Music." Ph.D. dissertation, George Peabody College for Teachers, 1967.

Ingalls, David M. "Francis Scala; Leader of the Marine Band from 1855 to 1871." M.A. Thesis, Catholic University of America, 1957.

Kirvin, Marten. "A Century of Wind Instrument Manufacturing in the United States." Ph.D. dissertation, State University of Iowa, 1962.

LeClair, Paul Joseph. "The Francis Scala Collection: Music in Washington, D.C. at the Time of the Civil War." Ph.D. dissertation, Catholic University of America, 1973.

McCormick, David Clement. "A History of the United States Army Band to 1964." Ph.D. dissertation, Northwestern University, 1970.

Olson, Kenneth E. "Yankee Bands of the Civil War." Ph.D. dissertation, University of Minnesota, 1971.

Patrick, Stewart. "Minnesota Bands during the Civil War." Ph.D. dissertation, University of North Dakota, 1972.

Swanzy, David Paul. "The Wind Ensemble and Its Music During the French Revolution." Ph.D. dissertation, Michigan State University, 1966.

Thompson, James W. "Music and Musical Activities in New England, 1800–1838." Ph.D. dissertation, George Peabody College for Teachers, 1962.

Tiede, Clayton Howard. "The Development of Minnesota Community Bands During the Nineteenth Century." Ph.D. dissertation, University of Minnesota, 1970.

NEWSPAPERS

Baltimore Sun, 1855–65.
Boston Independent Chronicle, 5, 12 Nov. 1789.
Boston Journal, 1860–65.
Danbury (Conn.) *Evening Times*, 2 Aug. 1932.
Mankato (Minn.) *Semi-Weekly Record*, 1860–65.
Minneapolis Pioneer Press, 1860–65.
National Intelligencer, 1850–66.
New York Herald, 1859–65.
New York Times, 1855–66.
Pennsylvania Gazette, 22 Apr. 1789.
Philadelphia Evening Star, 1860–1900.
Philadelphia Universal Gazette, 10 July 1800.
Richmond (Va.) *Daily Gazette*, 1860–64.
St. Anthoney (Minn.) *Express*, 1850–64.
St. Paul (Minn.) *Chronical and Register*, 1845–60.
St. Paul (Minn.) *Democrat*, 1860–65.
St. Paul Minnesota Pioneer, 1850–65.
St. Paul (Minn.) *Pioneer and Democrat*, 1850–65.
Virginia Gazette, 13 June 1777.

Washington Evening Star, 1860–65.
Washington Post, 1859–65.

PERIODICALS

"The Bands of New York." *Music Trade Review* 2 (1876): 126–27.

"Band Joe Sweeney and His Banjo," *Virginia Cavalade*. Richmond, Va.: Richmond Virginia State Library. 2 (Summer 1952): 34–35.

Benton, Elizabeth C. "When Johnny Marched Off to War." *Selmer Bandwagon* 14, no 5 (December 1966): 2–3.

Berger, Kenneth. "Military Bands of History." *Music Journal* 14 (September 1957): 14.

Blum, Fred. "Music During the Civil War: A Preliminary Survey." *Civil War History* 4, no. 3 (September 1958).

"The Boston Band." *Boston Musical Gazette; a Semi-Monthly Journal, Devoted to the Science of Music* 1 (25 July 1883): 51–52.

"The Boston Brass Band." *Gleason's Pictorial Drawing-Room Companion* 1 (9 August 1851): 225.

Boyce, Joseph. "Cockrell's Brigade Band at Franklin." *Confederate Veteran* 11, no. 6 (June 1911): 271.

Brayley, Arthur W. "The First Brass Band." *American Music Journal* 5 (July 1906): 12.

Campbell, Henry. "The War in Kentucky and Tennessee As Seen by a Teen-Aged Bugler." *Civil War Times Illustrated* 2, no. 7 (November 1963): 26–29.

_____. "The 18th Indiana Battery Fights on From Hoover's Gap to Chattanooga." *Civil War Times Illustrated* 2, no. 9 (January, 1964): 42–45.

_____. "Union Bugler Found Chickamauga 'Terrible Battle.' " *Civil War Times Illustrated* 3, no. 2 (May 1964): 34–37.

_____. "Campaigning Through Tennessee." *Civil War Times Illustrated* 3, no. 5 (August 1964): 46–48.

_____. "Lilly's Battery Nearly Destroyed at Mossy Creek." *Civil War Times Illustrated* 3, no. 6 (October 1964): 46–48.

_____. "Skirmishing in East Tennessee, The Atlanta and Nashville Campaigns, End of the war...and home." *Civil War Times Illustrated* 3, no. 9 (January 1965): 36–39.

Camus, Raoul F. "The Heritage: Band Music of Colonial America." *Music Journal* 29, no. 6 (June 1971): 18.

_____. "A Re-evaluation of the American Band Tradition." *Journal of Band Research* 7 (Fall 1970): 6.

Chase, Charles Monroe. "A Union Band Director Views Camp Rolla: 1861." Edited by Donald H. Welsch. *Missouri Historical Review* 55 (July 1961): 307.

Cunningham, S. A. "Letter." *Confederate Veteran* 1, no. 4 (April 1893): 101–102.

Dodworth, Harvey B. "Band Music Then and Now." *American Art Journal* 31 (July 1880): 1.

Dwight, John Sullivan, ed. *Dwight's Journal of Music, a Paper of Art & Literature* 41 vols. 1881. Reprint. New York: Johnson Reprint Corp., 1968.

Felts, Jack. "Some Aspects of the Rise and Development of the Wind Band During the Civil War." *Journal of Band Research* 3 (Spring 1967): 38.

Fennell, Frederick. "The Civil War: Its Music and Its Sounds." *Journal of Band Research* 3 (Fall 1967): 28.

Forman, Charles V. "A Thumbnail History of the Marine Band." *Jacob's Orchestra Monthly* 23, no. 2 (February 1931): 89.

Fox, S. M. P. "Story of the 7th Kansas." *Kansas Historical Society Transactions* 7 (1902–03): 287.

"From Nursery to Battlefield." *Outlook Magazine* 107 (1914): 88.

Hamblen, David. "Early Boston Bands." *Journal of Music* 24 (December 1966): 32–33.

The **Land** *we Love, a monthly magazine devoted to literature, military history, and agriculture.* 6 vols. (May 1866–Mar. 1869). Charlotte, N.C.: J. P. Irwin and D. H. Hill [etc] 1866–1869. [Note: Founded and edited by caustic General D. Harvey Hill, this monthly magazine served as an outlet for reminiscences, official reports, and chauvinistic poetry.]

Lebby, Robert, M.D. "The First Shot on Fort Sumter." *South Carolina Historical and Genealogical Magazine* 12, no. 3 (July 1911): 141–45.

"Letters of a Badger Boy in Blue." *Wisconsin Magazine of History* 4 (1920–21): 209.

Marquis, Arnold. "Antique Instruments: A Civil War Band Lives Again." *Hobbies* 75 (September 1970): 49.

Mathez, Jean-Pierre. "The 19th Century Wandering Musicians from Salzgitter." *Brass Bulletin*, no. 13 (1976). Zurich, Switzerland: Heggenmacher, SA. pp. 106–115.

McBain, David. "The Royal Military School of Music." *The Musical Times* 48, no. 1372 (June 1957): 311–12.

"Letters of a Badger Boy in Blue." *Wisconsin Magazine of History* 4 (1920–21): 209.

Otey, Mercer. "Letter." *Confederate Veteran* 7, no. 9 (September 1899): 262–63.

"Progressive Improvement." *Euterpeiad: or, Musical Intelligencer. Devoted to the Diffusion of Musical Information and Belles Lettres* 3 (20 July 1822): 8.

St. Clair, C. E. "Letter." *Confederate Veteran* 19, no. 6 (June 1911): 271.

Stackhouse, David L. "D. W. Reeves and His Music." *Journal of Band Research* 5 (Spring 1969): 15.

Stephen, Wilhelm. "German Military Music. An Outline of its Development." *Journal of Band Research* 9, no. 2 (September 1973): 10–21.

Stone, James. "War Music and War Psychology in the Civil War." *Journal of Abnormal and Social Psychology* 36, no. 4 (October 1941): 559–60.

Sunderman, Lloyd F. "Sign Posts in the History of American Music Education." *Education* 62 (May 1942): 519.

Trigg, S. C. "Why the Band Played At Franklin." *Confederate Veteran* 19, no. 1 (January 1911): 31.

Welles, Gideon. "Fort Sumter." *Galaxy* [?] (November 1870): 613–37.

"The West Point Band." *Euterpeiad : or, Musical Intelligencer. Devoted to the Diffusion of Musical Information and Belles Lettres* 2 (18 August 1821): 4.

Winthrop, Theodore. "The New York Seventh Regiment, Our March to Washington." *Atlantic Monthly* 7 (June 1861): 744–57.

MUSIC

The American Veteran Fifer. Williamsburg, Va.: Drummer's Assistant, 1905.

"Bandbooks of the Port Royal Band." Sets 2, 3. Concord, New Hampshire: New Hampshire Historical Society.

"Bandbooks of the Seventeenth New Hampshire Infantry Regiment." New York: New York Public Library.

"Bandbooks of the Twenty-Fifth Massachusetts Infantry Regiment." Worcester, Mass.: The American Antiquarian Society.

Bruce, George B., and Emmett, Daniel D. *The Drummers and Fifers Guide*. New York: Firth and Pond Co., 1862.

Catalogue of Music, Band, U.S. Marine Corps. Washington, D.C.: Government Printing Office, 1885.

Cushing, Joshua. *The Fifer's Companion. No. 1. Containing Instructions for Playing the Fife, and a Collection of Music, Consisting of Marches, Airs, &c with Their Seconds Added*. Salem, Mass.: Cushing and Appleton, 1805.

Dodworth, Allen. *Dodworth's Brass Band School*. New York: H. B. Dodworth, 1853.

The Drummer's Assistant; Instruction for Beating English and Scotch Duties, Calls, Marches, and Tatoos. Dedham, Mass.: Herman Man, 1808.

Francis Scala Collection. Washington, D.C.: Library of Congress, Music Division.

Graupner, Gottlieb. *G. Graupner's Complete Preceptor for the Clarinet, Containing an Accurate Scale and Examples of the Best Fingering, to Which is added a Collection of the Most Popular Airs, Marches, &c. and a Concise Dictionary of Musical Terms*. 2d ed. Boston: Gottlieb Graupner, 1825.

Hazeltine, Daniel. *Instructor in Martial Music*. Exeter, N.H.: n.p., 1810.

Holyoke, Samuel. *The Instrumental Assistant, Containing Instructions for Violin, German Flute, Clarionet, Bass Viol, and Hautboy; Compiled from European Collections*. Vol. 2. Exeter, N.H.: Henry Ranlet, 1807.

Hubler, James, Jr. *The Complete Fifer's Museum*. Greenfield, Mass.: S. and E. Butler, 1807.

Narramore, William D., and Jewitt, A. *The Fifer's Assistant*. Boston: published by the authors, 1812.

Robins, Charles. *The Drum and Fife Instructor; in Two Divisions: Containing I. Instructions for the Drum and Fife, II. A Valuable Collection of the Most Approved Marches*. Exeter, N.H.: C. Norris and Co., 1812.

Robinson, Alvan, Jr. *Massachusetts Collection of Martial Musick, Containing a Plain, Easy and Concise Introduction to the Grounds of Martial Musick. Designed Principally for the Benefit of the Militia of the United States*. Hallowell, Me.: E. Goodale, 1818.

W. H. Shipman Collection. Des Moines, Iowa: State Historical Archives, Iowa Historical Library.

The Village Fifer; Containing Instructions for Learning to Play the Fife, and a Collection of Marches, Airs, &c. Exeter, N.H.: Norris Sayer, 1808.

DISCOGRAPHY

Bales, Richard. "The Confederacy." Columbia Records Legacy Series. National Gallery Orchestra and Choir. New York: Columbia Records, DL245.

Bales, Richard. "The Union." Columbia Records Legacy Series. National Gallery Orchestra and Choir. New York: Columbia Records, DL244.

Fennell, Frederick. "The Civil War, Fort Sumter to Gettysburg." Mercury Records, LPS2–901/LPS2–501.

"Making History Live." Civil War Military Band Music. Vols. I, II. Milwaukee, Wis.: Heritage Military Music Foundation.

Moses, Asch. "Ballads of the Civil War." New York: Folkways Records, F45004.

"Songs of the Civil War," Tony Randall, narrator; John Aler, tenor; Alan Baker, baritone. New World Records, LP202 PNW.

Warner, Frank. "Songs & Ballads of America's Wars." New York: Electra Records, EKL13.

Weaver, James. "19th Century American Ballroom Music, Waltzes, Marches, Polkas & Other Dances. Smithsonian Social Orchestra and Quadrille Band." Nonesuch Records, H-71212.

INDEX

ABOUT THE AUTHOR

KENNETH E. OLSON, Professor of Music at Austin Peay State University in Clarksville, Tennessee, specializes in the study of American music.